Be Your Own Strategy Consultant

Demystifying Strategic Thinking

Tony Grundy & Laura Brown

THOMSON

LEARNING ™   Australia • Canada • Mexico • Singapore • Spain • United Kingdom • United States

Be Your Own Strategy Consultant: Demystifying Strategic Thinking

Copyright © Tony Grundy and Laura Brown 2002

Thomson Learning™ is a trademark used herein under licence.

For more information, contact Thomson Learning, Berkshire House, 168–173 High Holborn, London, WC1V 7AA or visit us on the World Wide Web at: http://www.thomsonlearning.co.uk

British Library Cataloguing-in-Publication Data
A catalogue record for this book is available from the British Library

ISBN 1-86152-980-5

First edition published 2002 by Thomson Learning

Typeset by Dexter Haven Associates, London

Printed in the UK by TJ International, Padstow, Cornwall

Contents

List of tables and figures

Preface

Whilst there are many books on strategic management, there are few which succeed in giving managers, or students of management, a really digestible account of both:

- what it is
- how to actually do it.

The result is that managers, both with and without MBAs, fail to do much more than very basic strategic analysis. Even fewer succeed in developing effective implementation strategies. All are held back by difficulties of dealing with behavioural issues and by perceived financial constraints.

Be Your Own Strategy Consultant sets out to avoid all of these deficiencies. This book will demystify strategic thinking by providing you with a comprehensive set of techniques. Whilst accepting that there are times when a strategy consultant can be helpful, the ideal world projected is one in which managers themselves drive their own strategy process, with perhaps occasional process facilitation and skills development from the outside.

Our distinctive approach is as follows:

- The strategic thinking tools are integrated within a single and well-explained process (but not one that is 'strategy by numbers').
- Each tool has its applications explained within a detailed 'how to use' section – and there is guidance on when to use it (and possible drawbacks). Linkages are made to other tools in the process. This is followed with key questions to provide the reader with exercises for their own organization.
- A major focus on strategy implementation is provided, not just formulation.

- Drawing from research into the value of strategic thinking, and on strategic behaviour, we help you concentrate strategic thinking in the areas of highest impact.
- Case-study material drawn from major companies allows you to work through a number of tools – to reflect on their learning. This also encourages you to appreciate the open-ended nature of strategic thinking.
- Behavioural issues will be drawn out – so that strategic thinking is not merely looked at conceptually.
- A process for dealing with strategic projects is included.

Our techniques are also meant to be integrated into companies' management processes – and not just seen as aimed at a specific individual. To date they have proved their worth across a range of major companies, including Barclaycard, HSBC, the Metropolitan Police, Microsoft, Nokia, Royal Bank of Scotland and Tesco.

Once you have read this book, perhaps you might think about how those thought processes could be applied to your own wider organization – either within your own team or in other areas as well.

Finally, we would like to thank all of our clients for their enthusiasm and creativity in applying these approaches, and in helping to build what would seem to be an exciting approach. We would wish, if we could, to send these processes back in time to our earlier career stages, when we ourselves struggled to see the big picture.

Tony Grundy and Laura Brown
Goffs Oak, Summer 2001
e-mail: lbrown@ntlworld.com, telephone 01707 875999

Tony Grundy's public three-day 'Breakthrough strategic thinking' programme is run at Cranfield School of Management; for in-company events or strategic support generally contact the author direct.

PART ONE

Demystifying strategic thinking

CHAPTER ONE

Demystifying strategic thinking

Introduction – and a story of strategic thinking

In the very week when we first began to write this book, Britain as a country was in paralysis. Long queues of frustrated motorists snaked around major roads in an impatient wait for petrol. The Labour Government appeared helpless in the face of pending seizure of the entire economy.

The rapidity with which the petrol crisis struck took most of us by surprise. The selfless British public responded by buying up metal bins to store spare fuel safely away in their garages.

Fortunately for both authors, fate had left us in the Scottish Highlands running a strategic workshop. Our client had – with pre-science – opted not to run the workshop in Aberdeen, which came to a total standstill for three hours due to an invasion of farmers. Apparently the farmers managed to block two crucial bridges in Aberdeen, rendering the traffic solid. In other parts of the city they succeeded in halting traffic flows by driving tractors at four miles an hour repeatedly around several strategic roundabouts – for hour after hour.

Elsewhere, much of mainland Europe had also ground to a halt – with France and Belgium badly hit. A spontaneous revolt by an unsuspected alliance – the hauliers and farmers – proved instrumental in drawing our attention inadvertently to the higher cost of fuel – and diesel in particular.

The petrol crisis of September 2000 highlights some interesting contrasts about strategic thinking. First, the hauliers and farmers seemed to have excelled in the way in which they drew attention to their plight – and with maximum leverage. Second, the Government appeared not to have recognized the severity of the threat of disruption, even after the crisis was under way and gaining momentum.

For weeks the UK press had been campaigning against 'excessive' fuel prices – and duties. As the oil price rose the Government got more and more revenues.

In terms of strategic thinking, the hauliers and farmers appeared to win 7–0. Just as the country was beginning to turn against the protesters the crisis was put into abeyance. The protesters called off their action but threatened to reinstate it within sixty days unless the Government made some very real concessions. This was a rather cunning plan.

The Government, no doubt not wishing to seem weak or feeble, stated publicly that they could not give concessions, whilst no doubt privately working feverishly on ways of getting around the protest whilst still saving face. This backfired badly: the following week a chance remark on a Welsh Radio statement which claimed the protest was on again (it was 'a joke') spread rumour around the country in hours. Petrol ran out again and normality was delayed by another day.

Our story of the petrol crisis of 2000 highlights some interesting things about the phenomenon of strategic thinking:

- Strategic thinking is often harder in large and more bureaucratic/political organizational structures. It is often best done in smallish groups.
- Strategic thinking can often be done without an elaborate process – indeed too much process of the wrong kind can inhibit the creativity which is at its very core.
- Organizations often omit to think strategically even when the need to do so is staring them in the face.
- Getting the value out of strategic thinking sometimes does not require deploying vast resources and effort. Instead it depends on getting creative leverage out of ideas – to obtain at least ten things for the price of one. The petrol protesters were able to bring the country to a standstill by skilfully picketing key oil refineries.
- Strategic thinking demands thinking through not merely what you can do or need to do, but also what others are likely to do (not merely spontaneously, but also as a knock-on effect of your own actions).
- Strategic thinking involves a continuous scanning of the environment to identify disruptive change and the sudden take-off of opportunities.
- It also requires imagination, along with the willingness to tell stories about the future, which may or may not happen – scenarios which are a guide to further thought. By extending one's awareness in the future, far more insights about the possible are created.

So let us now define strategic thinking.

Strategic thinking is the stream of ideas and reflections which help managers to grasp the bigger picture and helps prevent them from getting lost in the wrong kind of detail. It is a fluid process which generates the insights, options, and breakthroughs to move the organization forward in an uncertain and changing environment.

Strategic thinking differs from narrower thinking, therefore, because it requires a fundamental shift of perspective, as follows:

Operational Thinking	Strategic Thinking
■ linear	■ iterative and unpredictable
■ deductive	■ inductive and intuitive
■ pre-programmed	■ creative
■ boundaries clear	■ ambiguous and fuzzy
■ safe	■ anxiety provoking

Unless managers are able to recognize the fundamental differences in perspectives between operational and strategic thinking, then they will almost certainly fall down a chasm between the two.

Strategic thinking has often been likened to the experience of flying a helicopter (or 'helicopter thinking'). A helicopter can bring access to a number of capabilities, not merely confined to flying:

■ The ability to lift up from the ground to see the bigger picture of what is going on.
■ The ability to land on, or just hover above, an important feature or detail.
■ Agility – the ability to navigate forwards, backwards, sideways, upwards and downwards.
■ Speed.
■ Surprise and concealment – the ability to conceal oneself behind a hill or other obstacle, and attack when the enemy is least expecting it.
■ Power – being able to attack with a variety of arms, machine guns, air-to-ground missiles and rockets.
■ Flexibility – performing a multitude of roles including attack, carrying troops, reconnaissance, etc.

The helicopter analogy is therefore more wide-ranging than just taking off and seeing the big picture from the air. Likewise, strategic thinking also embodies examining key strategic details, agility, speed, surprise, power and flexibility.

So what role does strategic thinking play in the ongoing management process? Strategic thinking plays a role at a variety of levels, as follows:

■ corporate strategy
■ business strategy

- business function
- strategic project
- managing yourself – at work
- managing yourself – in everyday life.

As we will see, in some ways the order of the above (at least in terms of frequency – if not in terms of importance) could be arguably reversed. For strategic thinking can be applied very frequently to oneself and to the immediate strategic environment.

Strategic thinking – becoming your own strategy consultant

In most complex organizations clarity over who should undertake strategic thinking – and for what reason – is ambiguous. In fact we would argue that anyone in a position of real business authority ought to be a strategic thinker.

This entails a significant development of capability for virtually all managers – right up to Chief Executive. But often the gap is filled by the strategy consultant. The strategy consultant may operate as an expert (diagnosing market opportunities and internal capability) or as a process facilitator. In the latter case the focus is primarily on stimulating, channelling and challenging strategic ideas and reflections.

Whilst strategy consultants of all types do add value – even despite the criticisms of some observers – wherever possible managers need to learn the black arts of strategic thinking. We are here in this book to accomplish that very goal – to demystify strategic thinking so that all managers can do-it-themselves.

Although business schools will no doubt continue to be the fountains of knowledge around strategic thinking, the torch should now pass to managers themselves. After all, it is they who stand to benefit the most from the helicopter take-off.

Who is this book for?

This book is for the practising manager who would like to think strategically. This may be because of difficulties in managing your current role, or because you are seeking a bigger and more challenging role but are not fully confident that this will be viable.

The book is also very relevant to management students where it can play an invaluable role in demystifying strategy. There are some excellent management texts on strategic management. However, to the student who is also a practising manager these may seem somewhat remote from everyday management reality. Our book – we feel – very much bridges that gap.

In particular, our book is conceived as being the ideal toolkit for dealing with any MBA project which has at least some strategic content – indeed most have. As such it is a potential 'Must-Buy' for nearly all MBA students for their projects (see chapter 13).

It is worth highlighting that the book contains a ready-made process for applying to your company's strategic issues. It is therefore not just for individual managers, but also for the team. Companies that have adopted some or all of these techniques to date include:

- BT (scenarios)
- CNU (managing change)
- Dyson Appliances (creativity management)
- Ford (acquisitions)
- Metropolitan Police (organizational strategy)
- Microsoft (implementation)
- Nokia (new product strategies)
- Prudential (managing for value)
- Royal Bank of Scotland (organizational strategy)
- Standard Life (strategic thinking)
- Tesco (strategic thinking and project management).

We hope that you can therefore get a number of things out of the book, including:

- A comprehensive set of techniques – which you can go back to and practise on with your issues.
- Case studies – where you will be able to grasp what it is like to 'Be your own strategy consultant'.
- Greater self-confidence in your ability to think strategically, and in your capability as a senior manager generally.
- Significantly accelerated thinking processes – so that you can achieve more in less time – and achieve more value-added results.
- Greater ability to ask the right questions in the context of a senior team.
- An enhanced ability to implement strategy.
- Where practised in a team context, greater ease of decision-making – and a significantly easier political environment.

Why strategic thinking is difficult – and cognitive limits

So, now let us take a quick look at some of the reasons why strategic thinking may appear difficult. Figure 1.1 captures this with a fishbone analysis. Here we start off with the symptom 'strategic thinking is difficult' – to the right of the fishbone. The root causes are shown as the fishbones to the left. (We will be exploring fishbone analysis further in chapter 5).

Figure 1.1 demonstrates a number of potential reasons, which are tested out in this book, to explain why strategic thinking might be thought difficult. Firstly, as we will see in chapter 6, the very nature of strategic thinking is frequently unclear. If we are not really sure what it is, and what it is not, then this will add to its potential difficulty.

FIGURE 1.1: Fishbone analysis: the difficulty of strategic thinking

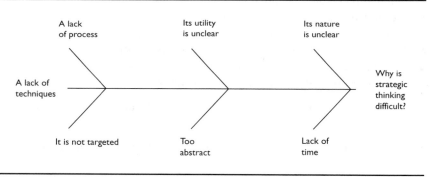

In addition, there may also be scepticism around its utility. If several of the management team are not actually convinced of its virtue then it again stands little chance of taking off.

There is almost invariably a lack of process applied to strategic thinking. A robust strategic process might have, for example:

- the process broken down stage-by-stage
- clear outputs at the end, and at each individual stage
- clear inputs (of data) at the beginning
- key strategic questions to guide discussion within each stage
- time set aside from daily activities (or sacred strategic space) for strategic reflection.

There may well be a lack of analytical techniques – other than rudimentary SWOT analysis – in use. Whilst techniques themselves will not provide the stimulus for strategic thinking, without some framework to separate out thoughts the end product is invariably not much more than a brain-dump.

We will also explore in chapter 6 another key problem, the tendency not to target the value of strategic thinking. If one were to target this value then one might be more alert to picking out truly strategic ideas, we believe.

Besides these factors, strategy is often considered at too high or abstract a level. A business strategy in its entirety is made up of many sub-strategies or 'mini strategies'. Quite often it is more practicable to deal intellectually with a strategy on a more small-scale basis. By breaking the strategy down into smaller domains it can be thought through far more effectively. A 'mini strategy' might be, for example, a specific project which you need to accomplish in your role, or perhaps a very specific market area which your organization seeks to expand in.

A common complaint that managers have is that there is a lack of time to engage in strategic thinking. Whilst recognizably managers are frenetically busy nowadays, this is often due in part to their lack of strategic effectiveness: not only are they not necessarily doing things the right way but they are doing a lot of the wrong things.

Facilitation of strategic thinking is becoming more common in leading companies, but there are still many sessions conducted by management teams which have no explicit facilitation and little informal facilitation.

Some organizations are also generally prone to fear – whether this is concerned with the market, new competitors or new technologies, current financial performance or internal restructuring. This fear is echoed at an individual level where there are concerns about future job progression or security. Fear acts as a huge dampener for strategic thinking.

Finally, managers operate under severe cognitive limits. Swamped by information overload – much of which is of a somewhat trivial nature – it becomes hard to clear the mind for more creative reflection.

Cognitive limits operate at both an individual and group level. It is sometimes said that the average person can hold five things in their head at once. A not-so-bright person can hold their attention on three. A genius – apparently – can hold as many as seven things in his/her mind simultaneously. This is often said to be the magic rule of five, plus or minus two.

As we know from theory on organizational learning (see, especially, Argyris, 1991), groups are often not as bright collectively as are individuals. Indeed, where those individuals are very bright themselves, arguably the result is even less intelligence as they typically pull and push the organization in different directions.

In large part because of these tough cognitive demands – and also in order to gain critical mass – it is advisable to limit the number of major strategic initiatives – or 'breakthroughs' to a maximum of three. This is in accordance with the Japanese philosophy of *hoshin* – which simply means breakthrough. *Hoshin* has been practised explicitly by a number of companies including TI Group, HP, Glaxo, SmithKline Beecham and on a perhaps less formal and explicit basis by Tesco.

Tesco's breakthroughs, for instance, that can be mapped from around 1994 to the present time appear in figure 1.2. These begin with Clubcard, the acquisition of William Low in Scotland, and customer service breakthroughs. More recently we see Tesco focusing on international expansion and conversion of stores to the 'Tesco Extra' format in the UK.

FIGURE 1.2: Strategic breakthroughs at Tesco 1994–2000

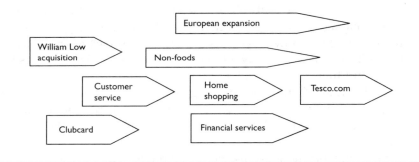

FIGURE 1.3: Breakthroughs: maximum possibilities

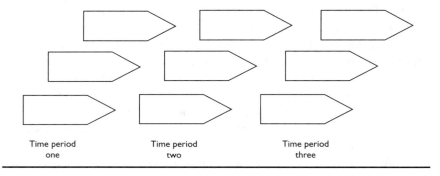

Whilst the rule of only three breakthroughs to be conducted simultaneously is a sound guideline, it may be possible to conduct up to three breakthroughs within each decentralized business unit. Also, once the breakthrough is well underway it is then possible to start new break-throughs. If a particular breakthrough takes, on average, eighteen months to come to fruition, this means that potentially an organizational unit can absorb six in three years.

Figure 1.3 is now a visual representation of these possibilities, showing that in theory it may be possible for an organization to implement up to nine breakthroughs in three years. This assumes that each one takes a year to launch and implement.

Overview of the book

In the next section we examine the key techniques for strategic thinking. This is split into:

Chapter 2 which focuses on external analysis, and chapter 3 which deals with competitive positioning. Chapter 4 then deals with creative options and breakthroughs. Chapter 4 includes a rich case study on BMW and Rover Group, in which you get the chance to imagine that you were the Chief Executive of BMW at the time of Rover's acquisition. What other options would you have considered aside from buying Rover?

We then turn in chapter 5 to demystifying implementation. In chapters 6 and 7 we draw upon further research conducted with both senior managers and a number of strategy academics to tease out how one might put a value on strategic thinking. In chapter 8 we give you a worked example of how strategic thinking facilitates strategic change – with Champney's Health Farm, again where you are invited to imagine you are its Chief Executive. In chapter 9 you can practise this further with the turn-around case of Marks & Spencer. Chapter 10 then takes a more specific look at how acquisitions can provide a vehicle for strategic change.

In our third section, we look at strategic thinking in practice. We first examine the impact of behaviour on strategic thinking in chapter 11, and draw out the implications for managing the process. Chapter 12 then examines in more practical detail how you can become your own strategy consultant. Chapter 13 then looks at how strategic thinking can help to steer strategic projects, and includes a rich set of checklists. There is also some practical help for how to define and deal with an MBA strategic project.

In the final chapter, 14, we take a refreshingly novel look at how strategic thinking helps deal with practical, everyday issues – both within work and in personal life generally.

But before we turn to the first stage of the strategic thinking toolkit – strategic analysis – let us explore our first case study, Dyson Appliances, to get a taste of some techniques.

CASE STUDY: DYSON APPLIANCES

From inventor to entrepreneur

Dyson's breakthrough in the carpet cleaning business demonstrates the importance of aligning all critical areas of the business both internally and externally to deliver value-based, sustainable growth.

In the mid-1990s, James Dyson, founding Chairman of Dyson, decided to take on other players in the domestic carpet cleaning industry with a rather different proposition. He decided to discard the taken-for-granted assumption that such devices needed a bag. Dyson decided that – far from adding value to the customer – the bag was actually an unnecessary cost and a bother to replace. Worse, Dyson contended that the bag itself actually reduced the effective power, and thus the performance, of the carpet cleaner. Dyson's new product, a distinctively designed, yellow, expensive and bagless floor cleaner, gained market leadership in the UK carpet cleaning market.

James Dyson invented and patented a device which enabled his cleaners to do without a bag, using a very fast circling vortex of air. The dust was drawn up into a perspex tube or cylinder where it was dropped. Periodically the user would empty out this cylinder without producing a small dust storm. (This is because of it being packed densely as it is drawn to the side of the cylinder as the air is circulated at high speed.)

Going for competitive knockout

Now Dyson could have stopped at this point in designing his strategy but he decided not to do so. Instead, he set about achieving a compelling customer pull, and a dominant competitive advantage. Intuitively James Dyson recognized that to leapfrog over companies like Hoover and Electrolux he needed to align a number of points of competitive leverage. Only then could he secure a financial advantage. Each one of the points of competitive leverage procures financial value.

So let us now represent these points of leverage using a pictorial tool called 'wishbone analysis'. The wishbone analysis in figure 1.4 highlights just how many points of competitive leverage Dyson focused on. It also emphasizes how dependent his strategic success was on areas where he had relatively low influence (for example, on the assumption that the major industry competitors would not change their mindset significantly). Figure 1.4 also emphasizes how Dyson did not just set about exploiting its strategy from a technology-led point of view. In particular, he experimented with marketing innovation to achieve a compelling advantage. (For instance, he offered his products at half price to electrical goods retail sales people to encourage trial.) Figure 1.4 in totality shows how well Dyson's strategic thinking and his strategic vision were articulated.

FIGURE 1.4: Wishbone analysis

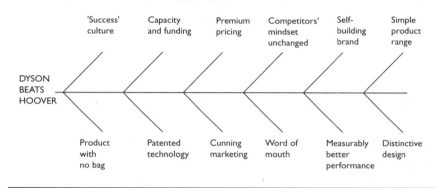

Turning competitive advantage into hard cash

Interestingly, this wishbone was not achieved in one fell swoop. Dyson had previously penetrated the Japanese market with a £1000 bagless machine. His UK entry strategy was based on the lessons of this experience, and in the mid-1990s this became a deliberate strategy, with a price of over £200. Developing an effective wishbone may require a number of iterations as the strategic concept is refined. The premium price of £200 was thus a key driver not only of Dyson's volume growth but also of his higher margins.

The results of this strategy were spectacular. In a short time Dyson had achieved a major share of the market. In two and a half years Dyson had moved from employing fewer than 20 people to employing 300, and, in 2000, reaching 1500.

According to *The Times* (8 February 1997), Dyson had reached a turnover of more than £100 million per annum in the three years since the launch of its core product, enabling him to buy a £3 million country house as his new home. Margins were rumoured to be of the order of those of The Body Shop in its heyday. His book, *Against the Odds*, is a fascinating account of this success.

Creating 'built-in success'

When a growth strategy is targeted at achieving real dominance, it is perhaps rare to find that this is achieved through getting only a small number of factors right. It usually involves getting a considerable number of things right, and having favourable circumstances and good timing.

Where strategic success proves elusive, this may well be where just one, two or possibly three factors were not aligned completely. Dyson's success was achieved by working backwards from customer value and by engineering his entire activities to deliver that value.

Some of these factors may be to do with the competitive strategy, some due to its implementation. James Dyson's own capability is the 'backbone' of the wishbone, being critical to implementation.

The various bones on the wishbone are interdependent. When they co-exist, additional value is created. For instance, the bottom bones of the wishbone deliver a natural and impelling demand for the product. The top bones help to lower its costs, increase its price, protect that price and facilitate expansion.

By taking wishbone analysis as a whole, various factors will differ both in their degree of importance and in terms of influence levels. This leads to a more in-depth analysis to extend the domain of our control over the strategic vision, helping identify (and reduce) the likely implementation gap. Another cut to the analysis is how uncertain these factors are.

In Dyson's case the assumption that the 'competitor's mindset is likely to remain unchanged' appeared to be both very important and something over which Dyson had low influence. Had Dyson's competitors been able to counteract directly, this might easily have destroyed value through much reduced volumes, reduced prices, increased discounting and by also pushing up operating costs. Therefore, a critical issue for Dyson was how he encouraged his competitors to believe that continuing to sell machines with a separate bag offered the best route forward. Obviously, the fact that he had a strong patent protection was a useful tactic. But by encouraging a public debate on the relative merits of 'the bag' versus 'no bag' he encouraged them to dig into (and become more committed to) their existing mindset.

If we now go back in time to the point where James Dyson evolved his own business case for this growth strategy, we could easily do a financial plan with:

- sales revenues = sales price x volume
- variable costs
- fixed costs
- working capital and capital investment
- cash flows and NPV ('net present value').

But, more importantly, the critical areas which drove the value of this strategy were:

- customers' perceptions of the superior value of the Dyson product and willingness to pay a premium
- the company's ability to satisfy premium customer expectations throughout all of its product and service delivery
- competitors' inability to compete head-on with Dyson or to evolve an alternative and more effective strategy
- Dyson's ability to harvest a good proportion of his product's premium price through its retail channels
- the company's ability to gain cost economies through scale and simplicity of the product range.

Over a protracted period of years Dyson tried to develop and launch the product which culminated in its launch period prior to 1995. The period 1994–95 saw a rapid development phase and 1996–2000 saw the product's exploitation. This called for some kind of review and reflection around 2000, perhaps leading onto subsequent change.

If we now stand back to look at the evolution of Dyson's wishbone, a review might now well be advisable, especially as Dyson faces a number of transitions. In Dyson's growth strategy, for example, key uncertainties lie in:

- Patents – which may expire.
- Cunning marketing which has been imitated by Electrolux.
- The word of mouth effect, which may no longer be as strong, the Dyson product being in part fashion-dependent and not quite as novel at the present time.
- Customers sometimes querying its 'measurably better performance' – which is very hard to measure objectively.
- Imitation of its design style, for example, by competitors.
- Competitors' mindsets changing (for example, many competitors sell a single-cyclone model although in a court case won by Dyson in late 2000, Hoover was asked to withdraw its look-alike 'Vortex' range).
- Premium pricing now under some pressure from discounting.

In addition to these particular wishbone alignment factors, we will leave it to the reader to query whether other factors might be by now both important and becoming increasingly uncertain. Figure 1.5 can be used to position these assumptions. Also, the factors driving Dyson's external and internal growth are perhaps not now so favourable, unless new products or technologies are brought out that are equally attractive to customers.

FIGURE 1.5: Uncertainty-importance grid

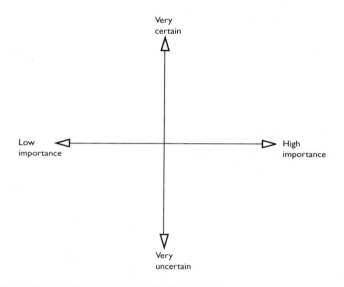

So, whilst Dyson Appliances has been a most dramatic and successful growth strategy to date, clearly its competitive challenges are now mounting.

The above case on Dyson underlines:

- The ongoing need for strategic thinking – to avoid complacency.
- That competitive advantage has to be continuously reinvented.
- The rewards from a quantum level of competitive advantage are quantifiable – and in economic terms.
- Two key strategic challenges are a) to know your customer better than they know themselves, and b) to always be in a position to outguess and to pre-empt competitors.

Conclusion

Strategic thinking is an essential ingredient of any senior manager's capability. It is qualitatively different from operational thinking – and can be very difficult unless one is prepared to shift mental gear into 'helicopter thinking'.

Organizations and individuals have quite restricted cognitive limits. This therefore demands techniques and processes to break strategic thinking down into some structural steps. These steps need, however, to be managed as a fluid, intuitive and creative process, rather than one which is overly analytical, linear and primarily data-driven.

References

Argyris, C., 'Teaching Smart People How to Learn', *Harvard Business Review*, May–June 1991.

Dyson, J., *Against the Odds*, Orion Business, London, 1997.

PART TWO

Everyday strategic analysis

CHAPTER TWO

Demystifying strategic analysis, part 1: the external environment

Introduction

Strategic analysis is so frequently seen as something to be tackled in a relatively ad hoc process of meetings and discussions. Most managers feel uncomfortable using formal tools except, for instance, SWOT analysis.

Yet strategic options are now so much more complex, uncertain and demanding. Managers owe it to themselves, their staff and their shareholders to tackle strategic analysis in a professional yet non-bureaucratic way. In this chapter we show how this is possible, giving hands-on guidance on which tools of strategic analysis to use, when and why.

Some (but not all) of these tools are to be found in most good books on strategic management. However, several existing concepts are taken further here. New tools and concepts are added. These have been discovered through working with managers to help them analyze their strategies over the last fifteen years.

This chapter includes the following tools and concepts:

- gap analysis
- SWOT analysis
- PEST analysis
- growth drivers (within the market)
- the five competitive forces
- uncertainty grid analysis (with uncertainty influence analysis)
- the uncertainty tunnel (and scenarios)
- re-writing the industry rules – the industry mindset.

But first, many books exhort managers to 'think strategically' or prescribe 'strategic leadership' to 'helicopter' out of tactical day-to-day management. But few address the way to make this happen. Where strategic analysis tools are explained this is most frequently done conceptually, rather than with illustrations showing how to use the tools during day-to-day management of strategies for growth.

In this and the following chapter there are a number of reader exercises which allow you to practise the techniques on your own issues. Do take the time out to do this – otherwise you will not get the maximum value from this book.

Gap analysis

Gap analysis is one of the least well-used tools of strategic analysis. It is still quite rare (even in the new millennium) to see it in formal use. Frequently corporate plans are based more on aggregating separate, tactical plans for achieving more profit, rather than by creating stretching, but completely viable, business strategies.

An example of gap analysis for a maturing company is illustrated in figure 2.1. Here we see the core business activities facing competitive pressure and a fall in growth rate, squeezing operating profit. Although international development and new business activities may fill part of corporate aspirations, there still remains a significant gap.

FIGURE 2.1: Strategic gap analysis

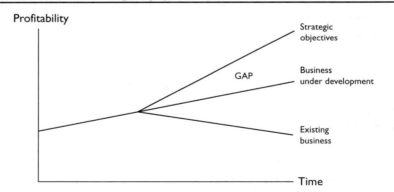

Whilst gap analysis can be very useful – if not essential – unless it is coupled with additional techniques of strategic analysis it is likely to be optimistic and unsupported by robust strategies based on solid competitive advantage.

Indeed, in certain industries managers have been known to just throw ideas – almost at random – into 'the gap'. Jokingly, we refer to this sometimes as 'CRAP analysis', which means:

■ creating
■ artificial
■ plans

to signify that all too often initiatives aimed at filling the strategic gap are not thought through.

The key benefits of gap analysis are that it:

■ provides a very clear focus for sketching your aspirations for the business
■ links in with the strategic breakthroughs required in order to move the business forward
■ emphasizes the longer and medium term and is not just confined to the shorter term.

The disadvantages of gap analysis are that it:

■ is frequently used on its own – without supporting techniques
■ typically results in superficial thinking, rather than in truly creative analysis of potential breakthroughs.

FIGURE 2.2: SWOT analysis

Strengths   Weaknesses

Opportunities   Threats

Gap analysis can be used for a wide number of applications, including:

- Sales gaps – both short and medium term.
- Profitability gaps – for three-year planning value gaps – for targeting shareholder value creation either at the corporate or business level.
- Customer value gaps – the gap between what customers expect and what we deliver.
- Competitor gaps – for understanding how we match up to our competitors.
- Cost gaps – for targeting strategic cost reduction.
- Organizational gaps – for understanding gaps in capability.
- Change gaps – for understanding the gap between where we are now in the change process and where we want to be in the future.
- Personal development gaps – between present and desired capability.

EXERCISE

For one of the above gap areas:

- Where are you now?
- Where do you currently think you want to be?
- Where do you actually need to be, given external and internal change?
- Therefore what is your gap?
- What are the options for closing it?

Following gap analysis, the next step may be to perform a SWOT analysis. Strengths and weaknesses are more typically the internal variables of strategic position. Opportunities and threats are more typically the external influences on a company. A typical format for a SWOT is shown in figure 2.2.

EXERCISE: SWOT ANALYSIS

Taking one of your business areas, do a SWOT analysis. Now, using the above strategic dos and don'ts, what further insights can you glean from the SWOT, and especially what is its 'so-what?'

SWOT analysis

The origins of SWOT analysis are unclear, but we do know that it was used as long ago as the 1960s. SWOT analysis is easy to use and remember, but because it was perhaps the first strategic analysis tool this does seem to have crowded out other – possibly more valuable and also complementary – techniques.

SWOT analysis is by now a frequently used and indispensable tool, providing a number of provisos for using SWOT are met. These are summarized as the following list of strategic dos and don'ts.

Strategic dos

- Make continuous and explicit comparisons with your external competitors (or internal substitutes), to reality-test your assumed strengths and weaknesses.
- Where you are unclear as to whether a particular variable is a strength or a weakness, separate these two aspects out, listing one as a strength and one as a weakness.
- When dealing with product- or service-related strengths or weaknesses, make sure that you 'think as if you are the customer' – assessing the strength of weakness from the customer's perspective. This invites having the equivalent of the 'out-of-body experience'.
- Rate your degree of strength and weakness on a scale (of, say, 1–5) so that you get a handle on how strong you are, or how weak (likewise with opportunities and threats).

Strategic don'ts

- Do a SWOT analysis without highlighting the key areas which are most important for competing effectively.
- Be unduly self-critical of particular areas of the business when from the outside of the company you are perceived as being strong (for example, by your customers or competitors).
- Think that compiling a SWOT analysis equates with actually having a strategy.
- Assume that SWOT necessarily completes the strategic analysis (you will need to complement it with other tools, particularly those which uncover unexpected areas of opportunity or threat).
- Complete the SWOT analysis without standing back and saying 'What patterns have emerged about the overall business position, e.g. we are in need of turnaround, and what bigger options for strategic development does it now suggest?'

As you will see, SWOT analysis is rarely self-sufficient and needs to be utilized along with other strategic analysis tools. Having witnessed innumerable SWOT analyses produced without the benefit of the above 'strategic dos and don'ts', SWOT analysis reminds us of the phrase used by many estate agents to describe a property where quantity is a substitute for quality: 'deceptively spacious'! So many SWOT analyses are voluminous without really distilling the key strategic issues and options. Indeed, doing a SWOT analysis is actually pointless without drawing out the 'so-what?' from it. The 'so-what?' can include, for example:

- A succinct statement about whether your position is competitively:
  - strong
  - average
  - weak.
- Specific options for developing the strategy.
- Patterns within the SWOT analysis, for example where:
  - there are many opportunities, but you have a weak capability to exploit them
  - there are a number of threats, and your specific weaknesses make you vulnerable
  - you have major strengths which might allow you to seize specific opportunities.

Some thinkers jokingly refer to SWOT as a 'stupid waste of time', which seems a little unfair considering how central SWOT has become in management practice. More fairly, we could call a raw SWOT the 'superficial work of teams'. Nevertheless, we do need to be especially careful with SWOT – because of its very subjectivity.

One particularly helpful way of representing a SWOT is to use vector analysis to represent the pattern of strengths and weaknesses, and of opportunities and threats. This format was originally used by Lewin (1935) to represent 'forcefield' analysis – within change management (see chapter 5). Here the relative strength and importance of strengths versus weaknesses is shown as a series of arrows. The upward arrows denote strengths (or opportunities), and the downward arrows denote weaknesses (and threats). These are illustrated in figures 2.3 and 2.4.

EXERCISE: REFINING YOUR SWOT

For the SWOT analysis which you did earlier, using the vector analysis approach (see figures 2.3 and 2.4), what further insights does this generate about your overall strategic position?

The balance of opportunities/threats and of strengths and weaknesses can now be plotted (for different businesses) on a SWOT Grid (a new technique) – see figure 2.5.

FIGURE 2.3: Strengths and weaknesses analysis
— using forcefield format

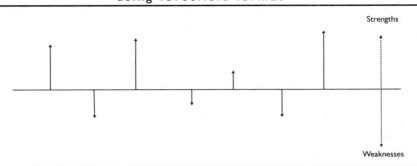

FIGURE 2.4: Opportunities and threats analysis
— using forcefield format

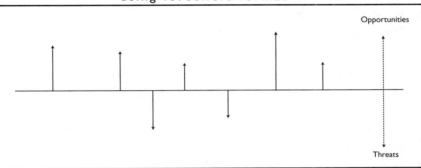

FIGURE 2.5: SWOT grid

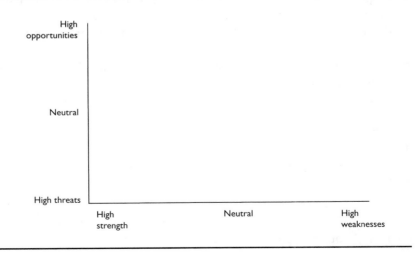

This uses the weighted judgements from figures 2.3 and 2.4 to plot the overall positioning of a business unit in terms of its:

- potential and vulnerability: opportunities and threats, versus
- its relative strength.

To summarize, the key benefits of SWOT are that it:

- is easy to use and provides both an external and an internal view of your strategic position
- provides a quick way of generating some key strategic issues
- helps to provide a context for the gap analysis
- most managers are familiar with it.

The key disadvantages of SWOT are that it:

- can be highly subjective – unless it is checked out by further analysis and data collection
- is often unprioritized
- frequently generates a lot of information without real interpretation
- is often done at too high a level of analysis.

The tool can be linked to other techniques (coming soon) as follows:

- Strengths and weaknesses – linked to competitive positioning and competitor analysis.
- Opportunities and threats – linked to PEST factors, growth drivers and the five competitive forces.
- Threats – linked to the uncertainty grid.
- Opportunities, threats and weaknesses – linked to the attractiveness-implementation difficulty grid (AID analysis) – see chapter 5.
- Opportunities and threats – to the 'Market Attractiveness' dimension of the General Electric (or GE grid) – see chapter 3.
- Overall patterns from the SWOT – linked to the strategic option grid (chapter 4).
- Weaknesses: linked to fishbone analysis – to diagnose why a weakness exists (chapter 5).

SWOT analysis can be used at the:

- corporate level
- business level
- departmental level
- project level
- personal level.

Amplifying the final point, SWOT is an excellent starting point for analyzing your personal career strategy.

EXERCISE: SWOT ANALYSIS 2

For either the departmental, the project or the personal level above:

- What key patterns come out of the SWOT (what is its 'so-what?')?
- What key options come out of this thinking?
- What further data or analysis work should you now do to reality check your SWOT?
- What is the 'One Big Thing' that you have probably missed in the SWOT?

Once we have done an initial issues analysis, based on gap and SWOT analysis, we might now begin to scope the potential for strategic break-throughs in the business. Here a 'strategic breakthrough' is defined as: 'A specific programme of strategic action which will produce a step-change in the company's competitive position, its financial performance and/or in its capability'.

The idea of 'breakthrough' comes originally from the Japanese philosophy of *hoshin*. As described, this simple philosophy states that any organization can only realistically accomplish between one to three strategic breakthroughs within a specific time period (for instance of eighteen months to two years). (Where an organization is broken down into more than one relatively decentralized sub-unit, each sub-unit can perhaps itself accomplish between one to three.)

There are several reasons why an organization can only implement such a small number of breakthroughs. This is due to:

- the need to concentrate resources to achieve a critical mass
- to enable strategies to be easily communicated
- to mobilize sufficient intent and power within the organization
- to help managers to understand what is really, really important.

The last reason is worth amplifying: organizations are not well-known for their powers of collective intelligence. Indeed, organizations full of allegedly 'bright' individuals (like hospitals, universities, business schools and management consultancies) are notorious for being difficult to manage.

Strategic analysis (and decision-making) in such organizations is like pulling teeth – without anaesthetic. We have often thought of this as being the syndrome of 'self-cancelling intelligence' – intelligent moves by some stakeholders are cancelled out by equally intelligent, counter-moves by others.

One of the reasons why the law of breakthrough analysis is of such small numbers therefore (one to three at any one time) is because of the organization's cognitive limitations (as we described in chapter 1). In cognitive psychology it has been said that:

The average person can hold up to five things in their head at any one time. Whilst a genius can hold seven things in their head at one time. But a below average person can hold just three things in their head at any one time.

Hence the rule of cognitive psychology of 'five plus or minus two'.

Because (as we have already seen) organizations – notwithstanding how bright the individuals are within them – can only cope with limited complexity, we are therefore confined to going for the maximum number of strategic breakthroughs as just three.

Environmental analysis

Below are listed three complementary tools for assessing the economic attractiveness of a particular growth opportunity:

■ PEST analysis – the key political (and regulatory), economic, social (and demographic) and technological factors shaping industry change.
■ The growth drivers in the market which are generating or inhibiting market growth.
■ The five competitive forces – the impact of entrants and substitutes, buyer (customer) and supplier power, and competitive rivalry between existing players.

PEST analysis

Taking PEST analysis first, figure 2.6 displays the key ingredients of PEST. Note that the various PEST factors should not be analyzed completely separately, but need to be looked at in terms of the pattern which emerges (again, do a 'so-what?' for it). For example, PEST factors might be used to predict the broad impact of recession on an industry such as retail, as follows.

■ Political factors: following an election, interest rates go up (to choke off economic demand, which was previously overheating).
■ Economic factors: the impact of a fall in GDP (gross domestic product) causes tax income to fall, public expenditure to rise (to fund unemployment costs) and thus income tax rates to rise. This in turn puts additional restraint on consumer demand, especially in discretionary retail purchases. As unemployment rises rapidly this acts as a brake

on consumer spending and also shrinks those areas of the market, which are highly price sensitive.

■ Social factors: concerns about security of jobs, higher income taxes and lower real increases in pay put a squeeze on sectors such as holidays and restaurants.

■ Technological factors: information technology plays a major role in helping companies to shed jobs, thus putting an increased and continuing squeeze on economic demand.

The above highlights how the apparently separate ingredients of PEST need to be examined to see how they might interact together to assess their overall impact.

FIGURE 2.6: Using PEST analysis

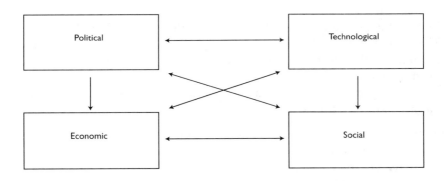

EXERCISE: PEST ANALYSIS

For one business area of your choice:

■ What are the current PEST issues impacting on it?
■ How might future PEST issues impact on it?
■ What is the 'so-what?' from this analysis?

The key benefits of PEST analysis are that it:

■ Focuses the attention on some of the wider changes in the environment – even outside your own particular market.

■ Draws attention to some of the softer issues – like the political (and regulatory), and the social.

■ Helps us to gain a better understanding for external conditions for growth in a market.

The key disadvantages of PEST analysis are that it:

- sometimes merely highlights the obvious
- can absorb time which might have been spent understanding strategic variables, which are more important.
    PEST analysis links to a number of other techniques, particularly:
- SWOT analysis – to provide input to opportunities and threats
- growth drivers – to provide core assumptions for the conditions (outside the industry) for market growth.
- the strategic option grid (chapter 4) – for helping to understand the strategic attractiveness of a particular option
- the uncertainty grid – which can be used to prioritize issues.

Growth drivers

The next area of analysis is the main growth drivers within the market. The PEST factors will identify some of the key drivers of growth which are outside the industry, but in addition those within the market itself need to be examined.

Growth drivers which are inherent in the market can include a variety of things, for example:

- Service innovation: a new market (or segment) may be more attractive to customers than the existing one, either because the need is now delivered in a cheaper or better way. For example, telephone or Internet banking and telephone insurance might offer customers either a cheaper or better service (or, arguably, both), than existing more expensive or inflexible providers.
- Technology innovation: a new technology (for instance, mobile telephones or personal computers) may enable the customer to satisfy previously unserved needs or ones which were at best inconveniently served in the past.
- Increased learning about products or services: there may be an increase in awareness among customers that the product or service exists, and how its benefits can be extracted. Once customers have learned more about these benefits, this is likely to increase the frequency of usage.
- Price reductions: as a market expands, growth can feed up on itself as companies gain economies of scale. The benefits of these economies are then passed on to the customer in the form of lower prices. These lower prices can then induce penetration of new customers and/or

increase frequency of purchase. Or, a single competitor might break rank and reduce its prices, causing a surge in demand and increasing its own market share.

■ Scarcity of substitutes: shortages of other means of satisfying needs can generate an (often unsustainable) increase in market or segment growth. For example, in times of economic boom the demand for external consultants frequently increases due to internal skill shortages within companies, not necessarily because they have anything particularly wonderful to offer.

We would stress here that growth drivers are those factors which actually influence the growth in aggregate market demand. To maintain the purity of the technique external growth driver analysis should not embrace internal growth drivers and brakes. The key reasons for this are as follows:

■ It is likely that your analysis will then divert too much towards internal thinking.
■ The resulting analysis will be less helpful for external market forecasting, as you will now have a mix between external and internal growth drivers.
■ Growth drivers are one of the three main inputs to positioning your business on the GE grid (see chapter 3). Unless you have a reasonably pure analysis of the external market it will be relatively difficult to perform an accurate positioning of each business unit.

The growth drivers do not merely tease out forces impacting on volume, but also on value. One can easily be faced with a situation of a market experiencing good volume growth, but where prices (in real terms) are coming down. This may either slow market growth considerably or possibly even make the market shrink.

Where you do wish to use the growth driver format to capture internal growth capability it is imperative to do a separate analysis for the internal growth drivers – the factors enabling or constraining a company to grow from a capability angle.

Besides its use for business analysis, growth drivers can be used for understanding the sustainability of internal business expansion – which may be fuelling your job security and promotion opportunities.

So, how important are the growth drivers inherent in the market which are not already detected by the PEST factors? The answer is, they can be very important indeed. Growth can be generated by spontaneous increase in demand by customers or by industry innovation. Or the wider PEST factors can provide an environment conducive to growth. But even the PEST analysis may not always pick up the potential for growth driven by technology through innovation within the industry. (The 'T' of the PEST factors is normally aimed at detecting trends outside the particular industry.)

Also, when using the 'S' (or 'social and demographic trends'), this does not always identify key market trends such as changes in buying criteria, and method and frequency of use.

Once all the key PEST factors and growth drivers within the market have been identified it is essential to evaluate their combined effect. Here a pictorial representation of the overall growth drivers provides stimulus for debate. This is accomplished through a vector analysis (where arrows are used to represent the strength of growth drivers) which are now explored in more depth.

Vector analysis is a way of mapping the impact of forces for growth in an industry. The length of the vector arrow represents the perceived strength of the force driving growth.

Taking a graphic example of growth drivers let us examine the growth in the share price of dot-com shares in 1998–99. Here, the main growth drivers were: the huge growth in usage of the Internet (during 1997–1999); the perceived possibilities for reducing costs and thus reducing price (as at Amazon.com); media hype; the rise in dot-com shares began to feed on itself, creating a self-fulfilling prophecy; also the 'emperor's new clothes syndrome': no-one appeared willing to question the fundamental economic logic of this boom.

FIGURE 2.7: Growth drivers: dot-com market

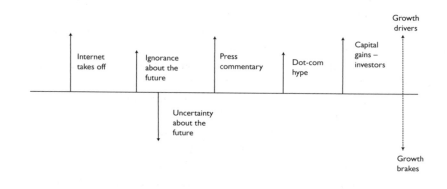

The growth drivers of dot-com share prices are shown in figure 2.7 (as at 1998–99). But by mid-2000 through to 2001 sentiment had reversed. It would appear that the growth in Internet usage was perhaps a necessary – but not a sufficient – condition of revenue (and margin) generation. What was also needed was:

- a preparedness by customers to make transactions through the Internet (either directly or indirectly – i.e. via Internet advertising)
- confirmation that this demand was actually both massive and reasonably profitable
- well-managed dot-com companies able to deliver real shareholder value – not so much later, but preferably sooner.

The conditions were not met, big-time.

Figure 2.8 now plots the new growth drivers (and brakes) in late 2000 through to mid-2001. The growth in Internet usage takes on a much lower and weaker importance. The mounting losses of dot-com companies (and in many cases the sheer absence of revenues) reversed sentiment. Once the rot in sentiment had set in, this became a self-fulfilling disaster.

FIGURE 2.8: Growth drivers: dot-com market

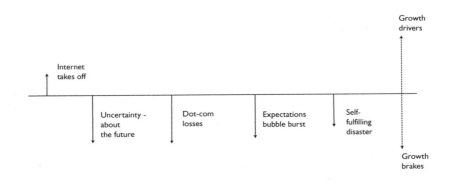

To get a sense of perspective in this acute turnaround, even one of the most 'successful' companies, Amazon.com, experienced a share price collapse of over 90 per cent.

In conclusion, growth drivers are an essential tool for thinking strategically about the external market. Many managers find it actually easier to use than Porter's forces (coming next) and actually use it more frequently. (This is not to downgrade the importance of the five forces, but to highlight that to Be Your Own Strategy Consultant you may need to take on board techniques which are not quite within the strategy mainstream.)

EXERCISE: GROWTH DRIVERS

For one market area:

- What are the external growth drivers (and brakes) and, using the vector approach, what do these suggest about future prospects for growth?
- For your own business: what does an internal growth driver analysis tell you about your overall capability to respond to that growth?

Growth driver analysis has the following key benefits:

- it helps you to do a reality-check on assumptions of market growth
- it gives more objective input to potential 'exit' decisions – by checking out whether assumed growth in a market is a reality or merely a mirage
- it may identify possibilities for actually influencing the growth of the market – rather than just being passive.

Its key disadvantages are potentially:

- that without further research it is subjective
- frequently, managers using it do a brain-dump of the past or present growth drivers, rather than the future.

Key techniques which link to growth drivers include:

- SWOT analysis: to suggest further opportunities and threats.
- PEST factors: to provide a better context for the analysis.
- The five competitive forces: to help identify situations where high competitive pressure in the industry is latent – and just ready to explode. This may occur when growth drivers go neutral or reverse (as in mobile telephones in 2001).
- The uncertainty grid: again this helps to prioritize the growth drivers.

The five competitive forces

The five competitive forces (Porter, 1980) provides an essential technique for analyzing your past, present and future competitive environment (see figure 2.9). These five competitive forces comprise:

- entrants (the threat of)
- substitutes
- buyer power (i.e. of customers)
- supplier power
- competitive rivalry (between existing players and, indeed, yourselves).

FIGURE 2.9: These forces determine industry
profitability…

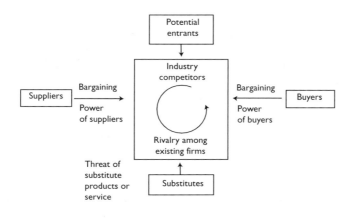

When Porter published his work it took almost five years to gain significant top management attention, and it has taken another 15 years for his five competitive forces to get even 50 per cent of the attention that SWOT currently has. (Judging from this and management's conservatism in picking up powerful strategic thinking techniques and running with them, it will be another 20 years before growth driver analysis [first published in Grundy, 1994] becomes general management currency. That is something of a shame considering how it might have helped dot-com company investors.)

To help demystify Porter's five competitive forces, let us take a look at an industry neglected by most strategic commentators – one ripe for transformation.

Illustrating the five competitive forces

CASE STUDY: AN UNUSUAL CASE – THE FUNERAL INDUSTRY

In analyzing a perhaps unusual industry – that of funerals (or, more explicitly, burials and cremations) – it can be seen that overall a relatively favourable picture emerges (see figure 2.10). The European industry is ripe for strategic breakthrough, even though the total market volume is actually decreasing (as people are living longer and longer) – in the US the market has already been transformed (source: Grundy, 1994).

FIGURE 2.10: Porter's five competitive forces
— a forcefield format

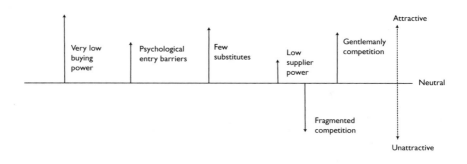

First, buyers have relatively low bargaining power. When some-one dies, to sort out the funeral and other arrangements is usually an urgent process. Death is what sociologists have described (rather clinically) as an 'unscheduled incident'. Furthermore, the buyer is in the perhaps unusual position of paying for the burial indirectly – from the deceased's estate. The buyer (the deceased's relatives) may also be emotionally affected by the death. The buyer is thus unlikely to be in a state of mind conducive to driving a hard bargain, to shopping around or going for a lowest-cost burial. This might look conspicuous in front of other relatives. In short, this situation of low buyer power is of clear advantage to players in the undertaking industry.

As Jessica Mitford (a critic of the funeral industry for many years) explained on UK Channel 4:

> The funeral transaction is unlike any other. If you buy a car or a house you discuss it with everybody, you shop around, and you consult. But if you have got a dead body in your living room then this puts a different complexion on things. You are likely to call the first under-taker who comes to mind.
>
> Once he comes in there and gets the body, that's the end of it as far as he is concerned. In other words, you are very unlikely to insist on someone else after that.
>
> The nature of the transaction is that you are probably in a fog of misery. You are not quite in your right mind and very susceptible in fact to all that the undertaker has to tell you; after all he is the expert.

This is compounded by the fact that when there is a death in the family then there is a lot of guilt feeling around – 'Oh dear, I wish I had been nicer when he was alive' – that kind of thing. And guilt feelings are very much what the undertaker counts on in selling his merchandise.

The fact is that people can be easily talked into something they don't need and cannot afford.

Second, 'substitutes' to a conventional burial in modern society have not really existed – at least in the UK (except of course the substitutes of going for cemetery versus crematorium options). The do-it-yourself burial is not socially acceptable. 'Substitutes' are therefore relatively unimportant – currently. (In a number of other industries this is similarly the case, but when using the five forces tool managers spend a lot of time trying to brainstorm substitutes. However, there is a caveat here that in certain industries potentially important 'substitutes' can be easily glossed over because managers haven't thought about the industry from the customers' perspective and also deep enough about innovation possibilities.) But this may be largely due to ignorance. Jane Spottiswode (UK Channel 4), author of *Undertaken with Love*, recounted a do-it-yourself (DIY) experiment with her husband's body:

> Well, the only real difficulty was getting a coffin, because I started with local undertakers and, shock, horror, they said 'We only provide it as part of our full service'.
>
> So then I tried the undertakers' suppliers, and the same thing happened. But then I found one, they thought it was a bit unusual. I got the coffin. It was chipboard and it was £36 plus VAT.
>
> Friends of mine had a Volvo, and they didn't want me to pick it up in my Mini – it wasn't quite the thing; we put it in the loft until my husband died because we knew there was no way he would live – he had lung cancer.
>
> When he died, after various tribulations we put him in the coffin and we took it and him to the crematorium. The funeral cost us just under £200 for everything.

Apparently (according to Channel 4) in the UK you can bury a body in a back garden (and don't even need a coffin) – but you do need a death certificate (but check the legalities first). You may also need to check out that the decomposing remains are unlikely to affect local water supplies. (This is what separates humans from Sandy and Hazel, the gerbils buried in one of our back gardens.) In the UK there is now even a movement of DIY funerals – 'The Natural Death Centre' (*Sunday Times*, 8 January 1995, 'Style', p.10).

Interestingly, the issue of substitutes highlights that the five competitive forces are not necessarily the same in each market – either by type of customer or by geography. For example, on a visit to Egypt one of the authors had the dubious fortune to be staying with a family who had experienced a sudden bereavement.

The owner of the village – a local Egyptian – came running in one night, shaking. His father had died, and the big issue was how to get his body to its destination within 24 hours. He seemed overwhelmed with a sense of urgency (or, more technically, Tom Peters' 'A Bias for Action' [Peters and Waterman, 1980]) and underwhelmed by grief (no doubt that would take hold after the funeral).

His imperative was to organize the relatives, the entourage, the funeral, the grieving – and all within hours (if not minutes). In Egypt, it would appear, you did not have the option, you had to do it yourself. The fact that this one force is different causes a whole set of different market dynamics in Egypt.

Continuing our story, entrants (our third force) may not be attracted to the funerals industry because of its traditionally gloomy image. On the other hand, real entry barriers may not be so high, particularly where a determined player enters by acquisition (as is now happening in the UK). Acquisitions may therefore enable entry and thereby shift the entry barrier indicator from being a 'favourable' force to one which is 'slightly less favourable'.

Howard Hodgson (a former UK undertaker – and now millionaire and author of *How to Get Dead Rich*) reflects on how business was done in the industry 20 years ago:

> It was very much a cottage industry, it was very much, other than the Co-Op, family, small. We needed to buy these [businesses] locally in order for us to have a strategy, which went from strength to strength. In fact, by 1990 we had established 546 outlets in the United Kingdom and were the largest funeral directors in the country.

This entry/acquisition strategy yielded some very tangible economies of scale for Howard Hodgson's business. He continues:

> There were considerable economies of scale. The average family firm of funeral directors had to have a hearse, probably two limousines, and conduct five or six funerals a week. The capital equipment was used once a day. By acquiring firms in the area and rationalizing, we were able to get one of these limousines to go out five or six times a day each.

Besides Howard Hodgson, a major entrant is Service Corporation International (SCI) of the US. Bill Heiligbradt, president of SCI (a nearly $1 billion company worldwide) said on UK Channel 4:

> We have found [in Australia]... that people have chosen to spend more on funerals. I would again emphasize the word chosen, it has been their choice.
>
> What we are here to do is to offer services and merchandise that make people feel better at a tough time in their lives...So the fact that our revenues have grown [per funeral] in Australia is because the Australian public desired it. In the UK that's our goal as well.

Apparently (according to Channel 4) funeral prices since SCI entered the Australian market increased by 40 per cent. Even where pre-paid funerals are involved, this can apparently increase industry profitability as the supplier reaps the fruit of receiving pre-paid investment funds. Estimates by the *Sunday Times* ('Style', 8 January 1995) of the value of just 25 per cent of funerals being pre-paid were put at £5 billion. This obviously suggests both a major threat and opportunity for investment institutions like insurance companies.

The pre-need market offers potential not merely for capturing value before death, but also for value added by pre-planning tailored funerals. Apparently in some cultures this has been the norm in the past. In China, for example, over 100 years ago all funerals were pre-planned, with individuals taking up to 20 years to refine the exotic detail of their funeral plans (*Mail on Sunday*, 20 May 2001).

Fourth, suppliers may have some bargaining power (especially in restricting space for graves or even for cemetery plaques), but there appears nothing special in the supply of hardware like coffins, hearses or the provision of flowers. (The one exception is perhaps the availability of land for burials.) This again is a favourable force.

Fifth, existing firms in the industry are currently relatively fragmented (few having significant market share, even locally against one another). Also, competitive behaviour is restrained given the cultural norms of the industry. Thus we would rate competitive rivalry overall as favourable, but as relatively important. So if rivalry were to increase significantly, this would have a big impact on the industry.

So, taking the five forces as a whole (see figure 2.10), it can be seen that the industry is currently relatively 'favourable' in providing the conditions for players in that industry to make a good, longer-term profit. Here we use a vector analysis format to do two things in one:

- to sort out whether a force is favourable (upward arrows) or unfavourable (downward arrows)
- to prioritize its importance.

This analysis suggests that:

- if already in the industry, longer-term profit should be good (unless entrants move in and restructure the industry or unless buyer power strengthens)
- if rated against other industries for identifying avenues for strategies for development, it might be considered to be an (inherently) attractive one to enter
- critical success factors such as building one's brand (to keep entrants out) and perhaps seeking a differentiation strategy can be readily identified.

The relative attractiveness of the undertaking industry has not escaped the attention of new players. Even as long ago as 1994 changes were mooted in the industry in a feature on 'The New British Way of Death' appearing in *The Times* (20 November 1994). This feature contrasted the clinical and gloomy British approach to the death business with innovation in the industry in France.

Around 1990, Michael Leclerc (who was part of the Leclerc family famed for their French supermarket operation) opened his first 'Supermarché de Mort' in Paris. By 1994 he had 60 supermarket franchises, 200 smaller shops and one-third of the French funeral business. In 1995 he entered the UK.

Michel Leclerc's business concept was to 'apply the technology of the food supermarket to the funeral industry'. In place of black, the Roc Leclerc colour scheme is blue and yellow, and in place of dim bulbs and heavy velvet curtains is strip lighting and stripped pine shelving. All the paraphernalia of death is on display, with a price tag. The main things they could offer, Mr Weller (the UK franchise manager) said, 'are choice, economy, and no hidden extras. We aim to charge between 20 and 30 per cent less than elsewhere but, above all, to offer the widest possible range, which our customers can view without the pressure of having a funeral director at their shoulder.'

Monsieur Michel Leclerc himself said on Channel 4:

We will try to reduce prices by between 40 and 50 per cent, because to me prices in England are very high, and I think we will quickly expand. I don't see what can stop us.

As Jane Spottiswode (the Channel 4 expert on DIY funerals) also said:

Why don't Texas and MFI and all those firms that profess to be do-it-yourself experts stack flat-pack coffins; stick-it together yourself. Again I was laughed to scorn. I received quite a nice letter from Sainsbury's who thought it was a good idea, but not for them.

Unfortunately, Michael Leclerc's new business did not prosper in the UK, presumably because he overlooked certain PEST factors (especially the 'social' – the very traditional, British culture). Also he may have entered at the wrong place – Catford, in South London – which was perhaps not the most trendy and innovative place in the UK.

A key lesson from this case is that you do not just have to have a good strategy – it has to be implemented at the right place, at the right time, and in the right way.

Coming back to the opportunities for expanding the very narrow, do-it-yourself substitute niche, one might be surprised to discover that:

- In principle, if one were able to secure a cheap burial site one could achieve a 'lowest cost' grave for 'as little as' £300 (including a cardboard coffin for £49.50). To this you would need to add the funeral service itself – still coming in at the cheapest at £645. More recently (*Sunday Times*, 'Style', 8 January 1995) the lower cost burial options have been exalted as 'environmentally friendly', saving the burning of hundreds of thousands of coffins each year.
- Alternatively, you might opt for a more conventional and, by comparison, up-market burial for over £4,000 (with an expensive oak coffin at around £2,000).
- Burial at sea is a novel proposition – this option saves the graveyard or cemetery cost, but requires 'boat hire with precise navigation equipment' (presumably to avoid the coffin turning up by mistake on a public beach) – a minimum of £3,000.

What emerges therefore from our industry analysis is a cosy industry structure ripe for innovation and restructuring, offering better quality at a much more acceptable price. To go one better than the Leclerc business concept, one might even imagine the possibility of a telephone-based funeral service or Funerals Direct PLC (perhaps called 'Death Direct' would be too unsavoury). This concept might offer the advantages of speed, simplicity, openness (about price) and flexibility. To update this to the dot-com era, perhaps this could be entitled 'Directdeath.com'.

Another competitive force which might change in this industry is the bargaining power of customers. There is near-local monopoly or oligopoly of undertakers. An assumption here is that bodies cannot really be moved around very far because of twin problems of refrigeration and speed (why do funeral vehicles never seem to exceed five to ten miles per hour? In Egypt they do a minimum of 60 miles an hour, such is the sense of real urgency). But there is no physical reason why bodies cannot be transported quicker (if colder) to a central location prior to collection for the actual funeral. Even cost would not be a major issue if one had a national network with high market share (supplementing the 'Directdeath.com' concept above).

Using the five competitive forces

Before we leave this example, there are a few more general and serious points which need to be made.

- When doing the five competitive forces you must try to put into the back of your mind which particular player you are. Otherwise the analysis of the industry itself will become confused with your own particular position. (Your own competitive position is best addressed by doing a second analysis to check out the critical success factors which emerge vis-à-vis your business.)
- You may need to do more than one analysis using the five forces, depending on whether you have in effect one industry, or more than one industry or market to analyze. For example, in the car market you need to do separate (although related) analyses for the executive and smaller volume car market. These two markets have quite differing characteristics (and inherent attractiveness). In the funerals business do a separate analysis for a) the pre-need market, b) the funeral, c) the aftercare market, and d) for a new, dot-com market.
- You need to look at how the competitive forces interact with one another rather than in isolation. For instance, buyers may seek to enter the market (via backward integration). Or suppliers may also seek

entry (via forward integration). Equally, buyers may look wider for sources of supply (if competitive rivalry is low), enticing new entrants in. Finally, new substitutes might be sought where buyer power is low.

■ When the industry changes significantly it is frequently not because of one competitive force, but because of changes to two or possibly three forces combining together.

Besides its use for strategic positioning of existing business, the five competitive forces provides an essential analysis for evaluating any new strategy. This is even if the 'market' or 'market segment' seems to be very similar to existing ones. Also, strategies for growth can frequently entail changing the industry structure. For example, this might involve introducing new substitutes or restructuring the industry through acquisition. Or industry change might occur by innovation in cutting out players in the industry chain, or by radically reducing costs (especially in mature and competitive industries).

Figure 2.11 now performs a segmentation analysis of the five competitive forces, helping you to be more discerning about which business areas are worthwhile being in, and which you should not be in, which you might be in – if certain preconditions are met.

FIGURE 2.11: Porter's five competitive forces and market segmentation

	Market 1	Market 2	Market 3	Market 4
Buyer power				
Entry threat				
Rivalry				
Substitutes				
Supplier power				
Total score				

Figure 2.11 helps us to refine Porter's rather generic presumptions about the attractiveness of a particular industry.

Further analysis can be done for:

- different geographic markets
- different channels to market
- different end-user industrial sectors.

EXERCISE

For a business area of your choice:

- For each of the five competitive forces are these:
  - favourable (three ticks)
  - neutral (two ticks)
  - unfavourable (one tick)?
- Taking the five forces as a whole (and your total number of ticks), what is the 'so-what?' from this, for instance in terms of:
  - its overall attractiveness
  - its critical success factors (for competing)
  - your specific options (for coping with these forces, or for changing the mindset of the industry)?

Finally, there are two further practical refinements of Porter's five forces which seem to have gone unnoticed by strategy theorists:

- It is possible to consider the extent to which each one of Porter's forces is favourable versus less favourable over time. This can be represented in a competitive forces over time curve (see figure 2.12). Here the degree of favourability is plotted over a particular period in the industry's life-cycle – perhaps over three to five years (or perhaps, in the dot-com industry, between three to five months). Figure 2.12 shows bargaining power over time increasing as a market matures quickly.
- Another cut to this is to look at how the five forces may change over the customer life-cycle. This thinking applies especially to the bargaining power of the buyers, substitutes and to competitive rivalry. Figure 2.13 illustrates this with reference to a) where the customer gets more and more locked into a supplier – for example, in a major consultancy project – or b) where the customer gets wise and learns (over a series of transactions) how to extract more value from it.

Porter's five forces are valuable for understanding your customer's industry. This can give significant edge to your marketing efforts, and to the design and delivery of products and services.

Industry dynamics can also play an important role. One of the criticisms that can be levelled at Porter's five forces analysis is that it appears as a static model. Although this was never intended by Porter, it needs to be demonstrated how the competitive forces can be used dynamically.

FIGURE 2.12: Competitive-pressure-over-time curve

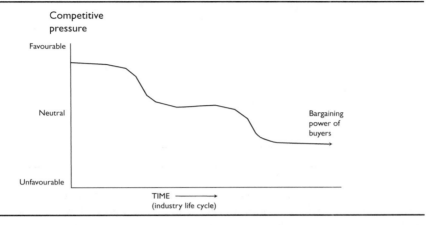

FIGURE 2.13: Customer bargaining power (over time)

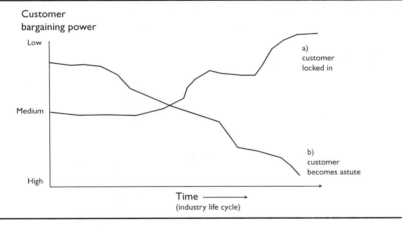

Figure 2.14 shows how the competitive forces can be used dynamically. The competitive forces need to be overlaid against:

■ the economic cycle
■ the industry cycle.

Figure 2.14 was born during some inspired moments of reflection by a number of Scandinavian managers from Partek. Partek manufactures and markets trucks, tractors, logging and defence equipment, and other systems throughout the world. (Partek's home base is Finland.)

FIGURE 2.14: The industry life-cycle and the five competitive forces

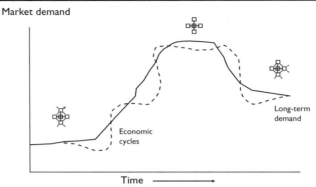

This picture shows an industry life-cycle overlaid with the economic cycle. The effects of the economic cycle can be pronounced, as in the early 1990s recession. Note how the Partek managers show the five forces moving from favourable or neutral to adverse (circled as they move to the right). The picture produces almost a cartwheel effect.

As one of the Partek managers put it:

> The real challenge is that senior managers need to hold in their mind not just the economic cycle, but also the five competitive forces. They also need to be able to map the longer-term industry cycle against the competitive forces – which do change. In our markets, because the effect of the economic cycle can be significant, we have to be able to think ahead and be very flexible to operational changes.

To summarize, the main benefits of the five competitive forces are that they:

- are much more incisive in analyzing competitor opportunities and (particularly) threats than a SWOT analysis
- can provide a prophetic view of industry changes (especially in margin levels) and in competitive structure and financial performance generally
- can give real insights into potential strategic options and into critical success factors
- can provide more substance for performing scenario development
- help to prioritize the areas which it is most/least important to compete in.

The disadvantages of the five competitive forces are that:

- Porter's framework looks daunting and complex (they can be remedied by using the shorthand version of 'competitive pressure' – which, of course, means thinking about the bargaining power of buyers, suppliers, entry barriers, rivalry and substitutes).

- Where the forces do not show a too bright or rosy picture managers' strategic thinking ends in a cul-de-sac. If the industry does not seem to be particularly attractive what can managers do about it (except look for another job in another industry)? Well, they might at least consider changing the rules of the game (see next section) or in being selective in what they do or do not compete in. Or, they may realize that to be profitable they need to have truly awesome competitive advantage.

One of the authors experienced this exact dilemma when creating a strategy for a training company of which she was a director.

CASE STUDY: BUSINESS PLANNING AND COMPETITIVE MYOPIA

Whilst I was finishing my MBA I needed to draw up a business plan for the training company of which I was operational head.

We had two markets – public courses and in-company. Our position in the public courses was strong, but we were weaker in-company, where we had lower volumes and inadequate client relationship skills. The dilemma was: shall we focus in the business plan on developing public courses, which was a mature market, or should we have risked focusing mainly on in-company?

The five competitive forces analysis came out as follows:

	Public course attractiveness		In-company attractiveness	
Buyer power	Medium	✔✔	Low	✔✔✔
Entry threat	High	✔	Low	✔✔✔
Substitutes	Medium	✔✔	Low	✔✔✔
Rivalry	High	✔✔	Medium	✔✔
Supply power	Medium	✔✔	Medium	✔✔
Score	9 ticks		Score	13 ticks

Note: here I have had to be careful with the ticks; for instance, if buyer power were 'high', this would score 'low attractiveness' (or one tick), as this is a negative.

Clearly, the in-company market was more structurally attractive (and also had much more positive growth drivers). There was a big difference in entry threat between each market, and also public courses exhibited greater bargaining power of buyers and there were substitutes (electronic learning). In-company won hands down.

Unfortunately, my boss seemed to believe that the public courses were easier and cheaper to develop (he had not done either the growth drivers or the five competitive forces analysis). A few months later I left the company but was able to monitor its market development.

Over the next nine months a number of new entrants (conference companies) entered the (now almost saturated) public course market, putting pressure on my former company's public courses.

It was fascinating to monitor the impact of these new entrants in real time – showing how practical and relevant a five competitive forces analysis can be.

The uncertainty grid

One way of now testing the external and internal assumptions underpinning a strategy is by using a qualitative importance-uncertainty grid (see figure 1.5) (derived from Mitroff and Linstone, 1993). Using this grid, managers can plot the key assumptions driving the value of any strategic decision. These can be external and internal, soft and hard assumptions.

Having selected a sub-set of these assumptions, these are now prioritized by using the grid (which can be a flipchart, a white board, or a piece of paper). Once assumptions are carefully and skilfully defined, it is possible to debate the relative importance and uncertainty of these various assumptions (using a flipchart, the assumptions can be easily moved around using post-it notes).

These assumptions are defined in terms of 'the future world being okay'. For example, if we were using it to understand the uncertainties of getting to a meeting in London on time, assumptions would be defined as 'the trains will run on time', rather than 'the trains will not run on time'.

A frequent mistake (when first using the grid) is to have some assumptions defined positively and some negatively. This makes it impossible to judge usually the overall downsides to a strategy. An example of this would be 'Kings Cross Station might be closed' (a negative assumption), and 'there will be no London Underground strike that day' (a positive assumption).

At the beginning of the investment appraisal, key assumptions are likely to be mapped in the due north and northeast quadrants. Upon testing it is quite common to find one or more assumptions moving over to the danger zone in the southeast.

Figure 2.15 actually relates to the new product launch. The extra sales volume from existing customers is very important, but also considered relatively certain. Sales to new customers are considerably more uncertain (but also very important) – shown in the southeast of the grid (figure 2.16). Product launch costs are somewhat less important and also reasonably certain (shown just slightly northeast of the centre of the grid).

FIGURE 2.15: The uncertainty-importance grid (example)

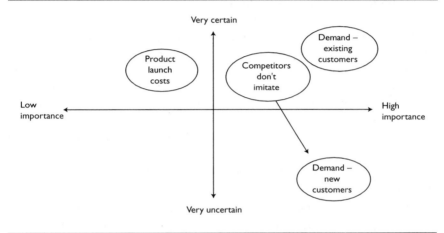

FIGURE 2.16: The uncertainty-importance grid (analyzed)

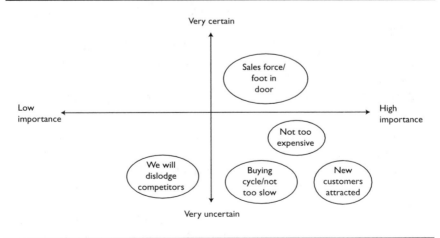

Interestingly, a more fundamental assumption – implicit in managers' minds but brought out by discussion of the grid is – that competitors will not imitate with a better product in year two.

In this case, the assumption is shown as beginning life just west of the product launch costs assumption (relatively certain and less important), but actually heading southeast.

The uncertainty grid is very helpful for targeting data collection. This should be aimed at learning more about those assumptions which are either most important, more uncertain, or both, and note those bits of data which are just easier to collect.

The uncertainty and importance grid is also a vital tool for evaluating assumptions prior to undertaking key financial sensitivities. This tool helps focus these sensitivities towards the critical uncertainties (for example, to new competitor entry). A 'sensitivity' is defined as being the financial impact from a change on either a value or cost driver (see, also, chapter 5). For example, following on from the uncertainty-importance grid, successful imitation of the new product by a competitor might well reduce prices by ten per cent in years two and three, and reduce volume sales to new customers by half.

The uncertainty grid is often misunderstood by managers for a number of reasons:

- Their mindset is one of putting on the grid what they will actually do to achieve the strategy. Whilst it is perfectly possible to use the grid in this way, when we are conducting preliminary strategic analysis this would be inappropriate and premature.
- Managers are not used to thinking explicitly about their assumptions, as these are taken for granted.
- Managers find it very hard to think about, let alone to creatively imagine, the future.
- Sometimes they want to put probabilities on the grid, rather than leave it as more qualitative – especially if they come from a more technical background. But the point of the grid is to think through (unquantified) degrees of uncertainty rather than to focus on more easy-to-quantify risks.

Ultimately, 'importance' can be subjected to some financial analysis – based on the likely financial impact. But experience tells us that the grid is more powerful when left initially unquantified. (Value and cost drivers, or performance drivers, can help to go beyond 'importance' in more depth – see chapter 5.)

The uncertainty grid can be used either before a decision, during implementation, or for post review. Indeed it is perhaps at its most power-ful when tracking live implementation of a strategy. Here assumptions which were implicit previously often crystallize in a startling and unexpected way – as being both most important and as most uncertain.

The uncertainty grid can be used for:

- evaluating specific strategic decisions
- investment decisions
- acquisitions and alliances
- business reappraisal and turnaround
- strategic change programmes
- strategic breakthrough projects generally
- new market entry
- product development
- diversification
- e-commerce strategies.

At a personal level it is also useful for evaluating future career strategies and personal relationships.

It has relationships with a number of other techniques, including:

- SWOT – helping us to assess and prioritize threats. It also helps check out whether your strengths are really that important, and whether you are certain they really are strengths or not (as a basis for targeting market data collection).
- The strategic option grid (see chapter 4): as input to the 'uncertainty and risk' criteria.
- For scenario development.
- For use with importance and uncertainty-over-time curves (see the later section on scenarios).

The key benefits of the uncertainty grid are that:

- it helps to identify the vulnerables and blind-spots in a strategy
- it helps managers to focus on the future, rather than on the present
- its simple format allows it to be used at a very intuitive level – so that paper representation is not really essential.

Its disadvantages are that:

- it is somewhat counter to the mindset of many managers who need to practise it a couple of times to make it work
- managers are sometimes unsure as to what level of analysis it should be used at.

To help with the latter point, it can be useful to do a micro-level uncertainty grid (like that shown in figure 2.16), and then to break down one of the assumptions using a separate and more detailed uncertainty grid.

For example, in figure 2.16 we break down the assumption that: 'We will make sales to new customers' into:

- 'new customers will be attracted to it'
- 'our sales force can get their foot in the door'
- 'it will not be simply too expensive'
- 'we will be able to dislodge competitors'
- 'the customers' buying cycle will not be very slow'.

It is really helpful to make the assumption as specific as possible. For example, we could turn 'Competitors will not imitate it successfully' into 'No competitor will have comparable market share through imitation within two years of launch'.

The effect of being as specific as this is to shift the assumption on the grid – often on both axes.

Finally, asking the question 'What is the one big thing we have missed' can be extremely helpful in covering blind-spots.

An associated technique is also the 'Uncertainty-Influence Grid' (figure 2.17). Here the horizontal axis is low uncertainty versus high uncertainty. The vertical axis is high influence versus low influence. Again we plot the key assumptions on the grid of the world going well.

FIGURE 2.17: The uncertainty-influence grid

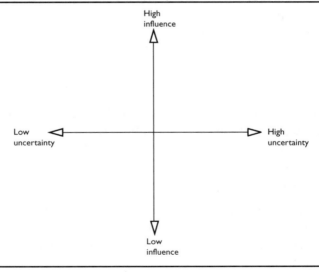

The danger zone here is with those assumptions which are both most uncertain and over which we have low influence. Once we have identified the respective positionings we then:

- focus corrective action on those areas which are most uncertain but over which we have greatest influence
- focus our creative thinking on those areas which are most uncertain and over which we have least influence (through the Cunning Plan and through the creativity techniques contained in chapter 4 – forthcoming).

Scenarios

Scenarios have been well popularized for many years (particularly by Shell managers and planners), but for many the notion of scenario development appears difficult, time-consuming and one of uncertain benefit. It is perhaps ironic that the most effective tool for dealing with uncertainty is rarely used because managers are so uncertain as to how to use it, and about what value it will be. In fact, scenario development can be rapid and add disproportionate value relative to effort.

The key questions which are now therefore addressed are as follows:

- What are scenarios?
- How can scenarios help?
- How can scenarios be developed – and quickly?

Scenarios:

- are internally consistent views of the future
- focus on discontinuity and change (not on continuity)
- also involve exploring how the underlying systems in the business environment may generate change
- are views of how the competitive players (existing and new) might behave.

Scenarios are not static and comprehensive views of the future. Scenarios are in many ways more like a video film – they are of necessity selective but contain a dynamic storyline. Scenarios thus contain a series of views (pictures) of the future. This is fruitfully presented as a series of pictures, not as a single one. Also, there is a storyline which enables these pictures to hang together.

The story can be run (again like a video film) forward or, alternatively, backward. By replaying the story you can work backwards from a particular scenario to see what events might bring about a particular outcome. (These events are called 'transitional events'.)

Just as 'strategy' is frequently defined as a pattern in a stream of (past and current) decisions, so a 'scenario' is a pattern of future events, and of the interaction between customers, competitors and other key players in the industry.

Next, although many managers understand change they are frequently bemused by the idea of 'discontinuity'. Discontinuity simply means a major break between past and future. Discontinuity can occur imperceptibly (for example, just as a train may be switched from one line to another). Or, it can happen abruptly – with a big jolt (or, even in its most extreme form, through derailment).

Scenarios naturally involve a lot of thinking about how the external environment actually works. For example, how might a change in regulation bring about market growth, changes in prices and margins, the levels of competitive rivalry and the pattern of competitor dominance? This is not about just applying standard PEST or competitive forces analysis and looking at the output in a static and isolated manner; it is very much about looking at industry dynamics, the impact of lags (for instance in recognition of what is going on and subsequent behaviour) and in changes in the industry mindset.

Finally, scenarios are not about creating abstract pictures. (This is not modern art.) As in cartoons, scenarios show players in the market doing specific things and behaving in specific ways.

Scenarios are therefore not an excuse to make broad or vague generalizations – as they are pictures they have a clarity about them which will enable recognition. Managers need to know which world they are entering into – the resolution thus has to be sharp, not fuzzy. In Ansoff's terms (1975), they provide ways of picking up, amplifying and interpreting weak signals in the environment.

Scenarios, like all pictures, will thus have a foreground and a background, some features of central interest, and others which are more peripheral.

By now it should have become evident what scenarios are not. Scenarios are not:

- mere forecasts
- projections from past trends
- fixed or rigid world views
- complete in all details
- static.

When doing scenario analysis for the first time with a management team, it is imperative to make these distinctions – particularly to avoid the rabbit warren of projections and forecasts.

Scenarios can help in a number of ways. Scenario planning at Shell is principally known for its very 'big picture' analysis – particularly for global or industry-broad scenarios, or for country-specific scenarios. In addition, managers can also perform issue-specific scenarios (for example, the impact of regulating/environmental pressure). Or one can do scenarios specific to a particular strategic decision.

Scenarios can thus be used for:

- acquisitions and alliances
- strategic investment decisions
- strategic projects
- strategic change
- organizational change
- our personal career.

For example, some time ago a major company wanted to explore how one might set about accelerating scenario development. The company had used scenarios to a limited extent in the past, but had found them to be slow and arduous to create.

The challenge set was this: how could one create a small number of scenarios for a key market in under a day?

A small (but hand-picked) team was assembled, which included the representatives, technical experts and planning staff – and an external consultant. (The consultant's task was to design and facilitate the process, not to give expert input on scenario content.) Once the issue had been defined, a number of key questions aimed at probing views of the future were defined. These were supported by the process in figure 2.18. It is also useful to have two small teams working in parallel on the scenario – with core common assumptions but with deliberate divergence at the later stages of the process.

Figure 2.18 begins by setting the broad background to the scenario. Just because it is looking at a scenario of the future doesn't mean that all assumptions are left open.

FIGURE 2.18: A scenario generation process

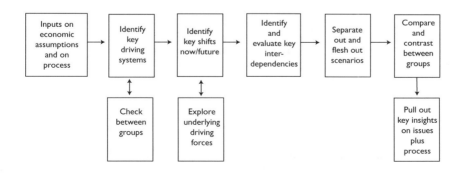

Next, the key driving systems impacting on the environment are identified. For instance, for the do-it-yourself UK retail market (in the late 1990s) the following was identified:

- changes in social and demographic lifestyles (e.g. the breakdown of the 'nuclear' family)
- the impact of the housing market
- change in leisure patterns
- the pattern of rivalry in the market place (for example, now that the grocery chain Sainsbury's has bought the out-of-town, DIY retailer, Texas, in the UK).

This kind of analysis is best done in a pictorial way. Figure 2.19 outlines some pictures of this industry. This figure highlights not merely the complexity of the external systems impacting on the industry, but also the influence of key clusters, particularly those around the housing market and the economy, family leisure patterns, and also competitive rivalry.

FIGURE 2.19: Scenarios for the UK DIY markets (late 1990s)

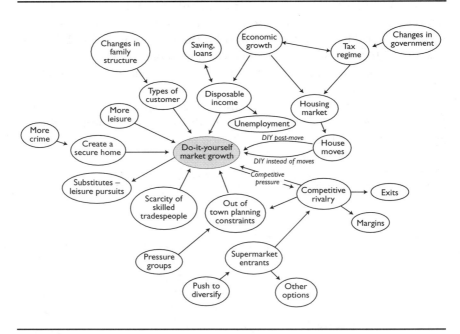

Here is a quick run-through of the scenario storyline, which was written in 1995 for the period 1995–2000:

- Labour government, with slightly higher taxes but with these eroding the incomes of income-rich people, but not specifically DIY fanatics
- reducing unemployment, making it hard to get tradespeople to do things at a reasonable price in the home
- so that the (now) dominant player, Sainsbury's, begins to make very good profits out of DIY, especially as no new sites can be opened (due to planning restrictions)
- so profitability per outlet goes up.

Once this analysis has been performed, it is then possible to identify those variables which are likely to be particularly unstable (that you can annotate as a green 'U') and high impact (and annotated as a red 'I'). Variables which are either or both U and I may then suggest some possible key shifts between 'new' and 'future'.

Another phase is to identify the biggest and most sensitive areas of interdependency. This helps identify these clusters of variables (and thus the shifts in 'from … to') which, once begun, could have an unstoppable momentum.

In order to separate out and flesh out specific scenarios, it is useful to turn once again to the uncertainty grid. This enables the identification of the one or more assumptions which are both extremely uncertain and very important. This assumption (the 'danger zone') normally suggests a specific scenario route.

A practical issue is the need to make sure that each scenario work group works together as a coherent team to define and then evaluate each assumption and its positioning. Frequently managers are tempted to delegate the positioning of each assumption to different individuals who would then work independently. This may lead to confusion over both what the assumption really means and why it has been positioned in a certain way. It is often faster and more effective to work together as a small team rather than to do fragmented individual work.

Once that route is chosen, fleshing out the various scenarios involves reviewing the key interdependencies, the potential major shifts and then creating a storyline about how the scenario could actually come about. This storyline would entail considering things like the following:

- What will the industry (or niche, or organization) really look like?
- How will the key players behave?
- What transitional events might bring this scenario about?

A most useful technique is to role-play competitors and how they might behave in the storyline of the scenario (and, for that matter, other key players like major customers, suppliers or the regulator). This helps inject more life and dynamism into the scenario picture.

Once a small number of scenarios have been developed, they should be then exposed to cross-testing by the two teams. This will help:

- reveal why particular assumptions were thought most important and most uncertain (and, conversely, those which are less important and most certain);
- draw out the implications for strategy, and for the critical success factors;
- begin to bring out the financial implications of the scenario.

Financial analysis does have a role to play in scenario development. This should not be so much a part of artificial sensitivity analysis (or 'playing the numbers game'), rather than the opportunity to begin to value and cost out the impact of a particular scenario, not only on your particular business but indeed on the whole industry. Some key lessons from scenario development in the past show that you need to:

- bring line managers and planners together to create scenarios
- examine key shifts in your views of the world
- ensure that financial analysis feeds directly into planning/decision-making processes
- avoid too many views of the future (preferably keep to two)
- manage concerns that 'we will never get the right (precise) answer' – scenarios are not about doing forecasts
- use few analysis tools – also avoid lots of detailed data input – free the mind to be creative
- refine and revisit scenarios, especially where new signals are detected in the business environment.

Scenarios can be used for a variety of business and organizational applications, including scenarios for an organizational future.

Expanding on the last example a little further:

CASE STUDY: ORGANIZATIONAL FUTURES AT A MAJOR TELECOMMUNICATIONS COMPANY

In the mid-to-late 1990s a major telecommunications company decided to try to see into its future. Using the uncertainty grid an assumption that 'it will be possible to run the organization on just a third of present staff' was tested out.

It was believed that whilst this assumption was very important, it was equally very uncertain-certain, but this was purely due to internal political blockages rather than for business reasons.

Uncertainty is dynamic and figure 2.20 helps to understand the phases of scenario development, its speed and impact. Figure 2.21 also maps the way in which uncertainty changes over time. On the vertical axis we see the degree of uncertainty – whether it is low, medium or high. The horizontal axis is the time dimension. Figure 2.21 is an example of how uncertainty might increase and then actually decrease significantly – once the impact of change in a market has worked its way through. An example of this would be a global economic turnaround which initially causes confusion generally. This culminates in a financial crisis, exhibiting great turbulence and uncertainty. Subsequently the major world economies stabilize and consolidate, and uncertainty reduces.

FIGURE 2.20: The uncertainty tunnel

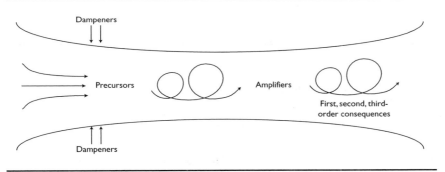

FIGURE 2.21: Uncertainty-over-time curve

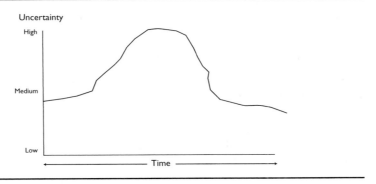

This curve can be plotted either for the total uncertainty of a particular strategy, or for that of a particular assumption. In order to place some prioritization on a particular assumption, we can then map its importance over time, using figure 2.22.

FIGURE 2.22: Importance-over-time curve

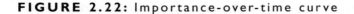

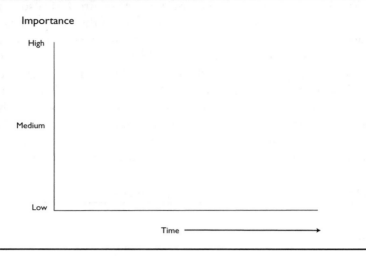

These subsidiary techniques can help support the scenario storyline – which we discussed earlier.

The benefits of scenario development are that:

- they can help one to 'see around corners' – helping to cope with uncertainty
- they make managers more sensitive to and alert to changes in their external (and internal) environment
- they get managers to 'think future' – in a way which conventional planning often does not
- they encourage one to think about 'How can we create a desired future?'

Scenarios are linked to other tools as follows:

- Wishbone analysis – here they help to construct a desired future.
- PEST analysis, growth drivers, the five competitive forces, motivator – hygiene factors and competitor profiling all help in telling stories about the (external) future.
- AID, forcefield analysis, stakeholder analysis (see chapter 5) help in imagining internal futures.
- Fishbone analysis – can help to identify events which lead to negative scenarios.

Re-writing industry rules – the industry mindset

Whilst Porter's five forces give an excellent overview of existing industry structure, they can lead us to take this structure as read. However, it is usually possible to challenge this structure through examining what has become the sixth force (to add to Porter's five), that of the industry mindset (Grundy, 1995).

'Industry mindset' can be defined as: 'The expectations and assumptions about the competitive rules of the game and the levels of financial returns in an industry.' The key ingredients of our definition are as follows:

- Expectations: the broader beliefs about how the industry is likely to behave and develop. These expectations may be completely appropriate or widely appropriate.
- Assumptions: the specific beliefs about industry and how to compete within it. These assumptions are frequently implicit and not thoroughly tested or debated.

The industry mindset plays a major role in shaping industry change (as in the funerals business), thus transforming Porter's five competitive forces model from a static into a much more dynamic model. Figure 2.23 adapts Porter's forces by showing how these five forces interrelate with each other and also how the industry mindset is at the very hub of competitive pressure:

- positioning the industry mindset as the central, sixth force, which plays a profound role in shaping the other five competitive forces;
- explaining how the other five forces interact with one another.

FIGURE 2.23: The industry mindset

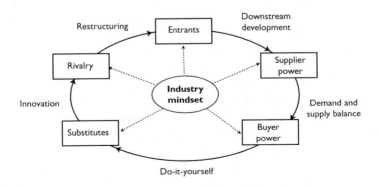

To illustrate the final point, buyer power is closely linked to substitutes (via companies deciding to do-it-yourself) and also to supplier power (via demand/supply imbalance). Also, entrants may restructure the industry, impacting on rivalry. (Porter's own account of the five competitive forces perhaps underdevelops the role of these inter-dependencies. By placing rivalry at the heart of his model, and with the other forces feeding into it, the other interdependencies are lost.)

Or suppliers themselves might enter the industry via downstream development.

Finally, substitutes and rivalry might together provoke fresh industry innovation. Few players with longer-term stake in the industry will sit idly by and watch their market position significantly eroded by new sources of competition.

The industry mindset can play a profound influence over industry dynamics. The prevailing industry mindset may send signals to players adjacent to the industry, attracting new entrants because of prevailing growth and profit expectations. (For instance, going back to the undertaking example, the cosy environment has now attracted new entrants, who have entered by acquisition.)

Also, rivalry is intensified by the 'copycat syndrome' – particularly when there are relatively uniform perceptions of what recipes currently make money. The copycat syndrome is often manifest in tactical pricing, culminating in a price war.

The industry mindset may also have an impact on the role of buyer power and also upon substitutes. This impact can occur by influencing buying criteria and also the switching criteria of buyers. Buyers may have narrow perceptions about what substitutes are available and inaccurate expectations about how new substitutes will perform. They may also make assumptions, for instance, that their purchase will not result in rapid obsolescence.

For example, in the mobile telephone market in the 1990s, first-time customers had poorly defined buying criteria initially. They had even less well-defined switching criteria. Having made their first mobile telephone purchase, within a matter of months they learnt of the full cost burdens, the limitations of the hardware (and the particular system it is reliant on). Perhaps within months (or even weeks) the customer might become aware that substitute systems (as well as the actual telephone itself) exist. In a relatively short period the buyers' switching criteria are likely to crystallize, based on their learning about the opportunities and often severe limitations of the product. The naivety of buyers' criteria is illustrated by one of the author's personal experiences. Tempted by a 'free connection deal' he was unaware of the £50 disconnection fee he was asked to pay to a well-known supplier to get rid of hardware which did not meet official performance standards. (His eight-year-old son kindly offered to dispose of the handset into the local River Cam.)

By 2001 rivalry has gone up considerably, buyers are very discerning and the mobile telecommunications companies have become far more responsive and innovative.

This example highlights how easily the five competitive forces analysis might easily fail to identify a key driver of industry change where the five forces are analyzed as a quick snapshot.

Finally, industry mindset plays a key influence over the power of suppliers through the fear factor. As anyone who has run a business knows, the fear factor of not securing the business plays a key role in undermining supplier power. When using the five competitive forces model it is remarkable how rarely 'supplier power' is credited with much competitive significance. This is probable due to the erosion of this power by the fear factor.

Certain interactions between the five forces have already been explained, so we focus now on the new elements.

- Entrants: these may introduce better and/or cheaper substitutes and may broaden buyer choice, giving them more bargaining power.
- Rivalry: intensifying rivalry may either squeeze suppliers' prices or may encourage closer collaboration via partnerships in order either to facilitate differentiation or low cost strategies.
- Substitutes: these might take existing suppliers out of play. This underlines the importance of thinking about substitutes both within your own part of the industry chain, but also either up or down the chain.
- Buyer power: this might intensify rivalry through buyers increasing the extent to which they shop around. Also, buyers might be tempted into developing upstream in the industry chain by entry strategies.
- Supplier power: here the overall demand/supply balance is a very important factor in adding to, or subtracting from, the negotiating power of suppliers.

Summary of key points

The analysis of the external environment raises many points to reflect on:

- Gap analysis is absolutely essential in order to get a sense of the need for new strategic thinking in the organization.
- SWOT analysis needs to be tested out using the other techniques and also with some selective, external data collection. It is also imperative to draw out its 'so-what?'

- PEST analysis helps to detect disruptive environmental change – and may highlight fresh opportunities.
- Growth drivers are essential to help understand the inherent attractiveness of markets, to detect changes, to proactively help grow the market, and to assist in forecasting sales generally.
- The five competitive forces help to ensure that we focus on the quality of a particular market – and also its competitive dynamics – rather than just its growth. It also helps in predicting and understanding possible changes in our margins, and more proactively can be used to develop strategies to protect and enhance these.
- The uncertainty grid, the uncertainty-influence analysis, and the uncertainty tunnel help us to detect and to understand key vulnerabilities – both occurring within the environment and within our own strategy as well. These techniques also help us to explore the dynamic effects of uncertainty and also to develop more flexible and robust strategies.
- The industry mindset (or our 'sixth competitive force') reminds us not to take the industry structure and its behaviour as a given, but to explore new and innovative ways of competing which will both shift the industry in our favour and give us real competitive advantage.

Conclusion

Analyzing the external environment can be relatively demanding. But providing that the task is broken up step-by-step the potential for identifying external breakthroughs is enormous, particularly through challenging the industry mindset.

References

Ansoff, H.I., 'Managing Strategic Surprise by Response to Weak Signals', *Californian Management Review* XVIII, p.p.21–23, Winter 1975.

Grundy, A.N., *Breakthrough Strategies for Growth*, Pitman Publishing, London, 1995.

Lewin, K., *A Dynamic Theory of Personality*, McGraw Book Company, New York, 1935.

Mitroff, I.I. and H.A. Linstone, *The Unbounded Mind*, Oxford University Press, Oxford, 1993.

Peters, T. and R.H. Waterman, *In Search of Excellence*, Harper and Row, New York, 1980.

Porter, E.M., *Competitive Strategy*, Free Press, Macmillan, New York, 1980.

CHAPTER THREE

Demystifying strategic analysis, part 2: strategic positioning

Introduction

In this second chapter on Demystifying Strategic Analysis we now look at how we analyze our own strategic positioning. One of the central tenets of strategic management is that one must draw a very clear distinction between:

- how inherently attractive one's markets are to be in
- one's own relative competitive strength in those markets.

In this chapter we examine a number of key techniques, including:

- motivator-hygiene factor analysis
- competitor analysis
- the GE grid.

Motivators and hygiene factors

An important clue in resolving problems of measuring value is the distinction between motivators and hygiene factors. This also enables us to explore the dynamics of value capture. (The idea of motivators and hygiene factors is imported from Herzberg's theory of motivation.)

Hygiene factors are the basic standards of product and service delivery which, unless delivered, will create value destruction. Where hygiene factors are not met they detract from value – and the buying impulse. Equally some activities may detract from the core delivery of value. Motivator activities excite customers distinctively and are the sources of differentiation. It is likely that hygiene activities will (at best) just pass on their costs to total value. Motivators contribute more to total value. One way of distinguishing motivator activities from hygiene activities is to adapt forcefield analysis to the task.

In figure 3.1 the conventional 'enabling' forces become the motivators, and the 'constraining' forces become the hygiene factors not being met and distractors. The relative size of the arrow (or vector) is a visual indication of the actual strength of indicators and hygiene factors (from a customer's perspective). This tool can be used either to help predict customer buying behaviour or to perform customer benchmarking of value added by the firm.

The picture of the motivator-hygiene factors which we have drawn may be deceptively simple.

FIGURE 3.1: Motivator-hygiene factor analysis: businessman contemplating a BMW purchase

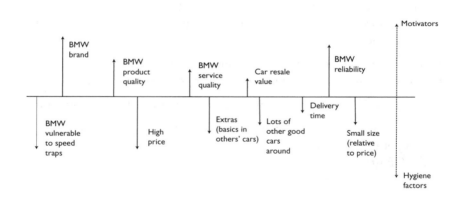

What you will need to think through is:

- Is the factor really a motivator or merely a hygiene factor (often managers put in 'motivators' things which are simply hygiene factors met to different degrees)?
- How important is that motivator or hygiene factor?
- How well is it met (or not met)?

Notice the need to break down the second and third of these.

We make no apologies here for the apparent complexity at work – we believe that the technique is only slightly complex because of the complexity within customers' own value criteria.

Obviously, at some point, a motivator-hygiene factor analysis needs to be checked out by some empirical research – with customers.

To illustrate, one example of a motivator for aeroengines is superior engine performance. An example of a hygiene factor is safety. Simon Hart, Head of Strategic Planning, Rolls-Royce Aeroengines, explains a particularly motivating role of differentiated engine performance – distinctive reliability. This motivator actually encouraged a major airline to switch to Rolls-Royce:

> It is a rare event for customers to switch – we have had some switch in our favour, but it is a fairly rare event. In the particular case in point (of switching) it was because of the reliability. We have a very, very reliable one. And this particular customer – because there was a lot of night flying involved, and it had to get in and out with a very high level of despatch reliability – he actually chose to switch from a competitor's products to ours.

The pattern of motivators and hygiene factors is specific to a customer (in relation to a particular supplier). As this pattern alters considerably between even individual customers this explains why, even when a firm offers a very high use value, but at a relatively low price, still some customers will buy from elsewhere. It also underlines the importance of building and reinforcing customer-specific motivator activities – to discourage switching.

CASE STUDY: THE CASE OF THE HOME SHOPPING STRATEGY

A few years ago a major retailer was looking at the possibility of developing a home shopping strategy. A consultant was hired to run a workshop for the home shopping team. Before the workshop he decided to interview his wife (now ex-wife) about what would turn her on – and off – about home shopping.

He found her in the garden where she was pegging up the washing. He first asked her what her views were on the turn-ons of home shopping and also what she would be prepared to pay for it.

With a peg stuck in her mouth she managed to say:

'I dunno'.

This told him that probably many potential customers were relatively unaware of the benefits of home shopping, and also what it would be worth paying for it.

He then asked her what would turn her off. She thought for a few seconds and then, eventually taking the peg out of her mouth, said: 'Well, if they were to turn up ten minutes late when I was doing the school run that would be the end of it.'

Armed with this second insight, the consultant took to the workshop with input that logistics would be absolutely critical (something which was not necessarily self-evident at that stage).

The above illustration highlights that small, rich samples of customers can be very informative.

Where it is not practicable to collect market data until late on, another technique is to perform 'psychic market research'. This entails asking yourself: 'If we were to ask these questions of this kind of customer – and with my out-of-body experience on full – what can I imagine they would say?'

Try this approach sometimes: it can prove uncannily accurate, quick and cheap.

Motivator factors are those aspects of customer value which currently:

- are sufficient to cause switching behaviour from a – merely average – alternative source of supply
- would make it psychologically difficult or unthinkable to switch to another source of supplier.

Hygiene factors are those aspects of customer value which:

- although insufficient to cause a customer to switch from another source of supply, are quite likely to cause switching out
- are frequently the kinds of things which the customer would prefer to pay to ensure they were met.

To help you arrive at a more objective assessment of the motivator-hygiene factors it is essential that you try to have – in *X Files* style: 'the out-of-body experience', by being your own customer. This entails seeing the world through their eyes and agendas – from their surface preferences down to their deeper anxieties. For example, if a client is thinking about buying strategy consultancy, motivator factors (from their perspective) are likely to be:

- strategy becomes easy
- I resolve my key dilemmas
- it helps me get my next job.

Hygiene factors (which might not be met) include:

- the consultant does not look cleverer than me
- the way he/she facilitates does not make me embarrassed.

An everyday instance of hygiene factors not being met is demonstrated by call centres, which keep you waiting – for indeterminate periods frequently – and then have the nerve to ask you to be patient! In our minds the thought is constant: 'You are wasting my time so that you can reduce your costs, and have the arrogance as a supplier to believe that your time is worth more economically than mine.'

Another quick example of hygiene factors-not-met is that of a retailer, whom we will call 'Poppadom Electricals' who has display stock of videos and TVs. The display stock is not for sale, but when there are frequent stock-outs no-one puts a sign up to say 'product currently unavailable'. So the poor customer can spend half an hour choosing a model and wait for a further five minutes only to be told that it is unavailable: their case being 'our stock systems can't provide the data'.

Motivator factors also require illustration, as they are not obvious, as in the following example.

CASE STUDY: THE SAD CASE OF THE MAZDA XEDOS

One of the authors was formerly besotted with a sleek Japanese saloon, the Mazda Xedos. He had two Xedos cars in succession, and besides having a very driveable car, a distinctive turn-on was being able to flash his headlights at other, similar Xedos owners to signal kinship; it was like being part of an informal Xedos club. (Because there were so few Xedos cars around this was still meaningful.)

Sadly, after several prangs (the Xedos used to implode at the front at the slightest impact), which resulted each time in a cost of £2,000 to replace the front and the radiator (at impact speeds ranging from 3–15mph), the author becoming virtually uninsurable, and the decision to switch was made, on the basis of the hygiene-factor not being met.

Staring at a nice grey Mazda Xedos replacement (for his now finally, written-off car), the hygiene factor not being met (the soft front) was simply too much to bear, and at last he bought a different car.

Driving his new Audi A4 around he is still tempted to flash his lights at other Mazda Xedos, but it would be no longer appropriate, and might unwittingly prompt road rage, so he has stopped.

At the business level, motivator-hygiene factor analysis can be used for:

- developing marketing strategy
- developing services strategy

- product development
- acquisitions due diligence
- scenario development (especially to understand future customer needs)
- internal service benchmarking
- HR strategy – attraction and retention strategies.

It can also be used for defining your own criteria in selecting suppliers, or in making an acquisition.

Additionally it can be used for understanding the criteria likely to be applied by an interview panel (when you are applying for a job).

EXERCISE: MOTIVATOR-HYGIENE FACTORS

For one of the above areas for application:

- What are the key motivator and hygiene factors not being met (given present delivery competence)?
- How could these factors now be met differently?

The benefits of motivator-hygiene factor analysis are that:

- it gives you an outside-in perspective on your competitive advantage
- it prioritizes customer value both in terms of importance and the extent to which value is being created (or, indeed, destroyed)
- it allows you to think ahead about future value creation in the industry, thus pre-empting your competitors.

Its disadvantages might include that:

- it can become too subjective unless one is fully capable of having the 'out-of-body experience', and unless some market data is collected.

Motivator-hygiene factor analysis can be used along with:

- SWOT analysis – to discriminate between (and prioritize) outward-facing competitive strengths and weaknesses
- growth drivers – to understand these more – and at a micro-level (where demand is created)
- buyer power – to understand how this can be managed more effectively
- competitor profiling (coming soon) – to set criteria and to help prioritize these
- GE grid – to help determine competitive positioning.

Competitor profiling and competitor analysis

Competitive profiling and competitor analysis help you to assess how well you are competing vis-à-vis specific competitors.

The various aspects of competitive advantage can be scored as 'strong', 'average' or 'weak' or alternatively as a 1–5 point scale (see figure 3.2) with 5 being 'very strong' and 1 being 'very weak'. Figure 3.2 contains some generic bases for competing which have been implemented successfully in over a hundred companies. Despite this success, it is important to tailor these to the important factors in your own particular situation. The relative importance of the factors can be assessed by weighting some factors as being more important than others. This analysis needs to be done relative to one or more key competitors, otherwise it is prone to subjectivity.

FIGURE 3.2: Competitor profiling

	Very strong	Strong	Average	Weak	Very Weak
	5	4	3	2	1
Brand image					
Product performance					
Service quality					
Innovation drive					
Cost base					
Supporting systems					
Support skills					

As an example of more specific competitive strengths, a major international hotel chain identified the following specific dimensions:

- brand name and service reputation
- locations
- booking systems and services
- reception service
- ancillary facilities
- room quality
- food (and beverages) quality
- cost base
- personalized customer service.

Specific criteria can be derived (indirectly) from environmental analysis (especially the five forces) and also from customer value analysis. The other big thing to input is analysis of factors impacting on costs.

Below are some useful pointers to adding a more objective bite to the analysis.

- For aspects of perceived superior value: test out whether particular customers or market segments do actually perceive you as superior to a particular competitor.
- For actual value (of product or service): disaggregate the dimensions of this value and compare line-for-line with a key competitor.

When doing this it is vital to ask (once you have listed out your factors) the question: 'What is the one BIG THING that we have forgotten?' Usually there is one big thing – and sometimes this is where you are weak and competitors are strong.

In interpreting the criteria in figure 3.2, the following points are worth reflecting on:

- Brand strength – is not just about brand awareness but whether this is perceived as an attractive brand halo by customers. (Before its privatization, British Rail was a very well-known brand but one which lacked a favourable reputation.)
- Product performance and value: this focuses on perceived value for money of the core product.
- Innovation effectiveness: this is not just about being innovative, but actually delivering real results from it – either through adding more value to customers or reducing costs, or being able to develop strategically more rapidly.
- Systems: these are the IT and non-IT routine processes for delivering value through the organization.
- Skills base: these skills comprise general management, commercial, financial, marketing and sales, operations, IT and HR skills.

Competitor profiling can be used for:

- identifying specific strategic breakthroughs
- business planning
- analyzing strategic investment decisions
- acquisitions
- alliances (to help assess complementary and relative strength)
- market entry strategies.

And, more specifically:

- to help position your business portfolio on the GE grid (making it less subjective)
- challenging internal patterns of resource allocation (you may be competitively weak in an underfunded way).

It can also be used to check out your own personal competitive advantages and position. Here useful headings might be:

- leadership capability
- management skills
- technical knowledge
- business knowledge
- IT literacy
- interpersonal skills
- networking and political skills
- financial skills.

EXERCISE: COMPETITOR PROFILING

For one key competitor of interest:

- Where are they positioned on the competitor profile?
- Where are you positioned?
- What is the 'so-what?' from this, for example in terms of:
  - overall positioning and relative vulnerability?
  - possible strategic breakthroughs for your company?

The choice of which competitor(s) to analyze is an interesting issue. This is very far from being self-evident. You can choose the competitors to examine based on:

- likely threat
- ease of attack
- potential to learn from them.

It may be useful to target a competitor (or new entrant) on the basis of these criteria and the degree of ignorance – although it may seem to be a bad idea to analyze a competitor you know relatively little about, this can be illuminating.

It is especially interesting to put a new entrant in the profile.

When displaying the positions of competitors do please avoid putting more than two competitors at once on the grid. Even three competitors can become visually difficult and confusing. A practical tip here is to use a blank acetate with the competitor format on. You then create (using a blank acetate and a felt pen) zigzag pictures for each competitor in different colours. By overlaying any two competitors on the standard acetate you can mix and match the positionings.

It is crucial to do your competitors first because otherwise you may be biased by perceptions about your own positioning.

The GE grid

We now need to examine the position of different business units within the corporate portfolio. (This can also be done for mini-business units within a larger business). This can be done by using the GE grid – so named after General Electric, the successful US conglomerate.

FIGURE 3.3: GE grid

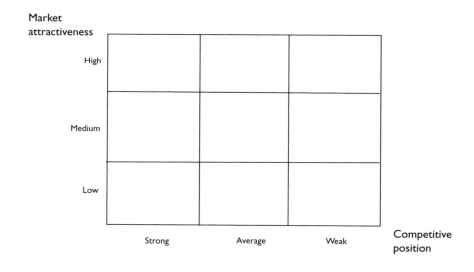

The GE grid (see figure 3.3) splits positioning into:

- market attractiveness
- competitive position.

'Market attractiveness' is the combination of three main factors:

- PEST analysis
- growth drivers
- competitive forces (including the industry mindset).

Obviously you will need to take a view on the relative importance of each of these forces. In the earlier example of the training company in chapter 2, the competitive forces are probably slightly more important than the growth drivers. Also, PEST factors were relatively important, as demand for courses was primarily triggered by regulatory change – which had actually slowed, reducing demand. The point here is that you need to judge relative importance very much on a case-by-case basis.

Market attractiveness gives an overview of whether a particular market (or segment) offers longer-term financial returns on a par with, greater than, or less than other industries. These 'other industries' are ones which either you are already part of or might conceivably enter. Wider still, you can make comparisons with dissimilar industries which a key factor of production – finance for investment – could be in.

The best way to distinguish the market attractiveness from your own competitive position is as follows. Imagine the strategy development director of Venus PLC landing on earth for the first time in his or her spaceship with £100 million in freshly minted £50 notes to invest. What industries does he/she invest in? He would possibly avoid many declining industries downsizing because of economic constraints, their ecological pressures and where there is relatively fierce competitive rivalry (for example, coal mining). He might be more interested in the home entertainment, communications and computing market – an emerging, possibly fast-growing industry with perhaps more relaxed (currently) competitive rivalry. Or perhaps as part of a cunning plan he might seek to revolutionize – and make even more attractive – the funerals industry. By testing out market attractiveness he would perhaps be able to screen out investment opportunities even before considering what kind of competitive strengths he might be able to attain in a new business venture.

Figure 3.3 allows the separation of two variables of total market attractiveness from competitive position. The vertical, left, axis depicts 'high', 'medium' or 'low', total market attractiveness. The horizontal axis picks out 'strong', 'average' or 'weak' competitive positions. The GE grid thus enables a multitude of factors to be compared simultaneously.

The GE grid enables you to:

- position an existing business, having analyzed its market attractiveness and competitive position
- compare it with other business units
- evaluate new business opportunities
- reposition a business – from right to left on the GE grid, or even (by shifting the business' market focus – diagonally northwest, in a turn-around strategy, or by continuous improvement

- challenge the adequacy of investment to achieve such a repositioning (both long-term investment and revenue costs with longer-term benefits)
- compare your positioning with other key competitors operating in the same or differing market segments.

To position a business effectively on the GE grid you will also need to take some view of its competitive position. The following ten key criteria will usually suffice (as a checklist).

- brand, image and reputation
- simplicity of product/market focus, or alternatively a relevant and broad offering
- relative market (or niche) share
- product and service performance
- distribution channels
- cost base
- responsiveness (but this doesn't mean reactiveness)
- technical and non-technical competencies
- financial strength
- management skills.

EXERCISE: THE GE GRID

Using the above criteria, where would you position one or more of your business areas on the GE grid?

What is the 'so-what?' from this, especially in terms of potential options for repositioning the business, and their benefits and costs?

The GE grid provides key benefits which:

- help to understand present financial performance and to predict future performance
- scope the amount of investment to protect and develop the business
- can help provoke innovative strategies for changing the industry's mindset
- help to prioritize strategic decision-making and resource allocation
- help to re-evaluate existing business units.

Its possible disadvantages are that it:

- can be subjective – unless of course a more detailed appraisal of the criteria for market attractiveness and of competitive strength is made
- can provoke fear – few managers feel comfortable if their business unit is positioned towards the southeast of the GE grid (low market attractiveness and weaker competitive position)

- can, if used too much as an analytical tool (rather than as the starting point for innovative thinking), inhibit questioning about how the industry and/or competitive positioning can be transformed.

Having said the above, provided that the GE grid is not used in isolation, it is an excellent technique for taking a 'helicopter' view of business positioning – it also gives a solid starting point for innovative thinking.

The GE grid can also be used at a personal level for:

- analyzing job attractiveness
- analyzing your own competitive position (either for getting that next job, or for actually doing it after you have got it).

EXERCISE

For a job you are either contemplating doing now or in the future:

- What is its inherent attractiveness? (Consider its prospects for career growth – tailoring the growth drivers, and what degree of organizational pressure will it put you under? Also what are the likely returns?) – Vertical axis.
- What is your personal competitive position (considering your actual competencies, your 'brand', the strength of your CV and its likely implementation difficulty)? – Horizontal axis.

Before we leave the concept of competitive advantage it is worthwhile saying more about its sustainability. A key task is to protect competitive advantage once this has been gained. The danger is that competitive advantage is regarded as a 'thing' that you create and then maintain or develop. Many sources of competitive advantage are, however, less tangible. They are continually being recreated, frequently on a daily basis. In particular, sources of advantage, such as the following, are ongoing processes, and need to be supported through ongoing organizational learning:

- building corporate image
- responsiveness to customer demands externally
- internal responsiveness
- problem diagnosis and solving – whether this is tactical or strategic
- capturing and evaluating, and exploiting new business opportunities.

These processes are becoming increasingly important relative to more tangible sources of advantage: e.g. assets; market share; products. This shift from tangible towards less tangible sources of competitive advantage occurs as the service element in value added by the business goes up, and as businesses become more complex and interdependent.

In the long run, softer sources of competitive advantage may account for the majority of variance in the performance of companies in the same sector. This is not to say that the more tangible sources of competitive advantage are not important, they clearly are; but the software of competitive advantage is becoming primary in many cases. Tangible sources of competitive advantage allow you access to the pitch in a meaningful way, but the 'competitive game' is increasingly decided by the softer sources of advantage – especially in the long run.

Speed also offers potential for sustaining competitive advantage. The following illustrates some important ways in which time (or speed) plays a major influence in shaping competitive advantage and offers new ways of configuring breakthrough. Speed is important in:

- reducing the length of time taken to develop and launch a new product or service
- achieving faster yet smoother integration of new acquisitions
- securing quicker turnaround time of customer enquiries and confirmation of transactions
- accelerating major change programmes through the use of task forces and by project management
- speeding up the business planning cycle without undermining the quality of decision-making.

Speeding up activities without detriment to quality, and without increasing costs demands much more effective learning and feedback in the management process. Without continual and open learning, accelerating processes may result in costly errors.

Time-based competitive advantage (Stalk, 1990) has close resemblances to some key themes within project management. Project management tells us that quality, cost and time are three variables which need to be continually traded off against each other. To illustrate this, where there is continual attention to quality cost may be under-emphasized. Where a process is accelerated it is often thought that costs will increase due to problems associated with activity compression. However, costs can often be reduced by accelerating activity. In addition, customer value can be increased, speeding its delivery.

The organization which is able to deliver a more responsive service may, in turn, reduce customers' costs or risks. This benefit might be converted either into premium pricing or into greater volumes. Alternatively, a more responsive service may reduce the tendency for customers to switch to other suppliers.

Summary and conclusion

Strategic analysis is an essential ingredient in breakthrough strategies for growth. Strategic analysis can help identify and evaluate opportunities both within and outside the current domain of corporate activity.

The first step is to gain a more deepened objective understanding of the market (or industry) structure, and how it is changing and the underlying dynamics. Once a realistic assessment of competitive position has been made it is then possible to target and cost out how strategic repositioning may be achieved. Where it is intended to build a new business from scratch then again the investment costs and effort needed can be established much more realistically.

We need to check out not only current competitive positioning but also sustainable competitive advantage, otherwise your strategy development is likely to fail.

EXERCISE

For one of your key businesses, ask the following questions:

- What is the overall gap between the current state of your business (in terms of sales, profits, cash flow and competitive position) versus where you want it to be?
- From the SWOT analysis of your own business, what growth opportunities exist where you could achieve and sustain genuine strategic advantage?

We now summarize the key tools and their uses.

Tool	Use
Gap analysis	■ Setting stretching strategic objectives
	■ Implementation planning and measurement
SWOT analysis	■ Brainstorming
	■ Issue analysis
	■ Presenting strategic position
PEST analysis	■ Analyzing industry environment
	■ Scenario analysis
	■ Generating critical success factors
	■ Input to GE grid
Growth drivers	■ Industry analysis and change
	■ Analyzing product/market opportunity
	■ Input to GE grid

Five competitive forces	■ Analyzing competitive environment ■ Input to GE grid (vertically) ■ Generating critical success factors
Industry mindset	■ Predicting industry change and competitor response ■ Understanding the other five competitive forces
GE grid	■ Business positioning (existing) ■ New opportunity – evaluation ■ Understanding investment requirement ■ Appraising possible divestment
Motivator-hygiene factors	■ For understanding customer value ■ For generating customer-led breakthroughs
Competitor profiling	■ Input to GE grid positioning
Uncertainty grid	■ For developing scenarios ■ For testing specific strategic decisions

Summary of key points

Whilst there are fewer techniques to learn for competitive positioning, the following key learning points can be drawn out:

- Motivator-hygiene factor analysis is imperative for gaining a more customer-focused perspective, and for generating further breakthroughs.
- Competitor profiling can be used to track your own position, and also to generate further breakthroughs.
- The GE grid allows you to position your existing portfolio of strategies and to evaluate new ones – also providing a health-check on potential financial attractiveness.

References

Lewin, K., *A Dynamic Theory of Personality*, McGraw Book Company, New York, 1935.

Stalk, E., *Competing Against Time*, Free Press, Macmillan, New York, 1990.

CHAPTER FOUR

Creative options and breakthrough strategic choice

Introduction: the creativity process

Strategic choice is above all not merely the product of strategic analysis. The techniques in chapters 2 and 3 will not provide either the necessary or the sufficient conditions for evolving a breakthrough strategy. You will also need to become creative in your strategic thinking – which involves a major element of imagination and play. This may not come naturally either to you or to your team, who probably spend the vast majority of their time on tactical management.

The creative process entails a good deal more than merely brainstorming. Brainstorming (whilst laudable as a means of generating ideas), typically produces a mass of disconnected, disjointed and largely unrelated ideas. This mass of ideas can actually cause more problems than it may solve. This is particularly true of unstructured brainstorming. This may release a lot of energy only to be replaced with frustration and confusion, especially around 'where do we go next?'

The creative process is best harnessed by using some thought triggers to develop strategic lines of enquiry – almost along the lines of detective work. Some of these lines of enquiry might require expansion, development or playful experimentation in combination with other creative thoughts. Creative thinking does have to be targeted, at least to an extent, otherwise it can go off in an inappropriate or unhelpful direction. Managers, therefore, need to relate the resulting stream of ideas back to the central thought of 'what are we trying to get out of all this divergent thinking, and what is its ultimate value likely to be?'

Figure 4.1 now maps out a more semi-structured creative process than mere brainstorming. This figure shows a non-linear process, a veritable cycle of creativity. This begins with our creating the right quality of thinking space to encourage creativity. This thought space is needed for two key reasons:

- To step out of everyday concerns and thought habits, and to allow for time and attention to develop the ideas more fully.
- To stretch our mindsets to embrace the possible – rather than to get ourselves bogged down in everyday clutter and in the detail of where we are now. This necessitates the search for both likely and less likely options. This process of search will then require a further phase of identifying the synergies between the key ideas which we have come up with. This search should then be followed up by a somewhat more analytical sorting-out process. Here we have the opportunity to narrow the lines of enquiry to a small number. The next step is to then go through the process of synthesizing the ideas to bring out the best combination. Our next step is to simulate how it will be a success (or not), especially during implementation, perhaps through telling stories about the future.

FIGURE 4.1: Creating strategic options

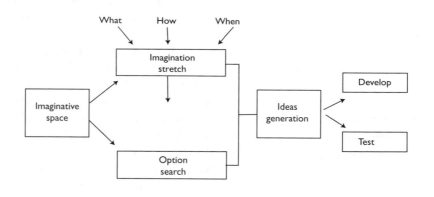

Finally, we need to think about creative ways in which we might build support for the idea's go-ahead, and for its implementation.

In our next section we now describe some recipes for creating lines of strategic enquiry – with our '55 ways' of being creative. We then turn to the evaluation of strategic choices and further refinement of these ideas using the strategic option grid, where we also explore the impact of decision-making styles on strategic thinking. Finally, we apply the strategic option grid to the case of BMW/Rover.

Creativity techniques

All of the techniques contained in this book contain at least some element of creativity (for example, when we are using the GE grid to understand the present position of a business this can also be used to think about how a business unit might be radically repositioned). Visual approaches like the GE grid usually do enhance creativity. But in addition to these more visual approaches it is also possible to use some less formal stimuli for generating creativity. These are best laid out in the following 55 recipes for being creative. They consist of:

- general lines of strategic enquiry
- challenging the constraints
- working backwards from customers
- beating your competitors
- challenging the industry rules
- creating greater degrees of freedom in the organization.

General lines of strategic enquiry

The recipes below are mainly concerned with generating sufficient vision and detachment from the detail.

The recipes below give you general suggestions for becoming more creative:

- 'Work backwards from the result, not from where you are now'. It is always a good idea to start by thinking about what you actually want to achieve, rather than just by throwing up a good idea.
- 'Imagine the future – and how you succeeded in it'. Instead of beginning in the present, try the thought experiment of being in the future. It is frequently much easier to work back from the future rather than forwards from where you are now.
- 'Look at existing practices as if you were an alien visitor'. Most industries can be revolutionized by simply seeing their practices as 'strange', as if you were an alien. For instance, one major bank in Ireland actually instituted 'alien away-days' to look at its markets from scratch. This enabled it to fundamentally question its existing marketing strategy, shifting it towards a greater focus on human need as opposed to packaged products.
- 'Frequently go back to what you really, really want (the Spice Girl strategy)'. The problem with much conventional strategic analysis is

that analyzing where you are now can root your mindset in your current position rather than in possibilities and in potential. The Spice Girl song of going for what you really, really want reminds you to go back to your stretching goals. This is especially useful in a difficult situation and one which is emotionally or politically sensitive.

- 'Practise helicopter thinking – avoid getting bogged down in detail'. A similar recipe is to remember to think as if you have a helicopter perspective. This can jolt you into a bigger appreciation of the context of an issue, and of the possibilities which it affords.

- 'Maintain emotional detachment from any situation which is a mess'. The least helpful thing to do is to get too emotionally involved in the issues or the options. One approach is to imagine that the issues are not in fact yours but actually someone else's. Or imagine looking at them through the wrong end of the telescope, so that they appear to shrink in significance. Questioning resources deployed in a strategy can be a more fruitful line of enquiry.

- 'If you were to invest more resources, would this give disproportionate value?' One approach is to relax the resource-based constraints associated with your current strategy. This may lead to a strategy with a bigger scope, which exhibits greater economies of scale and dominance.

- 'Zero-base your strategy'. Alternatively, one might take away (mentally) all of the currently committed resource, and then reassemble new and perhaps different resources according to a new 'cunning plan'.

- 'Start from a very low resource base and build up from this'. Linked to the above, a slightly more relaxed approach is to start again from a low base of resources and then increase them.

- 'Simplify the process'. Whilst processes may be seen as the area of operational management, often by doing something differently and more simply one can transform a strategy. Not only might this reduce cost and be faster but also this might add more customer value: complexity can often get in the way of realizing value.

Challenging the constraints

Challenging the constraints can invariably lead to some fruitful lines of enquiry. These prompts help you to step outside your current frame of reference.

Many of the resistances to strategic thinking are due to taken-for-granted constraints:

- 'Wherever there are constraints get more, (and not less) excited (the "Joy of Constraints")'. Whilst it is probably too late to write the equivalent (in strategy) of the famous book 'The Joy of Sex', a useful substitute would be perhaps 'The Joy of Constraints'. In other words, if someone says 'We can't do that', then instead of just accepting that, become mentally and emotionally challenged to think of a way around it, especially with the cunning plan.
- 'If there is a constraint, think why it is there and how it can be avoided'. More specifically, it may help (rather than by resorting to simplistic brainstorming) to consider why a constraint exists in the future. Fishbone analysis (see chapter 5) can help you here. In the same breath, by determining why it is there you are probably halfway to avoiding it.
- 'Focus on constraints one at a time, always beginning with the most critical one'. This is a prescription from Goal Theory (Goldratt, 1990). Instead of staring at each constraint simultaneously it is necessary to pick them out one at a time, to challenge and dissolve, usually beginning with the hardest. If that one is simply too daunting, pick off a number of the easier ones first.

Working backwards from customers

Customers are potentially a fantastic source of strategic inspiration – and one which is frequently ignored because it is felt embarrassing to ask customers what they think you could or should do.

Customers are a wonderful source of strategic thinking. It has been put that they are your unpaid strategy consultants.

- 'Have the out-of-body experience – do psychic market research'. Before conducting extensive market research, why not think about what your customers are likely to come up with anyway – were you to do market research. If you are able to enter fully into this simulation, which we call the 'out-of-body experience', then often you can elicit customers' attitudes, needs, and what they are (and are not) prepared to pay for almost as well as in doing actual market research. This approach has the advantage of avoiding conducting extensive market research into the wrong thing. Even if you are going to conduct market research, this is a useful preliminary step in order to help define the best questions.
- 'Be your own customer (physically)'. In most markets you can actually be your own customer. This is easiest in retail, financial services,

leisure, publishing and telecommunications. But even in the business-to-business market you can make an enquiry to your own company (or to a competitor) and live through at least the front-end of the process. The main reason why companies do not use this approach seems to be down to fear. Fear that one might find out that one is not as good as the average. But discovering such a thing is precisely the kind of learning which can lead to strategic thoughts.

- 'How can you add more value to your customer?' Following on from an out-of-body experience, now think about how you can add even more value to your customer and if you were a customer, what other needs do you have which are either not currently being supplied or are being supplied poorly? Are you delivering value throughout the customer's main phase of consumption? What experiences both before and after that core phase can you also service?

- 'How can you avoid destroying or diluting value?' Most writers focus on value added, but by simply avoiding the destruction of customer value, or even merely its dilution, this can in turn generate real competitive advantage. Imagine, for example, if you were running a management course in a British hotel, a facility with no builders banging away, no sudden intrusions of staff chinking coffee cups whilst you are in mid-sentence. This is, unfortunately, just a dream. On one occasion one of the writers was running a 'mission impossible' course in London – which turned out to be 'mission very impossible'. The hotel's garbage collectors parked immediately outside the room with the van engine running noisily. One of the writers leapt out of the back door to investigate, finding the cab empty with no driver! He was minded to re-park the van himself and might well have done so had not the attendant returned!

- 'If you are creating lots of value, capture more of it'. Interestingly, many companies create value but sometimes fail to fully capture it. This might be due to highly competitive market conditions, or it might be due to a lack of innovative positioning and pricing.

- 'When is most value created/least value created over time? (Plot a value-over-time curve)' – see chapter 5. One specific approach is literally to draw a curve of value added (as perceived by the customer) over his/her experience of the product or service. This is particularly useful for exploring customer value associated with services. For example, if a supplier was delivering a major consulting project, when would value actually be realized? Unless a clear picture of this is gained then it will be more difficult to justify the investment.

- 'How can something be made more convenient to buy?' By just taking away the difficulties of buying something this can lead to increased sales. Alternatively, by making it easier for the customer to buy more (both mentally, emotionally and physically), this can facilitate sales volume.

- 'How can something be more absolutely irresistible to buy?' More stretching still, set yourself the mental goal of making your proposition so compelling that it actually becomes irresistible. This can often be achieved by skilful management of the buying experience – and its psychology – on top of an already highly attractive product and service base. The buying process is, after all, a mental rehearsal of what consumption will be like, to a large degree, so how can you give a flavour of that experience – what is your bait?

- 'How can customers sell you on your behalf?' Getting your customers to sell you is a great way to leverage your network of intangible resources. In the consulting industry this is called having a 'fox'. The role of the fox is to go down the holes in the organization to tell you where the rabbit is – you do not need to know how to find them yourself. The fox is not only willing, not wanting to get paid, but is also very good at it. But you must delight the fox first.

- 'What cunning plans would build customer or channel lock-in, preferably without them knowing it?' Perhaps this one has a slightly manipulative feel about it. But in many competitive markets you may need this tip. To achieve this you do need to identify either the things which will really turn the customer or channel on, and then get them addicted to these. Or, it may be that you skillfully create switching costs which would make it unthinkable to change supplier. Obviously customers and channels are not stupid, so things (like a dependency on technology support) are likely to be spotted; less tangible things may not be. So, for example, building a very close personal relationship on the basis of both trust and excellent delivery can build significant switching barriers.

- 'Get customers to think of the financial value of your differentiated product or service'. In marketing it is not always self-evidence that one should think about how much financial value the customers actually see in your delivery. You can indeed ask them 'What is it actually worth to you?' For instance, when the major supermarkets in the UK set up home shopping, a key issue was to consider what it was worth to customers to receive shopping at home. (This is, of course, a separate, if related, issue to what they would be prepared to pay for it.)

Beating your competitors

Competitors, too, can be a source of significant inspiration – not merely to copy them but (ideally) to get tangibly better than them.

Your competitors are equally fertile territory for you to generate new strategic thoughts.

- 'Study your competitors – but then do things even better', Competitive analysis is not particularly done well by many companies. Some do no formal competitor analysis at all. Doing competitor analysis is however only the first stage to asking the question: 'How can we do things even better – that is either better than how they do it or better than how we do it now?'
- 'Learn from how things are done in other industries'. Other industries can be fertile grounds for creative thought. For instance, many years ago one of the authors helped the British Post Office to think through how it could protect its cost centres by organizing a lunch with Securicor service managers, who were able to suggest not building bullet-proof centres but put forward ways of deceiving criminals so that they did not actually know where the real cash was.
- 'Can you build barriers to imitation?' Whilst all of us strive to create competitive advantage it is not always so obviously important to protect against imitation. The best forms of protection are to built multiple levels of naturally reinforcing competitive advantage (once known as the 'Onion Model' of competitive advantage – Grundy, 1995). Here, whilst in theory each level might be imitated, imitating all the layers of competitive advantage would be very difficult indeed.

Challenging the industry rules

Besides the 'alien approach', which we saw earlier, challenging the ways in which value is created and captured – and how resources are managed – typically provokes powerful lines of enquiry:

- 'How can you change the rules of the game?' The rules of the game are not fixed – and you can change them. Imagine, for example, if you were starting an estate agency industry from scratch at the present time. Would you have expensive BMWs for your senior sales agents? Would you be clearer about who your agents are actually working for to improve integrity and confidence (estate agents frequently work for both seller and buyer – they are in reality 'double-agents')?

- 'If the rules of the game are changing in the future, how can you do this now?' Rather than respond negatively or defensively to industry change, use scenario story-telling to see into the future. Then work out ways in which you can manifest that future yourselves – to beat competition.
- 'Abandon any existing mindset (at industry, company and personal levels)'. More systematically, begin by letting go of your existing mindset. This mindset can be multi-layered. Forget not only how the industry does things currently – and the company – but also how you do things and even think about things.
- 'What would really put your competitors off-balance?' Following on from earlier thinking on competitors, identify strategies for getting (and keeping) them off-balance. Temporary price reductions are unlikely to achieve this goal, but a series of well-phased products and/or service enhancements might.
- 'Where a competitor might find something difficult to do, how could you make it easy (for you)?' True competitive advantage often does not come from anything superbly innovative but from doing something really, really well – that comes to you naturally – but which a competitor is likely to find very difficult to implement. The proviso here is that it must be strategically important!

Creating greater degrees of freedom in the organization

There are a number of ways of generating radical challenge within the organization – dealing with the art of the possible. Indeed, there are many ways of loosening up the organization to think more creatively about the strategies as we now see.

- 'Have a "Strategic Amnesty"'. A powerful approach is to spend some time (even if just 20–30 minutes) with the team to talk about, and to let go of, past strategic failures. Usually there has never been the time or the safe opportunity to do this. By calling this a 'Strategic Amnesty' it is easier to flush things out and to let them go.
- 'Imagine you just started in the organization today'. This is a similar thought process to having strategic amnesia. Here you forget your own experience, the agendas and thought patterns the result of the organization's socialization. At the same time you can still access the

knowledge you have gained from your experience – so you can have the best of both worlds. Besides being a fruitful line of enquiry for competitive strategy, this is also helpful in doing a strategic review (for yourself) of your own role. Coupled to this is an experiment of 'if we were not in the market already, how would we now enter it and with what business model?'

■ 'Think about what natural turn-ons may exist – for customers or stakeholders (what is the "bait"?)'. In our later chapter 4 on Implementation, we examine in greater depth the need to analyze stakeholders' (or customers') agendas. Here we need to focus specifically on those things which will tempt commitment.

■ 'Eliminate unnecessary turn-offs'. Here we focus on avoiding those things which may put off the key stakeholders (or customers).

■ 'Where you have apparently low influence over something important, how can you get more influence?' In any situation our attention is likely to be drawn to those areas over which we have most apparent influence. It is less obvious that in fact one can often get further at a creative level by focusing instead on at least some areas over which we have little influence – and then trying to work out cunning plans for gaining more influence over them.

■ 'Forget that anyone might be against your solution – deal with that later'. Stakeholders can sometimes be troublesome, and this can crowd-out your thought space to think differently. One tactic is to simply forget that they might either be against you or even that they exist. Whilst influencing stakeholders is of course very, very important, this needs to be handled mentally quite separately.

■ 'Hunt for natural enablers which are latent in the situation'. What this means is that in diagnosing a situation that there may be some degree of freedom but the real breakthrough in thinking is to ask what hidden energies or resources can be drawn out of a situation.

■ 'Create "white space"' – set aside exclusive time to focus solely on the problem'. A major perceived problem is frequently the sheer lack of time for strategic thinking. The result of this perception is that managers flit from problem to problem like super bees but rarely actually resolve any specific problem. Instead, one should focus on a single issue at a time. Also, you do need to allocate sufficient time which is completely clear of other concerns, to address it. This can be done whilst travelling, in hotels, or even in traffic jams (but watch the car in front – after two new radiators to one of our cars it was decided to focus more on the road and less on problem solving).

- 'Force yourself not to do anything else until you have solved at least one chunk of the problem'. This is a tough one, requiring considerable mental discipline. But unless you are able to apply discipline in strategic thinking the best you can hope for is partially resolved problems.
- 'Do allow yourself to think out loud – even if an idea may seem silly to others'. This is a classic technique – which helps not just creativity but also to diffuse organizational politics. It should be prefaced perhaps by saying, 'I know this may be a stupid thought, but would you mind if I just think out loud?' This tactful approach gets people to listen and to be more open and sympathetic.
- 'If you can't think of a creative idea, who might?' This prompt is absolutely not a last-ditch one. Indeed, you should always think about who might be able to get you to your goal of having strategic thoughts about a particular issue.
- 'Explain the problem to someone detached from it'. A related approach is simply to talk through the problem with someone else. This is invariably helpful – and not merely to get direct input. The verbalizing of the problem often in itself generates strategic thinking.
- 'If you are stuck, leave the problem and go back to it later'. Leaving a problem for a while may seem to be counter-intuitive when it is really bothering you. Paradoxically, however, this is frequently the best way of resolving it.
- 'If you have got a really good idea, how can you make it even better (aim for "Total Cunning")?' Here we move from normal management (which we can describe as 'running' – that is, very hard to stay still – through 'cunning' and finally through to 'stunning', that is exceedingly clever and innovative).
- 'Ask your unconscious mind to look for a solution'. An advanced approach is to ask your unconscious mind to work on it for you. With practice this usually dissolves up to half (or more) of the problem – and with a 90 per cent reliability level.
- 'Look for analogous solutions from other spheres of life'. Many people unconsciously draw help from analogies in other domains of thought, for example from military action or from sport. This is really quite helpful and can actually cast new light on a problematic situation. What you are in fact doing here is constructing an analogous model with refreshingly new and powerful characteristics.
- 'Imagine you are your own consultant, advising yourself'. This is one of our favourites. Because we both are management consultants it is sometimes actually hard to think outside the box about our own

strategy. That is why it pays to conduct a special version of the 'out-of-body experience' – of imagining you are your own management consultant. It is useful to couple this with, say, a thought experiment that you are starting your first day in the organization, or that you are re-entering the industry from scratch.

- 'Break down complex problems into chunks and deal with one at a time'. Implicitly we have referred to this technique throughout these creative checklists. This requires segmenting it into parts – and perhaps even into separate problems; we will go into this in depth in chapter 5 with 'Fishbone analysis', which diagnoses each problem's root causes by asking a chain of 'why-why' questions.

- 'Look for a process of solving the problem first, not necessarily the solution'. Einstein once said that the essence of genius was not to solve a problem but to understand the best process for solving it. In a Columbo-detective context, this is about working out recipes for generating fruitful lines of enquiry (for example, here we think about the possible motive for a murder, identifying all of those who might have known the victim, was there anything in the victim's life or recent activities that seemed dubious or out of character?). So, for example, if sales are drifting down and you are losing market share then a useful process might be to examine who or what might be actually eroding your market share.

- 'Don't do brainstorming without a method of processing the ideas (especially screening).' Relatively unstructured brainstorming is often not terribly valuable. Brainstorming, if indeed you are to do it, does need to be accompanied by some screening methodologies (for example, either the strategic options grid – see the next section, or the AID analysis – see chapter 5).

- 'Remember that creative management must contain Play and Fun'. Lastly, you will need to set the style of any creative session so that it is not 'management-as-usual'. Set aside a separate room where you cannot be disturbed – preferably off-site – and please, please could you turn off those mobile telephones. (Thanks.)

As a final preliminary step before moving onto the strategic option grid, let us show how these have been applied to a most remarkably interesting industry – the funerals business (which we touched on in chapter 2) in connection with Porter's five competitive forces.

Imaginary exercise – A funerals start-up

Imagine that you are 45 and have just been liberated (the new word for 'made redundant') from a senior director role in a major corporation. You have received a pay-off of £100,000 as your contract provided for premature termination – in this case due to a takeover of the company.

Unfortunately a close relative has just died, and you are disenchanted by the premium price, the narrow range of funerals options, and the way in which the whole affair was conducted.

You do not wish to go back into another high-flying, big, corporate job as it is simply too stressful. So, you hit on the wonderful idea of starting up a funerals business. How would you enter the market?

If set the above as an examination question it would be very tempting (as most managers are) to race into the 'What' and 'How' of the start-up. But this is not really the most effective approach (although it might be efficient, short-term). Instead, a superior approach (the 'Einstein Way') might be to establish some lines of enquiry. Some useful ideas would be:

- Work backwards from customer need: what do they want but they are not getting, and what is being delivered badly or inefficiently?
- Which customers do you wish to target? – Here the segmentation is quite complex, for example you can distinguish between:
  - unpredictable versus predictable deaths (e.g. terminal illnesses)
  - different age ranges
  - different income and wealth levels
  - multi-cultural variations
  - religious, agnostic and atheist (the latter two categories being substantial)
  - pre-need versus after the event (i.e. the death) customers.
- What needs are you going to meet:
  - mourning
  - remembrance
  - (possibly) celebration – why does it have to be so depressing?
- What psychological and economic value might a customer place on a wonderful funeral? (and how could you price this?)
- Which activities will deliver value:
  - the funeral itself
  - body collection, storage, and disposal
  - body presentation and preservation (embalming and cryogenics)
  - catering (for the living)
  - grief counselling (both after and – in terminal cases – before death)
  - wills (for everyone – as death is a certainty)
  (and how might you do these differently?).

- How?
  - insourcing of activities (see above)
  - outsourcing of activities
  - joint ventures.
- What are the possible distribution channels?
  - a retail network
  - telephone call centre (but one which is pleasant and does not keep you waiting!)
  - the Internet
  - a sales force or agents.
- Which geographic markets will you enter and why? (It does not have to be where you currently reside – nationally and internationally.)
- What routes might you use to develop your strategy, for example:
  - organic development
  - joint venture and partnerships
  - acquisitions
  - franchises.

The above is quite a formidable list of lines of enquiry. Each one may give rise to some interesting options. But together they may well generate some very different propositions to those which exist currently.

For example, some rather wonderful new business models created by managers using this exercise include:

- Remembrance.com: a website-based business focusing not on the burial but on remembering someone's life. This might appeal to the famous or the seriously rich, like Bill Gates of Microsoft.
- Out-of-the-box.com: an Internet company helping devise tailored and innovative solutions for where to place your remains (for example, in satellite orbit). (Or Dyson – James Dyson enters the market with a technology: 'Say Goodbye to the Coffin'.)
- Military funerals for veterans: this includes being dropped in a special lead coffin in the sea from a rented-out Hercules.
- 'Fun-Erals' – the fun way for atheists to exit life.

Whilst these ideas are obviously off-the-wall, by stretching our imagination in this way we would have a good basis to generate some stretching ideas.

The additional creativity checklists which deal with things like competitors, constraints and organizational issues, would also be useful here, as the senior director in the exercise might get cold feet quite quickly – due to perceived scale and risk.

This would therefore require self-challenge over the scale of resources that could be made available. Potentially, the margins and return on capital on a business venture of this type could be quite significant. This might suggest that it could be possible to interest venture capitalists, especially if the business were to become national.

To evaluate strategic options we now turn to the strategic option grid.

The strategic option grid

Our favourite book on strategic management is not by one of the strategy gurus such as Michael Porter, Henry Mintzberg or Hamel and Prahalad. Surprisingly it is *Winnie The Pooh* (Milne, 1926).

The book begins with a teddy bear being dragged unceremoniously downstairs. The story goes as follows:

> Here is Edward Bear going down stairs, bump, bump, bump on the back of his head. It is as far as he knows the only way of coming downstairs but, sometimes he feels that there really is another way, if only he could stop bumping for a moment and think of it... [p.1].

This indicates the importance of always obsessively looking for other available options, and therefore at strategic choice.

Organizations seem hell-bent on pursuing strategies which patently are not working, and which are destroying shareholder value. Reasons for this myopic vision include the following:

- excessive commitment to the past investment in a specific strategy
- difficulty in injecting learning into the organization's decision-making;
- the lack of a deliberate, as opposed to an emergent or even 'sub-mergent' strategy (Mintzberg, 1994; Grundy, 1995)
- failure to manage stakeholders and their agendas.

This section on the strategic option grid looks at:

- styles of strategic decision-making
- strategic attractiveness
- financial attractiveness
- implementation difficulty
- uncertainty and risk
- stakeholder acceptability.

Before we look at the various ingredients of the strategic option grid, let us take a quick look at how styles of strategic decision-making impact on strategic thinking generally.

Styles of strategic decision-making

Many organizations focus on reactive, tactical decision-making rather than on making more balanced strategic choices. In addition to day-to-day financial pressures (especially that of delivering the current year's profit target), senior managers are afflicted by many personal and political agendas.

We call these agendas the 'PASTA' factors (personal and strategic agendas) – see chapter 11. They are very much like white and green pasta. When cooked, the pasta becomes tangled, sticky, and messy. Something similar happens in organizations when personal agendas become hopelessly intermingled with strategic agendas. Managers even lose sight of the origins of these agendas (Grundy, 1998) and they may fail to challenge the logic of their decisions.

Unable to agree on an overall framework for strategic choice they then 'muddle through' their strategy on a highly tactical basis. The result is frequently strategic drift, as they become unable to cope with external competitive challenges, resulting in tactical fire-fighting and financial decline.

The decline of Marks & Spencer (see also our case in chapter 9) and Sainsbury's in the late 1990s illustrates how a vicious cycle of tactical decision-making can result in weaker performance and thus further desperate tactics. In fact, much decision-making in business seems to be of a tactical rather than strategic nature. Contrast figure 4.2 which illustrates a tactical style of decision-making with figure 4.3, which is based on strategic choice.

In figure 4.2 we see a combination of tactical error, competitor attack and internal complacency producing a spiral of tactics, weaker performance, further tactics and even weaker performance. In figure 4.3, notice that, instead, in addition to carrying out an objective examination of our current strategic position, we also need to think about the future competitive environment and also future competitive position.

This will then generate some more challenging and exciting options for the business, and these will then need to be evaluated and prioritized. The evaluated options will become strategic breakthroughs (that is, external or internal programmes which make a major impact on competitive position and financial performance, and areas for continuous improvement). The number of these strategic breakthroughs will be relatively small. Typically there will be only one to three in a particular business area over a particular time period of somewhere between 18 months to three years. This follows the Japanese philosophy of break-through, or *hoshin* (Grundy, 1995), which we mentioned in chapter 1.

FIGURE 4.2: Tactical decline

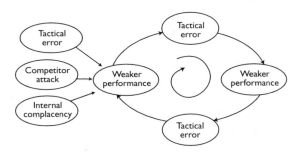

FIGURE 4.3: Strategic choice

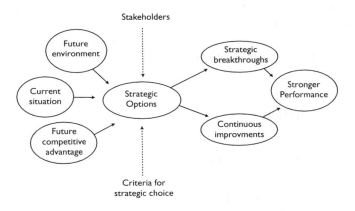

The criteria for strategic choice need to be predefined and explicit, rather than loose and unstructured. The strategic option grid (see figure 4.4) allows personal and strategic agendas to be thoroughly unscrambled. This enables us to put more order and flow into the strategic decision-making style – but without making it inflexible and bogged down in a planning bureaucracy.

The row headings of the strategic option grid are generic criteria for appraising strategic options, and the column headings are strategic options (more than four columns can be used if necessary). Sometimes options are created by combining other options (and so, for example, option 3 could be a combination of option 1 and option 2). Each option generates a different pattern of stakeholder influence, and thus of stakeholder acceptability. Each of the boxes on the strategic option grid can be scored high, moderate or low to indicate the option's over-all attractiveness. (Note that the areas of uncertainty and risk and implementation difficulty have to be scored in reverse, that is, something that is 'highly difficult' is given a 'low attractiveness' score.)

Figure 4.5 shows an example of the use of the strategic option grid. It scores the telephone enquiry system of a railway that was to be privatized. Option 1 (closure) was strategically and financially attractive, but it was uncertain, difficult and less acceptable. Options 2 and 3 (cut costs and increase prices, respectively) looked marginally more attractive, but it was option 4 (obtain more centralized funding, raise prices and cut costs) which saved the organization.

Before we look in more detail at the criteria (which can be tailored to your specific business or decision) it is important to stress that the strategic option grid is merely the starting point for thought. Even with what would appear to be a weak option, if we were to apply the creativity technique outlined earlier, we might well be able to craft a better option.

We now look at strategic choice criteria in more depth, and especially at the influence of stakeholders.

Strategic attractiveness

'Strategic attractiveness' can be defined according to a number of factors including:

- market growth (present)
- market volatility
- competitive intensity
- future market growth
- fit with own capability
- fit to own brand
- likely edge over competitors
- scale of opportunity
- focus or possible dilution of own strategy.

These criteria can be represented visually. One useful way of picturing them is to tailor forcefield analysis (Grundy, 1995) based on Lewin's much earlier technique. In this system, upward vertical lines are drawn in proportion to the perceived importance of positive strategic attractiveness factors, and downward vertical lines indicate the relative importance of the negative factors.

FIGURE 4.4: Evaluating strategic options

Criteria \ Options	Option 1	Option 2	Option 3	Option 4
Strategic attractiveness				
Financial attractiveness*				
Implementation difficulty				
Uncertainty and risk				
Acceptability (to stakeholders)				

* Benefits less costs – net cash flows relative to investment

FIGURE 4.5: Strategic option grid for railway telephone enquiry system

	Closure 1	Cost cutting 2	Price rises 3	Options 2 and 3 plus more funding 4
Strategic attractiveness	✳✳✳	✳	✳✳	✳✳✳
Financial attractiveness	✳✳	✳✳	✳✳✳	✳✳✳
Implementation difficulty	✳	✳✳	✳	✳✳
Uncertainty and risk	✳	✳✳	✳	✳✳
Stakeholder acceptability	✳	✳✳	✳	✳✳✳
Total score	8	9	8	13

Figure 4.6 illustrates this technique for a hypothetical acquisition of Marks & Spencer by Tesco in 2000. The analysis would help key stakeholders make a much more informed and objective strategic choice. It suggests that such an acquisition would be very much a mixed bag, and our verdict based on this analysis would be that acquiring Marks & Spencer would be of dubious strategic attractiveness for Tesco.

FIGURE 4.6: Strategic attractiveness: acquisition of Marks & Spencer by Tesco

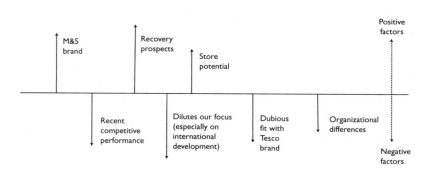

In addition to the factors mentioned above, the GE grid described earlier in chapter 2, along with related analysis techniques, is a great help in going deeper into these criteria.

Financial attractiveness

Financial attractiveness is based on the key value and cost drivers which underpin a strategic option. A value driver (which we explore further in chapter 4) is defined as 'anything which directly or indirectly generates cash inflows, present and future, into the business' (Grundy, 1998). A 'cost driver' is defined as 'anything which directly or indirectly generates cash outflows, present and future, out of the business'.

These value and cost drivers can again be represented visually using forcefield analysis. Figure 4.7 shows the analysis for the hypothetical acquisition of Marks & Spencer by Tesco. (More formally, this technique is described as 'performance drivers' in chapter 5.) Key criteria here could be:

- incremental sales volumes generated
- premium pricing achieved
- discounts avoided
- costs reduced
- costs avoided (for example by having one head office rather than two)
- accelerated or retarded strategy development
- share price impact.

Note that while the impact on share price criterion is not strictly a cash inflow or outflow to the business, it does impact shareholder value directly. As it happens this force has a very negative impact in this analysis.

Our verdict based on this analysis would be that the acquisition would be moderately financially attractive.

FIGURE 4.7: Financial attractiveness: acquisition of Marks & Spencer by Tesco

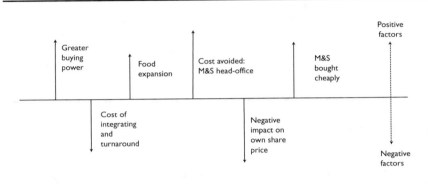

Implementation difficulty

Implementation difficulty needs to be anticipated over the total time of implementation, and not just during its early phase. Again figure 4.8 illustrates the inherent difficulty of the hypothetical acquisition of Marks & Spencer. Typical criteria of difficulty include the following:

- inherent complexity
- clarity of implementation strategy
- determination and commitment
- resistances
- availability of resources and skills.

More specifically figure 4.8 draws out the enabling and constraining factors relating to the acquisition.

Our verdict based on this analysis would be that the acquisition would be very difficult, and thus of low attractiveness in terms of the implementation difficulty criterion.

Implementation difficulty can also be assessed using the difficulty-over-time curve (see chapter 5).

FIGURE 4.8: Implementation difficulty: acquisition of Marks & Spencer by Tesco

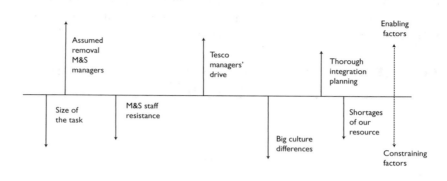

Uncertainty and risk

Detailed factors for uncertainty and risk are diverse, and are specific to the context of a particular option. Some generic factors are:

- environmental uncertainty (will external conditions change?)
- management uncertainty (can we make it work?)
- cultural uncertainty (will people adapt?).

Figure 4.9 shows an analysis for the Marks & Spencer acquisition, which looks highly uncertain and is of low attractiveness.

The uncertainty grid (see earlier chapter 2) will help you to get a more objective handle on these judgements.

FIGURE 4.9: Uncertainty and risk: acquisition of Marks & Spencer by Tesco

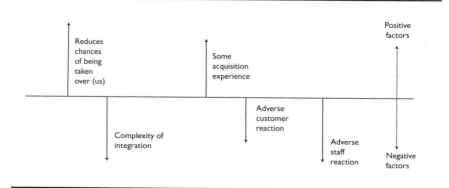

Stakeholder acceptability

Having worked through the previous four criteria (it typically takes managers a relatively short period of time to do this, at least in outline), we are in a better position to examine the stakeholder agendas. Here we can take one of two approaches to the analysis. Either we can do another forcefield analysis (see figure 4.10), which will average out the stakeholder agendas, or we can analyze the agendas stakeholder by stakeholder.

FIGURE 4.10: Stakeholder agendas: acquisition of Marks & Spencer by Tesco

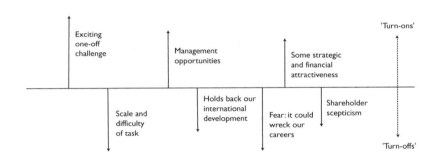

Figure 4.11 gives a useful overview of where Tesco's internal stakeholders would be likely to be coming from in the Marks & Spencer acquisition, and it shows some overall hypothetical inferred agendas. It demonstrates that while the strategy would have some 'turn-ons', there would also be some substantial 'turn-offs'. This kind of analysis can be used to reflect on 'do we really want to do this, and do we want to do it for the most appropriate reasons?'

The type of analysis shown in figure 4.11 can help us to disaggregate the agendas of the individual stakeholders. If we widen our thinking about stakeholders not only to those who have an influence over the decision, but also to those who are involved in implementation, and are the victims of implementation, this is a more informative practice (see Piercey, 1989). To determine the attitude of the stakeholders, we need to imagine (as fully as we can, in a kind of out-of-body experience) that we actually are the stakeholders. Otherwise, we may misread the stakeholder agendas. The technique of stakeholder analysis is again explored further in chapter 5.

Figure 4.11 separates out the influence and attitudes of the stake-holders in the hypothetical Marks & Spencer acquisition. Assumptions underpinning it include the following:

- Tesco shareholders would be likely to be nervous about the possible distractions of the acquisition
- Marks & Spencer middle managers might not be against Tesco as it might offer them a fresh regime.

FIGURE 4.11: Stakeholder positioning: (hypothetical) acquisition of Marks & Spencer by Tesco

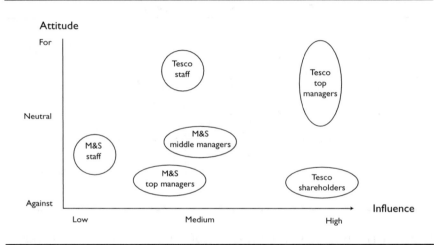

A forcefield analysis for each group of stakeholders could then be conducted (for any of the ellipses in figure 4.11) to determine their turn-ons and turn-offs. Sometimes the outcome of critical strategic decisions is based on the micro-agendas of a very small number of stake-holders. This again highlights the imperative to separate personal and strategic agendas.

Our verdict based on these analyses would be that the stakeholder acceptability of the acquisition would be medium to low.

Applying the strategic option grid

Standing back from the strategic option grid, there are a number of potential ways of using it. First, one can use it on a stand-alone basis to sort out high level options. These might be options for a) what to do –

where these options are quite separate, b) what to do – when there are a variety of routes to achieve the same goal, and c) implementation options. Where options for 'different things we can do' are across the top of the grid, effectively the 'options for how to do it' are in a third dimension behind the page. All (ultimately) need exploring.

Secondly, the grid can be used before using the more detailed techniques contained in the rest of this book. Thirdly, the grid can be used after using the more detailed techniques (GE grid, uncertainty grid, etc), and perhaps also after some selected data collection.

The advantage of not doing detailed analysis up front is that more options can be thought through, and also this will minimize commitment to a course of action. (Typically, when data is collected commitment to the course of action tends to increase.) The disadvantage of the more high-level approach is that in the wrong hands this might be subjective.

Possible drawbacks of the strategic option grid

Whilst the strategic option grid is a potent technique for group or for individual decision-making, it needs some caution:

- In assessing strategic attractiveness, users will often rate highly simply because they are attracted to the opportunity or decision. In reality, however, the option may be unattractive due to its unfavourable GE grid positioning and thus to market attractiveness, likely competitive position, or both.
- Financial attractiveness may be considered low simply because the decision requires longer-term investment. But provided that future returns are good, there are simple grounds for giving a more positive judgement.
- Implementation difficulty may be underestimated as only the early stage of implementation is thought through.
- Uncertainty and risk: again, key uncertainties may not be uncovered, resulting in a bias to optimism. This requires further analysis using the uncertainty-importance grid (see chapter 2).
- Stakeholder support: unless the positions of key stakeholders (now and in the future) have been thought through in detail, then the view might be either under- or over-optimistic.

Conclusion

Through formalization and visualization of the criteria for strategic choice, and in particular a formal stakeholder analysis, hopefully more informed choices can be made.

The strategic option grid will also help you to become more creative – generating additional options. We take this further in chapter 8, where we generate options using the 'optopus' grid for Champney's (see figure 4.12 for the generic characteristics of this grid) – which suggests eight ways of developing lines of enquiry generally.

FIGURE 4.12: The 'optopus' (or option octopus)

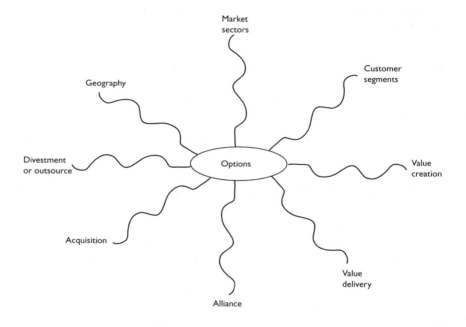

Once you have identified some interesting options then wishbone analysis (see chapter 1) can be used to develop the thinking behind them, from 'cunning', hopefully, to 'stunning'. Our experience of using the strategic option grid suggests that some options, which do not come out particularly attractive on first scoring, can turn out to be much more attractive when they are done slightly differently.

Summary of key points

The key points from this chapter are:

- There are many ways of generating creative options, including zero-based thinking, the 'out-of-body' experience, or taking the 'alien perspective'.
- Each of these strategic options can be explored in a structured way using the strategic option grid.
- Each of these options is only as good as 'The Cunning Plan' which you have developed for it.
- Each of its criteria can be tested quickly using the 'forcefield analysis', vector format.
- The robustness and potential vulnerability of your judgements need to be thoroughly tested out.

References

Goldratt, E.M., *Theory of Constraints*, North River Press, Great Barrington, Massachusetts, 1990.

Grundy, A.N., *Breakthrough Strategies for Growth*, Pitman Publishing, London, 1995.

— *Exploring Strategic Financial Management*, Prentice Hall, London, 1998.

— *Harnessing Strategic Behaviour – How Politics Drives Company Strategy*, Financial Times Publishing, London, 1998.

Milne, A.A., *Winnie-The-Pooh*, Methuen, 1926.

Mintzberg, H., *The Rise and Fall of Strategic Planning*, Prentice Hall, London, 1994.

Piercey, N., 'Diagnosing and Solving Implementation Problems in Strategic Planning', *Journal of General Management*, vol. 15, no 1, (Autumn 1989), p.p.19–38.

■ **CHAPTER FIVE** ■

Demystifying implementation

Introduction

Many strategies fade (or fail) in companies because of strategic (implement-ation) droop. Although the analysis may have been sound, the choices made, so many strategies end up in effect in a state of corporate impotence.

Managers schooled in the art of tough business and financial analysis (especially those who love to focus on objectives, targets and controls) are extremely prone to overlook implementation realities. But it is precisely the soft issues which frustrate and bog down strategic implementation.

But are we destined to struggle forever to overcome implementation droop (of strategic proportions)? We think not. The implementation link requires a little more than a single question: 'Can we do it?' It also calls for organizational analysis to help drive both the decision and the implementation process.

This chapter therefore focuses on demystifying a number of techniques, including:

- performance driver analysis
- fishbone analysis
- from-to (or FT) analysis
- how-how analysis
- attractiveness and implementation difficulty (AID) analysis
- value and cost driver analysis
- value-over-time curves
- forcefield analysis
- difficulty-over-time curves
- stakeholder agenda analysis
- importance and influence analysis
- influence-over-time curves.

But let us take brief look at the implementation process.

The implementation process

Figure 5.1 defines the five stages of implementation for strategic development. These stages are as follows:

- Diagnosis: what is the scope of the opportunity (or threat)? What are its objectives, and possible benefits, costs and risks? What is the overall implementation difficulty and who are the key stakeholders (at a high level)?
- Options – and the cunning plan: what cunning options are available for implementation?
- Planning: for these options, how attractive are they versus difficult to implement? What key activities are needed, and with what resources?
- Implementation: is implementation proving effective and, if not, why not? What new implementation forces and stakeholders have come into play, and how might these be handled? Do the original objectives need revisiting and are these more easily met by other strategies? If so, what are the costs of refocusing efforts?
- Learning and control: is the implementation on track in terms of its intended competitive, financial, operational and organizational effects? Did you achieve what you set out to achieve? If not, what were the factors you might have controlled, or attempted to influence, but didn't. Or, do you need to revisit and change your recipes for developing strategies for growth (or for their implementation)? Finally, were the implementation difficulties much greater than envisaged and, if so, why?

FIGURE 5.1: Managing the strategy process

To summarize which strategic thinking techniques are appropriate in managing each stage of the implementation process, consider the following:

Diagnosis	Cunning options	Planning	Implementation	Learning and control
Performance drivers	AID analysis	Value and cost drivers	Forcefield	Fishbone analysis
Fishbone analysis	Stakeholder analysis	How-how analysis	Difficulty over time	Wishbone
Performance drivers		AID analysis	Stakeholder and agenda analysis	Performance drivers
FT analysis		Value-over-time curve	Influence analysis	FT analysis
Forcefield and stakeholder analysis			Forcefield and stakeholder analysis	Forcefield analysis

The techniques which we have already explored are as follows:

Diagnosis	Cunning options	Planning	Implementation	Learning and control
PEST factors	Wishbone analysis	Gap analysis	Wishbone analysis	Gap analysis
Growth drivers	Strategic option grid	Wishbone analysis	Uncertainty grid	Wishbone analysis
Competitive forces	Uncertainty grid	Uncertainty grid		Uncertainty analysis
Competitor profiling				
Gap analysis				

EXERCISE: DIAGNOSING IMPLEMENTATION

For a past area of implementation which you have been involved in, ask the following questions:

- What were the strengths and weaknesses of each phase of the implementation process, particularly:
  - diagnosis;
  - cunning options;
  - planning;
  - implementation;
  - learning and control?
- What 'dos and don'ts' can you distil for the future? Look at some tools for diagnosis, for creating cunning options, for planning, implementation, and learning and control.

Performance driver analysis

Performance driver analysis helps to diagnose organizational performance, either externally or internally, or both. A second way of analyzing business and financial performance is to identify the key performance drivers using a tailored version of forcefield analysis (see later in this chapter).

Performance drivers here are drawn as vertical arrows and brakes are shown as downward arrows. Figure 5.2 illustrates this with reference to the perceived performance drivers of Rover cars, based on external data synthesized around late 1995.

FIGURE 5.2: Rover cars: performance (around 1995)

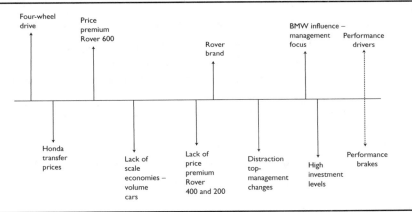

Although this method does not purport to be an exact picture of Rover's performance drivers it does yield some important concerns about the medium-term attractiveness of BMW's acquisition of Rover, even if there were longer-term opportunities beyond this analysis.

Performance driver analysis can be used for:

- analyzing a group's performance
- understanding a business unit's performance
- understanding a team's performance
- analyzing an individual's performance.

Performance driver analysis is especially helpful in turn-around situations.

In many ways, performance driver analysis is more incisive than SWOT analysis as it focuses on those factors which have an impact on economic value generation of a business. This gets us away from the 'nice-to-haves' which often cloud up the 'strengths' of SWOT analysis. Also, with the vector format the performance drivers are automatically prioritized.

The key benefits of performance driver analysis are:

- the 'so-what?' drops out much more readily than in a SWOT analysis
- it is already prioritized
- it can be linked more closely to financial planning
- it gives a better feel of the overall business context before addressing a specific business problem or bottleneck (so that we do not simply respond reactively to a problem)
- it makes judgements on performance less of a personal issue.

The performance drivers are, in effect, scored according to their importance multiplied by their relative strength or weakness.

There is a close parallel here with the process of motivator-hygiene factors (see chapter 3).

Performance driver analysis is linked to other tools as follows:

- Gap analysis: it helps understand why there may be a performance gap
- SWOT analysis: it turns this into a sharper, more incisive analysis
- PEST, growth drivers and the competitive forces can all be translated into external performance drivers
- motivator and hygiene factors and competitor profiling can help to generate internal performance drivers
- FT analysis (coming later in this chapter): performance drivers can help identify the 'from' and also where you might want to go – the 'to'.

Fishbone analysis

Fishbone analysis is a very quick and easy way of going behind the more immediate definition of the problem or opportunity. For instance, figure 5.3 illustrates why strategy is frequently not well implemented. This can be done to a variety of reasons, or underlying root causes. These include, for example, having too abstract a strategic vision, not fully thinking through implementation, or through having too many unprioritized projects.

There are some important guidelines for using fishbone analysis. The dos are:

- Identify the symptom of the cause and position it over towards the right-hand side. Where there are a number of possible symptoms you might need to analyze several problems (and thus draw up several fishbones). Or, you may need to summarize a number of issues into a single, overarching fishbone.
- Make sure that the root causes are the real root causes (or at least quite close to their being root causes). If you can still ask the question 'Why?' then you are still at the level of a symptom.

- Use your common sense to understand at what point you should cease going back up the causal chain. Thus 'lack of leadership skills' for most purposes is a satisfactory root cause rather than going back to 'the Board appointed the wrong leader' or 'there were no really suitable candidates'. (You do not need to go back to the dawn of time to necessarily scope and diagnose a problem.)

FIGURE 5.3: Fishbone cause analysis

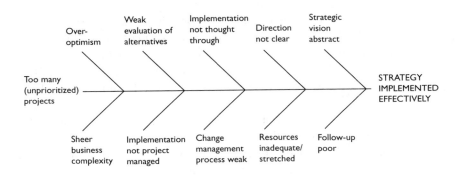

The don'ts are:

- Don't worry about whether the fishbone causes should go vertically or downwards – there is no special priority in where they are positioned – they are all equivalent. Most fishbones are more complete if they are drawn up in a creative flow, rather than in some pre-structured manner. If you do want to prioritize the fishbones, write the root causes on post-its and then move then around, perhaps in order of priority of difficulty, or degree of influence, or perhaps their attractiveness.
- Don't clutter up the analysis with sub-bones off a main fishbone on the very same sheet of paper. This produces a visually complex, messy, and hard to interpret picture. Where appropriate, do the analysis of a particular mini-fishbone for a particular cause on a separate page.
- Don't forget to consider the external causes as well as the internal root causes, and also the tangible versus the less tangible causes of the original symptom.

One of the major objections to fishbone analysis is that it is merely a list – so what other value does it add? (This is an objection sometimes raised by those who appear inherently sceptical of the value of strategic thinking tools.) Our main responses to this view are that:

- The fishbone itself is a powerful device for mapping causality and it is not therefore just a brainstorm – it repeatedly asks the 'why-why?' question, picking up more and more of the causal system of the problem. This generates more ideas than a simple list because:
  - The 'why-why?' question stimulates further thinking about root causes – either at a deeper level or more laterally (and into other areas of the organization).
  - Each fishbone can usually be traced back to its sub-fishbones. (With a list each point is usually the end of the analysis and thus is not analyzed in greater depth).
  - Subsequently each fishbone can be prioritized using, for example, the AID (attractiveness-implementation difficulty) analysis or the importance-influence analysis (see our explanation later in this chapter). This effect can be powerfully shown as an overlay of two acetates, one on top of the other, the first acetate being the fishbone and then the second one on top being its prioritization. Here one shows the fishbone first and then, once that has been explained, one moves onto talk about its prioritization.
- The fishbone is a visual device, making it easier to communicate (especially to top managers) and generally of much more interest.
- With a list the symptom tends not to stand out from the root causes. Also, a common tendency (without using a fishbone) is to talk around general issues rather than real causes.

Having used fishbone analysis for nearly ten years to diagnose strategic issues we realized that a number of generic factors were at work. These factors interact as a system which we now call the 'root cause system'.

The ten main generic systems which appear to be at work are:

- the competitive environment
- operations (internal)
- the wider environment
- the customer
- resource availability
- decision-making
- politics
- culture and style
- structure and skills
- financial imperatives and pressures.

Figure 5.4 now plots the main interdependencies of these systems. By creating a variety of fishbones for quite different issues it is quite usual to find a small number of themes coming up over and over again.

FIGURE 5.4: Root cause systems (generic)

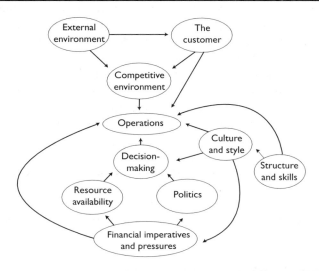

Often these are interrelated. We suggest that you use this picture to stimulate thinking about the possible root causes, or as a quick check on their completeness. The following illustration is a most interesting example of root cause systems at work.

CASE STUDY: ROOT CAUSE SYSTEMS AT BP, 1989–2001

At BP in the late 1980s there was an increasing sense of organizational drift. Decision-making was perceived to be slow, the culture and style of the organization was highly bureaucratic, and it was felt that there was perhaps too much internal politics. Resources were not always well-allocated, as the Group (then) used accounting-based (financial) measures for its business plans and for control, whilst cash flow analysis was used in isolation for longer-term decisions. This created some confusion in strategic priorities.

BP was able to operate this way, and to still succeed, largely because of an absence of fierce competition, generally favourable oil prices, and its strong cash flow from its rich North Sea and Alaskan oilfields. (One example of its paternalistic culture was BP's canteen lunch. This was once said to be 'the best five-pence lunch in the City' – BP introduced identity cards partially, it was believed, to keep out unwelcome students. Many staff then spent their lunchtime savings on a few lunchtime pints, not helping with decision-making speed but maybe dampening organizational politics.)

Quite clearly BP's malaise was due to complacent culture, and it was for that very reason that in 1989 the new chairman, Bob Horton, instigated BP's 1990 'culture change' project. In parallel with that initiative there was considerable structure changes, investment in management skills and asset changes, divestment and cost reduction in operations. Financial plans and targets became value-based – that is based on cash flow generation (BP was one of the first exponents of value-based management – Grundy, 1992). BP then made a number of shrewd and successful acquisitions, propelling it (some would say) to its current position as the world's number two oil company.

Figure 5.5 now plots the key root cause systems at work within BP's strategic change 1989–2001. These capture the interdependencies between root causes.

FIGURE 5.5: BP strategic change 1989–2001: root cause systems

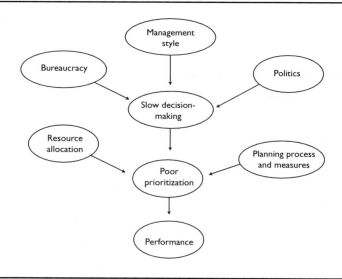

The BP case fishbone analysis exposes some major management dilemmas. Where there are some underlying problems, such as culture and style, or leadership, then do you attempt to deal with them as a separate programme or initiative, or do you attempt to manage around them, minimizing their effect?

The answer to this tough question depends to a large extent on the situation. Where there is a real determination to tackle these issues from the top – and an ability to actually deal with implementation difficulties or barriers on the way – then there is hope in tackling them directly. Where this is not in place it may be better to work bottom-up on individual issues – until the time is right to take the bigger ones on.

In the words of the HR director of a water company undergoing strategic change (to some senior managers who were asked to champion change):

> What we want you to be like is like the Vietcong: resourceful, innovative, sometimes patient and hidden, but always ready to dart out and fight when and where you can actually win. You will prepare for the grand battle – but later.

Here we see the HR director not wanting to confront the biggest issues head-on yet, but beginning to start introducing change – doing this by stealth.

Even where it is entirely appropriate to tackle a big change challenge head-on it is still worthwhile breaking it down into specific breakthrough projects. For example, in the mid-1990s the supermarket chain Tesco was simultaneously hit by the effects of prolonged recession, government restrictions on new out-of-town supermarket expansion, and a price war triggered by new entrants.

Out of a number of breakthrough areas one in particular – culture – was chosen for a new focus. Initially it was unclear as to how to tackle this and what was likely to come out of it. This breakthrough went into a process of transformation into practical projects to improve operational performance, which would in time improve culture. These included:

- Tesco superior customer services: through 'one-in-front' (if a queue of more than one customer built up, where possible further check-outs would be opened)
- service training for front-line store staff
- investment in management training (often with a behavioural focus)
- simplification of processes at head office (making the retail head office interface easier to deal with, thereby reducing the sense of there being 'two cultures').

Sometimes fishbone analysis can actually inhibit creative thinking, however, by reinforcing the 'it is a problem' mindset. One more creative approach is to see each problem as an opportunity – as a chance to get additional value out of the situation, and in cunning ways.

For example, at the time of writing both of the authors were engaged in working on a major longer-term project to develop the strategic thinking skills of a services firm. Such was the demand that between us we were spending a considerable amount of time per year with one client. Clearly if there were to be a sudden recession this might happen to affect that client more than others, our client contact might move on or take ill, or budgets might be suddenly scaled back.

The natural psychological response was to see this as a 'problem'. But the real problem would be not to lose that work but to have insufficient time to replace it (or ideas). Both of us however had several on-the-shelf ideas for further strategy development and we realized that a sudden drop-off of this work might be instrumental in bringing about a new phase of development. (Not that we were unhappy, of course, with the present situation.)

Another lesson is that sometimes the fishbone you are drawing appears so difficult that you are dragged down with a sense of depression and energy loss. Even if this is beginning to happen it is a very sound idea to start to think of the whirring blades of imaginary helicopters, lifting you off into the entirely different thinking space, towards the Spice Girl approach of 'What is it that you really, really want?'

CASE STUDY: STRATEGIC AMNESIA AT A MAJOR COMPUTING COMPANY

A few years ago one of us was facilitating a series of key account strategies at a major computer company. One part of the account had fallen badly behind budget and the fishbone was looking more depressing by the second. In a state of inspiration, the facilitator ripped off the flipchart, throwing it to the side of the room, saying:

> This is so bad I am going to give you strategic amnesia: if you were to forget being in this key account and be looking to enter it from scratch, what would you want to achieve, and how would you achieve that through a re-entry strategy?

At a practical level, the key benefits of fishbone analysis are that it:

- helps diagnose a problem in much greater depth, helping to scope strategic issues much more effectively
- usually goes halfway (at least) towards suggesting solutions
- reduces the tendency for managers to talk about the same issues over and over again – just using different words creates greater confusion and slows progress significantly
- communicates the scope and the key reasons for the problem in a politically neutral way – it is an essential technique for managing upwards

- provides a means of linking strategic analysis with implementation (for example, by taking gaps within a competitor profile – see chapter 3 – and using a fishbone to tease out the detailed causes which need to be addressed)
- allows you to go freely up and down levels of analysis without getting irretrievably lost down the rabbit holes.

Its potential disadvantages are that:

- it can reinforce the 'it's a problem' mindset
- managers do tend to restrict themselves to solving the causes of the problem with fishbone analysis, rather than examining where they might be (the 'cunning plan')
- unless a fishbone is prioritized (which we will see later), it only takes you a limited way forward.

Fishbone analysis links with other techniques are as follows:

- Gap analysis – to understand the causes of the gap.
- SWOT analysis – it helps to explore weaknesses and threats at a deeper level (the same can also be done for PEST problems, or for asking 'why is the bargaining power of buyers strong?' – seeing that as a symptom – or 'why are new entrants a threat?' – yet another symptom linking with Porter's five forces).
- The GE grid: to explore why a market is attractive (or less attractive) and equally why competitive position is strong (or weak).
- Motivator-hygiene factor analysis – to explore the reasons for hygiene factors not being met.
- Competitor profiling – to analyze why a competitive gap exists.
- Uncertainty grid – fishbone analysis can tease out why an assumption is either a) very uncertain, or b) very important.
- Importance-influence analysis – here we can diagnose out why we (currently) have low influence over something, with a view to gaining more influence.
- For the uncertainty tunnel – to analyze the precursors of change (as root causes), and also what causal factors may trigger future transitional events to take us into a new state of the world.
- For forcefield analysis (coming later in this chapter) – to explore why a force is constraining.
- For stakeholder analysis (again coming later) – to explore why a key stakeholder is against.
- For cost drivers – fishbone analysis can be used to explore the problem 'why are certain costs too high?' – as an alternative format (to cost drivers).

Fishbone analysis can also be coupled with wishbone analysis. Having first drawn a fishbone analysis one then does (for a particular root cause) a mini-wishbone analysis for what would have to go right to actually fix the problem (see figure 5.6). This mini-wishbone contains not only the things that would need to go right over which we have relatively high influence, but also those things over which we have lower influence. This we call a 'fish-wish' analysis.

Finally, it is useful to highlight that fishbone analysis can be of considerable help in structuring problems. Generally several problems hide inside each other but are interrelated. This invites us to split them up although they remain linked. We call this 'piranha analysis' – to highlight the fact that whilst smaller problems can appear to be more manageable, they can be actually deadly and ferocious (hence the piranha analogy).

Figure 5.7 gives an excellent example of this, using a relationship problem as its focus. Relationship problems are endemic in complex, changing organizations (not to mention in personal lives), and strategic thinking is a vital tool in helping you deal with them.

Typical relationship difficulties occur with your boss, with a subordinate, or with a close rival.

Figure 5.7 splits into four piranha problem areas:

- what do you yourself bring to it
- what do others bring to it
- the current organizational context
- the past organizational legacy.

This problem structure forces you into assessing what you brought to the situation. Besides helping you become more objective, it also focuses on some things which you ought to have much more influence over – yourself!

The 'context' should generate some thinking about what is currently going on around the relationship, for example restructuring, performance pressures, inconsistent organizational priorities. The 'legacy' can, in some situations, be very important as it helps to understand how the problem might have developed and how this might have been at least partially caused by past organizational mistakes.

Having used the piranha, it is not unusual to witness a partial or even a complete turnaround of a relationship, especially if it has been shared openly between both sides. (It is also very helpful here to use the wishbone analysis to create a vision for a much better working relationship and the alignment factors for it to go right.)

Let us now leave fishbone analysis by reflecting on what one manager said of it: 'Unless you pull a problem up by its roots, like a weed it always grows back'.

FIGURE 5.6: 'Fish-wish' analysis

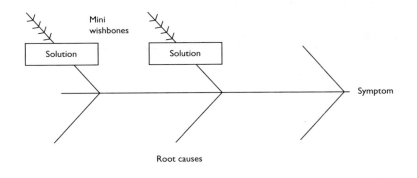

FIGURE 5.7: Fishbone analysis of relationship difficulties

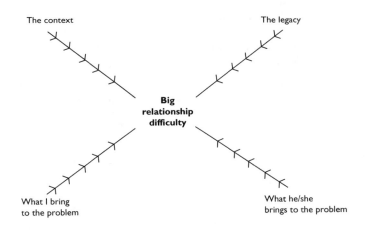

From-to (FT) analysis

FT analysis helps us to scope the extent of the strategic project which you are working on, in terms of its breadth and its degree of stretch.

FT analysis is another useful tool for scoping the extent of implementation, especially for organizational change or for operational development. When a development project has a significant impact on 'how we do things around here' or the 'paradigm' (see Grundy, 1993), then it is essential that at least a rudimentary FT analysis is conducted.

The 'paradigm' embraces a raft of organizational processes, some of which are 'hard' and tangible and some of which are 'soft' and intangible. See figure 5.8 for a generic FT analysis.

FIGURE 5.8: FT analysis

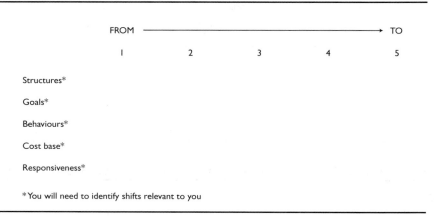

For example, managers within Prudential Life administration used an FT analysis based specifically on the paradigm to scope their organizational change project. This helped them to get their minds around the 'soft' as well as the 'hard' factors, as follows.

Paradigm	From	To
Power	Restricted	Resides at the lowest appropriate level
Structure	Hierarchical	Flatter
Controls	Instinctive and 'seat of the pants'	Measured objectives
Routines	Retrospective-looking	Live and forward-looking
Rituals	Loose plans	Structured plans
Myths	The 'Mighty Pru', 'Life Administration is OK'	Real world
Stories	Our job well done	Delighted customers
Symbols	Status hierarchy	Rewards for performance
Management style	Aloof	Open

This kind of analysis can also be used to monitor the progress of a project, perhaps using a score of 1 to 5 with 1 being the 'From' and possibly 5 being the 'To'. (In some situations, however, we might well be starting off with better than a 1, as we might already have made some progress towards our goals, prior to embarking on the project. Equally, we might wish to go all out for a 5, although a 4 or even 3 might be more realistic and acceptable, depending upon the situation.)

The Prudential example of from-to analysis is very much a more 'gourmet' approach. We see a semi-structured approach being used to generate the key shifts which the strategic project is aimed at delivering. A simplified approach is to quickly brainstorm the froms and tos in a way much more specific to a particular project. Our main caveat here is that you really must think about the softer factors which are needed to shift, for example, behaviours, attitudes and mindset generally.

To perform an FT analysis you need to carry out the following steps:

- What are you trying to shift? (the critical categories)
- By how much are you trying to shift them? (the horizontal from and to shifts)

By now it may have become apparent to you that FT analysis is essentially an extended form of gap analysis (see our previous section). Because it breaks the gap down into a number of dimensions, it is generally more specific than gap analysis and is frequently the next step on.

EXERCISE: FROM-TO ANALYSIS

For one area of strategy implementation of your choice and in particular one for which there is already an existing state of affairs which you are trying to change or shift:

- What are the key dimensions which you are trying to shift?
- What are the extremes of these shifts (from left to right), i.e. where have you started from originally, and where would you like to end up ultimately?
- Where you are actually now? (Note: this does not have to be a 1.)
- Where do you want to be as a result of this strategic project? (Note: this does not have to be a 5.)
- What specific actions or interventions might make each shift feasible?

The key benefits of from-to analysis are:

- it gives a clear and more complete vision of the extent of the potential difficulty that achieving that vision may give rise to
- it can be used to actually monitor strategic progress
- it is a very useful technique for communicating what needs to be done, or for exploring the implications and for getting greater buy-in
- more specifically, it is especially helpful in presenting business plans.

If it does have a drawback, it is that managers may struggle to come up with their desired categories for development and change (presumably because of a lack of clarity and ownership).

FT analysis links into a number of other techniques as follows:

- It can be used to summarize changes in the external market place, for example by drawing from PEST factors, growth drivers, the five competitive forces and the industry mindset.
- It can help to move from a performance driver and/or fishbone analysis to a programme of development and change.
- It can help give an overview of the more detailed 'how-hows'.
- It helps break down any gap analysis.
- It can be used prior to forcefield analysis and stakeholder analysis to scope likely implementation difficulty and the level of stakeholder support.

How-how analysis

How-how analysis is useful in the detailed planning of implementation. It is also useful in finding a way forward which might not have been thought about before.

Figure 5.9 gives an example of a how-how analysis, where until this picture was drawn up managers perceived that there was no way that the cost of bought-in motors could be reduced.

While fishbone analysis works backward from the current situation to find out how and why it exists, how-how works forward to see how it can be resolved in the future.

FIGURE 5.9: How-how analysis

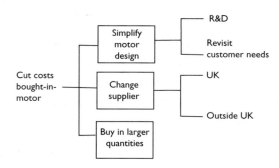

How-how analysis adds the most value when you have not really thought very hard about the detailed implementation steps that will be needed to achieve something. But even when you have thought about this, it will also be useful just to help identify the less tangible as well as the tangible aspects of implementation, especially:

- positioning
- communicating
- influencing
- team-building.

How-how analysis will also help to get some approximate order of the likely sequence in which things need to happen – and potential critical paths.

'How-how's' major benefits are that it is common sense and that it exposes assumptions about what actually has to happen, reducing blind-spots. Its key potential disadvantage is that is can tell you little more than you already know, if you have thought about something really well already.

'How-how' analysis links to other tools as follows:

- it may help to go from the fishbone's root causes to some potential implementation solutions
- it can help to operationalize the various shifts which have been identified in the FT analysis
- it can feed into the AID (or attractiveness-implementation difficulty) analysis (coming next)
- it can help scope the likely value and cost drivers (coming soon).

Attractiveness and implementation difficulty (AID) analysis

By looking at the relative attractiveness and its difficulty of implementation one can now begin to evaluate strategies at a micro-level, from a number of perspectives:

- one can prioritize a portfolio of strategic activities, any one of which can be undertaken
- mutually exclusive strategic activities can be prioritized
- different options for implementing the concept can be evaluated
- the different parts or activities within an activity can be prioritized.

The AID analysis grid subsumes both 'strategic' and 'financial' attractiveness into the variable of 'attractiveness' (the vertical axis) from the strategic option grid. Implementation difficulty and stakeholder acceptability are combined in the horizontal axis of implementation difficulty (see figure 5.10).

Beginning with the vertical dimension of attractiveness one can now expand on the final bullet point above.

FIGURE 5.10: AID analysis

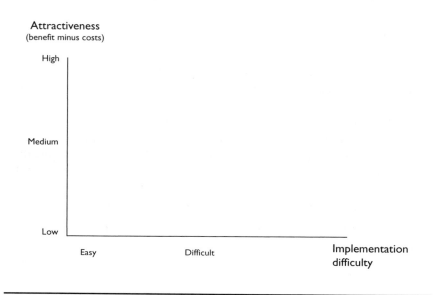

Only uncertainty is left out of the AID grid – so we have a much simpler prioritization technique but one that does however omit uncertainty.

The strategic option grid and AID analysis are not mutually exclusive. The option grid can be used first to evaluate different strategic options (either for different projects or for different ways of implementing a specific strategy). Then the AID analysis might evaluate and prioritize sub-parts.

It is sometimes the case that some parts of a possible strategy can be undertaken without doing others. For example, buying a business is a project but the constituent parts of the business can be regarded as sub-projects to be retained or possibly disposed of.

Even where a strategy does consist of a number of discretionary sub-parts, which are not discretionary (such as a training strategy), it is still possible to display their individual positionings on the AID grid. Without doubt some parts of the training will be more difficult to implement than others – and will thus have different positionings horizontally on the AID grid.

Thinking now about the vertical dimension of attractiveness, each part of a training strategy may vary in its relative benefits, and in its relative cost. For example, a training project might have the following profile:

	Benefits (B)	Costs (C)	Attractiveness (B)-(C)
Pre-diagnosis	High	Medium	Medium
Pre-work	Low	Low	Low
Main programme	High	Medium	High/Medium
Interim support	Medium	Low	Medium
Follow-up programme	High	Low	High
Ongoing support	High	Low	High

The AID grid enables trade-offs to be achieved between strategies. The vertical dimension of the picture focuses on benefits less costs. The horizontal dimension represents the total difficulty over time. This time is the time up until delivery of results, and not of completion of earlier project phases. This tool enables a portfolio of possible projects to be prioritized. Figure 5.11 illustrates a hypothetical case.

Strategy A is seen as being both very attractive and relatively easy to implement. This project is non-contentious and will probably be given the go-ahead. Strategy C is relatively difficult – it will probably end up being zapped unless it can be reformulated to make it both a lot more attractive and easier.

FIGURE 5.11: AID analysis

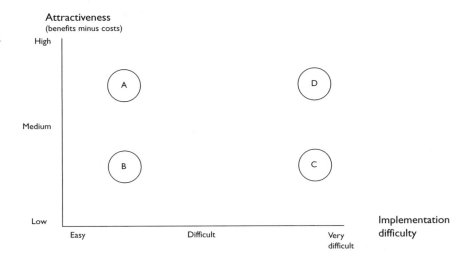

Strategy D presents the biggest dilemma of all. Although it appears to be very attractive it is also very difficult to implement. Yet managers will tend to focus on the attractiveness of the project rather than its actual difficulty. And that can occur even though they have gone through the IMF and stakeholder analysis thoroughly.

When using the AID tool at HP this happened to us twice. Quite separately, two 'D' type strategies were identified and as managers spent more time analyzing them, commitment to action levels built up.

Although neither of the projects went ahead – in their existing form – both the author and the (then) internal facilitator Stuart Reed, had to be relatively strong to convince the teams that some further refinement was necessary.

Stuart Reed said at the time:

> I had gone through with them (the managers) both the implementation forces and the stakeholders. Although it did seem to be an attractive project our two organizational tools were telling us 'it is not going to happen'. I think because the managers were going through the analysis tools for the first time (and hadn't actually tried to implement it) they hadn't quite realized that it really wasn't going to happen.

Strategies in the northeast zone do present us with some interesting management dilemmas. Following up one HP school of thought (number 1, as above) one viewpoint is that it is unlikely to be worthwhile to do these projects as realistically the organization will lack the commitment to drive them through. However, a second HP school of thought is that such projects merely represent a challenge for creative thinking – as long as they are potentially very attractive it may be very fruitful to do this.

At HP another senior manager re-examined a strategic project with which one of the authors had been personally involved some eighteen months earlier. This potential strategic project concerned a business process change and a restructuring. At the time the position of this strategic project was due east on the AID grid, (i.e. medium, attractive and very difficult).

This strategic project went into suspended animation for around eighteen months. On further contact with HP we discovered that the new senior manager had solved the problem both creatively and decisively by outsourcing the process rather than by internal reorganization. The project thus shifted from due east to northwest, that is: high attractiveness, low implementation difficulty.

We uncovered a third school of thought working with Pioneer UK, the hi-fi company. Its Japanese managing director said to us: 'Perhaps we should do that project *because* it is difficult.'

Initially, we wondered whether this was perhaps an example of management heroism. On reflection, however, this philosophy fitted in well with the notion of Breakthrough Management, or *hoshin*. Here a breakthrough is frequently something that is both highly attractive and very difficult to implement. (Whilst breakthroughs do not have to be very difficult to implement – just hard for others to imitate – they frequently are.)

A particularly cunning plan is to target projects which, whilst they are likely to be between very difficult to mission impossible for others to implement, we will find them easier. Here mission impossible (or MI) is just off the page to the east of the AID grid.

If we do decide to target projects, which are very difficult, then following the *hoshin* philosophy it is important to narrow the focus to a very small number of projects within a specific period of time. It is very unlikely that more than three can be undertaken simultaneously without distraction of organizational attention and loss of energy generally.

The positionings on the AID grid are likely to be relatively tentative unless tested out using other techniques. For example:

- the 'attractiveness' of the project may require further analysis using value driver and cost driver analysis (Ultimately, this attractiveness can be financially quantified, albeit perhaps approximately.)
- the implementation difficulty can be tested out using forcefield analysis and stakeholder analysis
- the difficulty over time can be visualized using the difficulty-over-time curve.

A useful rule of thumb for the less experienced user of the AID grid, or for those who have not used forcefield and stakeholder analysis to check out their horizontal positioning, is that:

- if you think the project is easy, it is probably difficult
- if you think the project is difficult, it is probably very difficult
- if you think the project is very difficult, it is probably mission impossible (or MI).

(One manufacturing company invented a fifth category which is even worse than mission impossible, but because its letters are identical to a well-known UK furniture retailer and have other negative, albeit humorous connotations, we will leave this to your imagination.)

Another technique is to tell scenario stories about the evolution of the project over time. This may help to tease out its likely trajectory on the AID grid. For example, many projects start out with an assumed northwest position (very attractive and easy), but then zigzag south and east to the southeast (low attractiveness and very difficult).

A final point on AID analysis is that this technique can be used to prioritize each of the bones of the fishbone (or, indeed, the wishbone). This can be done either using a separate AID picture or – and this is neat – actually along the edges of the fishbone, as mini-AID pictures with a cross drawn of the positioning.

To summarize, AID analysis can be used:

- to prioritize strategic breakthroughs as a portfolio
- to evaluate business plans
- to evaluate the sub-components of a strategic breakthrough or project
- to track (in real time) an area of strategy implementation.

Its key benefits are that it is a:

- quick and easy technique to use
- visual way of representing and debating priorities.

Its potential disadvantages are that:

- it can be subjective, unless it is accompanied by further analysis – for example of value and cost drivers (for attractiveness) or of forcefield analysis (for implementation difficulty)
- it can just represent existing thinking on a breakthrough, rather than more creatively, the Cunning Plan.

AID is linked to the following other techniques:

- Value and cost drivers (or performance driver) analysis help us to scope 'attractiveness'.
- Forcefield analysis helps us with 'implementation difficulty'.
- The root causes on the fishbone can be prioritized individually using the attractiveness-difficulty criteria. (This can be done as per the overlay of the two techniques in figure 5.12.) Here the 'attractiveness' and 'difficulty' are concerned with resolving that particular case generally as opposed to that of a very particular solution.
- AID analysis helps us to prioritize the from-tos of the FT analysis.

Value and cost driver analysis

Value and cost driver analysis helps us to get a better steer on the 'attractiveness' of a particular strategic breakthrough.

A 'value driver' is defined as: 'anything outside or inside the business which either directly or indirectly will generate cash flows – either now or in the future'.

A 'cost driver' is defined as: 'anything outside or inside the business which either directly or indirectly will generate cash outflows – either now or in the future'.

FIGURE 5.12: Fishbone with AID analysis

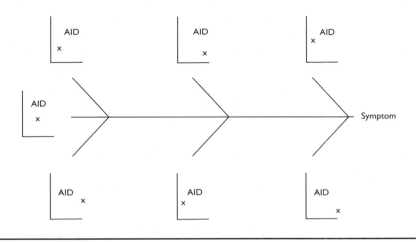

Examples of value drivers include:

■ customer loyalty
■ a lack of competitive pressure
■ a unique product
■ a value-creating technology.

Examples of cost drivers include:

■ complexity of operations.
■ poor quality
■ bureaucratic processes and structures.

Value and cost driver analysis can be used to restructure a company's cost base strategically (Grundy, 1998), to avoid costs being managed primarily on a short-term basis, and in isolation.

Figures 5.13 and 5.14, which depict a value and cost driver analysis for supermarket trolleys, is an excellent example of this. Here we see the value drivers being split down into 'value to the customer' and 'company value' – to give the macro-level value drivers. The macro cost drivers have a different split, these being analyzed over the new wonder-trolleys' life-cycle of costs. Other cuts to the cost analysis are:

■ cost by activity
■ cost by process
■ cost through the transaction cycle.

Most managers using value and cost driver analysis for the first time tend to copy relatively slavishly whatever example is given to them.

Whilst this usually comes off, it is important to realize that the structure of value and cost drivers will vary according to the specific situation.

To illustrate this let us look at a second example. In figures 5.15 and 5.16 we see the value and cost drivers of our (small) consultancy potentially investing in a website in 1999. We were sceptical as to its potential value (at that time) not only in terms of 'will we get more business?' but also 'will it be the quality we are targeting?' Also, being very busy already, the obvious point was how we would accommodate much more work.

This value and cost driver analysis was done in around six minutes in a café in Edinburgh, overlooking the castle. Tea and croissants were consumed simultaneously, highlighting the fact that these analyses can be done very, very quickly.

The figures were illuminating. The key insights (which were not there before) were that:

- more value was likely to be added (at least in the medium term) from selling more to existing clients (by getting them to look at our website) rather than by new hits
- new hits might come from companies which were geographically distant, costing more in travel time and inconvenience
- the costs of maintaining the website could exceed set-up costs, as would the cost of our time to input into the design
- there were considerable downside costs through competitors seeking to copy our products
- the protective value was intriguing: if one did not have a website how would one track lost business to competitors with websites?

FIGURE 5.13: Value drivers – new supermarket trolleys

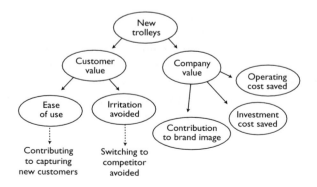

FIGURE 5.14: Cost drivers – new supermarket trolleys

FIGURE 5.15: Value drivers – website

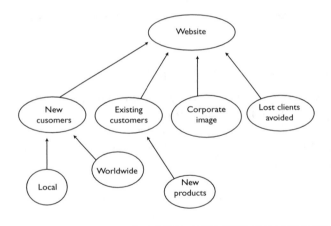

FIGURE 5.16: Cost drivers – website

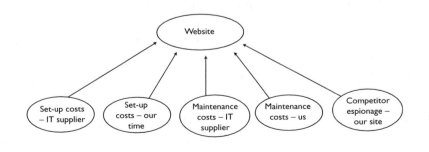

On the basis of the final bullet point above we decided to continue to monitor this possibility closely but not to go ahead yet.

Value and cost driver analysis is essential for anyone doing a business case, especially before doing the financial numbers. (Imagine how wrong our numbers would have been had we not done this analysis!)

It can be used for a variety of applications, including:

- acquisitions
- investment decisions
- cost management
- change projects.

It can even be used for evaluating projects in our personal life (see an analysis of the value and cost drivers of living with a new partner – Grundy and Brown, 2001).

Its key benefits are:

- it provides a key bridge between strategy and finance
- it helps to stretch thinking laterally about less obvious areas of value and cost
- it is highly flexible.

The key linkages with other techniques are as follows:

- with the strategic option grid: to test out why something is felt to be 'highly attractive' financially, or not
- with AID analysis (coming later): to test out assumed 'attractiveness'
- with performance driver analysis: to analyze an individual performance driver in depth
- with the 'importance' dimension of the uncertainty grid / the importance influence grid: to test out relative importance of both value and cost drivers.

Forcefield analysis

Forcefield analysis is a technique which brings to the surface the underlying forces which may pull a particular change forward, which may prevent progress, or even move the change backwards. These 'forces' can be separately identified as 'enablers' or 'constraints'. But neither set of forces can be adequately identified without first specifying the objectives of the implementation.

When managers first see forcefield analysis they often read it as being some form of extended cost-benefit or 'pros and cons' analysis, which it definitely is not. Forcefield analysis is simply concerned with the difficulty of the journey which a strategy is likely to make throughout its implementation.

The difficulty of this journey, like that of any other journey in life, has nothing to do with the attractiveness of reaching the destination. The only sense in which it is permissible to incorporate the perceived benefits of a strategy as a forcefield enabler is insofar as:

■ there is actually a genuinely attractive business case for the strategy and one which has turned on key stakeholders
■ key stakeholders are attracted by the strategy for other reasons.

The most effective way of evaluating the forces enabling or constraining achievement of the strategy's objective is to represent this pictorially. This picture represents the relative strength of each individual enabling or constraining force by drawing an arrowed line whose length is in proportion to that relative strength.

A horizontal version of forcefield analysis is depicted in figure 5.17. Note in this case that, on balance, the enabling forces appear less strong than the constraining forces. This particular analysis is for a telecommunication company's strategic plan. It shows that although many of the plans, processes and programmes had been put in place, it was nevertheless difficult to envisage implementation being a complete success. Subsequent events suggested that implementation difficulties at the company were very severe.

FIGURE 5.17: Forcefield analysis: telecommunications company

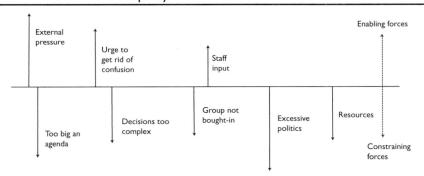

The example of the telecommunications company highlights one important truth about forcefield analysis, namely that:

■ the degree of ease of the strategic project is only in proportion to the extent of your pre-existing CUNNING IMPLEMENTATION PLAN.

Managers who have not already thought hard about the phases of difficulty and about options to get round potential hurdles (for example, push versus pull strategies) may be doomed to suffer a very difficult project.

As a rule of thumb, one would wish to see the enablers outweighing the constraints by a factor of at least 1.5 to 2 overall, in accordance with the principle of military dominance. Otherwise we should be concerned and potentially worried that implementation droop will set in.

Also, any stoppers really must be addressed, otherwise implementation won't happen. During – and before – implementation the key implementation forces should be continually monitored to ensure that none threaten to 'go critical' and become a 'stopper'.

The next issue that arises is how to evaluate the relative strength of the various forces. Two methods used successfully in the past include:

- scoring each force as having 'high', 'medium' or 'low' impact
- scoring each force numerically on a scale of 1 to 5.

Where a team may wish to change its mind (and does not wish to spoil its artwork), then by using post-its the length of the arrows can be changed.

Most groups of managers work comfortably by using the high, medium or low scoring method. In exceptional cases (for example where managers have scientific backgrounds or have an inherent love of quantification) the numerical 1 to 5 scale appears to fit more comfortably.

One of the common objections to forcefield analysis is that the whole scoring exercise is 'highly subjective'. This feeling normally occurs within the first ten minutes or so of any analysis exercise. It arises usually because all that managers have done is to identify that a force is an enabler or a constraint without exploring key questions including:

- Why is it an enabler or a constraint?
- How important an influence is it on the change process (and when)?
- What underlying factors does it depend upon in turn?

This highlights that any forcefield analysis is dependent on many assumptions, many of which are implicit. A more successful and less 'subjective' analysis will have brought to the surface, shared and agreed these implicit assumptions.

A number of pitfalls need to be avoided in the use of forcefield analysis for managing strategy implementation, which include:

- Focusing primarily on tangible (as opposed to less tangible) implementation forces.

- Missing out major constraints because the team wishes to paint an 'ideal' rather than a realistic picture of the change (we return to these issues in a moment).
- Failing to identify a 'stopper': that is, a change which has such a powerful impact that it is likely to stop the change in its tracks. 'Stoppers' should be drawn either as a thick black arrow or, alternatively, as an arrow which goes right to the bottom of the forcefield analysis and 'off the page'. (This assumes that you are using the vertical format for forcefield analysis.)

A 'stopper' can be defined as an influence which will effectively put an end to the initiative either through direct confrontation or passive resistance. (Implementation may fail because of 'limpet management' – just as one constraint is loosened another in effect reasserts itself.) Also, there may be cases where a specific enabling force can be made strong and prove decisive in moving the strategy forward. This kind of force may be described as an 'unblocker' and can be drawn as a very long (or thick) positive line upwards on the forcefield picture.

There may also be instances where a negative and constraining force can be flipped over to make a positive force, and in so doing transform the picture. For instance, if an influential stakeholder (who is currently negative) can be turned around in favour of the change, this can provide a major driver in the strategic project's progress. To prioritize which force to focus on, begin with the most presently limiting (or constraining) factor. This is the first key tenet of the Theory of Constraints (Goldratt, 1990).

A useful tip is to look beyond the existing enabling forces to the context of the implementation itself. Within that context, ask yourself whether there are some latent enablers which, if brought to the surface, could be used to unlock organizational energy. For example, if staff feel overburdened with work then a restructuring which is geared not so much to reducing cuts but to reducing organizational stress and strain is likely to be most gratefully received.

Or, by using a 'pull' strategy to get staff's ideas on future organizational processes in advance of a restructuring might flush out some really good ideas for simplification. It might also get staff on board as they see these ideas already incorporated in the plans for the new structure.

This is the second, major tenet of the Theory of Constraints, which is that within any really difficult situation there is buried somewhere within it some latent, naturally enabling force.

Forcefield analysis can be used for implementation in virtually any domain, including:

- business plans
- change projects
- acquisition integration
- strategic reviews (as a process)
- organization development.

The key benefits of forcefield analysis are that it:

- encourages you to think about difficulty as opposed merely to attractiveness
- helps you to focus on the context and process for implementation, rather than its context
- gives an early warning of 'mission impossible' projects.

The key disadvantages of forcefield analysis are that it:

- Is sometimes too much of a snapshot of the short and medium term. This can be remedied however by a later technique of the 'difficulty-over-time' curve.
- Can be incomplete – which might give you the misleading impression that implementation is not too difficult really (this can be availed by asking the question again, 'What is the One Big Thing which we have forgotten?).

The key linkages with other techniques include:

- With AID analysis – to test out the assumed level of difficulty.
- With the strategic option grid – to help test out your views of implementation difficulty.
- With stakeholder analysis – to understand the context for change more deeply.
- With 'how-how' analysis – to analyze the difficulty of specific activities.
- With fishbone analysis – by using fishbone analysis to ask the question for major constraining forces, 'Why is this so difficult?'
- With the uncertainty grid – to tease out the most dubious implement-ation assumptions.

Difficulty-over-time curves

Whilst forcefield analysis is very good at tackling short and medium term difficulty, it may not stretch managers' thinking about the longer-term dynamics of implementation.

To address this issue we need the 'difficulty-over-time' curve (see figure 5.18). This plots the precise degree of difficulty (easy, difficult, or very difficult) over time.

FIGURE 5.18: Difficulty-over-time curve

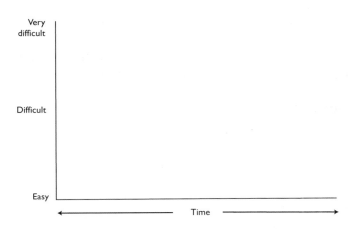

Sometimes implementation gets easier over time, but more commonly it gets more difficult. This can occur at all kinds of different stages, perhaps as a steady incline or, alternatively, difficulty could climb a little, then fall back before getting really, really difficult.

This reminds one of the authors of his experience on a rollercoaster in Los Angeles. It appeared to be two rollercoasters, one small and one which was quite awesome. He thought he had gone on the small one until he went over the first peak to see the very big one right ahead. The experience was amplified by the fact that it was very quiet and early in the day. Indeed he and his companion were the only two people on the ride. So they couldn't get solace or company from other people's screams. Nor would they have probably been missed had they fallen out – until the bodies were found.

A rollercoaster strategy of this kind can be just as bad as you are not prepared for the sudden onrush of difficulty as implementation proceeds.

The difficulty-over-time curve can be plotted either for the total difficulty of the implementation activity or project, or for just one constraining force. The difficulty-over-time curve is most helpful when creating scenario storylines for implementation.

The key benefits of the difficulty-over-time curve are that it:

- is dynamic, and helps to stretch our thinking about the future
- is easy to visualize mentally.

The difficulty-over-time curve has the following linkages to other techniques:

- to forcefield analysis – it provides a visual way of thinking about the various forces through time
- to AID analysis – it helps to think about where a strategic project might shift to
- in conjunction with stakeholders – to examine how the difficulty of dealing with them is likely to change over time.

Stakeholder analysis

Stakeholder analysis is another major tool for analyzing implementation (Piercey, 1989; Grundy, 1993).

A stakeholder is an individual or group who either has:

- a decision-making role
- an advisory role
- an implementing role
- a role as a user or as a victim.

Stakeholder analysis is performed as follows:

- first, identify who you believe the key stakeholders are at any phase of implementation
- second, evaluate whether these stakeholders have high, medium or low influence on the issue in question (You need to abstract this from their influence generally in the organization.)
- third, evaluate whether at the current time they are for the project, against it, or idling in 'neutral' (see figure 5.19).

In order to estimate where a stakeholder is positioned approximately, you will need to see the world from that particular stakeholder's perspective. From experience over the years we have found that the best way to convey this is to ask managers to have in effect an out-of-body experience – not quite literally, of course!

This involves not merely trying to sense the surface attitudes of stakeholders to a particular issue but also the deeper-seated emotions, focus, anxieties and even prejudices. Figure 5.20 represents those levels which all need to be thought through.

Later on we illustrate how a specific stakeholder's agenda can be mapped using stakeholder agenda analysis, which is another application of forcefield analysis.

FIGURE 5.19: Stakeholder analysis

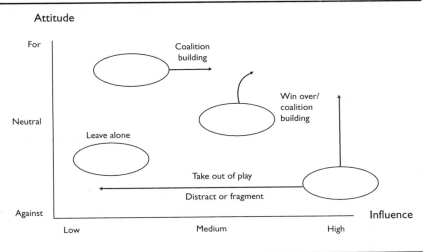

FIGURE 5.20: Levels of agendas

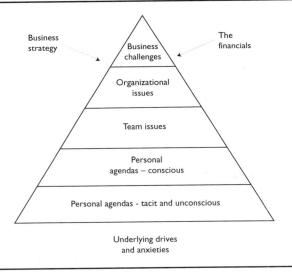

To bring home the point that stakeholder analysis really does involve having the out-of-body experience, we usually go as far as even showing an acetate of the two television stars of *The X Files*, Mulder and Scully! From experience, managers who literally do take the perspective that 'I am the stakeholder' are typically at least 50 per cent more accurate in their analysis.

The above-mentioned three steps give a good 'first cut' of the pattern of stakeholders. The cluster of stakeholders depicted on a stakeholder grid (see figure 5.19) should then be assessed to see what the overall picture looks like, particularly:

- Is the strategy an easy bet?
- Or is it highlighting a long slog?
- Or, finally, does this seem like mission impossible?

For instance, if most of the stakeholders are clustered towards the bottom part of the stakeholder grid, then you clearly have a mission impossible on your hands (unless the stakeholders can be repositioned).

Another difficult configuration is where there is an equal number of supporting stakeholders (with lower influence), i.e. in the northwest of the picture, to those against (but having higher influence) – in the southeast. Once again, this means that implementation is likely to experience major difficulties.

Finally, where you have a large number of stakeholders floating in neutral in the middle of the picture, this very neutrality can present major problems due to organizational inertia.

It is a particularly useful idea to position yourself on the stakeholder grid, especially if you are the project manager. This helps you to re-examine your own position – and your underlying agendas – which may be mixed.

Following your tentative, first-cut analysis, you should then move on to the next phase:

- First, can new stakeholders be brought into play to shift the balance of influence or can existing players be withdrawn in some way (or be subtly distracted)?
- Second, is it possible to boost the influence of stakeholders who are currently in favour of the project?
- Third, is it possible to reduce the influence of any antagonistic stakeholders?
- Fourth, can coalitions of stakeholders in favour be achieved so as to strengthen their combined influence?
- Fifth, can coalitions of stakeholders antagonistic to the project be prevented?
- Sixth, can the project change itself, in appearance or in substance, and be reformulated to diffuse hostility towards it?
- Seventh, are there possibilities of 'bringing on board' any negative stakeholders by allowing them a role or in incorporating one or more of their prized ideas?

■ Eighth, is the pattern of influence of stakeholders sufficiently hostile for the project to warrant its redefinition?

Once you have done the stakeholder analysis it may well be worthwhile revisiting the forcefield analysis to either introduce one, or more, new forces, or to revise earlier views. The forcefield analysis will now incorporate all of the enabling and constraining forces, including some of the more political and the less tangible ones.

Often a particular stakeholder may be difficult to position. This may be because his/her agendas might be complex. It is quite common to find that it is only one specific negative agenda which has made a stakeholder into an influential antagonist.

Where there are very large numbers of stakeholders at play on a particular issue, this may invite some simplification of the implementation. For instance, the implementation project may need to be refined, perhaps even stopped and then restarted, in order to resolve an organizational mess.

In order to use stakeholder analysis effectively you may need to set some process arrangements in place where a team project is involved. First, the analysis may be usefully performed in a 'workshop' environment so as to give the analysis a 'reflective' or 'learning' feel. This will help to integrate managers' thinking on a key strategy. It may also be useful to devise code words for key stakeholders in order to make the outputs from this change tool feel 'safe'. On several occasions managers have decided to adopt nicknames for the key players. An element of humour will help to diffuse the potential seriousness of performing stakeholder analysis.

CASE STUDY: STAKEHOLDER ANALYSIS

A major financial institution was introducing some new processes which were fundamental to its operations. It decided to use the stakeholder analysis technique to identify who the key stakeholders were on the project, and where they were likely to be positioned.

The half-day workshop began by identifying the key stakeholders. No less than thirty-one stakeholders were defined. At the end of the exercise the question was put: 'Who is the one big stakeholder which we have forgotten?' The answer was there were actually two big stakeholders omitted, being:

■ the customer
■ the media.

The moral: unless stakeholder analysis is used in strategic thinking, your implementation could easily fall over as key players may be overlooked.

So far we have used stakeholder analysis in a relatively static manner. But obviously key stakeholders are likely to shift over time – and early support for the project may therefore evaporate. A number of things need to be anticipated therefore, namely:

■ Senior managers' support is likely to be very sensitive to the perceived ongoing success of the strategic project as it evolves. Any signs of failure are likely to be accompanied by suddenly diminishing support.
■ New stakeholders may enter the scheme, and others might disappear.
■ Certain stakeholders may increase in influence, or even decrease in influence.
■ Where the project changes in its scope or in its focus significantly, stakeholders will then change their positions.
■ Stakeholders' own agendas might change due to external factors outside this particular project. For example, other projects might distract them or result in a reprioritization of agendas and of this project in particular.

Due to the above it may be necessary to review stakeholder positions at least several times during the lifetime of the project.

As a final note, obviously the stakeholder tool should not be used for covert personal and political purposes. Its purpose is to help get things done in organizations and not to obtain personal advantage for its own sake.

For further analysis it is possible to examine how stakeholders may change over time by plotting:

■ their attitude over time (ranging from 'against' through to 'for');
■ their influence over time (ranging from 'for' through to 'against').

This is depicted in figure 5.21.

Also, it is possible to prioritize which stakeholders to focus on by plotting:

■ their level of influence on this issue, and
■ our degree of influence over them.

In figure 5.22 we see the two axes plotted. Note that one should try to evolve strategies for gaining more influence over those stakeholders who are most influential – and who we have currently least influence over.

One thing to watch with stakeholder analysis is that you do not make fixed and rigid assumptions about stakeholders' attitudes. Using the grid over many years leads us to believe that often managers have a pessimistic bias – assuming that certain stakeholders will be against. In fact, they are often in neutral due to overload of existing agendas or due to perceived resource constraints.

FIGURE 5.21: Stakeholder attitude and influence-over-time curves

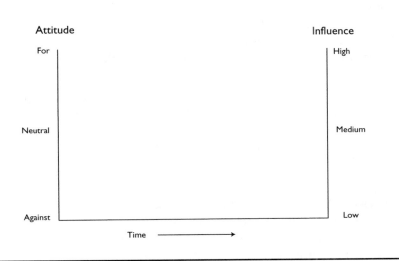

FIGURE 5.22: Influence over stakeholders grid

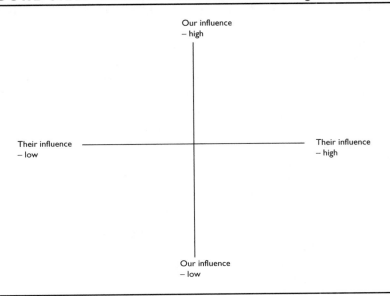

When confronted with positionings of themselves as 'against' they are often slightly surprised. The lesson here is that often many organizational agendas are actually more fluid than is perceived. This is actually good news for strategic thinkers who may feel there is little real chance of their ideas being actually implemented.

Stakeholder analysis is useful:

- at the very start of a strategic process – even as early as the ideas stage
- at the strategic options stage
- when performing detailed planning
- during mobilization of implementation
- mid-way or at the latter stages of implementation
- after implementation – to draw out the learning lessons.

Stakeholder analysis is also particularly useful for focusing on communication strategy. Here it will help you to identify which stakeholders to communicate with, when, how and with what message.

The key benefits of stakeholder analysis are that:

- it deals effectively with the political issues associated with strategy
- it encourages mental agility and the ability to take a variety of perspectives on an issue (through the out-of-body experience) simultaneously
- it defuses organizational politics and makes particularly sensitive issues discussable, sometimes called (by some colleagues at Cranfield) 'the zone of uncomfortable debate – or the 'ZUDE'.

Stakeholder analysis is linked with the other techniques as follows:

- Fishbone analysis can be used to ask why is a particular stakeholder against.
- Wishbone analysis can be used to identify all the things that would have to line up to influence a key stakeholder.
- How-how analysis can break down the tactical steps required to influence either a collection of stakeholders or an individual stakeholder.
- The uncertainty grid can be used to rate your assumptions that a stakeholder is 'for' in terms of how important this is, and also how certain/uncertain.
- Stakeholder analysis can also be used to deal with political uncertainties through the uncertainty tunnel (see chapter 2).
- Stakeholder analysis helps you to arrive at a more accurate appraisal of 'stakeholder acceptability' per the strategic option grid (see chapter 4).
- Stakeholder agenda analysis (following) helps to go under the surface of these assumptions.
- AID analysis or importance-influence analysis can prioritize which stakeholders to influence.

■ Forcefield analysis can help to understand the overall difficulty and potential for influencing a stakeholder (what things make this easier, and what things make this more difficult).

Stakeholder agenda analysis

Stakeholder agenda analysis now helps you to go down a level deeper – to the agenda of a specific individual, distinguishing between positive agendas (or 'turn-ons') versus negative agendas (the 'turn-offs') – see figure 5.23. We saw this earlier in chapter 4.

FIGURE 5.23: Stakeholder agenda analysis

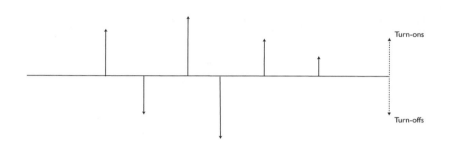

Stakeholder analysis has a very high potential for frequent, everyday use. Besides being applied at a macro-level on the bigger strategic issues it can be used on projects, for meetings generally, and for even drafting a simple letter or e-mail, or making a telephone call.

The major benefits of stakeholder agenda analysis:

■ It can be used to help identify one's own position on something and why one is in a dilemma.
■ It helps you to make a business case or to make a strategic presentation.
■ It can help you to get a new role – either inside or outside the organization.
■ It can suggest what the deeper agendas of the organization are, so that you can target your activities in strategic thinking to the 'hotter spots' – thereby avoiding unnecessary frustration.

Stakeholder agenda analysis has the following linkages:

- With the uncertainty grid: how certain are you that a key individual is 'for' something, for your assumed reasons?
- With the attractiveness-difficulty grid: how attractive is it to persuade a particular individual to shift their agenda – and how difficult is this?
- With the strategic option grid: as an overview of the influences on one's thinking before scoring and prioritizing the key options.
- With the five competitive forces: to help understand the agendas of potential entrants, rivals, buyers and suppliers.

Importance and influence analysis

Importance and influence analysis helps us to look at the extent to which we have control over various strategic factors, or we do not have control (see figure 5.24).

FIGURE 5.24: Importance-influence analysis

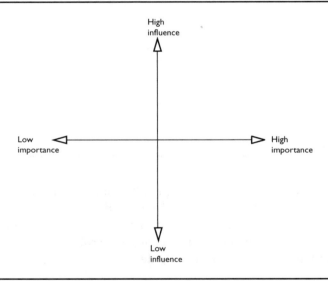

Most attention is often drawn to those areas which we have most influence over – and which are most important – rather than those which are both most important and where we have least influence (the south-east of the importance-influence grid).

Yet it is frequently possible – through creative thinking – to get at least some influence over these areas.

For example, one department at British Telecom was responsible for strategic advice (Grundy, 1998a), but when they put their issues on the grid they found that most of them were indeed positioned in the southeast. This suggested a number of things: first, that they needed to build their own influence over the organization. Second, that they needed to develop their competence so that their input on these issues was naturally sought by many stakeholders. Third, they needed to form coalitions with other areas of the organization to deliver these activities. Fourth, they needed to cut down what they were trying to do so that they could provide more leverage where it really mattered.

Importance-influence analysis can be used:

- as part of a scenario development process
- when influencing stakeholders: to determine where the pivotal points of influence might be
- to challenge one's own mindset that some things are simply beyond one's control.

The key benefits of importance-influence analysis are that it:

- forces managers to think more proactively about what they can do about issues
- helps them scan their own external and internal environment and acts as a focus for action.

The key linkages of importance-influence analysis with other techniques are:

- With wishbone analysis – it can be used to highlight those alignment factors over which there is least influence. This can be useful to assess both vulnerability and also where you should think harder about how to create more influence.
- With performance driver analysis – again this can be prioritized for action, picking off the higher influence areas first.
- With external analysis generally – PEST factors, growth drivers, the competitive forces, can all be prioritized using the importance-influence grid (likewise the 'threats' of SWOT analysis).
- With fishbone analysis – again this will help to prioritize which of the root causes to focus on. Usually one would begin with those which are most important and over which most influence was exerted.
- With stakeholder analysis – to help debate how the most important stakeholders over which you have least influence could be influenced.
- With the uncertainty grid – to split out the 'most uncertain/most important' quadrant to determine what you can do most about (through influence).

A common problem for up-and-coming innovative executives is that they will get caught between:

- Trying to influence their peers (who, like themselves, have lower influence).
- Trying to influence the very top person (about their pet projects or ideas generally). He/she may wish to listen but may be reluctant to make any decision unless all of senior management are brought in.
- Feeling outside the inner circle of the senior management team, not seeing a real way to have influence over them.

Here the manager would probably have low to medium influence over his peers because they too have their own bright ideas – and in any event these stakeholders would be of low influence. The chief executive would be of high influence, but in practical terms perhaps not as influential as the main body of the senior team. Also, being at the middle levels your influence would be modest. But crucially you would have lowest influence over the managers who themselves have the highest influence – the main senior managers. This calls for a major reorientation of your focus.

Summary of key points

- The five key stages of strategy implementation are: diagnosis, options, planning, implementation, learning and control.
- At each stage there are a number of tools that can be used. Some tools work for different stages – so they can be used more than once.
- Performance driver analysis and fishbone analysis can be very helpful in turnaround situations.
- Fishbone analysis can be used to diagnose problems with considerable complexity, and can be used to uncover the systems at work between root causes.
- From-to (FT) analysis will help you to explore the scope of strategy implementation, to determine the level of desired stretch. It will also help you to communicate it within the organization and to monitor progress towards goals.
- 'How-how' analysis then breaks down each shift within the from-to analysis into manageable steps.
- Attractiveness-Implementation Difficulty (or AID) analysis is needed to prioritize particular strategic actions.
- Value and cost driver analysis then helps test out your assumed 'attractiveness' in more depth.
- Forcefield analysis and the difficulty-over-time curve then tests out its difficulty.

- Stakeholder analysis identifies the key stakeholders, positions them, and also suggests new influencing strategies.
- Stakeholder agenda analysis enables you to go another level deeper, to explore a particular stakeholder's ambitions and anxieties.
- Their attitude and influence can be plotted over time using the attitude-over-time and the influence-over-time curves.
- Stakeholders can also be disaggregated into:
  - those who have greatest influence
  - those we have greatest influence over, and
  - those who are least/most important (see the importance and influence grid).

References

Goldratt, E.M., *Theory of Constraints*, North River Press, Great Barrington, Massachusetts, 1990.

Grundy, A.N., *Corporate Strategy and Financial Decisions*, Kogan Page, London, 1992.

— *Implementing Strategic Change*, Kogan Page, London, 1993.

— *Exploring Strategic Financial Management*, Prentice Hall, London, 1998.

— *Harnessing Strategic Behaviour – How Politics Drives Company Strategy*, Financial Times Publishing, London, 1998.

Grundy A.N. and L. Brown, *Strategic Project Management*, Thomson Learning, London, 2001.

Piercey, N., 'Diagnosing and Solving Implementation Problems in Strategic Planning', *Journal of General Management*, vol. 15, no 1 (Autumn 1989), p.p.19–38.

CHAPTER SIX

Valuing strategic thinking, part 1: the academics

Introduction

Strategic thinking often fails to meet its expectations. This is, however, generally because strategies are frequently not implemented, or are implemented poorly. Another reason is because managers are unsure about how strategic thinking actually creates value. Because 'strategy' is often perceived as relatively intangible and qualitative, the idea of actually putting some financial numbers on strategic thinking (or on strategic thought) may never have occurred to most managers.

To enquire deeper into this topic the authors conducted in-depth, qualitative research into how five strategy managers and five strategy academics saw the links between strategic thinking and value creation. The five senior managers were drawn from a variety of industries – each of which was facing rapid external or internal change (or both).

In this first chapter on the value of strategic thinking we look at it through the perspective of a number of academics.

Strategic thinking is seen more and more as a central issue on the organizational agenda. But it would seem less clear that it is a 'must-do-rather than as a 'nice-to-have-and-nice-to-do and ancillary process'. Whilst strategic thinking may help to alleviate organizational boredom, how do we put it actually at the very heart of management's attention? Our answer is that if we were to truly understand the economic value of strategic thinking it would be obvious why we should all be doing it – and lots of it.

But how can we understand its true value?

Our first step in exploring the value of strategic thinking is to therefore understand what 'value' actually is. For this we need to look at value-based management.

Value-based management

Value-based management emphasizes the need to put a value on strategy. Whilst the focus of value-based management is clearly on managing economic value (or the net present value of the future cash flows from a strategy), these cash flows are frequently difficult to target or measure. But as strategic thinking is (at least initially) an intangible, let us look at how we can begin to put a value on it.

One viewpoint is that instead of there being a single way of coping with intangibles there were often too many different ways of estimating their value (Grundy, 1992). These can be evaluated by:

- Identifying what generic kind of intangible it belongs to (for example, is the intangible concerned with the value of a future opportunity, or does it protect the existing business, or is it 'intangible' because it adds external customer value – and there is resulting uncertainty about how much of that value will be captured).
- Next, working out how value might be captured or crystallized in the future.
- Identifying specific measures or indicators that the value has materialized.

A more specific approach is to identify specific value and cost drivers – along with the preconditions of getting them aligned (Grundy, 1998). To achieve this we need to isolate the key value-creating activities which might generate value (for example, strategic thinking might avoid strategic errors and help to prioritize resource allocation, etc). Having looked at this we should then ask how much value might be created if this value-creating activity were effective – and if it were not frustrated by organizational conditions or other extraneous failings.

Having done this, we could then estimate the value of complete alignment, i.e. where strategic thinking is not only effective and incisive but also translates into equally effective implementation. We should then compare this wonderful ideal world with the 'base case' (Grundy, 1998), i.e. this is where strategic thinking is not effective, or simply does not get acted upon. An assessment of the difference between both worlds could then be made, potentially, if only in broad, financial terms.

To find out some clues as to how to put a value on strategic thinking, seven key questions were asked:

- How do you believe strategic thinking might add value generally?
- What value (i.e. economic value) might it generate (in each case)?

- What specific factors are likely to enable or constrain the specific ways in which strategic thinking actually adds that value (using a forcefield analysis)?
- In practice, what additional value (if any) tends to emerge (as opposed to being deliberate) from strategic thinking?
- What value tends to be unrealized, and why (using a fishbone analysis)?
- To what extent do:
  - management distraction
  - dilution of outputs
  - defensive routines
  inhibit its realization?
- What could be done to get more value from strategic thinking, and how?

The study enabled ten key categories of influences on creating value of strategic thinking to be teased out, as follows:

- meaning (of strategic thinking)
- business value
- context
- thought value
- prioritization
- core process
- process drivers
- supporting structure and skills
- supporting processes
- soft value.

These are now shown in figure 6.1.

Figure 6.1 also shows the main interdependencies between high level influences.

'Meaning' was important as the meaning of strategic thinking was somewhat unclear. Business value itself was segmented by type and was also broken down into specific categories like emergent, latent and contingent value.

'Thought value' was also important in its own right, with strategic thinking helping managers to construct a better ordered and more appropriately focused view of their business. Prioritization was, in itself, of significant value.

The 'core process' high level category contained a variety of sub-categories. These ranged from permission (on thinking strategically) and ownership through to the use of jargon and the physical conditions around the activity.

There were also a number of process drivers acting on the process including leadership, agendas, defensive routines, destruction and time constraints.

Supporting processes included project management, setting measures, and formal recognition of successful strategic thinking.

FIGURE 6.1: Strategic thinking categories

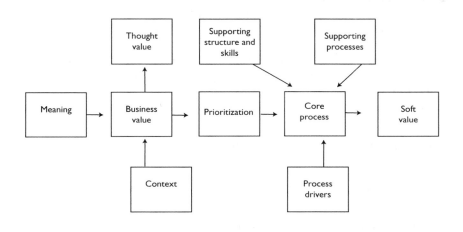

FIGURE 6.2: The value of strategic thinking: academics' perspectives

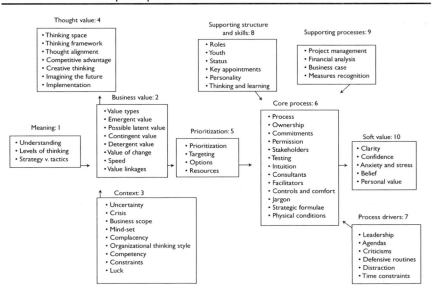

Finally, 'soft value' covered clarity, confidence, belief and reducing anxiety and stress. Potentially, strategic thinking could be of personal value, too.

This framework is then broken down into sub-categories, which are represented in figures 6.1 and 6.2.

We now look at:

- what the academics said
- what the senior managers said (in chapter 7)
- the implications for valuing strategic thinking.

Inevitably this chapter is more analytical than the others in this book. Nevertheless, there are many practical implications which we draw out as 'so-whats?'.

The academic perspective

In this section we examine the views of the academic respondents. This will cover:

- the meaning of strategic thinking
- business value
- context
- thought value
- prioritization
- process generally
- process drivers
- supporting structure and skills
- supporting process
- soft value
- conclusion
- summary.

The strategy academics (from Cranfield School of Management) that were interviewed were:

- Professor Cliff Bowman (CB)
- Dr Tony Grundy (TG)
- Murray Steele (MS)
- Pauline Weight (PW)
- Phil Davies (PD).

We now show the categories which emerged from the academics.

The meaning of strategic thinking

In 'the meaning of strategic thinking' we cover the definition of strategic thinking, the levels of strategic thinking, and the confusion over strategy versus tactics. The meaning of strategic thinking is considerably far from being self-evident, which is most interesting.

Definitions

Respondents felt that 'strategic thinking' was actually ambiguous. Their following definitions cover the standard ingredients of strategy, namely that is:

- broad
- about the whole organization
- about change and alignment of the organization to its environment
- about the real world – it is not theoretical as such.

> I think it links for me to what strategy is about. It is long-term, it is breadth. (PW)

> …I think what it [strategic thinking] should be about is when you are thinking about the overall strategy of the organization and the implications of what is happening, and what you do about it. (PD)

> Well, strategic thinking is a concept. You have to link it to something to make it real. (PW)

One academic draws our attention to the ambiguity of strategic thinking. He is also sceptical about whether a rational strategic planning process will be useful in practice:

> But even that [strategic thinking] as we saw at the beginning – isn't clear. (CB)

> As we said in the preamble, we need to define 'strategic thinking'. I think there is value in having a sense of direction, especially for senior managers and directors. Now how they get that sense of direction is another question. Rarely – in my view – does that sense of direction come from a rational planning process. (CB)

So, it does appear that the meaning of 'strategic thinking' could be clarified further:

- highlighting it is a cognitive process which is separate from the strategic planning process
- it might manifest itself differently whether it is being generated by an individual, a team or the wider organization
- it can go on quite independently of the formal planning process.

Levels of strategic thinking

We see that strategic thinking can happen at any level in the organization. One might even reverse the mindset that strategic thinking should happen most frequently at the top – perhaps the strategic thinking should happen at middle to more senior levels – where ideas are born and where implementation is carried out:

> For a start, strategic thinking should be a part of any successful organization. It is not just something that only the Board does, or that only certain people are able to do. It happens not just at the corporate/business strategy level, but also at the project level and at the personal level. So, debates about a person's career are essentially considered of a strategic nature. (TG)

This suggests that the value of strategic thinking may be currently limited at least partly because of confusion as to who should be doing it – and also of its narrow association with top management levels.

Strategy versus tactics

Whilst the strategy versus tactics issue is expanded on in the next chapter, here we see that a preoccupation with tactical detail may be done in part to defensive routines:

> If people don't agree with what is happening then they are likely perhaps to go down the rabbit holes. They are likely to resist it so they are less likely to think about the future. (PW)

One potential cause of limited value coming out of strategic thinking is therefore that its very meaning is only partially clear.

The 'so-whats?' of this are that:

- strategic thinking should go on at all times in an organization;
- it must not be regarded as owned (either exclusively or primarily) by one sub-section in the organization.

Business value

We now look at the value to the business from strategic thinking, as follows:

- types of value
- latent value
- contingent value
- detergent value
- change value
- speed
- value of linkages.

Types of value

Strategic thinking might have an emergent value. Unlike the formal process of strategic planning where there are deliberate outputs, strategic thinking is perhaps more likely to create value in spontaneous ways:

> You mean you can get some value as a by-product. Yes, it does happen, if you pursue (for example) a particular technology path and then you find a new application, for example. It does happen. It is a tricky one, that. (MS)

> I think that strategic thinking has a value in spotting the unexpected. (TG)

Here we see (surprisingly) value – even of an emergent nature – having a quite measurably economic quality. However, the nature of deliberate versus emergent value is a hard one to distinguish:

> I am not sure that we always capture the value of deliberate strategic thought, but with emergent thoughts it is probably even more difficult unless one is alert to it. (TG)

This suggests that the full value of strategic thinking comes through a collection of ideas (or thought streams) rather than through a single, big strategic thought. Also, it is not easy at all to differentiate between value which is deliberate and pre-intended from a strategic thought value which emerges more or less accidentally.

Latent value

Whilst managers may well have had strategic thoughts, the value may be unrealized – just latent:

> Like in government or art, people come up to you with something that they have been thinking about for a very long time. Strategic thinking had gone on maybe all of their lives. And it was only at that time that the opportunity … the value came out.

Whilst strategic planning has a specific time-frame, strategic thinking is not so constrained and may also be in gestation for considerable time (this being a difference between the two):

> What looks like a very off-the-cuff decision might have gone on as a result of thinking – which you weren't aware of – which went on quite a while before … It might have come from something which happened years before. What came out as a beautiful clear idea had actually been gestating for a very long time. (PD)

As the value of the strategic idea may be not determinate at a point in time, its value may not be fully appreciated. This might suggest that to help managers focus more on its value one might first ask 'what value came out of strategic thoughts in the past?'

Contingent value

Value may be contingent simply because of organizational contingencies:

> It is contingent, the right idea at the wrong time – it has got to be different enough to show the value but not so different that people are not going to know how to do it. (PD)

This also implies that the value is ultimately contingent upon implementation. The corollary of this is that for certain ideas to have value they must be implemented.

One way to assess the value of strategic thinking might be to try to put an economic value on a strategic thought, or thought stream – given some assured, contingent conditions:

> And, to say 'what was the value of strategic thinking?' I asked them at BT to think about the value and they said, 'Oh yes – there was that little idea to set the value of identifying the Internet as a strategic issue – that was quite important for BT's business'. Can people put a value on that? Or on the value of Tesco's e-commerce strategy, potentially now worth between one and two billion pounds? How much did the one value four years ago contribute to that value? If it was only 1 per cent that would have been worth £10 million. (TG)

The above quotes show that it may be possible to estimate the value of a strategic thought – but realizing that value is contingent on its effective implementation, and on its timing, and on organizational conditions generally. We should perhaps also differentiate between the value of specific strategic thoughts and ideas and the value of a set of thoughts, and finally the value of the strategic thinking process itself.

Detergent value

Besides more positive creation of value, strategic thinking might help to reorganize or reorientate a business (its 'detergent' value – Grundy, 1995):

> In one situation I was consulting with a Board on where it should go with its two key businesses. What was interesting – it was absolutely clear – was that they didn't want to be in one business, but they didn't quite know how to say it. There was a moment in the bar and they said, 'Well, why don't we get out of it?' The analysis had been done but the decision happened in literally a microsecond.

> The thinking they had done allowed them to make the right decision. (PD)

Here it was perhaps easier to put an economic value on the thoughts, as they were clearly contingent upon some action, i.e. change. Further, where detergent value is involved, as this is more tangible, it might be easier to put an economic value on it as opposed to other forms of value (such as emergent and contingent).

Change value

The next examples show how strategic thinking can lead to value creation by acting as the catalyst for strategic change:

> Remembering now a strategic management seminar for a conglomerate, and two blokes were sat there and each discovered that the other had something that they wanted. One guy was trying to sell certain products and the other guy was struggling to find a supplier. [elaborates] The fact that they were thinking strategically was the catalyst for that. (PD)

Speed

An interesting area of value is speed. Accelerating management debate and decisions could lead to more effective change and development:

> The other thing is, will this ever generate something; will anything happen? In my experience these things may take place down the line. But the strategic thinking has allowed you to take action quite quickly. (PD)

It would be intriguing to ask managers what the economic value of acceleration might have been. Indeed, our representative from Tesco (see next section) volunteers that this aspect is particularly of value.

Value of linkages

The idea that strategic thinking adds value by purely linking a range of management actions is an interesting one. Without this linkage one could well imagine confusion resulting. The effect of confusion could be quantified through the costs of disruption, duplication and possibly even conflicts:

> It has added value in some clear examples. It is almost like a 'Road to Damascus' experience, where suddenly you see a 'Wooh!' and it becomes clear, and everything changes. So it is the start of clarity. (PD)

> An example was at a major retailer, where I was working with their non-food business on their strategy. And then I subsequently went to work with the home shopping people. During the home shopping workshop, the goal was to work on home shopping. But when I reflected on it at the time there were some opportunities for the non-food business, which was constrained by space. And when you actually put those two opportunities together you definitely had a synergy between the two. And that was definitely a thought that wasn't expected in that strategic process. (TG)

Whilst hard to quantify, it would be interesting to estimate the potential cost (through confusion) of a lack of alignment of strategic activities. Clearly, this would require imagining a) the situation with the alignment, and b) without the alignment.

The 'so-whats?' from this are that strategic thinking generates value in diverse and not singular ways, and not just to create new strategies.

Context

The context section now looks at:

- crisis
- mindset
- complacency
- organizational thinking style
- luck.

Crisis

Crisis is an important catalyst for strategic thinking, mentioned by several respondents.

Mindset

Mindset is also mentioned as being an important constraint on strategic thinking adding value:

> The biggest constraint is almost inevitably the external mindset, the culture of the organization, especially of the top people. They don't tend to see new opportunities in the same way as younger people further down the organizations can see them. So the lenses through which they see external change are biased basically in favour of what they are currently doing. (MS)

This mindset is not just at the organizational level, but at the industry level too:

> The mindset of the industry – you have then got their awareness of the external world. It is filtered, all the time. We have – we don't need to change because everything is fine versus what does the Internet mean to our organization? How are we going to cope with this? So there is a line – fat and happy versus terrified, and obviously something in the middle. If you are totally terrified then you will probably do nothing. Rabbits in the headlights stuff. (PD)

Indeed, a possibility is that an entire industry may be – at least during a certain time period – relatively devoid of strategic thinking, thus restricting its opportunity to add value.

Complacency

Complacency is also put forward as being a major constraint on strategic thinking:

> And if the business is currently successful, there isn't the compelling need to turn the strategic thought into value anyway. And there may never be a moment in time when I have to do it, so then I can delay. (TG)

Organizational thinking style

The thinking style of the organization is suggested as being an important factor – either in enabling or constraining strategic thinking:

> Strategic thinking has, for me, a link to organic-type organizations. If it is a freethinking type of organization then their ideas will be enabled. And then we are back to whether this happens at all levels. (PW)

These assumptions require testing; a free-thinking organization might well be one which takes decisions in a reactive way to perceived opportunity. Equally, a more established organization might have considerable need for strategic thinking – in order to reinvent itself.

Luck

A problem with putting the value on strategy is that of luck:

> You can't judge the impact in financial terms that it has – you can only do that after the fact. That's the problem…Saying 'that was a good piece of strategic thinking there, particularly as you can get organizations ending up with successful situations not through any formal process whatsoever'. This is just out of luck or good fortune. They don't plan their way at all. (CB)

It is also felt that uncertainty creates big difficulties in targeting value.

> You might actually realize more value or less value because if the world is inherently uncertain and therefore inherently unknowable, then a great strategy might not work but a rubbish strategy can actually work better [elaborates]. (PD)

But perhaps if we were to consider the value of strategic thinking (rather than of the actual strategy) perhaps this may help to create luck. Luck may occur not merely through chance but also by the recognition of 'here is an opportunity – and it is this big'. Surely this falls into the category of strategic thinking.

The key 'so-whats?' from this are:

- Mindset and thinking style are major impediments to strategic thinking: this implies a need to abandon preconceptions and to adopt the new ways of thinking (which we saw in chapter 4).
- Strategic thinking may seem to be subservient to luck – but perhaps strategic thinking (if based on synthesis and creativity, and not merely on analysis) can and should be used to create luck.

Thought value

The section on thought value looks at the value created by strategic thinking through its contribution to management thinking clearly. This covers:

- thinking space
- thinking framework
- thought alignment
- competitive advantage (its recognition)
- creative thinking
- implementation.

Thinking space

Strategic thinking may add value just by encouraging managers to think (when they otherwise would not):

> Whether there is space in the organization for strategic thinking to take place. That links back to culture. Is this an organization which allows you time to think? (PW)

> A major reason why people come on programmes at Cranfield is to get away from work and to have a chance for a bit of a brain dump and a think. (MS)

But such thoughts – whilst seeming to be 'revolutionary' may nevertheless have only a latent value, as frequently they are not then implemented.

Thinking framework

It may also provide a framework for thinking (generally) – and one broader than a specific functional one:

> Secondly, there needs to be understanding of the industry context, and to some extent of the way in which you think about these things. The way we think about the context is conditioned by the tools we use. If I am an HR specialist I think of the industry in terms of turnover, demographics, pay rights. If I am a production engineer, I think of efficiencies. (PD)

Thought alignment

It also acts as a medium for synchronizing thought:

> …And that is one of the benefits out of the strategy process – they are thinking about the same thing. (MS)

This might help accelerate the management process, and avoid strategic confusion and mistakes.

Competitive advantage

In addition, it can help managers to focus decisions on areas where there is real competitive advantage:

> The strategic thinking bit does come in in recognizing what does give us advantage. (CB)

Creative thinking

Thinking differently is a key part of strategic thinking. Indeed, to some it is almost synonymous with strategic thinking. One respondent stresses the value of strategic play:

> I think people ought to stop thinking about their business and start thinking about things which aren't actually dangerous for them, to improve their thinking about them. People are very inhibited about thinking. Kids think about anything, and 'why is the sky blue?'. (PD)

> The real problem with thinking is that it can be thought to be playing. We are playing with the ideas; we are not getting anywhere – let's get on with it. You get comments like, 'Well that's all well and good, but what about the bottom line?' Or, 'I am sure that is interesting but we are trying to run a business here'. (PD)

> Well, I think it adds value in a general sense. Seeing opportunities and anticipating problems. And that's about breadth, about thinking out-side the box. It is more about creative thinking, which is part of strategic thinking. (PW)

The above underlines the creative element in strategic thinking, but do not help in identifying how this aspect of it can be encouraged. The more formal aspects of strategic analysis may not guarantee creative strategic thoughts. Creative value no doubt links to emergent and contingent value, too.

Implementation

The value which strategic thinking might play during implementation appears considerable:

> Some people may achieve part of the value by partial implementation of the strategic thought. Because, to get the full value out of the strategic thought there has to be alignment of all the key things as part of the system, partial implementation may not help. Perhaps 80 per cent implementation might only produce 20 per cent of the value. (TG)

The key 'so-whats?' from this are:

- Managers need to give themselves real thinking space (to kick-start strategic thinking).
- They then need some framework or tools to help them put structure in the process, rather than just attempt it 'freestyle'.
- Analytical thinking will not (of itself) generate strategic thoughts – this is perhaps why planning processes, planning departments, and indeed a good deal of formalized, remote-from-the-job training on strategy appears often ineffective.

Prioritization

In the section on prioritization we consider:

- setting priorities (generally)
- targeting (strategic thought)
- options
- resources.

Setting priorities

Setting priorities generally is mentioned several times as being a major problem which strategic thinking can address:

> You can have problems where you have got too many objectives and statements. That is just desperate thrashing around – like people with forty priorities. (CB)

Prioritization could mean not doing things and limiting action (rather like in a detergent value – see earlier):

> Strategic thinking adds value almost from what people are not going to do, because otherwise they will try to do too much strategically, and that will actually dilute the effect of that strategy, and you would not actually realize the value.
>
> People need to do fewer things (in order to add more value). One thing which is likely to enable it [strategic thinking] is if the organization is really overwhelmed by things that it is currently trying to implement – so it provides a focus. (TG)

The value of setting priorities might thus come in terms of:

- focusing on a smaller number of strategies – and doing them faster and better
- being able to make exit decisions more easily
- identifying (within a problem) where to focus the thinking and discussion
- conserving energy (not mentioned specifically above but an obvious consequence)
- helping avoid impossible to implement and/or severely disruptive strategies
- coping with the pressures of delayering.

Targeting

Targeting the value of strategic thinking is thought to be something that could be done, but probably is not done:

What is interesting here is that because people do seem to target the value of what is coming out of a strategic thought, they probably don't have them in the first place or, when they do have them, they are intoxicated by the ideas stream and do not get into the almost carnivorous role of what value can you get out of them. Maybe one should cut down the number of strategic thoughts so that we can get more focus. (TG)

This vacuum seems to be due (in part) to the fact that few have thought that 'strategic thoughts' might have an economic value:

Another factor is that no-one ever puts a monetary value on it. No-one says, 'hey, this could be worth £12.5 million – that idea'. There is probably a missing stage in the strategic thinking process of 'what is the value of that strategic thought?' (TG)

Not only is targeting important, but also deciding who will actually be responsible for cashing the value in – through moving it forward.

Options

One respondent is relatively conservative with regard to the value of formal reviews of strategic options, which are outside the core of existing strategy:

Organizations should be milking what they have got for as long as they can do it, and not wasting time trying to shift into something that they are not going to make anyway. (CB)

Another is slightly more positive, hinting at strategic thinking adding value by defining appropriate success criteria:

All we can say is we know what we shouldn't do…and what we are doing is actually helping. So what the value thing in thinking is you put in the criteria for success. (PD)

Resources

Interestingly, one respondent regards resources as less of a constraint:

It [constraints] is very rarely to do with resources. Most places have resources available. There is something around at the moment about not having enough human resources available. (MS)

In summary, more refined prioritization and more formal consideration of options might not only be beneficial but could link into managers' natural agendas – saving time and avoiding strategic mistakes. The key 'so-whats?' from this are that:

- The strategy tools we have looked at (especially in chapter 5 – the 'strategic option grid', and in chapter 6 (Attractiveness-Implementation Difficulty [AID] analysis) are so essential.
- Having strategic thoughts is always something which one should target for potential economic value, rather than seeing this as being rather restrictively quantitative and limiting.

Process generally

Process is itself quite complex and covers:

- process (itself)
- ownership
- commitment
- permission
- stakeholders
- testing
- consultants
- facilitation
- control and comfort
- jargon
- strategic formulae
- intuition
- physical conditions.

Process

We now examine:

- structuring the process
- relating it to other processes
- behavioural techniques and tactics
- strategic baggage – letting the past go
- tailoring the techniques
- setting expectations on what strategy entails
- defining ideal numbers (for group discussion).

Targeting value may require guidance – or some facilitation:

There are other workshops and management meetings where a lot is discussed but nothing is finished off. Where they do have strategic thoughts they are half-finished. If you look at the whole process of refining a strategic thought to the point at which you could do something about it, some are about 70 per cent, some are 25 per cent, they are all unfinished, they are all in bits. (TG)

However, without a process strategic thinking can lose direction and may also lack rigour:

> So you end up with probably more things which you apparently need to do than you do need to do, with actually less clarity on the what. Because managers do not realize that these thoughts are actually unfinished, you can't turn them into real actions and into real value. (TG)

Another interviewee stresses, however, the need for formal preparation, and for creating conversations about issues:

> Planned strategic thinking is – 'We are going to go away and do strategic thinking. We are going to go to a nice hotel and get a consultant talking' – like Tom Peters, or someone like you. If you go on your own – just simply going along to get some insights – but if you go collectively, as an organizational event, then clearly it is to address some problem, you have talked about it beforehand, you have not gone in there cold. So that is the formal side. But the informal side, that isn't planned, and that is often more valuable, and that often people say, going off, 'I am really worried about this situation', saying what do you think we should do? Or, I am really worried about this situation, I don't really know what we should do, or I don't understand why this is happening...and these are the ones where the quality of informal relationships...because that is what actually allows you to do it. (PD)

The ideal degree of formalization would thus vary depending upon organizational context. Nevertheless, it may be difficult – in the context of managers not well trained in strategic thinking – to apply it formally, at least in the first instance.

The strategic thinking process can be extended to other related processes:

> Also, having management processes with strategic thinking embedded in them, like at Tesco. That obviously does help. (TG)

The analytical process may need to be bedded into new and acceptable team routines and tactics:

> And people don't get embarrassed and shy about using a couple of tools, which means that you can have a more efficient and constructive debate about it. (TG)

But no amount of preparation will help if people carry with them strategic baggage:

> It is also about forgetting things – like that didn't work. There is an awful lot of that. A helpfully judicious dose of unlearning. And not trying to do absolutely everything yourself, because you can't. So I say: 'This is what

we can't do, this is not on the agenda. And these are one or two things that we will talk about'. The output is to improve thinking and to decide whether to take this on [elaborates on facilitators]. (PD)

In practical terms, it is felt that smaller numbers may help strategic discussions:

The other thing that helps is numbers, when you get beyond certain numbers you can't have a conversation. Maybe like a dinner party of eight people, it is lovely. When you get up to twelve it becomes two camps – you can't have a sensible conversation. It's about relaxing; it is about getting people to be comfortable. (PD)

Overall there appears to be a good deal to get right in establishing an adequate process to generate valuable strategic thoughts, including:

- some analytical techniques (carefully selected)
- behavioural tricks or processes
- a supportive culture
- a small(ish) group.

Ownership

Ownership is clearly a key issue and a perceived imperative:

Another enabler is when middle levels of management have had an input in the first place to the bigger strategy. (TG)

But at the end of the day they have to sort out their own destiny. They can't pass the buck to a consultant or to a generic solution, or to a system (from a book). Unless the top team actually believes it to the point where they will actually change their behaviour, then it [the plan] is just an artefact. (CB)

Whilst ownership is clearly of importance, we are not sure (from the above) how this ownership can be improved: this seems to be a blanket term for trying to get people to think the same way. But assuming the strategic thought is sensible in the first place, buy-in might be an enabler of value.

Commitment

Likewise, a precondition of strategic thinking adding value is top management commitment:

Lack of commitment by the top management. Er, the culture of the organization. Frequently a misalignment between the top level of management, the next level down, and so on. They find that they think that they think that everyone is thinking about. (MS)

Permission

But more than commitment one also requires permission (by top management) – to have strategic thoughts within the organizational context:

> Permission … (is an enabler). There needs to be permission to think about it. They don't want to be asked to go and do some strategic thinking – but someone says this is what you mustn't think about'. (PD)

If permission is lacking, then the value generated can be severely constrained:

> Whenever you run a workshop and the permission isn't there, you always stay at that place, you never get into the detail. (PD)

Stakeholders

Engaging key stakeholders in the process is of central importance, and not secondary significance:

> If someone has to get other people enthused as well, there may be the team, many stakeholders, that is going to be another potential frustration. And I think that that frustration works back into behaviour. It is as if past frustration might have become so great that they might not have the capacity to have the strategic thought. (TG)

Testing

Linked to facilitation, testing out ideas is seen as a critical value-creating activity (within strategic thinking):

> It is almost about having a difficult tutorial with someone who keeps on asking the questions. It is Socratic. For me it is something which is, it is the difference between a rambling essay and a tight piece of work. It is something that is quite precise, quite hard-thinking.
>
> I see my role like a philosopher, I am challenging people's definitions of the role around them, so that they think much more clearly about it and so that they are not just simply doing whatever everybody else is. (PD)

Besides creativity, at the other end of the spectrum is also therefore testing and challenge.

Consultants

The issue of the role of consultants provokes some interesting responses by the academics – who appear generally lukewarm to their involvement (perhaps out of genuine causes for criticism or perhaps a touch of rivalry

– between the academics and the consultants). Nevertheless what is said supports the hypothesis that managers can – and should – strive to be their own strategy consultant.

> You need to have quite a detailed understanding of the organization to – I think – come up with a viable direction for it. This is because consultants can't do it for you. This is because consultants won't know the detail, even if they trample all over the place for three months, they won't know. So I don't believe in consultants. (CB)

But another interviewee feels that strategic consultancy can play a positive role:

> Which probably means that strategic consultancy of that kind, unless it is conducted at top-level, is probably not going to have the potential value that it could have. (TG)

But others take a different and more sceptical view:

> They then get disappointed because you don't give them the answers that they expected, and then you get a sort of learnt helplessness, where people learnt about strategy and planning, and then give it to consultants to do. That takes the risk out of it.
> They [the consultants] attempt to get the answers that fit their solution. (PD)

So whilst (expert) consultancy is largely dismissed as not adding significant value, facilitation does seem to play a role in adding value – to strategic thinking. It remains to be seen if the managers think the same.

Facilitation

Facilitation is seen as being a very helpful catalyst in the strategic thinking process:

> There is one other factor – the ability of the facilitator, and once again it is about fit. There is the style of the facilitator and the process – do these actually fit? Do they want to listen? And the process also includes how people have been asked to come to the event, how has permission been reflected in how people have been asked to come to the event. And it depends on whether he stops and says, 'I trust you' and goes away, or whether he stays and is empowering. (PD)

Control and comfort

A novel idea is that of taking people out of their normal comfort zone – and where they can control their mental processes:

One thing is to get people out of control in the sense that everyone wants to be in control. You think differently when you are out of control. (MS)

Holding a strategic management session at the edge of a precipice might be justified. (MS)

Jargon

Jargon can either facilitate or inhibit strategic thinking depending on organizational culture and whether it is used well or abused:

In fact, when people get criticized for not doing strategic thinking (and this comes from my one-to-one experience), it seems to be more to do with how they make presentations in management, and the way in which they talk. They talk about operations, about getting things done and not about big-picture stuff. And they may not use the right jargon. (TG)

The danger with strategic thinking is that if it is too complicated it is a private language. (PD)

This jargon might unfortunately therefore make the strategic ideas much harder to communicate.

Strategic formulae

Specific formulae for generating strategy (like Porter's generic strategies) are frowned upon by one interviewee:

Everything that is a formula (another constraint) is almost by definition wrong (for example, the generic strategies). So it is really about uncovering what is actually successful in the business and trying to understand why...on the basis of that move forward with a time horizon of not more than two years. (CB)

Physical conditions

Interestingly, the physical conditions of the 'strategic thinkers' (and of the participants) is seen as an important potential enabler or constraint:

One of the things that could be done to improve the quality of strategic thinking is to improve the physiological and physical aspects of it. It sounds a really obvious point. People ought to be rested, they should not bring their mobile phones with them, they should feel that they are ready to focus. I take them for a walk outdoors [elaborates]. (PD)

An interesting line of enquiry therefore is whether managers' physical energy and general state of well-being may detract from strategic thinking. Also, the physical setting might signal symbolically to managers that a different style of thinking is called for.

Intuition

Intuitive insights are felt to be an important ingredient of the process:

> It is very difficult to allocate the success of an organization to a particular type of thing, to a particular strategy. Success comes from a whole host of reasons. In my view planning *per se* does not necessarily help. I think insights are very much more important than any planning process. (CB)

> We are into this wonderful management skill of judgement. If you have got a team of people trying to move forward from A to B, and you always have members who have never got enough detail to move forward, then it may be necessary to explore further opportunities, which may be right or it may be wrong. (PW)

In summary, there were mixed views of how formal the strategic thinking process should be. There was agreement that soft factors, like ownership, permission, stakeholder alignment, were required but an emphasis on facilitation rather than on consultancy input.

The key 'so-whats?' from this are:

- Managers do need some structure for strategic thinking.
- They also (in the current skills climate) need facilitation (and this is not a 'nice-to-have').
- The strategic thinking process is often more important than its content, and much more attention is needed to get this right.
- This may also require a jolt out of the conventional mindset. (There may be a variety of ways to achieve this. For example, the author's style is to use humour to shift managers out of their conventional world view – hence the emphasis on 'avoiding rabbit holes', 'the cunning plan', and 'the Spice Girl approach to strategy' that we saw earlier in our book.
- Strategic thinking does, however, have to be grounded in everyday reality. We must always ask: 'what is the 'so-what?' of strategic thinking?'
- Appallingly unfavourable environments (for strategic thinking) are to be avoided.

Process drivers

The next section on process drivers discusses:

- leadership
- agendas
- criticisms
- defensive routines
- distraction
- time constraints.

Leadership

It would have been surprising if leadership had not got a mention at some point:

> I can then – the leader – decide things, I can set an agenda. I can say 'You can't do that but you can do that'. In the absence of that clear view then everyone is thrashing around. (CB)

Leadership's role is to signal that 'strategic thinking is okay':

> The leader's presence is all about permission. But often they are the worst person to be there because they are just going to take over and everyone has to listen and nothing ever happens. (PD)

Strong leadership may help or even get in the way of strategic thinking (by becoming too dominant):

> The style of leadership in the organization is pretty crucial. If it is a brutal style, that is going to make it difficult. If people are just expected to get on and do it [the strategy] then that is pretty impossible. Whereas if they are more receptive to the fact that some new strategic projects do need more resource and more time to deliver value, then that is important too. (TG)

Clearly, this indicates that leadership is not just about providing a signal that it is 'okay to do strategic thinking' but also requires of each manager leadership skills to take the strategy forward.

Agendas

Agendas are perceived as influencing the success of efforts at strategic thinking greatly:

> Unless it [the strategy] changes your personal agenda then it is not going to make any impact. (MS)

This is the case to a major, rather than a minor extent:

> If I am a manager in an organization with my personal agendas, and I have this strategic thought, it may never get up the agendas because you have always got more things to do. So it is a simple fact of time management. If that is not in place you are just not going to get a focus on the ideas that really matter. (TG)

Perhaps strategic thinking can actually help to dissolve limiting agendas, thus adding value:

> Around that it is using strategic thinking to mitigate organizational politics. Now that does not necessarily translate into economic value immediately, but by enabling people to do things, if we aggregate across the organization, that would be great. (TG)

However, follow-through to action may still be difficult, unless there is perceived to be an appeal to personal agendas:

> So you either don't do things at all, or wait until they drop from the current organizational agenda. And they are able to do that. Because their bosses aren't checking out that they have implemented those strategic ideas. (TG)

Agendas appear to play a key role in inhibiting the value of strategic thinking. Perhaps it would be possible to incorporate these agendas into the strategic thinking process more than in the past.

Criticism and defensive routines

The defensive routines that are triggered may halt strategic thinking in its tracks:

> I have seen some dreadful instances where people have presented some strategic thoughts in a [facilitated] conference and they have just been chopped away by senior people: 'We can't think that way, we can't do that', and getting very defensive. Even where we have set up behavioural rules, like not being political, personal, and we have all agreed to that and someone has criticized the strategy they didn't like and it has blown up. (TG)

Sometimes it may be necessary for the leadership to break through these barriers to get the value from strategic thinking.

Clearly, defensive routines are likely to be a major constraining force on creating value from strategic thinking.

Distraction

Distraction (with extraneous detail) may well impede value – whether this comes from attention being diverted or by strategic ideas simply not penetrating awareness. Managers may have fundamentally underscoped what is required to get the value out of strategic thoughts:

> They are too busy doing other things to give it attention. The whole thing about strategic planning is that people write a plan and they put it on the shelf and look at it twelve months later...[elaborates] (MS)

Much distraction may occur because of managers' time constraints:

> Management distraction is very simple, you have got so much time available and one of the problems is that people don't realize what is involved in doing it. It actually involves a lot more than that [a day]. You have to free up enough time. (PD)

Or, operational imperatives are simply the excuse for not doing strategic thinking:

> Management distraction typically is the short-term, operational agenda. It only causes a distraction where those executives don't believe in the strategy...When people say 'I haven't got time for all this strategy stuff' what they are really saying is, 'I haven't got the confidence to engage in the strategy process and I am hiding behind these urgent operational issues which I am really good at dealing with, but that's my excuse'. (CB)

Distraction factors are thus like a cloud of mist which clear, strategic thoughts have to penetrate in order to stand a chance of adding value.

Time constraints

Interestingly, time constraints were mentioned as a major barrier to strategic thinking, as evidenced by no less than three out of five of the respondents:

> A lot of the time you are just so busy, you don't have time; [you think] I am not clever enough, so I would simply do more work [cites a manager on a lap-top at 11 o'clock at night]. (PD)

> As an example of that managers say 'we must spend more time finding out what our competitors are doing but I am too busy shuffling paper'. (MS)

In degree of importance, it is possible that perceived time constraints might be one of the most important constraints on a) the process of strategic thinking, and b) turning this into hard, economic value.

The key 'so-whats?' from this are:

- that strategic thinking is absolutely integral with the need for leadership
- agendas must be managed proactively (reinforcing chapter 5's input on stakeholder analysis)
- dedicated time must be allocated to strategic thinking – until of course you are doing it more or less all the time.

Supporting structure and skills

A style of frenetic management does not seem to help either. In supporting structure and skills we deal with:

- roles
- youth
- status
- personality
- learning.

Roles

Surprisingly (perhaps), it is not even clear as to who should do strategic thinking – so the activity may get lost between the triangle of top management, (the official) planners, and middle managers:

> If people don't feel that that is their contribution in an organization, they feel they are an implementer, they work in an organization where the bright ideas are rewarded, then they can feel that they are not the right kind of cultural fit. (PW)

This leads to reflections more generally about what value managers add (within a hierarchy). One respondent suggests that the lack of strategic thinking in organizations questions what these managers are actually doing, and do they themselves add value?:

> A lot of people get promoted as a means of keeping them within the organization, and it is just hopeless in today's environment. A lot of people are unsuited to their roles; they were highly competent technically, but unsuited. Anyone who isn't directly involved in the production or in the service then one should ask some very serious questions about 'What are they doing?' ... You would save a lot of money by not having the hierarchy. (CB)

So, the lack of clarity of how senior managers should add value itself is a major inhibitor to strategic thinking. A further factor is the question of who should lead the strategic thinking process. The absence of a clear location for this responsibility seems to be another inhibitor on value creation:

It is about thinking differently, in new ways. And whose providence is it anyway? And who does strategic thinking? Who sees it as their role? Is it people in the strategy department, is it everyone in a strategic role? I think that's part of how the leadership role is given in the organization. (PW)

Youth

The relative youthfulness of managers also appears to be a key variable (with youth being associated with more free, creative strategic thinking):

You should get younger people involved in it, to open it up outside of the boardroom. You can actually involve what I call 'the value inter-faces'. You can recruit more young people to the Board, people who are maverick and different instead of being promoted on the basis of their past experience. (MS)

Whilst it is unlikely to see a one-for-one correlation between openness to strategic thinking and age, career life-cycle does seem to be a very probable factor influencing the process.

Status

Status also may be a major inhibitor – as one respondent pinpoints this in association with perceived level of strategic intelligence:

If you have got a mindset which says that people at the top must be clever, because that is why we are here, and all the people down there are thick, then there is no way you will credit the people down there. (CB)

Personality

Personality adds yet another variable, with respondents being fond of the personality tests of Myers-Briggs in particular:

…In Myers-Briggs terms, strategic planning is very 'J', whereas thinking is very 'P', keeping things up in the air, keeping options open. It is also about testing out our prophecies. (PD)

Perhaps personality tests could help encourage managers to work more effectively with their strategic thinking style:

And the people who get stuck and don't: are they people who are resisting change [elaborates]. They may not like change anyway. They may go on holiday to the same place for twenty years, and therefore they live their organizational life that way. They are very much in the present, rather than thinking about the future. (PW)

The above suggests the need to develop a more tailored instrument to diagnose strategic thinking.

Learning

Learning (about how to do strategic thinking) comes up – unsurprisingly – several times as a theme.

> The one big positive on the map is a lot of HR people and general managers are genuinely looking for more strategic thinking amongst managers, amongst the huge market change that is going on. There is a real hunger and need for managers to challenge those defensive routines. (TG)

Some of the value of formal strategic thinking may occur afterwards when managers get to confront the issue in everyday reality rather than in what might seem a surreal world of strategic thinking:

> Probably the learning takes place outside the classroom, outside the consulting process… And they go 'oh – yes' and they often forget where it is coming from. The value of an MBA or a workshop can be years down the line. (PD)

One respondent believes learning has a very positive influence – possibly (and especially with regard to implementation):

> If people have been trained in strategic thinking it would be an enabler, and so that they recognize that implementation is actually a very strategic issue. (TG)

It may also help managers to develop more all-round:

> Strategic thinking has to be of better quality. And one of the ways is to have better quality managers, so they are not just relying on their functional experience. It is actually quite a tricky thing because you have to know the [organizational] details and at the same time you have to think more broadly. And usually people are either one or the other. Few can do both. (CB)

The above the learning indicates that associated with strategic thinking seems to have a highly contingent and latent value and may not be realized unless the context supports it – and there is a more effective process too.

The key 'so-whats?' from this are:

- If strategic thinking is regarded as a key part of a manager's role (and on how he/she is judged on performance) he/she will probably actually do it – and a lot more.

- Different individuals have different levels of inherent strategic thinking capability. This needs to be recognized when undertaking team exercises on strategic thinking.
- Strategic thinking will not really happen unless managers are prepared to learn.

Supporting processes

Supporting processes include:

- project management
- financial analysis
- business cases
- measures
- recognition.

Project management

Project management offers potential as a vehicle to support strategic thinking:

> This is a health-check that it is potentially do-able. Certainly if that implementation is project-managed that would be an enabler too. (TG)

Financial analysis

Two of the respondents viewed financial analysis as being potentially unhelpful. For example, one told us:

> Anything that is overly numbers-driven is going to be a problem. I see a lot of planning processes that are extended budget exercises. The second constraint is where over-tangible elements of the organization are emphasized, largely because we know that the real sources of sustainable advantage, are likely (not) to be things we can measure. (CB)

It is still left open from the above about how financial analysis can help target the value of strategic thoughts.

Business cases

However, by doing a business case for an idea, this might help not only focus the strategic thinking but also target the value of the idea:

One example was for me to re-enter the market [consulting] from scratch. I might do this with a website positioning me as an international strategist. I might premium price this and get work I would otherwise not be able to have captured. All of these things would add tangible economic value. There might be some extra costs, like website, travel time, enquiries I did not want. So I could easily do a business case on what the idea is worth. (TG)

Measures

Measures can either help or hinder, depending upon whether they are applied appropriately:

So value tends to be unrealized if there are no criteria for success, and if we don't know what success looks like [elaborates]…No measurements – you have to measure it… (PD)

The issue of measurement of strategic implementation is a complex one, embracing concepts like the balanced score card. What is clear here is that there ought to be at least some 'success criteria' for adding value.

Recognition

As strategic thinking is often not recognized, it may not be as prevalent as it would be otherwise:

Strategic thinking being rewarded (would help). (PW)

Overall, there may be significant merit by financially appraising strategic thoughts, by seeing them as projects, pre-targeting and then measuring their benefits – and recognizing and rewarding them, too.
The key 'so-whats?' from this are that:

- other processes, like business cases and project management, do need to be deployed to get the best value out of strategic thinking
- if other things of value (like operational performance) are rewarded, then why not reward strategic thinking likewise?

Soft value

In soft value we look at:

- clarity
- anxiety and stress
- belief
- personal value.

Clarity

Clarity is seen as one of the major areas where strategic thinking adds value:

> It adds value to the people who report to them because there is some clarity there, and it reduces their ambiguity. (CB)

> The value comes where the clarity in the sense of direction actually does align with what is happening in the market-place…That clarity can reduce waste because it ensures that people are focusing on the things that are important, and not on the things that are less important. (CB)

This is mirrored in helping to avoid strategic mistakes (which is an area probably worth valuing in its own right):

> The [strategic] thinking gives you the confidence to make the right decisions and to also help you to avoid making the wrong ones. (PD)

Clarity could thus add value at the organizational, the team, and the individual level.

Anxiety and stress

Personal stress is another key area:

> It adds value to the individual because if they have a clear view of where the business is going, then it will reduce their anxiety and stress. (CB)

This is likely to be mirrored in the overall level of organizational stress.

Belief

Another area of softer value is belief:

> I think the interesting thing about why do people think differently or do things differently, as I have said, is do they have a belief in what is happening in the organization and they want to move forward? And that's very enabling. (PW)

But as we see above, unless belief underpins the content of strategic thinking, it is unlikely to be actioned and thus create value. Belief can be difficult at an organizational level – so that strategy is not implemented well. Lack of belief at the individual level could result in key staff leaving or not trying hard. Belief also clearly links with the concept of ownership covered earlier.

Personal value

Interestingly, value can be created by applying strategic thinking to a specific individual's situation at work – and to their career generally:

> Value can also be added to the individual. When running courses on strategic thinking, value can be added by applying it to things like 'what business they are (individually) in, and where should they go in the future, and their future career options. (TG)

This personal value is probably latent in many instances, as managers have probably not thought much about it.

The 'so-what?' from this is that:

■ All managers should look at the considerable personal benefit which strategic thinking will give them.

Summary

To summarize, therefore, we see the following implications coming out:

The meaning of 'strategic thinking' and its business value

Respondents were not entirely clear what 'strategic thinking' meant. This implies that, potentially, the literature itself is not so clear either, and managers may be even less clear.

Strategic thinking applies to many levels, not just to the top team or to larger areas of the business.

Value is frequently emergent, latent or contingent and may thus be diluted considerably. There is value simply through linking actions and also by speeding up the decision process.

Context

Crisis clearly acts as a spur to strategic thinking. This effect may be counter-balanced by mindset, complacency or by organizational style generally.

Luck may be a decisive factor in creating value from strategic thinking. But it may be possible to help create luck through appropriate positioning.

Thought value and prioritization

Thinking itself has a positive value – through creating space and a framework for understanding. Creative thoughts can have a distinctive value. Implementation is a potentially major area for value.

A very immediate source of value is to be found through better prioritization.

Process

There were mixed views on the benefits of having a deliberate process versus a less formal one. Conversations and networking between stakeholders were seen as helpful.

Who owns strategic thinking and provides the commitment and permission is key. Important sub-processes were testing and facilitation (although consultants were not generally seen as helpful – there was too much jargon). Getting physical conditions right was obviously vitally important.

Whilst intuition evidently plays a role, perhaps it could be better channelled.

Process drivers

Leadership was essential to help align agendas – but there was a case for engaging those personal agendas more openly. This might mitigate defensive routines and help defuse the effects of criticism.

Distraction generally – along with weaker time management – appears to be a major problem.

Supporting structure and skills

The roles of senior managers themselves appeared less than clear (in relation to strategic thinking – and even generally in what value they think they add). More youthful, thrusting managers might help (but would they have the necessary influence in the organization?).

Personality types were a major factor in influencing the effectiveness of strategic thinking. Whilst formal learning might help it was not clear (from these scenarios) how it could be effectively reinforced. We learn more on this in the next chapter.

Supporting process

There were significant opportunities to enhance strategic thinking through integrating it into project management, by pre-targeting its value and through measuring and recognizing its effective delivery through implementation.

Soft value

Soft value was a significant area of the value of strategic thinking, especially through helping create clarity, reduce anxiety and stress and increase belief (in future direction). It might also be of direct, personal and career value.

In summary, strategic thinking thus adds value through a complex, less tangible and haphazard process. By targeting it more specifically towards the creation of economic value, one might find greater clarity of discussion and focus in the process. A more focused and determined pursuit of this value might also help reduce organizational constraints in terms of mindset and management process.

The value of strategic thinking can also be seen at a variety of levels:

- The value of a very specific strategic idea.
- The value of a strategic line of thought (consisting of a number of strategic thoughts).
- The value of transmitting these thoughts (whether existing or new) – to prevent confusion in the organization or to just align the organization's mindset and actions.
- The value manifest through actual implementation.

Conclusion

In conclusion, there are major opportunities as well as constraints in getting economic value out of strategic thinking. Whilst strategic thinking can add value in a huge diversity of ways, there is a major challenge in aligning the thoughts, behaviours, practices, and support processes of the organization to deliver this value.

A major constraint was actually the ambiguity of what 'strategic thinking' actually meant. This ought to be an easy constraint to remedy, albeit one that requires extensive education throughout the management community. Perhaps strategy academics generally have some significant role in this?

Summary of key points

- Because strategic thinking is apparently an intangible its value is infrequently targeted. Nevertheless this value ought to be very clearly and specifically targeted.

- Strategic thinking does have a clear meaning, but its present ambiguity dilutes a lot of its value.
- Strategic thinking can add value at a variety of levels, and its value at lower levels can be considerable.
- Its value is manifest in a variety of forms, from latent value to contingent value to detergent value (sorting out past mistakes) through to its value in steering change.
- Strategic thinking often gains stimulus in a crisis, and in a steady organizational state is dampened by complacency and the prevailing mindset and thinking style.
- Strategic thinking has value simply through clarifying thinking – this requires sufficient thinking space, a framework for understanding how strategic ideas fit in, through alignment of thoughts, and through genuinely creative thinking.
- Strategic thinking is of major help in prioritization – especially of key options.
- Unless the appropriate support processes are in place organizationally, its value will be rapidly dissipated.
- This also requires skilful management of softer factors such as agendas and top management permission.
- To encourage greater strategic thinking demands considerable organizational change and more roles for younger, thrusting people.
- Organizational processes like business cases and recognition systems also need adopting.
- One of the biggest areas of value is soft value – including confidence, clarity and lower anxiety.

References

Grundy, A.N., *Corporate Strategy and Financial Decisions*, Kogan Page, London, 1992.

— *Breakthrough Strategies for Growth*, Pitman Publishing, London, 1995.

— *Exploring Strategic Financial Management*, Prentice Hall, London, 1998.

CHAPTER SEVEN

Valuing strategic thinking, part 2: the managers

Introduction

In our second chapter on the value of strategic thinking we go through the same influences that we saw in chapter 6. There are some new issues which emerge, and also the managers do have sometimes contrasting views to the academics.

In the final section we take a look at the key implications for the practice of strategic thinking and for its impact on strategic management generally.

Turning now to the interviews with senior managers a new set of sub-categories emerge, including:

Thought value	■ managing the future
Context	■ legacy
	■ technology
	■ growth
	■ timing
	■ acquisitions
	■ divestment
Core process	■ empirical feedback
	■ communication
Process drivers	■ power
Supporting processes	■ mentoring
Soft value	■ excitement

A surprise was that managers dwelt a lot less on process than the academics did. Although this may be because academics are more process focused, the managers have more actual direct experience of the process (see figure 7.1).

Turning now to a brief overview of the managers involved in the study, these include:

FIGURE 7.1: The value of strategic thinking

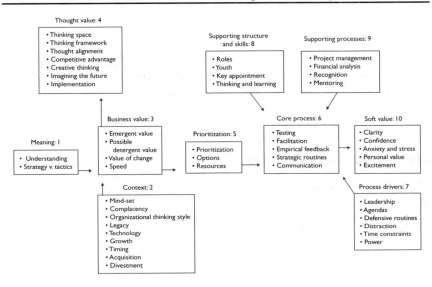

- Barclays: Steve Landsdown, Senior Manager, Corporate Banking (formerly corporate strategy manager, Group HQ) (SL)
- HP: Karen Slatford, Director and General Manager, Large Systems (Global) (KS)
- Lex: Lin Kendrick, Group Head of Management Development (LK)
- Tesco: Paul Mancey, Director of Tesco Direct (PM)
- Zurich Independent Financial Advisers (ZIFA): Joe Ranger, Assistant Sales Director (JR).

Over the past five years each of these senior managers had been exposed to some formal strategic training, either through a business school course or in-company programme, or via one-to-one mentoring.

We now turn to the categories.

The meaning of strategic thinking

The section on the meaning of strategic thinking covers:

- understanding
- levels of strategic thinking
- strategy versus tactics.

Understanding

'Strategic' is felt to be inherently bound up with time frames – and the future:

> I have never stopped to think what it [strategic thinking] is, although we always talk about it. For me, I think it is about time frames. One of the significant differences that I see between someone who is being a manager and someone who is being a director is their ability to think in time frames in which they should think. (LK)

Levels of strategic thinking

There are a number of levels of strategic thinking (as we see in this illustration from Tesco):

> We have used strategic thinking at a higher level as a basis to determine whether to enter the home shopping market. We have then used strategic thinking to determine which non-food markets to enter. At a lower level, we have also used strategic thinking to help us to identify which price and quality positions to adopt at each market. (PM)

Strategy versus tactics

The levels of strategy are sometimes seen as being distinguished by the concepts of 'strategic' versus 'tactical':

> The word 'strategy' can mean different things to different people and it is sometimes difficult to differentiate between a strategy and a tactic. Tesco is very, very clear about its top line strategy and the measures of success. However, delivering the top line strategy requires strategic thought to choose between the tactical options. (PM)

The term 'strategy' itself can dilute the value of true, strategic thinking, because of its ambiguity:

> I think 'strategy' is an unfortunate word. You need a different way of defining it. Because a strategy is a tactic depending upon where you are in the organization, you almost need a different way of defining it. (PM)

> People get confused. They think that tactical thinking is strategic thinking. People say they want to improve their strategic thinking but they don't allocate the time they need to do something about it. And there aren't the opportunities afforded them to really do [it] because we recognize and value action around here. We far less recognize thinking. And in an organization when it is all about action and doing, the strategic thinkers get lost, they don't want to be around…(LK)

The 'so-what' from this is that:

■ Once again, strategic thinking needs to be defined much more clearly, so that it will be used every day.

Business value

The section 'business value' covers:

■ emergent value
■ the possible
■ detergent value
■ value of change
■ speed.

Emergent value

Emergent value is see as being created through an openness to learning, but this is inhibited both by frequent organizational career moves, and because learning is not captured from other parts of the organization:

> Part of emergent value is how things work in practice. The value is being able to make mistakes and learn from them and to recognize successes them, and run with them. (SL)

The possible

Thinking about the possible exists, and can help to generate business value, but again the focus on the Today (internally and externally) inhibits the capture of this value:

> We don't have any of our businesses considering what the art of the possible is. We don't manage our customer data in the way that we could, there isn't a synergy across the group in the way that there should be; we could manage things...so we are dealing very much with today, we are managing the short term. It is a major constraint because our competitors will move well ahead of us. (one of the managers – anonymous)

Detergent value

At Barclays Bank 'detergent value' is seen to be a very tangible area where strategic thinking has generated tangible business value:

The economic value analysis suggested that the emerging scenario for this business was dominated by big investment banks. So we reached a fork in the road. We can either invest really heavily to try to rival the big investment banks, and we might just be able to realize value from doing that. The second option was to invest in reaching the scale of the Americans because there are other stronger opportunities for us in the UK. We would get more bang for our buck if we invest in the retail side of the business. (SL)

This 'detergent' value was obviously a very key management concern for Barclays in the recent past.

Value of change

Strategic thinking can add more value if managers screen out any change initiatives that are not self-evidently 'positive' or beneficial:

The value of strategic thinking in Tesco is its role in creating positive change for customers. (PM)

If strategic thinking and positive change is interlinked then it is very important for everybody to be very innovative in what they do. It is equally important to make sure that it is positive change and not negative, so it is in line with business objectives and what people want. (PM)

Speed

At Tesco's speed is seen as being a very major area where strategic thinking has added value. This is manifest in Tesco's expansion globally into non-food products, and into innovation in supermarket formats:

For me, it is remarkable that in five years Tesco has moved from being a UK-based supermarket chain to become an international mixed retail and services business. This rapid transformation is based on clarity at the top and a tremendous creativity and energy in making it happen quickly. (PM)

Within a couple of years Tesco will have 45 per cent of its space overseas, it is a dramatic transformation in what Tesco is. And that can only be done by firstly clarity at the top in the general direction, and also a great deal of strategic thought in applying it and making it work. (PM)

The key 'so-what?' from this is again:

■ strategic thinking adds value in a variety of ways.

Context

The section on context covers:

- mindset
- complacency
- organizational thinking style
- legacy (new category)
- technology (new category)
- growth (new category)
- timing (new category)
- acquisitions (new category)
- divestment.

Mindset

As for the academics, mindset may severely frustrate strategic thinking:

> Our culture rejects certain knowledge skills like marketing, less so now, but information management, etc [elaborates on change management]. (LK)

Complacency

More specifically, complacency acts as a major block against the value of strategic thinking:

> Complacency can set in. Rather than being dynamic and constantly changing then the complacency sets in and that's when we start to fall backwards. There may not be the will to change. (LK)

Organizational thinking style

There are a number of times organizational thinking style is viewed as a major inhibitor (and sometimes an enabler). For example, at ZIFA we see that:

> Without doubt you meet people in the organization who are cynical about it. I do think that that kind of approach is still prevalent in some people. There are a lot of people who are still relatively open-minded and young but there are still people within our business who are still relatively cynical about it. I think you need a more open-minded culture. (JR)

This thinking style is seen as determined by leadership style, by structure and by the spread of strategic thinking generally through the management population:

> The people side is also an enabler, and leadership. We have got a brand new leader in Barclays now and he is driving through a lot of change; he is an inspirational kind of character. (SL)

Legacy

At Barclays the existing resources legacy is such that more challenging strategic thinking is restricted simply on grounds of practicality:

> We have a legacy, which is a big constraining factor. We are really constrained by what we have got to work with, by our skills and by the infrastructure of the organization. (SL)

Technology

At Lex we see that technology operates in a similar way to the resources legacy. As the organization's competencies here are not technologically focused, again this inhibits strategic thinking:

> It is about where we are today, where are the constraints we have today, what are the things which are the enablers today, and how might they change, and over what sort of time-frame? What are the things that are coming into the environment, like technology? To think strategically today is to get a real grip on what technology will do to change the whole market place. What implication does that have in terms of something being very global? (LK)

Growth

But if these issues were addressed, the value could be obtained and become manifest by growth:

> The major value [in strategic thinking] would be our ability to grow. That is where the constraining factor is at the present time because we don't have a great strategic thinking capacity... (LK)

Timing

Appropriate timing is an interesting determinant of the value of strategic thinking. Strategic thinking done at an inappropriate time (relative to industry/organizational life-cycles) may fail to generate value:

> Timing is an issue – is the timing right? Because suddenly you can apply something like that rather than just think about it. (JR)

Acquisitions

Strategic thinking can add value through choosing the most appropriate pathway to corporate development, especially opting for acquisitions over organic development, or vice versa:

> In one of our businesses we have grown and grown by acquisition, but the value of those acquisitions hasn't been assessed...Other of our businesses have grown organically, but very few. The most profitable parts of our business have been grown organically. But it is only every now and again that we stop and consider that... (LK)

Divestment

Divestment (specifically) – in a similar manner to detergent value – can add value through strategic thinking:

> An enabler too was the sale of a certain part of our retail group...that in itself made a very big statement, and as a consequence of that we were recategorized on the Stock Market. As an enabler, in terms of mindset and recruitment, then that is reasonably important [mentions new members of the Board]. (one of the managers – anonymous)

The key 'so-whats?' from this are that:

- Once again, management of mindset and thinking style is crucial – and migration away from an onerous legacy.
- Strategic thinking can add most value when it is well-timed, and when it may be addressed to thinking laterally about investment and divestment options.

Thought value

The section on thought value covers:

- thinking space
- thinking framework
- thought alignment
- competitive advantage
- imagining the future (new category)
- creative thinking
- implementation.

Thinking space

'Thinking space' is very much on the minds of managers in relation to the value of strategic thinking. At HP this realization appears to have had a profound effect on one senior manager:

> Just taking a day out to do strategic thinking does make a difference, out of the day-to-day environment. Often, and this I what it is like for most people in a sales organization, you end up with weekly, quarterly, annual pressure and targets. And you get really stuck into those – the grunt and grind, and the minutiae. And you don't get chance to step back. (KS)

> It's that helicopter thing. Getting up in the helicopter and looking down. The thought that you are someone from Mars and have landed on Earth and doesn't have a clue – it gives you a completely fresh view. Looking from above – sometimes you catch yourself doing it. Sometimes I catch myself doing it in a meeting. I let them get on with it, and I go up, up. I have a look and listen. It is really good practice; you look at things from a completely different angle. (KS)

On one occasion, spending some time on strategic thinking does seem to have added considerable – and very tangible – value (at HP):

> That issue was a festering, gaping sore. Just sitting down and going through that (with a mentor), just taking me through that strategy grid, and taking me out of my day-job, it put the whole thing in context. (KS)

Thinking framework

At Tesco's, one manager feels that the concept of strategy could be broken down, so that it can guide thinking at a different number of levels:

> It helps me to consider a number of different concepts. It helps to have a clear framework and common language that can allow everyone to contribute. (PM)

Perhaps this quote implies it would be appropriate to think of strategy as the 'macro', 'mini', or the 'micro' levels:

> It gives us a framework to identify and agree where customer value and hence sustainable competitive advantage might lie. It also gives confidence to make decisions because the process is inclusive and thorough. Strategic thinking helps to explain why, rather than just giving what. (PM)

In sum, whilst strategic thinking does provide a thinking framework, the architecture of this framework needs to be elaborated, level by level.

Thought alignment

Once again, strategic thinking may help to align thoughts:

> I knew I was going to be doing things, but I couldn't get a strong enough connection to what I was going to be doing to get the value we needed in order to meet the objective. A kind of light bulb went on with this particular idea. This would accelerate our progress towards the objective rather than just making a regular contribution, as I believe training and development does. It doesn't feel very exciting most of the time. (JR)

Here the alignment can come through completing a gap – and by giving an implementation imperative (thus aligning with the need to perform some action):

> That one will definitely make it into implementation, mainly because I look after it! It has given me a focus on what we need to deliver next year. It just fits (from a timing and an ownership point of view) perfectly really. I was already grappling with the million things we could do in training and development – what can we do to really make a difference. That was a very welcome bolt out of the blue. This is the answer to what we need to do. Otherwise you can find yourself training and developing until you are blue in the face, but not being entirely sure what value it is adding. (JR)

Competitive advantage

Helping managers think more clearly about competitive advantage is a very common theme:

> And it probably did highlight a specific thought which we had not thought before, which was – interestingly – it got us down into further detail which was to have a strategy that increased the quality of our people. We highlighted one particular area that could give us particular competitive advantage. And that area was relationship management, so rather than train people in everything let us concentrate on the specific, because we believe it can give us a competitive advantage… (JR)

Thinking about competitive advantage can be facilitated by benchmarks, providing that those benchmarks are appropriate:

> From that, the question was, 'which areas of non-food do you choose to get into first, and what will it look like?' And the process of the strategic thinking was to develop the framework to make choices and to understand benchmarks. Another important element is having benchmarks to beat. (PM)

Imagining the future

Surprisingly in-depth thinking about the future (in an imaginary way) is explored as follows:

> So someone's ability to think strategically is linked into their imagination, their understanding, their freedom to think and to consider what the art of the possible is, what the probable is. But it is not just like sci-fi, it is within a framework. (LK)

Creative thinking

One respondent feels very strongly that directors' roles should be more creative:

> A manager is very much about doing, a director is very much more about thinking about what the art of the possible is, and according to the level they are at. And it is that more of the time should be spent on the thinking rather than the doing. (LK)

> You actually need to be lifted out of your normal frame of mind into a different structure and process and give yourself the permission to be different. That structured way of doing it works much better because it gives at the beginning, like a signal, the permission to do whatever you fancy. (JR)

Implementation

Implementation appraisal is, for one manager at HP, an essential part of 'helicopter thinking':

> So, being able to (often) go up in the helicopter, and then to come back and have landed on the ground, it seems to be pretty unusual to have that ability. People cannot seem to jump the divide. (KS)

> The thing about the helicopter is that you go up, and then you come down, and for me it is about being able to go up and down, and up and down the scales. (KS)

Our Tesco manager also sees strategic thinking as integral with micro-strategies and implementation:

> Strategic thinking can also be applied to internal ways of working, helping to free up time and resource for adding value activities. (PM)

So, strategic thinking – it would appear – can potentially facilitate strategy implementation, thus capturing more value from strategic thought.

The key 'so-whats?' from this are that:

- Thinking space, thinking frameworks and the patience to align strategic thoughts are crucial to delivering its full potential value.
- This value can be realized either through developing present competitive advantage, thinking about the future, thinking creatively or thinking about implementation.

Prioritization

The section on prioritization covers:

- prioritization
- options
- resources.

Prioritization

Strategic thinking is seen as adding value through prioritization at Tesco, Lex, and at Barclays (in order):

> It is a way of prioritizing different activities, deciding to move into one market rather than another. (PM)

At ZIFA it is not seen as necessarily adding to the existing burden of implementation, but as refocusing it:

> It depends how excited they are really, when what you come up with isn't, certainly in my experience, it is not 'extra', it is 'instead of'. It is not on top of everything else we have got to do. (JR)

In conclusion, more structured strategic thinking helps to add value by prioritizing management agendas and through better resource allocation.

Options

Appraising specific strategic options is an area of significant value added (as in Tesco's experience):

> And one of the techniques I use regularly is the assessment of the attractiveness of various markets or options. (PM)

> The strategic thinking approach that I take does not second guess the answer. It is a tool to open up the debate. (PM)

Resources

At Tesco, key strategic projects are given high strategic priority, thus giving the organization a clearer focus than it might otherwise have:

> Tesco has a Customer Plan that lays out the key initiatives that must be achieved. These initiatives have well-resourced project teams and receive a very high priority. (PM)

In summary, prioritization was a very important value-creating activity (from strategic thinking).

The key 'so-what?' is that:

- prioritization is a key vehicle for strategic thinking adding value
- but this presupposes that sufficient creativity in identifying options has been deployed.

Core process

This section on core process contains some new categories:

- empirical feedback
- strategic routines
- communication.

Testing

Testing the strategic thinking helps to refine its value:

> A useful technique for us is a straw man or an Aunt Sally. A straw man is usually circulated before a workshop to kick start a project and to start to gather the issues. The language of a straw man must be open and invite a contribution. (PM)

Facilitation

Facilitation is seen as generally very helpful in unleashing value at ZIFA:

> Before, we were coming up with a plan where we were pretty sure that our headings were correct, but what we were struggling to do was to get any sort of focus on the breakthrough areas. What happened on Thursday night was that our thinking became much more pinpointed on areas where we could make some extra value, to outstrip the market in some

sort of way. Where we could decide where we really, really want [laughing] to be, and make a difference, rather than just do the same things that everybody does, we might be able to do them that bit better. The focus on two or three areas was the breakthrough on Thursday night. (JR)

The above is a good example of where strategic thinking at an average level appears to have been raised to a higher level and thus created significantly more value through facilitation.

Empirical feedback

By actually implementing strategy and identifying the value added, this can actually add value through empirical feed-back:

It is interesting looking back. The Tesco non-food plan was based on strategic thinking. The aim of the plan was to become the positive choice for Tesco customers' non-food needs. Key issues included deciding which product categories to enter and how much space a category should receive. (PM)

With the benefit of customer feedback and a trading history, space allocation is based on learning. (PM)

Strategic routines

By building in strategic thinking to organizational routines, this can help to increase its value, as evidenced at ZIFA:

And I think you almost need to make it something about how you do things in an organization. That you actually regularly go back and have those creative sessions, because you need to pull yourself out of the drudgery of the day-to-day more than we probably do. We tend to have little light bulbs that go on every year or two. I think we would benefit from making it a regular part of what we do and actually setting aside regular time for being more off-the-wall. (JR)

But at Tesco's, away-days may only give an illusion of real strategic thinking which should add value on a day-to-day basis:

I think that there is a danger in leaving all strategic thought to away-days and seminars. Customer needs are changing constantly and we are faced with options on a daily basis. No-one tries harder for customers is a core Tesco value. Although not necessarily a conscious thing, strategic thought and positive change are an everyday part of Tesco life. (PM)

So, the appropriate kind of strategic routines may depend upon the experience which the organization has with strategic thinking and its culture.

Communication

But unless the strategic thinking is communicated step-by-step its value may be diminished:

> For me, strategic thinking makes sense and helps to explain decisions. Although there is also merit in the 'black box' revelation, it is riskier to invest in change that cannot be explained. (PM)

> It is about the intuitive side; one of the Group MDs didn't know why he knew what he knew but he knew, and he would just intuitively know that we should buy that business. And he couldn't explain it to the rational colleagues that he had around him. So that inhibited his preparedness to share his thinking, because he just knew. And how many times did he make a mistake? They were minimal. But how much more could he have done [if he could have explained his intuition]? (LK)

The key 'so-whats?' from this are that:

- strategic thinking should always be refined – by internal critique and by the lessons from experience
- it is at its best when it is built into regular organizational practice and culture, rather than made into peripheral, special exercises
- equal time is required to spell out the steps in the thought process.

Process drivers

The section on process drivers covers:

- leadership
- ownership
- agendas
- defensive routines
- distraction
- time constraints
- power (new category).

Leadership

Leadership is seen as being an important facilitator of strategic thinking:

> The people side is also an enabler, and leadership. We have a new leader in Barclays now and he is driving through a lot of change; he is an inspirational kind of character. (SL)

Ownership

At ZIFA, having the right people there (during strategic thinking) helps capture its value:

> You need to have all the right people there, so they will become brought into the thinking actually at the time that it happens. And they tend to share the enthusiasm more than if it is an idea that happens at a meeting where only one or two people are present, and then you have to go through the experience of selling it and repeating the thought processes. Often that makes it die a bit; it loses spontaneity. (JR)

A lack of ownership can reduce clarity and cause dilution (two other categories).

Agendas

To get maximum value from strategic thinking requires adjustment of management's agendas (as seen at Barclays):

> Dilution is quite a big issue ... You tend to find in organizations that there are quite a few people with a say and a voice. So they will have their pet projects, and you can have a bit of parochial influence, and this leads to dilution of outputs. (SL)

Defensive routines

In common with academics, defensive routines can prove difficult, as illustrated by our HP respondent:

> Strategic thinking can be frustrated by the team. In some cases the pace of change is going really fast. And some people say 'and this too will pass – we will drag it out as long as we can and it will have changed by the time we have to get to the end of it and have to implement it. Oh my God, this is too painful, how can I make this not happen to me'. (KS)

> They say, 'let us get a bit more data'. But you have to have the courage of your own convictions. (KS)

Just often it is like marshmallows. Sometimes you have got a group of people sitting around the table like marshmallows. If you push them in they kind of blob out again. They blob about like marshmallows – it is marshmallow theory. If you hold them over the fire though you get a kind of chemical reaction. (KS)

Once again, defensive routines seem to impact covertly rather than overtly, making it slower and more difficult to turn strategic ideas into real action and change, and (by implication) reducing energy and enthusiasm.

Distraction

Both ZIFA and Lex highlight the loss of potential value through strategic thinking becoming diluted:

I think we don't follow through on it enough. And we try to follow through on it in our own meetings, but you drift back. Your clever ideas and breakthroughs get a bit diluted at the next meeting that you are in, and you get very day-to-day and practical and the sales figures aren't where you want them to be. Or, right, you have got to batten down the hatches rather than taking the lid off and energizing, and that sort of thing. (JR)

We create distraction by people at the top of the organization starting new things: he will start that, and that, and that. And he will be creating distraction. (LK)

Time constraints

Without a pragmatic approach to strategic thinking, time constraints will frustrate its value:

In today's world, you know, we don't get a minute! But we can get a minute. With the e-mails and the Internet, and communication at every time of the day and night, the pace is getting faster and faster and faster – you don't get time to implement far-fetched or too academic or too theoretical ideas. You have got to be quick. (KS)

Power

Power, though important, is felt to be subservient to persuasion:

I don't think that strategic thinking is an exercise in power; it is an exercise in persuasion, but not power. (KS)

In conclusion, whilst important, process outputs were not as extensive as in the academics' interviews.

The key 'so-whats?' from this are:

■ Soft issues (like appropriate leadership, buy-in, management of agendas etc) are just as important as (if not more important than) the actual content of strategic thinking.

■ The outputs of strategic thinking need to be very simple and action-based.

Supporting structure and skills

The next section covers:

■ roles
■ youth
■ key appointments
■ training and learning.

Roles

If managers see their role as doing, not as strategic thinking, they may not add value through strategic thinking:

> We have a lot of people who think tactically, who are phenomenal doers. We have far fewer people who think strategically and that would account for why our share price is where it is, why we haven't got many new technology businesses. What we are very good at is building up a body of knowledge and information and applying that. Our core competencies are in old technology things, and we do them well. [elaborates] But what we want to be in the future is quite different to that. (one of the managers – anonymous)

Youth

The duration of organizational service is either an enabler or constraint of strategic thinking:

> You have a lot of long service, you have got traditional ways of doing things and that can inhibit things. This constraint is diminishing because we are recruiting different sorts of people. But it would have been a strong force. (LK)

Key appointments

A key area for intervention (at Lex and Tesco) to amplify strategic thinking is to make key appointments which will promote it:

> The last three appointments are people with sales and marketing backgrounds who understand service delivery and who are not finance directors. (LK)

> At Tesco we try to recruit people who share our values, which requires conceptual skills. (PM)

Training and learning

By training and learning support, strategic thinking skills (for example those associated with leadership) might be enhanced:

> Leadership is very, very important in strategic thinking. The previous leadership programme was around getting people to understand what leadership is about. The new programme is around leaders, and around managing change. We haven't had to do that in the past, but now we have to change. (LK)

> An enabler is the recognition of strategic thinking as an essential tool in the organization, and recruiting with the appropriate skills and training. (SL)

> The key 'so-whats?' from this are that:

- strategic thinking needs to be seen as an essential part of a manager's identity
- all appointments which entail an element of strategic thinking need to be screened for that capability.

Supporting processes

This section covers:

- project management
- financial analysis
- recognition
- mentoring.

Project management

Project management is a complex area – and may not seemingly add value if implemented inappropriately. Project management might not necessarily help strategic thinking if it is focused primarily on starting new initiatives:

> We have a lot of initiatives, projects, whatever, because we don't have strong project management skills. We are very imaginative – we start things, lots and lots of things, but very little actually gets completed. We don't see the value of these. (LK)

It thus requires a better process – as at Tesco:

> As Tesco becomes more diverse, cross functional projects are increasingly important. Cross functional projects are not easy to deliver and require effective sponsorship. We assemble a team to attack an opportunity and then we move them on. (PM)

> If you try to do change on a business-as-usual basis, then you have people working part-time on it. People close to the business are essential for developing strategy, but they often don't have the experience to implement it. (SL)

But at ZIFA there are concerns about project management resulting in overload – such are organizational time constraints:

> I think that's where it might get to become too difficult and then maybe you can potentially lose the value that you might have had. In fact, does it add workload, and I don't think it necessarily does mean that if you are doing it 'instead of'. But if you are making it into some kind of project-managed situation then that does add more [difficulty]. (JR)

At Barclays project management is seen as absolutely vital to help implement the strategy.

But conventional project management is insufficient – and needs an injection of strategic thinking skills at a micro-level.

More effective project management thus may need to:

- incorporate strategic thinking as a more integral process
- be accommodated for with a new pattern of resource allocation and with new organizational structures and processes.

Financial analysis

Financial analysis can provide an important steer to focus strategic thinking on areas of greatest value, for example at Barclays:

> It also depends on what the organization requires in terms of payback and proving things like lack of ability to take risks. In any strategy there should be an element of real risk. (LK)

This is mirrored at Barclays, but this has been accommodated into a new process of 'managing for value' (with shorter and longer-term trade-offs):

> The economic profit target is a constraint, but it also puts the focus, the target that everyone tests their ideas against. (SL)

Whilst managing for value appears to be a helpful way of addressing the short versus longer-term dilemma, it poses new challenges for managers. These include:

- being creative in strategic thinking – but also giving attention simultaneously to value creation
- managing and juggling with resource constraints.

Recognition

Recognition processes are also seen as essential in encouraging managers to think strategically:

> Strategic thinking is all very well and good but it is also vital to have effective performance management to support it. You have to ensure that people who deliver change through projects can have as fulfilling a career as traditional line managers. (PM)

Mentoring

Finally, mentoring might be a helpful supporting process, although this requires finding an appropriately skilled, supportive, and politically neutral adviser:

> You do need someone to bounce your ideas off, because you need some help to get out of the context into a more objective way of thinking. Or, just to get somebody to give you a different view. (KS)

> You could use somebody from inside the company I guess, a mentor or a coach. A relationship and trust would be needed. But I probably couldn't have dealt with that (specific) issue without getting some partiality, and avoid potential leakage as well. With most things which are really important, news travels really fast in our organization. You don't want to be sharing your thought process with someone who can pass on what your thinking is. You could find that the ideas turn into something which you hadn't intended, or might get misinterpreted, or which have implications in the business – you need to get outside. (KS)

The key 'so-what?' from this is that:

- strategic thinking is not a stand-alone process but needs to be married with operational, human resource and financial processes.

Soft value

The section on soft value covers:

- clarity
- confidence
- anxiety and stress
- personal value
- excitement (new category).

Clarity

Once again clarity is viewed as being a very important element of value. At Tesco's, clarity has had a big positive effect, especially in helping make strategies happen (implementation) and in increasing organization speed:

> Tesco's success is based on clarity of what needs to be done and a personal responsibility to take the simple vision and turn it into reality. (PM)

At ZIFA, strategic thinking simply helps to link actions back to core objectives, and to providing a clearer focus generally:

> Strategic thinking adds value by linking what you are trying to achieve, i.e. the objective, and what you are doing. And I know that sounds really basic, but that's what it is to me. People go off doing things which don't necessarily take them closer to their objective. (JR)

> Strategic thinking links the two things. And it also makes you think more creatively about how you can achieve the objective. (JR)

Confidence

Linked to clarity is confidence. At Tesco's, confidence adds value by turning latent value of a strategic thought into real value through implementation:

> Financial services are a good example of where Tesco has followed the customer into a new market. Having a practical approach has given Tesco the confidence to try things. (PM)

Anxiety and stress

The following example at HP highlights the severity of the effects of anxiety and stress when there are blockages in much-needed strategic thinking:

> It just completely wipes you out, in terms of your ability to concentrate on the day-job. And in my job a lot of it is about motivating people. People read every little sign, and if your mind is somewhere else, they know straight away. They interpret the signals as all sorts of things. So, that was worrying, and most of my team had spotted it. They were engaged in it, and the whole organization became paralysed. This had been going on for several weeks. (KS)

Personal value

The HP manager also illustrates how important strategic thinking has been in shaping her career:

> Well, helicopter thinking has done me good, because it has helped make lots of career moves for me [laughs]. So, somewhere along the line one must seem some correlation. I think helicopter thinking must have been one of the contributory factors. There are not a lot of people around who can balance the strategic and the tactical. There are a lot of people who can be very tactical, and there is another group of people who can be quite strategic. But getting the two things to come together is quite difficult. (KS)

Excitement

Strategic thinking can add value through generating a state of excitement – a quality possibly not easily found in many larger organizations today:

> But I think it is hard to replicate the excitement that you feel about finding the breakthrough. Actually that can be quite time-consuming to take them through the process which you have been through, especially if people are remote, and that can be quite hard work, getting them to the same place in their thought processes. (JR)

The key 'so-whats?' from this are that:

- immense value can be gained by aligning and harmonizing managers' mental and emotional states about strategic issues
- another aspect of its value is to stimulate and focus a sense of excitement which will energize the organization.

On the latter point, however, important caveats are that:

- this excitement is not built up for inappropriate action
- this state may wear off quite rapidly and may need further stimulus.

Summary

To summarize again from the senior managers' interviews, we see the following:

Meaning

'Strategic' is again somewhat ambiguous for managers, and warrants definition and breaking down by the level of thinking at macro, mini and micro levels. Strategy is not easily differentiated from tactics, and the overlap between both confuses managers somewhat.

Business value

The business value of strategic thinking is manifold, and is often easier to harvest for detergent value and where change is involved. Speed generally is perceived to be a key area of possible value.

Context

Context is seen as very influential, partly as a constraint (due to the extent of pressures impacting on the business from may directions both externally and internally, e.g. due to the legacy), but at the same time these pressures put a premium (if not an imperative) on strategic thinking.

Thought value

A very major theme is the need for managers to give themselves more thinking space – through strategic thinking, as found, for example, in 'helicopter thinking'.

By giving managers a clearer thinking framework – particularly about competitive advantage – strategic thinking can add very tangible value to managers. Unlike some of the academics, who were sceptical of more general recipes for strategic thinking, managers found strategic thinking frameworks helpful.

Creative thinking, thinking about the possible and imagining the future, were particularly highly valued.

Strategic thinking was felt to be best incorporated within and integrated into implementation, rather than being seen as 'blue-sky'.

Prioritization

Prioritization was seen as a huge problem for managers – and as an area where strategic thinking could add considerable value, especially in dealing with the resource allocation problem.

Core process

Whilst managers spent less time talking about process than the academics, facilitation was seen as very important, incorporating strategic thinking into everyday routines. Without adequate communication, much of the value of strategic thinking would be unrealized.

Process drivers

Leadership was seen as very important to facilitate the process – and especially to help overcome defensive routines and to get a more strategic set of agendas.

Managers could easily have a strategic thought stream only to find their outputs diluted by organizational distraction and time constraints. 'Power' was mentioned surprisingly little, and its importance down-played – which was rather surprising.

Managers generally felt that gaining ownership was very important, which was unsurprising.

Supporting structure and skills

Managers' views coincided closely with the academics in that they both thought senior managers' roles should be redefined to make them (genuinely) more strategic.

To help managers become more strategic, younger (and less cynical) blood was seen as important, along with intervention in key appointments, and supporting training and learning. Notably, training and learning were seen as a small (if important) part of the equation. This contrasts with some academics emphasizing the impact of MBA and executive development programmes.

Supporting processes

There was a very interesting diversity of views on how (if at all) project management might help. Some felt that strategic ideas needed to be project-managed into implementation – in order to extract their value.

One manager felt that project management could be counter-productive – as in her experience it tended mainly to increase workload.

Financial analysis was another mixed bag, with the Barclays manager suggesting it could be both very helpful (in targeting strategic thinking on value), but at the same time it could constrain thinking. It was felt that recognition systems need to encourage strategic thinking more directly.

Finally, mentoring offered a useful opportunity to support the process, although there could be difficulties in finding an impartial and competent mentor.

Soft value

Once again, strategic thinking was felt to add considerable value by its direct impact on the individual, for example to give them clarity and confidence, and by alleviating anxiety and stress.

Overall, there was generally a relatively close correspondence in the findings from both chapters between academics' and managers' views, with some differences in emphasis.

Overall lessons from the study

In this final section we look at:

- the key themes which came up
- the key implications for strategic thinking generally and for further enquiry
- conclusion – back to the question of the value of strategic thinking.

Figure 7.2 now shows us the full framework of influences on the value of strategic thinking, combining both academics' and senior managers' thoughts. A number of things stand out from this:

- Strategic thinking itself is a relatively complex process – and one which has previously not been well understood.
- There is a huge diversity of ways in which strategic thinking can add (economic) value. Analyzing these has now given us a way of targeting, monitoring and controlling whether it is actually adding value, and if not then why not.
- As strategic thinking is often associated with higher-level thinking it may not be so obvious that it can be targeted economically.
- Because many of these areas of value are at least partially intangible, the routes towards harvesting that value have perhaps not been very well explored.

Strategic thinking – the key themes

FIGURE 7.2: The value of strategic thinking: the big picture

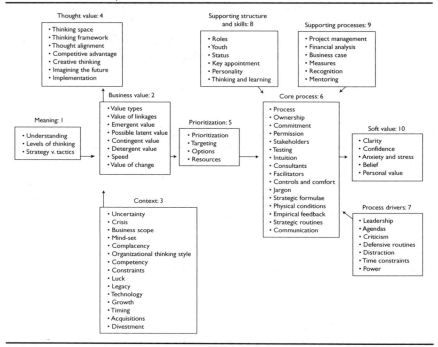

The key themes include:

- ambiguity of 'strategic thinking'
- levels of strategic thinking
- thought value
- pressure and bewildering choice – the maze
- prioritization
- organizational process
- soft value
- vicious versus virtuous cycles.

We now can cover the implication of each one of these themes from the point of view of:

- the current situation
- the future situation – and its potential value
- the key linkages to other themes
- the implications for strategic thinking generally.

Ambiguity of strategic thinking

The current situation

A number of the respondents were less than clear about what strategic thinking was, and equally its value. If the nature of strategic thinking is so relatively ambiguous then this is likely to be a very major inhibitor to capturing its value.

The future situation – and its potential value

Potentially, 'strategic thinking' is now defined as:

> the stream of ideas and reflections which help managers to grasp the bigger picture, and helps prevent them from getting lost in the wrong kind of detail. It is a fluid process which generates the insights, options and breakthroughs to move the organization at all levels forward through to implementation in an uncertain and changing environment.

Note that we have added 'at all levels' in the last sentence, and also 'through to implementation'. This reflects our findings that strategy is applicable at 'macro', 'mini' and 'micro' levels, and is equally applicable to implementation.

The value of this definition would be that:

- strategic thinking is now thought to occur both within and outside of the formal strategic planning process
- it is associated with streams of ideas – however partial and isolated – rather than necessarily with completed strategies
- it is linked with 'helicopter thinking'
- it is focused on choice (options) and action directed at breakthroughs (implementation)
- it is seen as being applicable at any level.

FIGURE 7.3: Thought value

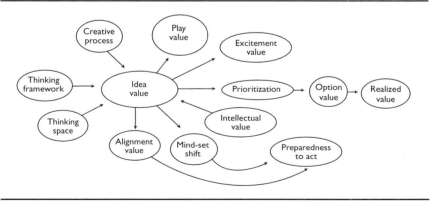

FIGURE 7.4: Prioritization

FIGURE 7.5: Soft value

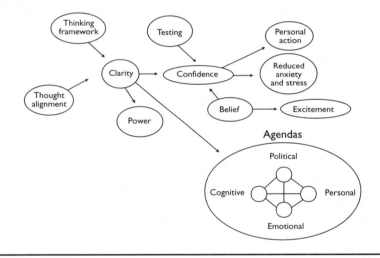

The key linkages to our other strategic thinking themes include:

- Because 'strategic thinking' has an unclear meaning, it is not necessarily associated with smaller-scale issues (mini or micro-strategies).
- Also, its ambiguity hinders targeting its economic value (figure 7.3).
- The focus on 'breakthroughs' would help with incorporating it into prioritization (figure 7.4).
- As it is now explicitly relevant to the individual, soft value may be enhanced (figure 7.5).
- Also, a more practical and immediate meaning might encourage a shift from a vicious to a virtuous cycle of strategic thinking (figures 7.6 and 7.7).

FIGURE 7.6: Vicious cycle of strategic thinking

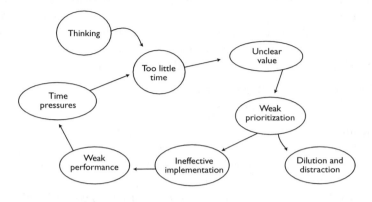

FIGURE 7.7: Virtuous cycle of strategic thinking

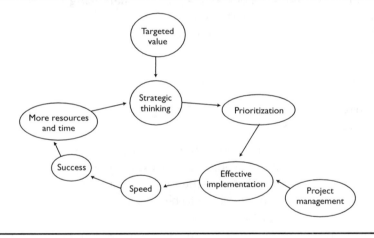

Levels of strategic thinking

The current situation

It was felt by interviewees that strategic thinking might be held back because of the lack of clarity of strategy versus tactics. Also, whilst strategy might be clear at one level, it might be unclear at other levels. For example, one might have a clear business strategy but an unclear corporate strategy, or a specific breakthrough project might have a clear strategy but the business strategy may be unclear. This might result in considerable confusion amongst managers.

The future situation and its potential value

By linking the various levels of strategy explicitly (through the strategic thinking process) it might become easier to manage and extract economic value. This would occur through improved alignment of that thinking – both across issues and organizational levels. Indeed, a constant focus ought to be (in senior managers' minds) on thought alignment.

The key linkages to other themes

Levels of strategic thinking link to:

- The ambiguity of strategic thinking – covered above.
- Its thought value: this could be enhanced through helping create greater thought alignment, more focus for the creative thinking process, more effective shifts in mindset, greater preparedness to act.
- Prioritization: prioritization at a variety of levels could be integrated – reducing management frustration and confusion.
- Organizational process: interventions to improve strategic thinking could be scoped more effectively – rather than being implemented at one level of the organization only.
- Pressure and bewildering choice within organizations generally: this might be alleviated.

Thought value

The current situation

Key findings here were that:

- Strategic thoughts have a highly contingent value. Because of the fragmentary and incomplete nature of existing thought process, much of the value is currently lost – the process being hit and miss (mostly 'miss') – and is often perceived to be down to 'luck'.
- Weaker links appear to be:
  - Getting the more creative process going (which may conflict with mindset, thinking style, culture and legacy) in the first place.
  - Providing the thinking space – the appropriate physical conditions and initial stimulus to get managers to think higher-level and/or differently.
  - Distilling the ideas into workable breakthroughs.
  - Gaining buy-in.
  - Securing sufficient resources (to harvest its value).
  - Mobilizing implementation effectively.
  - Coping with jargon and with generic strategic prescriptions which may not be appropriate.
  - Misunderstanding the potential and positive role of intuition.

The future situation – and its potential value

By more systematic attention to the process of crafting strategic thoughts into an economically valuable form, strategic thinking could become more effective. Also, by increasing the likelihood and extent of business and personal pay-offs, strategic thinking might be more fully brought into everyday routines.

The key linkages to other themes

Key linkages to other themes include:

- the ambiguity of strategic thinking would diminish, as the steps in the process would be spelt out and could be managed stage-by-stage
- by harvesting thought value more effectively, pressure and bewildering choice would become more manageable
- soft value could be obtained more easily – at the level of the individual
- again, the shift from vicious to virtuous cycles of strategic thinking (see later) could be encouraged.

Pressure and bewildering choice – the maze

Current situation

The interviews with the various managers highlighted graphically the difficulties of coping with change – from all directions. This made prioritization difficult and also undermined the preparedness to act to implement the strategy.

Future situation – and value

Whilst there were no ready remedies for resolving these difficulties, improving the strategic thinking capability throughout the organization – and not merely at the top – could help managers to find their way through the maze more effectively. This could occur, for example, through (figure 7.7):

- making key appointments – with a greater bias towards those who can think strategically and have a more strategically orientated personality
- strategic thinking and mentoring
- facilitation
- bringing strategic thinking into regular routines, for example into project management
- recognizing excellent strategic thinking – and its execution through breakthroughs more formally – and rewarding it.

The key linkages to other themes

The key linkages to other themes include:

- Because of unresolved bewildering choice it becomes much harder to create aligned strategic thoughts – and thus tangible economic value.
- Prioritization becomes extremely difficult – especially in the absence of formal strategic analysis techniques.
- The sense of being in a confusing maze compounds the problem of being unclear about the nature of strategic thinking anyway.
- Organizational processes supporting strategic thinking are likely to be inadequate.
- The vicious cycle of strategic thinking is perpetuated.

Prioritization

The current situation

There was some evidence of managers setting clear criteria for prioritizing options and resource allocation (Tesco and Barclays). But the decision-making process tended to focus on remedial or pressing areas of continuous improvement rather than on more challenging strategies (for example, at Barclays and at Lex). At ZIFA, it was perceived that new breakthroughs tended to get onto the menu if they slotted into some pre-existing agenda.

The future situation – and its potential value

By aligning the process for:

- delivering thought value (figure 7.3)
- prioritization (figure 7.4)
- shifting from vicious to virtuous cycles of strategic thinking (figures 7.6 and 7.7) one ought to see improved prioritization.

The key linkages to other themes

Links to other themes include:

- prioritization is a key part of organizational process
- it can also add considerable soft value
- without effective prioritization, thought value could be reduced.

Organizational process

The current situation

The organizational process (figure 7.8) is highly confused, and confusing, currently – both according to managers and academics. Strategic thinking skills are uneven and are typically inadequately supported.

FIGURE 7.8: Organizational process

Leadership and thinking styles are only partially in alignment with prioritization, and organizational action is both partial and frequently guided only in a loose way by strategic thinking.

The future situation – and its potential value

- Significant investment of time, resources, attention and in organizational change is required in order to establish a more effective organizational process.

    Potentially, given the few success stories of where strategic thinking has in the past generated economic value, the benefits of such changes could easily provide a payback this investment.

    The key link to other strategic thinking themes include:

- Improved organizational process would enhance thought value, soft value, help shift to a virtuous cycle of strategic thinking, and promote more capability in coping with pressure and bewildering choice generally.

Soft value

The current situation
Soft value, for example clarity, belief, reduced anxiety and stress, was seen as an important area of value by both academics and managers.

Whilst clearly some soft value was being harvested, there was clearly a lot of further potential to extract value from strategic thinking, both by individuals and by the organization generally.

The future situation – and its potential value

In future, it might be possible to add more value by managers at a micro-level seeing soft value (and not just business value – and thought value) as being a primary target of strategic thinking.

In particular, the refinement and clarification of agendas – at a cognitive, political, personal and emotional level will be seen as most helpful. More specifically, this would significantly enhance the perceived pay-off for strategic thinking, and thus the probability of managers engaging in it. This in turn would help them devote more thinking space to it and also help the shift from the vicious to virtuous cycles of strategic thinking.

A more conscious quest for the soft value of strategic thinking might also reduce anxiety and stress (and enhance the sense of excitement), thereby increasing organizational energy and the preparedness to act. It might also increase speed, which was viewed by both managers and academics as an important benefit of strategic thinking.

Key linkages to other themes

Linkages to other themes include:

- where soft value is actually captured this might encourage a more strategically focused thinking style
- the vicious cycle of strategic thinking could shift to the virtuous.

Vicious versus virtuous cycles

The current situation

In most cases studied (except Tesco, and to a lesser extent at Barclays), organizations seem to be locked into the vicious rather than the virtuous cycles of strategic thinking (figures 7.6 and 7.7).

In the vicious cycle (figure 7.6) there is relatively little effective strategic thinking. This resulted in unclear value, weak prioritization, dilution and destruction, and weak implementation and weaker results. This put additional time pressures on managers, discouraging them from actually doing strategic thinking, thus completing the loop.

Conclusion – what is the value of strategic thinking?

Now, going back to our key question, 'What is the value of strategic thinking?'

It was discovered that the economic value (to date) has been relatively unclear. Not merely was the strategic thinking process (and its underlying influences) not very well understood by individual managers, but even the definition of strategic thinking itself was ambiguous.

Value can come from:

- business value: for example as deliberate strategy, emergent strategy or through change
- thought value: through creating alignment within managers' thoughts
- soft value: through building confidence, reducing anxiety, and through building appropriately focused excitement
- prioritization (see below).

Managers were also found (largely) to be in a maze of strategic bewilderment when decision-making. Here they faced prioritization issues without a very clear strategic thinking process and one where resource allocation and other pressures and constraints had a tendency to drive out the more creative aspects of the process.

Indeed, it was not even particularly clear as to who should be involved in the strategic thinking process, when and how, and whether it did or did not apply equally to implementation. This is a strong hint to organizations to explicitly communicate that strategic thinking is something which can and should be done at all levels. Where any boundaries on strategic thinking are set then these need to be well communicated and justified.

So, whilst strategic thinking potentially might add tremendous value added, because of the very partial, isolated and fragmented way in which it is currently manifest and disseminated, much of that value was lost. This potential value was further dissipated by softer constraints, such as organizational thinking style, mindset, leadership, dilution of outputs, organizational destruction and a lack of direct personal pay-offs of doing it. The 'so-what?' from this is that organizations need to seriously question where they are genuinely interested in exploiting strategic thinking, and be more realistic about what needs to change to achieve this.

This suggests an equation for strategic thinking (derived from expectancy theory) of:

Effort = Perceived probability of success x (Business plus thought value plus soft value)

is a useful summing-up of the resulting answer to the question of:

'What is the value of strategic thinking?'

the answer being 'it is highly contingent, but potentially, with full organizational alignment, it could be vast'.

These two chapters have given plenty of pointers in terms of what needs to change in order to get real value out of strategic thinking. Unfortunately, organizations that are incapable of seeing this challenge could well end up in the following situation, depicted in Sun Tzu's *The Art of War*:

So when the front is prepared, the rear is lacking, and when the rear is prepared the front is lacking. Preparedness on the left means lack on the right, preparedness on the right means lack on the left. Preparedness everywhere means lack everywhere.

One would not wage a war without some sort of target measures, so why implement strategic thinking without targeting its economic value?

Summary of key points

The key points of this chapter substantially echo those of chapter 6. Additional points include:

- strategic thinking adds value especially through thinking about the art of the possible
- strategic thinking can add considerable value by simply speeding up organizational action
- the legacy from the past can prove to be a major burden on strategic thinking
- strategic thinking can add value through an obsession with competitive advantage
- imagining the future is one of the distinctive ways in which strategic thinking adds value
- strategic thinking frequently requires facilitation to draw out its full value
- where one puts a value on strategic thoughts that one has had, this closes the loop of empirical feedback and this encourages further strategic thinking

- away-days can become strategic routines and rituals, and may supplant the important activity of thinking strategically continuously
- data collection is sometimes used as quasi-strategic thinking as an unhelpful, disruptive and defensive routine
- weak follow-through is one of the major factors which dissipates the potential value of strategic thinking
- mentoring can help significantly to encourage and to reinforce, and to amplify strategic thinking
- confidence is one of the absolutely central ways in which strategic thinking can add value.

PART THREE

Managing strategic change

CHAPTER EIGHT

Strategic change at Champney's health resort

Introduction

Let us now turn to how strategic thinking helped steer strategic change at Champney's Health Resort. This illustrates not merely the behavioural and political aspects of strategic thinking but also how this can be turned into implementation. This case study is based on a documentary on BBC television in 1996 and also on interviews with Champney's managing director.

The case study shows how strategic thinking is crucial when managing strategic change, and particularly in turning strategic thoughts into options, then into overall strategic vision, strategic breakthroughs, strategic projects, and also financial results (see figure 8.1).

FIGURE 8.1: Strategic change: a process

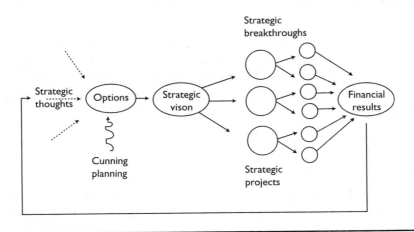

Background

Champney's Health Farm is located at Tring, Hertfordshire, UK. Champney's is a select, rural retreat for its members who reside principally in and around the Home Counties, England. Traditionally it is a most exclusive retreat, charging near-Savoy prices for its luxurious and relatively exotic services – in body and skin care generally.

But by the recession of the 1990s Champney's was suffering considerably. Falling demand meant that its cash flow had deteriorated to the point where it experienced an annual cash deficit of £1 million. Its previous owners decided that enough was enough, and sold out to foreign investors.

In business terms, Champney's was in the situation of a strategic turnaround. So its new, foreign investors decided that a new breath of life needed to be injected – to secure Champney's future.

In late 1995, Savoy-trained Lord Thurso was recruited to spearhead Champney's recovery. As its new chief executive, Lord Thurso set about formulating a turnaround plan which would secure Champney's a viable future. At this time Champney's also featured on a BBC2 production, 'Trouble at the Top'. Some of the quotes by Lord Thurso are taken from that television programme and some from interviews with one of the authors.

Because Champney's prided itself on its exclusive customer service, this turnaround strategy needed to be managed with great sensitivity to the people issues.

Strategic diagnosis

In the tradition of turnaround specialists, Lord Thurso set himself a tight deadline to formulate and project-managed his strategic turnaround plan. This was just one month. In the course of that month Lord Thurso was to spend the bulk of his time listening to Champney's various stakeholders, particularly:

- its members, and regular customers
- its staff
- its current managers.

A number of strategic projects were born out of Lord Thurso's strategic thinking, including people-related strategic projects (asterisked):

- sampling Champney's treatments (by Lord Thurso)
- simplifying management processes
- improving management reporting processes
- management restructuring*
- management recruitment*
- the communication plan*
- the strategic vision*
- developing a business strategy*
- customer database
- maintaining organizational morale*
- culture change*
- getting rid of Health-for-Life
- premises strategy
- the business case and its approval.

To begin with then, when Lord Thurso took over Champney's he weighed in at 16 stones. As a parallel agenda, Lord Thurso undertook to reduce this weight – coincidentally in parallel with what became Champney's own corporate slimming exercise. Most important in those early days for Lord Thurso was to sample the exotic, health-generating treatments, being his first project to help turn the business around.

FIGURE 8.2: Fishbone analysis of Champney's turnaround

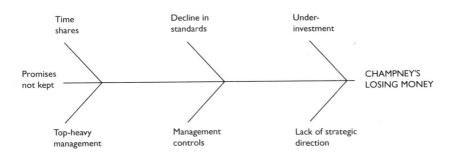

Lord Thurso's early diagnosis within the turnaround project indicated that Champney's suffered from a number of underlying problems (see our fishbone – figure 8.2). These included:

- a legacy of under-investment (and decay)
- a decline in standards generally
- an over-zealous attempt to market Champney's time-shares – to customers outside Champney's core customer base
- promises made to members which could not be kept
- a top-heavy management structure
- relatively poor (or inappropriate) management and financial controls
- a lack of sense of strategic direction generally.

Lord Thurso wisely negotiated a remuneration package which would not disadvantage him in recommending possibly unpalatable options – highlighting the linkages between strategic thinking and reward structure.

Reflecting on this situation (in an interview in 2000), Lord Thurso elaborated:

> There isn't any money and my job is to get the value out – bang, bang, bang. They take difficult decisions with ease. In a way, what I was doing was not far short of that. You arrive, the thing is absolutely bleeding to death and the shareholders are not going to be able to bale it out a great deal more and you have to have a plan for dealing with emergency situation.
>
> That's when you whip the patient into an ambulance and off to hospital.
>
> The thing was absolutely in the shit, that is a technical term. [Co-author and interviewer: 'Yes it is a technical term – it stands for Strategic Health in Trouble'.]
>
> When I first started I had an option, which was to recommend closing the business down, and I would be paid, I would have a kind of para-chute, so I was free to say: 'Look, I am sorry, I don't feel that the business is viable, the only way out is to chop it up and sell all the bits off… [recaps on the process during the first months].

Lord Thurso, on his first inspection of the property after taking over tells us (BBC2):

> It is clearly very tired. These rooms would have been considered five star when they were built but clearly the expectations of five star has changed. It is bland, it is grey, it is a very dead, dull room, it has no colour and it has zero on the excitement scale.

Also, Champney's strategic positioning itself seemed to be unclear:

> I have asked the question of everybody 'what are we selling?' and I get a lot of long-winded answers; the real answer is that no-one has thought about it.

He also reflects (1997 interview):

And I had also decided – it was as plain as day that the previous strategy, there was this wonderful name 'Champney's', which is true, it is the great opportunity. But what had been created in the past was the infrastructure for a £100-million-pound company even though it was only a £10-million-pound company.

It had all these people here who were called brand managers. And none of them understood what a brand was. And that was the extraordinary thing. None of them understood the elementary concept of a brand being a promise made to customers that has values and a character. If you said to them 'what does Champney's mean?' – the answer was, they hadn't thought it through.

Many of these issues must have been apparent almost as soon as Lord Thurso drove up Champney's drive. As soon as he arrived he found a mass of memos from his managers. Lord Thurso says (BBC2):

There are piles and piles of paper. It is a fairly classic thing. There are too many managers sending memos to each other. And I am suspicious of any company that is capable of generating so much paper when they are told they are expecting a new chief executive.

Also (1997 interview):

When I arrived here there were huge reports on everything. I said to them, 'Look, I just don't read them. I don't mind reading a novel by Tolstoy or Dick Francis, but I am not going to read that!'

The following reveals Lord Thurso's quite different management style:

I tend to communicate by getting up and sitting in someone's office. I loathe memos. In my last company I banned them completely for two months. I said 'the next person who writes a memo will be fired' – it was amazing, we didn't have a single memo written for two months. It was brilliant, people actually started talking to one another. (1997 Interview)

The above thinking clearly flagged up two significant strategic projects – simplifying management processes and improving management reporting processes.

At the same time management lacked the fundamental information that it required (BBC2):

We do not have good financial information; in fact not only is it not good it is actually awful. The management accounts that I have seen are mathematically correct but they are not informative.

So, besides simplifying the management process, a further strategic project would need to be improving management reporting processes.

He continued:

> There was a management structure which didn't work. The management reports were gibberish. I asked simple questions – 'do you know what your cash flow is?' and the guy couldn't tell me... They didn't produce balance sheets. They produced huge, thick reports, full of graphs, trend analysis. But the one thing that they didn't do was to produce reports where you could find profit, where you could find cash flow. I said we will really have to start from scratch.
>
> I remember sitting on the lawn on holiday wearing my Panama hat and a tee-shirt and my kilt, and smoking a cigar trying to read through two years of drivel, the management accounts... I can usually work things out and I just couldn't make it work.

But instead of rolling out a turnaround plan straight away, Lord Thurso spent precious time soliciting the views of all its key stakeholders, especially of its disgruntled customers. This enabled him not only to be absolutely sure that his chosen path was the right one but also, in behavioural terms, was owned.

This period of listening was primarily so Lord Thurso could establish a rapport with his new staff and thus to provide a platform for influencing them effectively (1997 interview):

> To be honest, I had already made up my mind before I arrived here what I would do. I had actually decided before the day that I started that I was going to take a million pounds out of the costs.

He continued:

> I wanted them to have thought that I had thought it through. They wouldn't have understood that I was capable of thinking it through very quickly, and that it was really clear what had to be done. It was really a very simple problem and it needed some pretty straightforward solutions.
>
> After I arrived I said 'I will have a month and I will take no decisions until the end of the month'. It was a good thing. I did fractionally amend certain decisions but 90 per cent of it was exactly what I had thought (previously).

Strategic thinking does not necessarily need a lot of time to accomplish. Nevertheless it is important to ensure that parallel strategic thinking occurs, even at a simplified level and at a slower speed in the rest of the organization. This does not come naturally easily to those senior managers who are particularly bright.

Lord Thurso realized intuitively that Champney's was the kind of situation which could so easily blow up if a number of stakeholders decided, rightly or wrongly, that he was 'the wrong man for the job'. Quite quickly Lord Thurso concluded from his own personal course of treatments that his operational staff were a real asset – to be retained, nurtured and grown. Lord Thurso says (BBC2):

> The closer I get to the front line the better I find the troops are. And that is very pleasing because if you have good officers and lousy soldiers you have got a lot of work to do, but if you have good soldiers and lousy officers, then you have to work to train or change the officers.

In some contrast, Lord Thurso found the management which he inherited, although up to the task of managing in a more steady state environment, not really up to a turnaround. The top-heavy management structure was not only an expense that the business could not afford; it also impeded the recovery plan, inviting two further interrelated projects – management restructuring and management recruitment.

Lord Thurso reflects in late 1997 just how serious the problems at the old 'head office' had become:

> And there was a business over there that had been completely neglected at head office. There was a flipchart in every office, which to me was a symptom of this very introverted style – the moment anybody had a meeting someone was on a flipchart. The whole thing was driven by the processes rather than by the objectives. If there were objectives they were tacked onto the process.
>
> People worked hard and interacted and interfaced and essentially went around in circles. There was no questioning of 'why are we here?' or 'what is the meaning of the universe?'
>
> It was quite clear that I had to make a very clear, that I had to make a very definitive statement that there was a complete change coming. It wasn't quite as bloody as it looked, because I re-deployed quite a lot of the people I had here back into the units. That refocused them on where the action was.
>
> I described it once as 'this head office was once a great black hole which sucked energy out of the units. Things vanished into it never to be seen again'. Whereas my idea of head offices is that it should be a tiny, tiny star in the sky, twinkling light down, completely out of the way.

Strategic options and vision

As Lord Thurso said (interview, 2000):

> I think life is all about circles and not straight lines. You can jump onto the circle anywhere you like. Number one, it is having a vision – call it a vision, call it an objective, call it a goal, it is the idea of where you want to go. The beginning of strategic thinking is where you are working out the vision strategy, then is mapping out the ways in which you could deliver that, like policies you put in place. Overall, a series of moves in chess is a strategy. Each move is a tactic.
>
> The leader has to ensure that there is a vision, that there is a clear idea. Whether the leader dreams that idea up himself or whether that idea is produced by a process of consultation, it doesn't really matter. He then has to make sure that there is a strategy for prosecuting it.

At this point it is now worthwhile doing an exercise on what you would see as being the possible strategic options facing Champney's.

This can be done at three levels:

1. options for competitive strategy
2. options for organizational strategy
3. options for the change process.

To help you to think about level 1, consider once again the following 'lines of enquiry': these are depicted as the 'optopus' or 'option octopus' (see chapter 4, figure 4.12):

- Which market sectors should Champney's be in?
- Where? (geographic options).
- Which customers should it target and what areas of value creation?
- Are there different means of value delivery and resource bases?
- Are alliance or acquisition possibilities?
- Might Champney's divest or outsource any activities?

Here we see the need to be quite creative and fluid in your strategic thinking. As Lord Thurso reflects (interview, 2000): 'The guy at the top must always be mentally in the future'.

EXERCISE: CHAMPNEY'S – OPTIONS FOR COMPETITIVE STRATEGY

Based on the case study so far, your imagination, and upon structured input from the 'optopus':

- What key strategic options can you think of for Champney's?
- How attractive are they on the strategic option grid (using the scoring techniques of three ticks means very attractive, two ticks means average attractiveness, and one tick means low attractiveness)?

EXERCISE: CHAMPNEY'S – OPTIONS FOR COMPETITIVE STRATEGY continued

- What overall scores do you get for the various options?
- Can you think of any ways of making these options more attractive (through the 'cunning plan')?
- What key vulnerabilities might reduce your option scores?

Note: a number of suggestions of possible answers are contained later in this book, somewhere, but it is advisable not to peep at these first.

This kind of reflection needs to be done in some specially created thought or 'helicopter' space (and time). Lord Thurso reflected (interview, 2000):

> The guy at the top is probably the only person spending his time thinking six to nine months ahead of the business. The most important single thing is thinking ahead…The first thing is one, with door shut, with phone switched off, gazing at this ceiling, running 'what-ifs' through my mind…

Turning now to organizational structure, assuming that you are going to reposition Champney's back to its traditional up-market focus, what future organization would you 'really, really want' (the Spice Girl strategy)?

EXERCISE: CHAMPNEY'S – OPTIONS FOR ORGANIZATIONAL STRUCTURE

- What key value-creating activities would you need in the future (say, over the next three years)?
- What likely roles would be needed to deliver these value-creating activities?
- How could you deliver these with least resources in the organization?
- What numbers of managers would this imply?

The implementation process

But knowing this posed a major dilemma for Lord Thurso if he were to move very fast and introduce a new, slimmed-down management structure, the shock might topple the organization, undermining morale at the cutting edge of customer service. In these situations there is probably no single 'right answer'. Arguably, by leaving the Champney's managers in suspense for one month, he prolonged the agony of uncertainty. But on the other hand, by at least listening to them over this period he would have a better idea of who was and was not able to make the transition – and also how many in simple, financial terms, he could take with him.

He continues (interview, 1997):

First of all I wanted a huge change and I wanted that to sink in quickly. I wanted the troops, the army in the resort to go 'Hey this guy might know what he is talking about!'

I also felt that I only wanted to do it once. I wanted it to be viciously quick for two reasons: one was to make a point and the other thing was to say to people, 'That's it. It is done.' And that undoubtedly worked.

Lord Thurso decided that Champney's above all needed a new strategic vision.

Strategic vision

Lord Thurso's own vision for Champney's is profoundly simple. Lord Thurso prefers the idea of 'vision' to 'mission' principally because mission statements are harder to grasp onto, particularly in terms of the behaviours which are implied by them (interview, 1997):

If you cannot remember a mission statement (I cannot remember our old one), if you have to refer to something, that's wrong. To me, any mission statement which is 'We will have care for our customers, be nice to our staff, be nice to grey squirrels on Sundays', you know, you have gone to sleep.

It has got to be something that encapsulated the spirit. 'Nowhere else makes you this good (Champney's)' – yes, it is a spirit statement. That's why, NASA – 'To get a man on the moon' – makes sense. At Champney's it is: 'Nowhere else makes you feel this good' – and that should apply to the staff as well.

Potentially, Lord Thurso faced major resistance to his plan, especially from senior managers who expressed their loyalty to the previous MD and to past strategy (during the television documentary). In business terms there was little alternative but to severely reduce the number of his central management team. Lord Thurso addressed the team as follows at a management meeting (BBC 2):

Please view my arrival not as something disastrous but actually as an expression of support by our shareholders.

The problem in a nutshell is that we are losing money. You are all intelligent people and therefore you will know that there will be a cost-cutting exercise. We have an expression in the fitness centre of 'no pain, no gain' but there will be pain.

We are, with the cost of head office, losing as a company approximately a million pounds in cash terms per year. It is my intention and target that by the end of the next year we will be cash-breakeven. The direction I have decided to follow is to put Champney's absolutely and without doubt at the top of the tree.

He had decided to tell them collectively of his decision so tha delivered two clear and separate messages. The first message was th there was an impelling need to restructure and reduce the managemen resource. The second message was to specific individuals – that they were, or were not, to be members of the future team. Within the restructuring project there would be two sub-projects – diagnosing current skills and defining the future skills needed to deliver the strategy. Indeed, besides developing an overall strategic vision, a further project was also required – developing a business strategy. Key sub-parts of this strategic project were: a marketing strategy for current activities, a review of wider strategic options, a customer services strategy, and finally a premises strategy. This was also related to a further strategic project: to enhance Champney's customer database.

Figure 8.3 represents this strategic vision as a wishbone analysis. This analysis highlights that the key factors which needed to line up to deliver the vision of 'Champney's' financial turnaround – through 'Nowhere else makes you feel this good' as:

- restructuring and cost reduction
- appropriate business strategy
- promises now fulfilled – through exit from Health-for-Life
- new management team
- staff enthused
- financial support for development
- appropriate investment
- word-of-mouth (resumes)*
- no major adverse environmental change.**

FIGURE 8.3: Wishbone analysis of Champney's (from 1996)

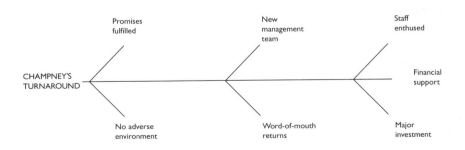

'erisk indicates factors over which Champney's had indicates those over which it had relatively _nt factor – no major adverse environmental _nalyzed down and positioned separately on the particularly for: no increase in competition, substitutes _jor threat, no major economic stagnation after 2000 etc.

_ing back now to Champney's change process, Lord Thurso _umber of options in communicating his strategy. One alternative, _nstance, would have been to speak to individuals separately – both _o communicate the need for the change and whether or not they still had a job. This alternative approach would have had the merit of removing the period of uncertainty during which his managers would have been concerned about their job security. But equally it would have meant that whilst Lord Thurso was interviewing his managers some would have heard about the organizational change sooner than the others.

These simple logistics highlight the behavioural implications of making a strategic change in an organization. For whichever way Lord Thurso played it, the effect on individuals' feelings – perhaps of hurt and fear – might have ramifications in their future and also that of the remaining team. Thinking through options in this area is always a major area for applying strategic thinking.

The impact of these redundancies was obviously severe on the managers. Champney's property manager, Willie Serplis, attempted to put a brave face on it as he came smiling to the television interview following his meeting with Lord Thurso. His smile quickly faded as he says (BBC2):

> Do you want to ask the question then…'How are you?' Not very happy. I just lost my job which is better knowing but what can I do? You want to be angry with someone or something but it doesn't make sense. You can dress it up in all the esoteric bullshit you know – downsizing, redundancy – but the reality is, for no fault of my own I have just been fired…

Lord Thurso himself looked emotionally strained when he was asked how he felt about this part of the process (BBC2):

> I would find it hard to sleep if I felt that anything I was doing was wrong in any way. I dislike doing it, but it is a necessary operation that has to be done on the company. All that one can do is to do it as humanely and professionally as one can.
>
> Most of them have been angry because at the end of the day we all like to think that we have a value in an organization and effectively when you are made redundant someone is saying that you don't have a value in the organization. When I say that it isn't to do with your performance it is to entirely do with the financial structure of the company, it actually doesn't help them very much.

One can imagine the atmosphere within the Management Block at Champney's as the reality sank in that it was the end of an era. Also those staying realized that they would be expected to achieve a quantum shift in the level of effectiveness – if the business were to come back into profit.

The above account highlights a further, short-term project: maintaining organizational morale.

It was then Lord Thurso's turn to address his operational staff. Lord Thurso appeared to be in a lighter mood as he informed his staff not merely about the severity of the situation but also of the fact that he was planning other job cuts. He continued:

> The last part of the strategy and the bit that does concern all of you is that New Court and the concept of a headquarters is going to be quite radically scaled down. There are 22 people sitting here and we have probably half that for the number of places that I actually have available. You are intelligent and you will have worked this out. And therefore some people are going to have to be redundant... And I do recognize the pain that this will cause you. I am sorry that some of you will be going, but please understand that it is nothing to do with you and your capability. It is simply about how this business has been run over the past few years and the requirement to put it on a proper cash footing.
>
> Finally, I would like to give you a little thought. All my life I have been involved in giving first-class service to people and I believe it is a wonderful thing to do. Be always ready to say 'yes' whenever a client or guest comes to see you and asks for something and you are tempted to say 'no'. Stop, think, and that will help us to create a level of service unheard of in this country.

And (interview, 1997): 'It is a tremendous culture change.'

Besides dealing with internal stakeholders, Lord Thurso had to manage the expectations of the Champney's members, whose business was needed to secure a successful future. These members had been disappointed in the past by its prior management who had, perhaps, set up expectations about improvements in standards that had not, or could not have, been delivered. Lord Thurso then decided to end the previous management's scheme for time sharing not only to those sales activities but also to buying-back the time share. Getting out of this business area proved to be one of the most difficult projects.

Lord Thurso was quick to realize that the Health-For-Life time-sharing scheme needed to be halted (BBC2): 'From what I have seen the constant push-push-push on Health-for-Life has given the wrong impression in the marketplace. I think maybe we should cut that right back.'

Apparently this was an issue which emerged only during his fact-finding. After being assured by his senior managers that there were not any other burning issues to be brought to his attention ('other than the cash flow' – said his finance director) he discovered that (interview, 2000):

> Some of the key issues I did not realize until later. The fact that the timeshare was totally critical and I would need to do that was something which I didn't realize. When I first got here one thought 'Yes, that's a time-share business; I will have to rev it up'.

He also determined that the physical facilities and amenities at Champney's did not provide a sustainable foundation for its future marketing strategy which was aimed at repositioning Champney's as an exclusive resort (BBC2): 'What a great architect friend of mine once described as the wow factor. What we have got here is the er factor. What we need is a wow factor.'

So, besides the organizational changes which Lord Thurso instigated, he also set about developing an ambitious project to revitalize the physical fabric of Champney's. This included:

- A major uplift in the entrance and facade to the central building – and to the driveway itself.
- A possible conversion of the Management Block to produce 20 additional treatment rooms. This, Lord Thurso hoped, would provide the spur to expand Champney's customers.

These renovations, Lord Thurso hoped, would provide a further benefit, signalling to Champney's employees that Champney's was genuinely going to be set on the road to a prosperous future.

Champney's strategic projects

But to achieve these plans, Lord Thurso needed to built the confidence of his investors who might well have thought that a turnaround was possible without major investment of this order. To achieve this he needed to produce a robust business case which, yet again, became a key project. Lord Thurso realized that to provide the basis for this confidence he would need to achieve a number of things:

- The restructuring of management had to be implemented successfully.
- Better financial planning and control needed to be stabilized – with the help of its new Finance Director whom Lord Thurso had brought in.
- Lord Thurso's restructuring would need to have delivered the required cost savings.
- Although a gap still remained (to break even) with these cost savings, this gap would need to be closed by expanding revenues.

■ To achieve this, the quality of service and standards generally at Champney's had to improve considerably – to the point where members felt a real difference and new members were brought in.

Although cost savings of half a million pounds per annum were achieved relatively quickly, it proved much slower to improve sales through improving customer confidence. But within one year Champney's managed to break-even. So, Lord Thurso was able to then put into effect his plan to obtain enough investment to reposition Champney's as an outstanding health resort.

The overseas investors were able to give Lord Thurso the vote of confidence he needed in order to move into Stage Two of the turnaround – a major upgrading programme – whose implementation became a further strategic project. So at last all the planks of Lord Thurso's future strategy were in place.

We have now told the story of Champney's strategic turnaround – but mainly from the point of view of the business. But if we look at this situation from a more behavioural point of view, we find that this dimension has perhaps even more importance than more tangible areas of change.

Implementing the strategic breakthroughs

The key three strategic breakthroughs for Champney's comprised:

■ a new strategy
■ an effective resource base
■ a responsive organization.

We will see these fleshed out in a later section, which summarizes the key strategic projects.

The key forces enabling Champney's change programme included Lord Thurso's leadership, the clarity of the strategy, and the support of lower-level operational staff. The most important forces were thus more behavioural in nature. These were represented in figure 8.4. These highlight that:

■ Lord Thurso had introduced a number of key enablers into the strategic change through his own leadership, a new strategy, a thorough restructuring and particularly in making some fresh appointments. (This was, in effect, a 'cunning plan'.)
■ Whilst there were a number of constraining forces, these were overall weaker than the enabling forces. Even these, Lord Thurso managed to eradicate or mitigate with his cunning change plan.

But, as we have said previously, we always need to ask the question 'What is the One Big Thing we have forgotten?' Probably it is the traditional culture of Champney's which was the missing constraining force from the 1998 picture we see in figure 8.4.

FIGURE 8.4: Champney's forcefield analysis

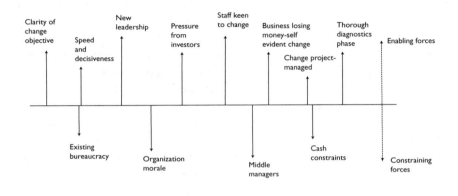

Lord Thurso's own larger-than-life character was a crucial ingredient in signalling that the changes necessary were very, very real. He reflects on the progress of his customer service project, which is also closely linked to the ongoing project of culture change (interview, 1997):

> But the key at the top should have a kind of evangelical fanaticism about what the strategy is. Unless you have this, you are not going to manage to convince people. For example, last year I called our plans 'Going from Good-to-Great'. And we didn't go from Good-to-Great, we got better. So I said 'This is Good-to-Great' part two. We could be back here next year doing part three or even part four. But one day we will get there and I ain't leaving here until we do.
>
> I believe that all human beings are capable of change for the better. This may be an optimistic view. But I therefore start from the premise that it is better to work with people rather than change them. I find that the grass on the other side of the fence is not often greener.
>
> When you are sorting out a business and getting the headcount right, yes you have to cut to get it right. But some people would go in and say, 'I can't work with that general manager' and fire them and get another one. And then after six months you get another one. Personally I prefer to say 'Why is this not working? Let us look at it and actually help this person.' I find that you then get staff who are more loyal.

But this involves recognizing that staff's agendas may not be nicely aligned with the vision. Lord Thurso tells us about the practicalities of achieving the necessary culture change- another project – to radically shift old behaviour patterns (interview, 1997):

> If I am honest with you I am only a small part the way through. All the things, these wonderful things that managers do, that is all part of our game. But the guy at the bottom says 'Sod you, I only have 40 hours to do my job'. What he is saying to you is 'If you want me to do this, give me a reason'.
>
> And that guy at the bottom isn't going to say, 'Wow, that guy at the top – he is a "zing", now I will suddenly smile at customers'. There has got to be something in it for him. And part of it is being controlled, led, cajoled, pushed into it. And a part of it is being rewarded, feeling nice, all of the rest of it. It is a huge culture change that virtually every company in this country needs to actually genuinely understand what a customer-orientated organization is. I have grave difficulty in thinking of a truly customer-orientated organization in the United Kingdom. I mean, there must be one somewhere.
>
> You do have to have a strategy. You can fight battles without a strategy and have success but it is a pretty haphazard thing. You have got to have a clear idea of where you are going, but equally you have to recognize that the achievement of the strategy will be a series of tactical steps.

It is also necessary to look at how implementation difficulty changes over time. Initially, Lord Thurso's turnaround project faced severe difficulties. But once the new structure was put in place, and one Lord Thurso's new vision for the organization had been unveiled, this difficulty would be mitigated. Figure 8.5 gives us an illustrated view of this difficulty, over the period 1996–2000.

As time progressed this difficulty increased at certain times as the organization found a new stability and sought to resist further changes. In turn this difficulty was then reduced once Lord Thurso's programmes to improve customer service and to shift attitudes began to bite.

Looking now at the key stakeholders who had an influence on this strategic change we see that:

- before Lord Thurso unveiled his turnaround project the balance of influence in the organization was against him (especially the existing middle and senior managers)
- but by introducing new stakeholders (including two new senior managers), exiting some old ones, and by appealing directly to the staff, the balance of influence was reversed – in Lord Thurso's favour (see figure 8.6).

Figure 8.6 is an impressive turnaround in the balance of power within the organization – again down to Lord Thurso's cunning plan.

FIGURE 8.5: Champney's: difficulty-over-time curve

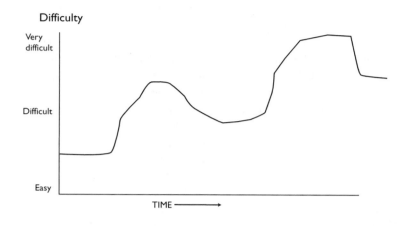

FIGURE 8.6: Champney's stakeholder analysis

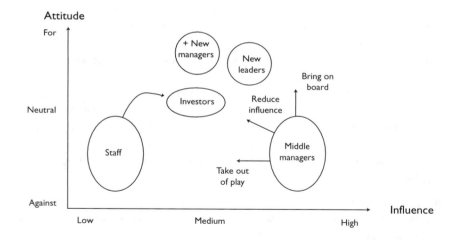

To understand the influence patterns of these stakeholders we must also bear in mind some additional factors:

- The agendas of stakeholders are not fixed but will change over time vis-à-vis the various projects as new issues arise and as perceptions change within the organization.
- At any point in time agendas may be fluid and ambiguous, particularly at the start of the turnaround. Key stakeholders, particularly middle managers, may not have any clear attitude at all. Although they may have some case agendas (such as 'I want to hang onto my job') these might be very limited. And even here, core agendas might be conditional on Champney's being seen as a congenial atmosphere to work in, given its new leadership. Never assume therefore that attitudes and underlying agendas of stakeholders are always givens.
- Individuals within one group will influence the agendas of others within the group. Through the informal network opinion leaders will signal their approval or disapproval of particular actions.
- You may need to break down the project into a number of sub-projects – as stakeholder positions will vary according to what is being implemented. For instance, a stakeholder may approve of Lord Thurso's plans to renovate the buildings, also approve of his plans to end the Health-for-Life promotion, but be violently against running a smaller department.

Besides Lord Thurso's management of the key stakeholders it is also worthwhile pausing to reflect for a moment on the impact of team roles and style, which will have an impact on the extent to which his team could now think and manage strategically.

Lord Thurso's own role comes over very strongly as being that of co-ordinator (or 'chairman'). He also combines both plant and shaper characteristics in his visionary skills. He exudes personal charisma and was able to carry a considerable number of stakeholders with him. His new general manager comes over (from the TV programme) as a shaper and completer-finisher. His new finance director appears to be a very strong monitor-evaluator, and his existing marketing manager an implementer and team-worker. (See also our discussion of the impact of team roles on strategic behaviour in chapter 11.) So, from even a small team base most of the roles appear well-covered, helping to provide a good behavioural base for future strategic thinking. (We will go back to this in the case postscript – based on an interview with Lord Thurso in late 2000.)

We will now summarize Champney's strategic change projects, which then provided the vehicle for turning strategic thinking into reality.

A summary of Champney's strategic change projects

Listing Champney's strategic change projects now according to the categories of 'strategic', 'operational' and 'organizational' they run as follows:

- strategic projects – for a new strategy
  - business strategy
  - marketing strategy – involving market research and brand strategy
  - business case
  - exit time-sharing
- operational and systems projects – for an effective resource base
  - sampling of services
  - customer service improvement
  - premises upgrade
  - management process simplification
  - management reporting
  - customer database enhancement
- organizational projects – for a responsive organization
  - management re-structuring
  - management recruitment
  - maintaining staff morale
  - culture change
  - communication plan
  - organizational skills diagnosis.

Later on we expand on the final bullet point above by examining some options for Champney's competitive strategy which have been thought about in the past.

Not only do the above strategic programmes gain in attractiveness through being part of a set of aligned and mutually supportive projects, they also gain through reduced implementation difficulty.

Key lessons from the Champney's strategic change case

In summary, the key lessons for using strategic thinking to help manage strategic change, and especially those that impact on people and behaviour specifically, are:

- Stakeholder analysis is absolutely central to managing the various strategic projects effectively. Accordingly, sufficient strategic thinking time should be devoted to analyzing the current and potentially future positions of stakeholders – and their driving agendas.
- Leadership is crucial in a situation where stakeholders are likely to actively resist implementation efforts. This leadership requires a degree of evangelical enthusiasm, a great practical tenacity in implementing that vision, and a continual openness to the environment of strategic change through strategic thinking.
- Achieving headway depends on building a sufficient 'stakeholder platform' to leverage off. This involved (at Champney's) key appointments of a new finance director and property manager – and winning over Champney's front-line staff.
- The difficulty over time of a strategic change or particular strategic project will vary over time. The shifts in difficulty need to be anticipated and managed rather than just coped with, which requires strategic thinking to sense the future.
- There are invariably more options which can be addressed through strategic thinking than most managers normally think about.

Champney's – some options for competitive strategy

A considerable range of options have come up over the years for what Champney's might have done (or might still do). These include:

- market sectors
  - the corporate market
  - the younger market
  - professionals, generally
  - the 'mass' market (but not necessarily down-market)
- geography
  - the US tourist market
  - middle-Eastern market
  - continental Europe
  - via franchise (on cruise liners)
- customers
  - the 'pamper yourself' customer
  - the stressed-out person
  - the exploratory, alternative treatments type
  - the health fanatic
  - men (in their own right)

- value creation
  - more focus on guiding customers through treatments
  - after-care – between visits, as part of a continual 'better life' process, e.g. through help-line, home visits
  - more focus on stress and life style
- change of use to, for example
  - a management centre
  - an up-market retreat
  - therapy for worn out, rich people, including pop stars, football stars
  - weekend dating activities
- value activities
  - franchising
  - smaller Champney's centres (actually now implemented)
- alliances
  - with a food company (to market Champney's brand)
  - with a restaurant company (who might deliver food to Champney's recipes)
  - with a cruise line or other up-market leisure providers
- acquisitions
  - to acquire and develop a second site, with a different catchment area (for example, in the north of England or in Scotland)
- divest or outsource
  - perhaps to sell some of Champney's land, as a highly exclusive set of flats
  - to sell Champney's to another buyer, either:
    - as soon as possible
    - after the business was turned around
    - on the back of the rise in property prices in 1998–2000
- to float all or part of the business.

Interestingly, the most common 'options' are 'to make Champney's more exclusive and to 're-market it to its core market', which is actually the option which Lord Thurso adopted.

Most groups underestimate the cost of this strategy (Champney's invested around £6.75 million) and fail to think through the possibilities for Champney's coming under greater competitive pressure. Also, Champney's traditional positioning might (some day) be not quite in keeping with customer demand.

Occasionally groups do come up with the 'sell the business' option, reflecting in part the tendency to hang onto what you have already got rather than thinking who might be the best corporate parent for a particular business.

Some lines of enquiry may open up then peter out. For instance, Lord Thurso reflects (interview, 2000):

> For example, we looked at opening restaurants. Now I am not saying that we won't open restaurants, but I have put it to one side for a while. We happen to produce stunningly good food.
>
> I have had conversations with a supermarket chain but at the end of the day...if you go to Birds Eye, for example, or Nestle...they very quickly say 'Actually, we can invent a brand and in the short term your name, Champney's, won't help us'. It is an area which remains of interest to me.

The range of options which can be generated for Champney's underlines the need to think much broader about 'options' through strategic thinking, than is conventionally done.

Each of these options can then be mixed with others through a mix-and-match process, for example Champney's could hold alternative treatment sessions at one-day sessions for professional, stressed-out people (with their partners), delivered through an alliance with an up-market hotel group.

Organizational strategy – options

When doing the exercise on organizational strategy no-one has ever wanted to keep the organization much as it was. Invariably, managers go for at least halving current numbers, and some take it down as far as six or even less.

Whilst Champney's delivers very high levels of service in comparison with other organizations, its value-creating activities are, if broken down, not unduly complex. Further, apart from IT there is little technology base (currently) to manage and develop.

The main roles which are often identified are:

- a managing director: to provide leadership, strategic thinking and challenge
- a general manager: to deliver day-to-day excellent service
- a financial and commercial director
- a marketing and sales manager (perhaps reporting to the financial and commercial director)
- an HR manager.

Breaking this down into sub-options:

- The finance director might have been supplied for the first nine months on a loan basis – to help sort Champney's out. After that a financial manager could suffice, once Champney's became steady-state.
- The HR manager's role might be part-time, subsumed into that of the general manager – supported with some outside HR consultancy.

It would be crucial that the financial and commercial director or the marketing and sales manager had the competencies to develop the sales database.

Here we see conventional structure thus semi-dissolving into fluid, strategic projects rather than making the assumption that for every value-creating activity there must be a role, there must therefore be an incremental person, and therefore there must be a cost.

Following the Champney's case study, the following exercise will be useful.

EXERCISE: REFLECTIONS ON THE CHAMPNEY'S CASE

- What parallels are there (if any) between Champney's organization and your own? (For example, in its strategic drift, its internal rigidities, and its focus on the internal environment over and above the outside world.)
- What parallels are there between Champney's strategic change process and the way change is managed in your own area, especially in the extent to which strategic thinking guides the change, or does not?

Conclusion

The Champney's case study gives us a fascinating real-time account of how strategic thinking can be used to guide strategic change. It also highlights that there may be many options which can be created – even in an apparently tightly constrained situation. These options can then be manipulated by 'mix and match' to evolve even better, and potentially cunning, strategies.

The case study also highlighted the equal importance of thinking through cunning options for implementation.

Finally, Champney's underlined the need to create a joint sense of personal and business need to do strategic thinking. Lord Thurso's final reflection is (interview, 2000):

There are very, very few people who just do that with no pressure at all [think strategically]. If you are comfortable, well-paid, good job, and good prospects on the horizon, where the company's making money, unless someone says growth is necessary then you won't think about it.

Summary of key points

The key points from this chapter include:

- Strategic change often demands a complex set of external and internal breakthroughs – all of which need to be skilfully prioritized.
- Fishbone analysis helps to diagnose the current situation very quickly and easily. This needs to be accompanied by active contact with customers, managers and staff in order to gain a clearer sense of what has gone wrong – and why.
- Whilst there were a considerable number of strategic options for Champney's, it was probably even more important to apply strategic thinking to the implementation process than it was to identify the 'perfect strategy' (assuming of course that such a thing actually exists).
- Organizational structure issues are perhaps best addressed through the Spice Girl approach of determining 'what do we really, really want?'
- It is imperative to have an overarching vision to guide strategic thinking about the implementation process.
- Strategic thoughts need (at some stage) to find a home in specific strategic projects.
- Strategic thinking needs to focus very much on finding the optimal communication plan (and style) for the strategy.
- Potentially, Champney's could have gone for a wider set of strategic options: usually there are many possibilities which need to be stored up as latent strategies – for the future.
- Stakeholder agendas need skilful sensing through strategic thinking.

CHAPTER NINE

Case study: creating improved performance at Marks & Spencer

Introduction

This case on Marks & Spencer (M&S) presents us with considerable management challenges. When a company as successful as M&S appears to lose its way then it is far from obvious as to the most appropriate strategy which it should adopt. It is all too easy to try to manage incrementally within the current mindset. Alternatively, in desperation sometimes strategies may be adopted which – although innovative – merely plunge the company into even deeper crises. In this case study we will ask you to Be Your Own Strategy Consultant – and to help evolve strategies to turn M&S around in 2001.

When writing an earlier case study on M&S in 1994 the use of the strategic thinking techniques flushed out some disturbing strategic patterns (Grundy, 1995). These highlighted that M&S was competitively weak outside the UK and was in great danger of complacency in its UK heartland. After the case was written, one of the authors showed it to a strategy professor at another business school for comment, which was

> It was a very good case. But I cannot help feeling that you have depicted M&S rather optimistically, and you could have been more critical.

Interestingly its author felt that what he had actually written could be seen (if anything) as highly critical. It seemed odd that the case could be construed as being 'too positive'.

For some years afterwards its writer (when running strategy seminars) when talking about M&S would suddenly duck down, pretending to have just spotted an M&S sniper on the roof opposite, out to get him. This was of course until the troubles at M&S burst into the open in the late 1990s.

The lessons from this earlier case are several:

- Firstly, it is often possible to 'see around corners' – being able to anticipate a change in fortune of a major and successful company using the strategic thinking techniques.
- Secondly, when some very real doubts emerge it is easy to dismiss them or tone them down rather than calling a spade a spade.
- Thirdly, when companies experience a major drop in their performance the seeds have frequently been sown earlier – and in some cases many years before.

To illustrate the last point, an external consultant was asked to run a seminar on innovation for M&S managers a decade ago (some of the rigidities in the M&S culture were already a source of difficulty). The workshop was not a success – for a number of reasons – not least of its being counter the M&S culture at the time.

A major stakeholder in the programme even suggested to the consultant during the workshop:

> I told you [before] that this wouldn't work. This [programme] is all about managing change, and we have already tried that.

Subsequently the consultant happened to bump into an ex-senior HR manager of M&S. Telling him of this story, the ex-M&S manager said: 'Well, I could have told you such a programme could never work at M&S. You just walked into a trap with no escape route.'

Coming back to the main part of our case study now, this is set out as follows:

- M&S – its position mid-1990s
- M&S – its position 1997-2001
- future options for M&S.

M&S – its position in the mid-1990s

In 1994 Marks and Spencer Plc was a very large, successful business with turnover of £6.5 billion and profits before tax of £851 million. Fourteen million customers then shopped at M&S each week.

M&S must have been exposed to many opportunities over the past ten to twenty years which would have been strategic temptation but had, by and large, chosen to build on its core business and capability.

Where M&S had come unstuck – in parts of its international development and in acquisition – is where it had stepped outside its (then) core capability. But these setbacks may well have prevented M&S from fully capitalizing on other avenues for strategic development, nearer to home, for example, into other service industries in the UK and elsewhere.

M&S's core business focused on high street retailing, and core products were clothing for all the family – women's, men's, children's. This 'general' business contributed nearly £3.8 billion of turnover. In 1994 it had also built a very successful niche food business which now amounted to a surprising £2.6 billion of turnover (40 per cent of the group). In the 1990s M&S had successfully diversified into personal financial services (although this business was still relatively small compared with the core). Growth had been primarily of an organic nature and overseas ventures (acquisitive and organic) had met with variable success. The most successful ventures appear to have been organic and have involved partnership with local companies from whom M&S had been able to learn.

M&S's gross profit divided by turnover (or 'gross margin') had increased from 32.8 per cent in 1990 to 35.1 per cent in 1994 – with no decreases year-on-year during the severe UK recession in the early 1990s. This was a truly impressive achievement and represented a very hard act to follow. How could M&S sustain this stretching performance into the late 1990s? This was to present a huge challenge.

M&S's annual report and accounts did not, unfortunately, give a breakdown of operating profit by type of trading activity – indeed M&S is not (legally) obliged to. However, it is safe to conjecture that the 20 per cent of business activities (by number of activities) which formed over 80 per cent of profit generation were (as an approximation):

- men's and women's clothing
- the food business.

This left home furnishings, children's wear, men and women's shoes, financial services and other products as generating probably around 20 per cent of profit. Also over 80 (in fact 87) per cent of activities were then located in a single country – the UK. Increasingly, M&S was beginning to source from non-UK suppliers, having overcome its earlier hesitation.

A summary table of M&S results is shown in Figure 9.1. This shows a remarkable stability in the mix of corporate business over a four-year period.

Its first half interim results for the 1994 year end highlighted relatively sluggish growth in food sales (at 3.9 per cent) relative to general business (posting an impressive 8.9 per cent growth). This highlighted perhaps the tougher competitive constraints impacting on its UK food business. It also highlighted why M&S might have been tempted into a major push for growth outside the UK.

If we go back even further in time (to 1985), M&S had achieved a compound rate of growth in turnover of around 8 per cent in nominal terms over nine years. On the other hand, during much of that period we saw fairly high annual doses of inflation, particularly in the overheated late 1980s and into the earlier part of the recession in the UK. So what was perhaps more impressive was M&S's stability and consistency of development rather than its percentage real growth *per se*.

TABLE 9.1: A brief summary of M&S financial performance

Turnover	1994 £m		1992 £m		1990 £m	
General	3786	58%	3371	58%	3221	58%
Foods	2632	40%	2358	40%	2306	41%
Financial activities	123	2%	98	2%	81	1%
	6541	100%	5827	100%	5608	100%
Operating profit	873		635		305	
Earnings per share	20.9p		13.5p		6.9p	

Source: M&S Annual Report and Accounts, March 1994

The main driver of increased profit growth over 1985 to 1994 was the improvement in operating margin, up from 9.4 per cent of turnover to 13 per cent. This kind of improvement could come in a number of forms – higher prices, fewer or lower discounts, or supplier productivity improvements/M&S holding supplier prices down, and delaying refurbishments. Much of that improvement came through M&S exercising its very strong bargaining position vis-à-vis suppliers. But if that were to be the case, then did M&S have much further scope to squeeze suppliers (or otherwise improve margins)? Did it need to seek other avenues for development to sustain its earnings growth? These were questions raised perhaps prophetically by commentators (Grundy, 1994).

M&S's recipes for success

M&S's success depended upon a philosophy of value for money, quality and service. It had built an extremely strong brand which had an appeal to a high proportion of the 'middle market' in the UK who had high brand loyalty. (To illustrate, M&S claimed to have 35 per cent of the British market for bras and knickers.) Its Marble Arch store was reputed to sell 19,000 pairs of women's knickers per day. Apparently one Arab customer arrived at the till with a rack of nightdresses, only to be told by the attentive M&S saleswoman 'These are all in different sizes' (he replied that 'so were his wives') (*The Times*, 10 December 1994).

M&S was very selective in having quality locations and relatively simple product ranges. It was also selective in the things which it did not do – for example, it did not (then) take other's people's credit cards and avoided high fashion, etc. It was also (justifiably) famed for insisting in the absolute best from its suppliers. According to one City of London investment analyst (on Channel 4):

> Being a supplier to Marks & Spencer is a source of unprecedented pressure, and some might say is interference from a customer in those businesses. If you are producing markets which are good enough to Marks, at a price which is acceptable to Marks, and the other conditions of being a Marks & Spencer supplier are satisfied, then being a supplier to Marks & Spencer is very, very profitable.

In the mid-1980s M&S began to lose ground to new competitors, such as Next, which targeted M&S and offered quality clothes with just that bit more fashion. This attack was good for M&S, which for a period regained much of the initiative.

M&S had also had a variable track record overseas and had had a number of disappointments both in North America (for instance in Canada where M&S traded for 22 years, according to the *Financial Times*, 1994) and in Europe. Like many companies which have developed a very strong market penetration of a single national country, M&S had found it hard to adapt its strategic and growth recipes to quite new and different business environments. For example, in Spain, it was said that while local people liked M&S underwear, etc, they found the original clothes offered 'ugly' (*Financial Times*, 1994). This invited the question as to whether M&S's merchandizing in Spain was originally driven by a tailoring of the UK offering, rather than by working backwards from local tastes.

Indeed, in a 1994 UK Channel 4 television programme on M&S, the scenes in the Valencian store suggested that the merchandizing strategy in its non-UK countries was built around the UK formula. It is as if M&S was aiming to convert non-Britons to the M&S, British formula. This might not necessarily be a bad thing – chains like McDonald's have created and imposed an international but US-based formula. But the M&S formula (especially in clothing) was likely to be heavily impacted by localized culture.

Whatever one thinks of this international development strategy, there is no doubt that M&S was seeking to exploit those opportunities in a big, albeit cautious way.

According to an investment analyst in the City of London (Channel 4):

> I think a much bigger proportion of its profits will come from continental Europe over the next 10, 15, 20 years. There is room for growth in France, maybe into Germany. But I also think that there are very exciting prospects in the Far East. It is already well established in Hong Kong and of course the great unknown is whether it might get into China.

In fact M&S intended to double its selling space in continental Europe over the next few years, with Germany and Italy (in addition to France and Spain) on the agenda. (The first German stores were announced in March 1995 – *Financial Times*, 28 March.)

According to Sir Richard Greenbury, then chairman (Channel 4):

> There isn't a retailer, a big one, in the world today that can probably say that he is going to stay in his home-based economy, and just do well there. I mean all the great retailers are having to face the facts that they have yet to take their skills abroad, one way or another.

Perhaps M&S was now much better placed to understand how to exploit its talents internationally than during its earlier experimental efforts. Maybe by recruiting more staff of other nationalities (especially in senior roles) would have helped, so as to adapt the M&S philosophy to other environments. This may seem to be a minor issue at first sight but could, in the longer term, be major as it shapes the mindset of management.

M&S's competitive advantage in 1994 was based (in order of ease of imitation, beginning with the most difficult things to imitate):

- M&S brand
- value for money (as of 1994)
- very high market share in niche markets (e.g. luxury food and women's underwear)
- supplier linkages and innovation
- systems
- sites.

M&S's brand is supported by reputation for value for money and also its reputation for customer service (and its supporting culture). Around these core advantages were clustered M&S's supplier linkages and innovation which were also core sources of competitive advantage. According to one City of London investment analyst (Channel 4):

> Marks has styled itself the manufacturer without factories... They probably do have the closest relationship with suppliers of any UK retailer.

Whilst this list of competitive advantages was impressive, these were potentially ones which could evaporate quickly. One analyst reflected on this (Channel 4):

> I think they are a very self-confident company, and provided that they remain self-confident and not complacent I don't think that that's a problem. But I think that retailing is a notoriously fickle business. You have to keep on reinventing it and reinventing it year after year, season after season. You have to make sure that your clothes are fashionable, that the styles and colour are what people actually want.

Some felt that (even then) M&S had become too rigid as an organization. Sir Richard Greenbury, chairman, espoused the dilemmas of maintaining discipline versus encouraging individual spontaneity:

> You must have discipline. You can't have everybody doing their own thing. And big businesses do become bureaucratic and they do become inflexible. But the day that they become so bureaucratic and inflexible that the free thinker, the maverick, the entrepreneur, the fellow or the woman who doesn't do it the conventional way... those people must be given an opportunity to express their talents.

But did he really mean it? According to one (brave) joiner from another retailer (a department store) who took another view (Channel 4):

> People just don't say anything. No-one will speak against the chair, because they say it shouldn't be done. You can just see people's faces changing (when you say critical things). People just don't believe you, when you say something bad about Marks & Spencer, so you just don't bother.

M&S also had some critical areas of competitive disadvantage as follows:

- M&S's perhaps had an over-cautious approach to managing its strategic development (at least in terms of organic development in the UK – except for financial services), and its culture generally.
- Its apparent lack of flexibility (for example in refusing to take non-M&S credit or debit cards [until very recently]).
- Its UK-centred mindset. This did not particularly affect its UK business but may have hampered its international development, perhaps seriously.

As regards organizational rigidity, let us note the comments of another analyst (Channel 4):

They [M&S] will certainly tend to be dismissive of criticism from outside. When you think about it, when a company is incredibly successful and Marks & Spencer has been, and still is, then your starting base has got to be, that what anyone outside is saying is potentially wrong, and that they know the best way to do things. They have been doing it like that for 20, 30, 40, 50 years and it works for them.

One of the most distinctive elements of this culture is the attention to microscopic detail at most senior levels. On the UK Channel 4 television programme, Sir Richard Greenbury, chairman, interjected at the start of a meeting to discuss current M&S foods to point out that:

I had the potato and leek [soup] last night and it has got lots of cream in it and it has got no potato in it. You know, if you have potato and leek then I like it to have a sort of powerful taste and it was, it was rich, it was too liquid, it just didn't gel with me.

As a result of this input in a later scene the food group merchandisers were seen taking notes of his comments as if they were about to change the formula.

Yes, this intervention was an example of M&S's great strength ('Retail is Detail'). But how could this level of detailed intervention be possible in the future if M&S were ever successful in generating up to a quarter, a half, or even more sales outside the UK? Could M&S truly become a substantial and successful international retailer with this apparently high degree of centralized, top-down direction and control in its merchandizing?

Also, the issue of M&S's (then) refusal to take other credit or debit cards might have been seen as justified in terms of the virtue of strategic choice – saying no to a costly strategy. However, the costs of excluding (or reducing) the business of many customers lacking M&S charge cards were considerable, if unquantified. Some customers maybe either have found it difficult or possibly too inconvenient to acquire M&S cards (for example, tourists). It has not always been the case that on seeing a Visa, Access or American Express card M&S have said 'I am afraid that we can't take that particular card, but if you would like to complete an application we may be able to issue you with your M&S card in about 5-10 minutes at customer services, where we have an online approval system.' Since then, M&S have addressed this issue if a frustrated customer asks the right question. Although this is now M&S's typical response, a credit card was previously seen as a threat, bordering on revulsion.

Again, the history of M&S's attitude to non-M&S cards was symptomatic of a twin competitive strength and weakness. As one analyst (Channel 4) put it:

You are looking at a company which essentially you have to characterize as a 'family dynasty', everyone is schooled in the history and in the traditions. I think the disadvantage of this kind of culture is that it can make it inward looking, it can perhaps breed a kind of arrogance.

Turning to M&S's international business, although M&S's brand strength had power and although M&S still had a clear market and product focus, it did not necessarily have complete fit with local cultures (or at least did not originally, as the various examples quoted earlier illustrated). Also, although M&S still had a strong supplier base this was offset by significant difficulties of logistics and attendant higher costs internationally. It was only in the late 1990s that M&S had been able to lift European sales. This success was achieved by exporting its 'outstanding value campaign' from the UK, and thus by reducing its prices and its margins significantly.

A specific competitive disadvantage in M&S international activities was the additional costs (prices were estimated as 20 per cent above the UK by the *Financial Times*) which M&S incurred because of its distance from the UK. But despite this cost disadvantage (relative to the UK), M&S still claimed to be 'unbeatable value' and not just in the UK.

Harder to remove still was M&S's UK-centred culture. According to their chairman, Sir Richard Greenbury, these attitudes were changing:

> One of the most exciting things amongst young people joining the business today is they think internationally. They are going to have to deal with a much more competitive, much more demanding trading climate. They are going to have to deal with customers who are not short of choice, or product at any price, of any quality, anywhere in the world. The consumer today is not just king, the consumer today is dictator.

One detects behind Sir Richard Greenbury's statement perhaps more a vision of the future rather than a reality in M&S. Its core management echelons were then staffed substantially by British managers.

M&S – its position 1997–2001

For most companies, competitive advantage needs to come from a number of sources and not just one. It is often the specific combination of competitive advantages that makes a company distinctive and which leads to superior performance.

The main ingredients of competitive advantage that lead to superior performance are:

- customer value
- lower cost
- greater speed, flexibility or responsiveness than our competitors.

This can be made more concrete by defining specific criteria:

- value – brand and reputation, market share, unique underlying skills and management skills
- cost – cost base, market share
- speed – distribution, unique operational skills and management skills.

M&S's traditional brand strength was supported by the M&S reputation for value for money and also its reputation for customer service (and its supporting culture). M&S's supplier linkages and product innovation were also its traditional sources of competitive advantage.

From the previous section, M&S had an impressively strong bundle of multiple and reinforcing sources of competitive advantage during the period of 1990-1996, but it had become somewhat bureaucratic and rigid, and not particularly receptive to change.

By around 1997, M&S's business portfolio was of varying competitive strength (for instance, between clothing, food, other items and financial services, UK and internationally). Although M&S had some impressive product lines, particularly women's lingerie and its niche foods business, this was offset by a number of strategically and (probably) financially less interesting business areas.

Financial services also represented a potentially attractive opportunity to M&S. The particular strengths which M&S brought to this arena were its:

- brand awareness (if tarnished in recent times)
- reputation for quality and, at the same time, value for money
- focus on a narrower product line.

M&S did not, around 1997, change its strategic direction fundamentally other than to change the design focus of its clothes in an attempt to become more fashionable.

During the period 1997–1999 a number of external market shifts (effectively external performance brakes) crystallized:

- Despite continued economic recovery, consumers became more discerning. Where they were asked to pay a premium, they appeared to want a brand and that brand was (at least in the young and middle-age groups) not M&S.
- Because of an increase in the sales of mobile telephones, computers (including access to the Internet) and in overseas holidays (through

cheap flights), a squeeze was put on the retail sector generally. M&S proved to be not well placed to withstand this.

■ Competition for up-market foods increased significantly, for example, by Tesco's 'Finest' lines.

■ M&S's international expansion (perhaps predictably) faltered, with a U-turn on investment in territories such as Germany.

■ New entrants to the UK retail market, like Gap and Matalan, began to take more share of the younger market, pushing M&S up the age range where it was under increasing attack from Next and Debenhams.

■ The fashion cycle was accelerating so that the two-seasons-a-year merchandizing process at M&S became unwieldy and obsolescent.

Meanwhile, M&S continued to pursue its international expansion plans whilst its UK position came under increasing attack. This was reflected in M&S's more recent results, as set out below:

TABLE 9.2: M&S financial performance 1997–9

Turnover	2000 £m	1999 £m	1998 £m	1996 £m
General	4629	4765	4811	4602
Foods	3201	3110	3157	3024
Financial services	365	350	275	216
	8195	8225	8243	7842
Operating profits	471	512	1103	1022
Earnings per share	13.2p	15.0	28.7p	26.2p

Source: M&S Annual Report and Accounts

M&S did make some major changes to its strategy in the period 1998-2000 as follows:

■ It decided to partially abandon its dependency on its traditional brand, St Michael. Ambitious plans to develop more exciting merchandizing ideas came from its 'Autograph' range. Trialled in its more prestigious stores, the plan was to get well-known designers to design expensive, up-market clothes to be sold in a separately demarcated section of M&S. (This strategy met with only partial success, and by 2001 signals were given that M&S was to rethink this strategy.)

■ Its previous chairman, Sir Richard Greenbury, eventually retired from the board. Sir Richard had overseen M&S's success in the early and mid-1990s, but now admitted (Money Programme, 2000) that its financial success was at least partially due to cost-cutting. With hindsight it was admitted that, given the investment in greater service by players like Tesco, this strategy might have been unwise. (Apparently the negative effects of this lower service strategy were not apparent to Sir Richard as stores would field all their part-timers on the days of his visits. He claimed not to have been aware of this practice.) Following considerable boardroom acrimony, Sir Richard was replaced by a successful retailer, Luc Vandevelde, who stated his aim was to turn around M&S within two years. M&S's advertising campaign (on TV and on billboards) featured a 'normal sized', but attractive, lady taking her clothes off to celebrate her size 14 body – aiming to appeal to Ms and Mrs Average UK. Unfortunately, Ms and Mrs Average UK did not want to identify with that image, so the campaign backfired.

■ M&S tried to enliven its underwear through joint ventures with Agent Provocateur, appearing to push aggressively into more adventurous and sensual markets. This again proved unsuccessful, and the M&S stand-alone lingerie shop pilot was halted. (Perhaps this venture was an over-reaction to the lady shareholder [see below] brandishing her bra!)

■ M&S recruited George Davies (ex Next) to form an alliance to create a new sub-brand, called Per Una. By May 2001 George Davies was reported to be having problems in timely sourcing for the new range.

By 1999, M&S's dividend per share was only just covered by current earnings, whereas in previous years it was twice covered by earnings.

In 2000, its profits after tax and after exceptional items were £258.7 million compared with a £258.6 million dividend, leaving a surplus of just £0.1 million. This break-even seems to be a rather amazing coincidence.

At one shareholders' meeting one angry shareholder and customer brandished an M&S bra, claiming that it was so fundamentally unexciting that it was no wonder that customers were alienated.

Whilst M&S still has an enviably well-known brand and a deep customer loyalty in some market segments, there is no question that its brand had been significantly tarnished.

The half-year results to September 1999 revealed that M&S had made a number of changes, aimed at influencing both internal and external performance drivers:

■ In management – its long-standing chairman left the board and a number of other top-level management changes were made. A number of television documentaries around the time suggested that Sir Richard was somewhat autocratic – based on sources inside M&S. His exit followed a boardroom battle which involved Keith Oates, then a senior director, making a pre-emptive strike for the chief executive's role whilst Sir Richard was away on holiday. Keith Oates also then resigned. A marketing director was appointed (for the first time) and was recruited from outside.

- In its supplier base – M&S moved fast to cut the less effective parts of its UK supplier base. Whilst this helped to reduce costs this also produced further bad publicity as thousands of manufacturing staff (not employed by M&S) lost their jobs. (Unfortunately, not all of these savings were to help M&S's bottom line, as they were needed to substantially reduce prices.)
- In marketing and promotion – M&S began to advertise more aggressively and to introduce more aggressive promotions.
- In its credit card policy – M&S decided to allow stores to accept credit cards for the first time in its history. This was to occur by spring 2000.
- Repositioning of the stores – by offering better value for money and improved service, and by better display and presentation of merchandise.

By late 2000/early 2001, M&S appeared to be in ever deeper trouble. According to the *Financial Times* (24 January 2001), Christmas trading had been even worse and, in the 16 weeks to January, group sales were down 3.1 per cent (down 5.1 per cent on a comparable store basis). Clothing, footwear and gifts were down 9.3 per cent. On the plus side, there was an improvement of 2.9 per cent in food. The 25 new concept stores were only 4 per cent ahead, despite expenditure of £60 million refitting.

Mr Vandevelde, executive chairman, had given himself two years to turn the store around but time appeared to be running out. Perhaps unfairly, one analyst, Tony Shirt of Credit Suisse First Boston said:

> You cannot really say that there is a strategy here at all… the only strategy seems to be not to completely muck it up, rather than to recover. Everything is being run very defensively.

In March 2001 M&S announced new steps to turn the company around, including (*The Times*, 30 March 2001):

- job cuts of 4400
- closure of many European stores
- closure of a small number of UK stores
- closure of the Direct catalogues business
- sale of half of its Manchester flagship store to Selfridges
- a share buy-back when property sales had gone through, Brooks Brothers in the US and Kings Supermarkets.

Its chairman asked for a further three years to successfully turn around the business. This would be through a return to a back-to-basics policy of 'classically-stylish' clothes aimed at the 35+ age group customers. (*Mail on Sunday*, April 2001.) Casual observation of M&S's actual customer base during lunchtime in its Marble Arch store in June 2001 indicated that around 90 per cent of its customers were between 35 and 60.

In May 2001, there were demonstrations outside M&S's Marble Arch store against its cuts and against the closure of M&S's European outlets (which appeared not to have been handled particularly well in PR terms). 2001 profits showed another fall of £36 million (on 1999) and Luc Vandevelde said he did not know whether sales would grow in 2002 (*Guardian*, 23 May 2001). In 2001 there was a further re-structuring charge of £335 million. This represented the third consecutive year of declining profits.

In a television interview Mr Vandevelde said that M&S's decline (before his arrival) had occurred over a five-year period and it would take about five years to reverse.

Some key statistics were:

- like-for-like sales – down by 2.6 per cent
- clothing and general merchandise – down by 6.3 per cent
- food sales – up by 2.6 per cent.

Luc Vandevelde also announced that M&S's head office would move to a new headquarters in Paddington Basin in around two years time, helping a change in culture.

Interestingly a new bonus scheme (the first of its kind at M&S) was to be introduced, offering big pay-outs 'even if M&S's profits continued to plunge' (according to reports). Apparently this was to ensure that successful business areas would not be penalized for poor performance elsewhere in the group. This attracted major adverse press commentary in May-June 2001.

Luc Vandevelde was (in 2001) still assembling his new management team, the last of the old guard having left. Roger Holmes, CEO designate (headhunted from Kingfisher in January 2001) was still finding his feet and was putting the final finishes to the new team. Press comment was concerned that this team lacked really experienced retailers with flair.

Thus, M&S still faces an enormous challenge to turn itself around. But now let us take this down to a more detailed level of strategic thinking as follows, especially in terms of its performance drivers.

The M&S case highlights a number of very major brakes on performance, each of which are ripe for further diagnosis, using fishbone analysis. These include:

- service standards
- dated store formats

- lack of appeal to many under 30s
- alienation of traditional customer base (especially women's clothes)
- limited success of re-launch through designer clothes/store upgrades
- slow time to market (new products) – an area now being worked on
- low price, reasonable quality and new entrants
- limited innovation in food
- lack of critical mass in new product areas (e.g. mobile telephones).

One might add to this further internal difficulties (and thus performance brakes):

- speed of internal change
- employee morale
- cost constraints
- supplier morale.

Future options for M&S

Clearly, in June 2001 M&S still faced a massive challenge to turn itself around – even in a three-year timescale. The repeated failures to deal effectively with problems had undermined external confidence not only in the organization but also in the leadership of its new chairman. The scale of the turnaround task was highlighted in a benchmarking visit by a group of managers to M&S's high profile Oxford Street store in London in January 2001. The managers found:

- The store was a rabbit warren which, given M&S's poor signage, was hard to navigate around.
- Its 'look' appeared old-fashioned, and attempts to brighten it up with a couple of TV screens showing videos seemed to create an even worse, patchy effect.
- Merchandizing was not well-displayed, with piles of unsold clothes cluttering up the stores, presumably left over from the sale.
- With one or two exceptions (with more healthy convenience foods) M&S's food range appeared almost identical to that offered ten years ago. M&S foods seemed to have been stuck in a kind of time warp.
- There was a tiny office bar situated at the back of foods in the basement (not the best place to generate footfall). This was unattended – spaces were there for three clocks showing the times in London, Los Angeles and Singapore. The Singapore clock was missing and the Los Angeles clock time was wrong. What had happened to M&S's famed attention to detail and discipline?

If aliens had visited this store (after being briefed on how successful M&S had been throughout 1975-1995) they would have had a real surprise – if not a shock. What had gone wrong?

Drawing the helicopter view out of this analysis, it would not have taken 700 pages of a strategy consultant's report (which was rumoured to have been presented to M&S top management in 2000) to have realized that: 'M&S strategy still needs to be fundamentally rethought' and 'Incremental tinkering with that strategy is not going to work'.

So we now invite you to perform (in the role of 'be your own strategy consultant') a mini-strategic review of M&S as at June 2001.

EXERCISE: TURNING AROUND M&S IN JUNE 2001 – IN TEN KEY QUESTIONS

1 If you had zero exit costs, which businesses at M&S would you choose to get out of?
2 Having identified these, what would be the cheapest/lowest risk ways of exiting them?
3 Which new products/markets (given M&S core competencies) that are likely to have higher margins could M&S now penetrate?
4 What stores base would you ideally like to have?
5 Would you reverse the decision to get out of M&S catalogues business (in order to capture demand left by selective store closures)?
6 Would you consider sub-letting M&S to other retailers or suppliers of services?
7 What kind of top management team does M&S now need and who would you bring in?
8 Could you/would you do a flotation of the foods business?
9 What other alliances (other than George Davies) might be of interest?
10 Who might you dispose of all or part of the business to and why?

Notes on the questions:
1/2 You might consider getting out of:

- shoes
- furnishings
- men's clothes
- women's fashion (outside lingerie).

3 Consider, potentially, home electronics (PCs etc), mobile telephones, holidays, estate agency, car sales (via Internet viewing), i.e. higher value items, perhaps even an in-store Financial Services Café (with free coffee). What products would an alien come up with? (Perhaps M&S could then be re-named 'Mars and Spencers' – to symbolize the blend of the innovative and the traditional.)
4 Consider reducing stores numbers by 10, 20, 30, 40, 50 per cent.
5 If you close, say, 20 per cent of stores, a way of keeping business would be the catalogue.

EXERCISE: TURNING AROUND M&S IN JUNE 2001 – IN TEN KEY QUESTIONS continued

6 Sub-letting: which out-of-town retailers might welcome a display area in M&S?
7 Would you want to change the chairman, have a different CEO, a stronger and more aggressive team of retailers?
8 The foods business might have greater potential for shareholder value creation. What would happen if this was a separate business and you then were to re-invent all other footage areas as a zero-base strategy?
9 You might consider an alliance with Tesco, or others.
10 Divestment – a hard one – who would want to buy M&S in 2001?

Conclusion

Even if you did not come up with an absolutely brilliant cunning plan for turning around M&S, it is highly likely that you generated some interesting options. Some of these options are probably ones which have not actually been thought about by M&S. This demonstrates that you truly are now well on your way on the road to 'Being Your Own Strategy Consultant'.

Summary of key points

- Strategic thinking allows you to 'see around corners' and to anticipate where current trends are headed, and how key uncertainties can crystallize and impact on your company strategies.
- M&S's very success exposed it to a potential demise, as in a state of success strategic thinking is often discouraged.
- Strategic thinking thus needs to challenge past recipes for success, and to evolve new ones.
- 'Strategic vision' (like M&S becoming a global retailer) can actually inhibit more fruitful and macro-level strategic thinking.
- Competitive advantage can quickly evaporate: strategic thinking constantly searches for ways of sustaining existing competitive advantage, and for creating new sources.
- Senior management must (at all costs) avoid the rabbit holes (witness the former chairman's leek and potato soup testing).
- Slow-burn changes in the external environment can gently then quickly accelerate, overcoming a company that has substantially lost its strategic thinking capability.

- Once a company has lost mental and emotional contact with its mindset it is inclined to commit itself to desperate deliberate strategies which are unnatural and will not work.
- In a turnaround situation, incremental strategies are no longer sufficient to deal with the situation and more radical thinking is required to resolve the external and internal crisis.

References

Grundy, A.N., *Breakthrough Strategies for Growth*, Pitman Publishing, London, 1995.

CHAPTER TEN

Acquisitions

Introduction

Acquisitions are a crucial area for strategic thinking. In this chapter we use this area as an example of how strategic thinking can percolate down to levels normally associated as being tactical, including detailed due diligence and acquisition integration.

This is done by examining as follows:

- acquisition logic and routes to corporate development
- acquisitions, alliances and divestment
- understanding our goals and present position
- evaluating options
- determining criteria – the dos and don'ts
- detailed evaluation – external
- detailed evaluation – internal
- sources of target
- linking strategy and valuation
- managing the deal
- post-acquisition integration – and learning.

In addition to this chapter, appendix I contains more on operations due diligence, and appendix II on the decision-making process – acquisition dos and don'ts.

A major thread through this chapter is the case of BMW's acquisition of Rover Group.

Whilst some acquisitions fail primarily because of poor execution, there are many which fail simply because of in-built design problems from the very start.

In this first section the key routes to corporate development are first examined, before moving onto the main reasons (good and not-so-good) for companies actually acquiring. The different types of acquisitions are explored before turning to how they can add shareholder value, using strategic thinking. Finally, the challenge of integrating perspectives is examined, along with the stages in the overall acquisition process and some critical success factors for getting this right. During this and other sections there are a number of short case examples, exercises, for you to complete, and (where appropriate) checklists to prompt reflection.

Acquisition logic and routes to corporate development

With businesses of all sizes facing competitive change in the 2000s, the pressures to find effective routes to corporate development have intensified considerably. Small, medium and very large corporations are inclined to thrust for growth. Here the mindset is often of continual growth, rather than in selective growth, coupled with ongoing review of opportunities to divest.

Some corporations, however, view their portfolio more like a deck of cards to shuffle in order to generate sustainable increases in shareholder value. All businesses can learn from this approach. For example, Granada Group will hold onto and develop a business unit as long as it offers an inherent opportunity to generate shareholder value, and as long as the corporate centre can add value to it. Whilst over the late 1990s a major thrust of Granada has been to rationalize, integrate, develop or sell off the Forte business-related businesses it acquired, its focus for the 2000s would appear to be media.

Granada is not alone in seeing shareholder value and portfolio management as being the driving force behind acquisitions and divestment. Groups like this appear to see their business almost akin to being strategic and financial escalators. If a division begins to slow down the pace of its development and capacity to generate shareholder value, it becomes ripe for divestment.

Consider now the following case of Virgin, which has skilfully timed its transactions to maximize shareholder value:

- Virgin is no longer in the pop music business, having sold out to EMI in the mid-1990s
- Virgin entered the airline industry in the early/mid-1990s to capitalize on the complacency of other major airlines
- Virgin sold 49 per cent of its share in Virgin Atlantic (to Singapore Airlines) at what would seem a very timely moment
- Virgin went into cinemas in the 1990s and sold out in 1999

- Virgin entered financial services in 1997 and announced plans to enter the mobile telephone market in 1999.

The corporate mobility of Virgin Group could be likened to a kind of 'Tarzan' strategy. Here the critical success factor is always to grab the correct next rope in the trees to swing to, simultaneously letting go of the last one (as it weakens). One moral of this is that acquiring a business may be forever, or it may be appropriate for a particular time period only. A second moral is that divestment is always a potential option: a particular business unit might be worth more (in either just real or just perceived terms) to a different corporate parent.

Unfortunately, many senior teams lack the strategic and financial mobility and astuteness of these more nimble corporations. Just as it is a very bad idea for your average businessman (or accountant) to emulate Tarzan, so it is potentially disastrous for the average corporation to go thrusting for growth, especially through acquisitions, and even more so without a robust process.

So why does all this interest exist in acquisitions anyway? There are a number of good and not-so-good reasons for making acquisitions. The good reasons might include:

1 To gain genuine and tangible economies of scale which will manifest themselves in lower internal or bought-in costs.
2 To extract corporate and business overhead which is adding little value, or which can easily be substituted by our own resource.
3 To acquire a distinctive product or set of services which can be easily sold through our own distribution channels without significant distraction.

Notice how specific and explicit these reasons are. Contrast them with your own. Also note the order in which they are listed, which is not probably the order which you were thinking of. Probably you would have listed these in the order 3, 2, 1. But the reality is that the realized value of most acquisitions is in the above order of 1, 2, 3.

Not-so-good reasons for acquiring businesses might be:

- To acquire market share (when market share increases will not necessarily result in gains in shareholder value).
- As a defensive measure (unless all other defensive options have been explored and exhausted – and even then if and only if it is better to stay in the business longer term rather than to exit).
- To satisfy the expectations of the stock market, which is expecting you to make a move of this kind.
- To satisfy a corporate restlessness to 'do something' – otherwise we will be going backwards.

- For a new management leader or team – to be seen as having done something significant, big, and bold, within the first 12 to 18 months.
- To fill a profit gap – without ensuring first that this will provide a genuine economic profit (over and above your cost of capital)
- To establish a presence in a market which is booming – at the moment
- To be responding to the fact that competitors are themselves acquiring (they may be foolish)
- To acquire a new competence (unless we are really, really clear as to how you will exploit this elsewhere in the group, and what hurdles preventing effective knowledge transfer might exist)
- To further your own (or the team's) personal career aspirations and/or agendas.

The sheer number of not-so-good reasons for acquiring underlines the importance of examining why it is (precisely) you might wish to acquire businesses.

Acquisitions, alliances and divestment

So, to begin with, on figure 10.1 we see the three major routes to corporate development as being:

- alliances
- organic development
- acquisitions.

FIGURE 10.1: Routes to corporate development

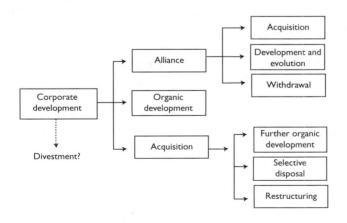

But notice how each route then branches off into sub-options. Thus, alliances can lead on into acquisition, development or withdrawal (i.e. divestment). Equally, acquisition can lead to further organic development or selective disposal, or to restructuring. Corporate development ought to be therefore very much a 'mix and match' process. Above all, we should ask the key questions: what do we want to achieve through our strategy? What strategic options are available, and which adds most/least shareholder value? Rather than: who should we jump into bed with (i.e. acquire or have an alliance with)?

In particular, successive management research studies unequivocally suggests that on average, acquisitions tend to destroy rather than add to shareholder value (Porter, 1987). It is invariably an uphill battle to generate shareholder value through acquisition, as any company that is strong and/or has lots of potential will typically be prohibitively expensive. For more on shareholder value see Rappaport (1986), Copeland et al. (1990), and Stewart (1991). Also, the buyer is likely to have far more imperfect information than the seller. Sadly, in general terms (except in a forced sale) divestment tends to generate superior shareholder value relative to an acquisition.

The lesson from this is that your management team must consider using strategic thinking – the full range of corporate development routes – and not merely acquisition.

Table 10.1 gives some perceived advantages and disadvantages of different routes to corporate development to be borne in mind before going down the acquisition route.

The table now warrants further expansion as well as a critique of its assumptions which may be partially erroneous.

First, organic development is often not perceived as being as exciting as other forms of corporate development – and slower. Whilst it does take some time to develop a company organically, the speed with which agile companies can move organically is impressive. Organic development can be a lot faster than managers might perceive it can be. It can also then surprise competitors and put them off-balance. Examine the speed with which Tesco has exploited its non-food and home shopping (over the Internet) – and other product innovations. Much can be done by accelerating organic development, for example by piloting a concept, by assembling a team of cross-functional, internal venture managers, or by modelling what the opportunity looks like in its future market, and then working backwards to arrive at a strategy.

Unfortunately, a major practical problem with organic development is that it may involve investing revenue costs (written off in the profit and loss account) to achieve its goals. This may put it at an unfair disadvantage

TABLE 10.1: Trade-offs: corporate development

	Organic Development	Acquisitions	Alliances and Joint Ventures
Advantages	Easier to control	Fast	Opens exciting opportunities
	Builds around core competencies	Extends competencies and opportunities	Transcends limited competence
	Lower risk	Surprises competitors	Surprises competitors
Disadvantages	Slower	Costly	Alliance may crumble
	May involve up-front revenue costs	Difficult and potentially risky, hits profits	Collaborators may dominate
	Unlikely to surprise competitors	Absorbs a lot of time	Doesn't give control
			Perceived lower quality earnings

to acquisitions and joint ventures. But if we are truly managing for longer-term shareholder value, then this should not be a real disadvantage.

But whilst acquisitions may well be fast to target, to negotiate and to do the deal, successful integration may take longer than expected, and success may be elusive. Far from being fast, success can be extremely slow indeed, as our later case material on BMWs acquisition of Rover illustrates.

Acquisitions that prove very difficult can not only absorb a lot of scarce senior management time (and thus destroy value), but may detract from other value-creating activities, especially:

- organic development
- alliances (which might sometimes achieve strategic goals more effectively and at lower cost)
- maintaining and protecting the performance of core operations.

Acquisitions and shareholder value (1) – types of acquisition

There are many ways of distinguishing between types of acquisition. These include ones which differentiate between ten variables:

- scope: 'in-fill' versus 'step-out'
- relatedness: 'related' versus 'diversification'
- geographic coverage: 'local' versus 'cross-border'
- style: 'friendly' versus 'hostile'
- company status: 'public company' versus 'private company'
- intention: 'deliberate' versus 'opportunistic'
- purpose: 'defensive' or 'protective' versus 'offensive'
- predictability of value: 'calculative' versus 'speculative'
- strategic mode: 'development' versus 'turnaround'
- management change: 'incremental evolution' versus 'management buy-in or bring-in'.

In terms of uncertainty and risk, the description on the left tends to be lower uncertainty and risk, and the description on the right higher uncertainty and risk.

The above highlights graphically the range of possible types of acquisition: by and large each acquisition has its own almost unique blueprint – unless of course you establish up front precisely which kinds of acquisition you are contemplating and stick just to those.

To give a concrete example, BMW's acquisition of Rover Group in 1994 could be characterized as:

- scope: step-out (four-wheel-drive and smaller cars) – high risk
- relatedness: medium to low – high risk
- geographic coverage: cross-border – high risk
- style: friendly – low risk
- company status: part of a public company – low risk
- purpose: a mixture of defensive and offensive – medium risk
- predictability of value: this was largely speculative – high risk
- strategic mode: a turnaround – high risk
- management change: initially some management, then managers brought in from BMW – high risk.

On six out of ten counts the acquisition of Rover by BMW was high risk, just two were medium risk, and only two were low risk This suggests that BMW had an immense challenge on its hands, irrespective of the particular issues peculiar to Rover Group itself.

To amplify some of these categories, by 'in-fill' we mean operations which are easily absorbed into existing operations, or which can be run along very similar lines (and without much special effort) as the other businesses. Generally speaking, these will be smaller in scale to step-out operations, which take one into new business areas (with certain exceptions).

'Relatedness' is driven by a number of factors, particularly:

- market relatedness (and similarly of customer needs)
- product and service relatedness
- relatedness of competencies.

On the question of geographic coverage, cross-border acquisitions are often more risky and uncertain because of a variety of cultural and regulatory factors. There is often less intimacy (of the acquirer) with local product markets and indeed with local labour markets. Add to that problems of physical distance and sometimes even of differences in time zones and you have a significant increase in difficulty, uncertainty and risk.

As for style, friendly deals are in a different ball-game from hostile bids. A hostile bid is much more demanding in terms both of preparation and of management time. One hostile bid could easily absorb the amount of time and attention from top management of ten friendly deals.

Turning to company status, public companies tend to be better regulated externally than private companies – having perhaps (although not always) management accounts and forecasts of greater reliability than in a private company context. Tax and legal matters are also likely to be administered more tightly. Stakeholders in public companies are likely to be slightly less emotional over their businesses than an owner/manager, who is likely to be more subjective about its value, and attached at a deeper emotional level.

With predictability of value, 'calculative value' occurs where it is possible to estimate – within reasonable limits of forecasting accuracy – the potential economic value of an acquisition. 'Speculative value' is where this estimation is less realistic. Examples of speculative values are the value put on dot-com companies in 1999 and 2000 (before the dot-com bubble burst), and also of the bids made for mobile telephone licences.

On strategic mode, whilst it is not always possible to discern whether a company actually is in a turnaround mode or not, warning signs could be:

- mature product life-cycles
- pending competitive entry by new sources of aggressive competition
- under-investment over a period of years in the business
- excessive cost cutting
- complacent management.

The above potential warning signs might be seen as characterizing Marks & Spencer over the period 1995–8, and could have been used as potential early warning indicators of turnaround.

Management change is a possibility: 'organizational evolution' means leaving the existing structure unchanged or making incremental changes. A management buy-in or bring-in means substantial or total replacement of the existing management team, either internally or externally.

Acquisitions and shareholder value (2) – value segmentation

Acquisitions, as has been pointed out, do not necessarily create shareholder value. But why is this the case? Acquisitions are frequently mismanaged because of the build-up of untested commitment, over-enthusiasm and the 'thrill of the chase' (Jemison and Sitkin, 1986). Anyone who has ever been involved in an acquisition should quickly recognize what we mean. It is very hard (even with the best of intentions) to maintain objectivity and complete clarity about the rationale and value of an acquisition once the process gets under way. Frequently it is the divesting company (and not the acquirer) that actually generates more value.

Understanding potential shareholder value creation is very much not simply a matter of playing around with the financial numbers. These numbers require concrete, strategic support and analysis. One useful framework to help us to think through the shareholder value of an acquisition strategy is that of the 'three Vs':

- V1 is the value inherent in the business strategy itself
- V2 is the value added through the particular deal
- V3 is the value created or destroyed through post-acquisition management.

The key test should therefore be: 'Why and how do you claim to be adding value through acquisition? Is it V1, V2 or V3 or some combination of these?'

Examining the three Vs (which are implicit in McTaggart *et al.*, 1994) closer, V1 can be assessed by evaluating a variety of parameters, which we expand on later.

The next 'V test' is V2: what is the value added through the particular deal? To arrive at V2 you need to assess the financial consequences of the strategy (in terms of anticipated cash flows), and also the underlying value of business assets and liabilities. To what extent are you paying more than, or less than, a reasonable value for these cash streams or assets?

McTaggart *et al.* (1994) describe V2 as 'the bargain value' of the acquisition. Some companies (notably Hanson PLC and Hanson lookalikes) have built corporate fortunes through exploiting V2 (and also, as will be shown later, V3). One very clear sign of V2 at work is where an acquirer buys a group for, say, £10 million, then makes disposals which yield at least £10 million, and is still left with one or more very profitable businesses.

In assessing the bargain value (or 'V2') you also need to take into account the underlying investment requirements and cost of changes necessary to sustain assumed cash flows.

V3 – the value added or destroyed during integration – is another tough test. Even where V1 and V2 are positive, V3 can be negative through ill-advised post-acquisition management.

Acquisitions and shareholder value (3) – process and critical success factors

Figure 10.2 now outlines the acquisition process in five key stages:

FIGURE 10.2: The acquisition process

- Strategy and objectives: unless an acquirer is very clear about its current strategic position and intent then the acquisition may have a spurious fit to the acquirer's goals.
- Search: unless very clear criteria are set for screening acquisition targets (strategic dos and don'ts) then the search process will be unfocused and misdirected.
- Evaluation: evaluation demands both qualitative and quantitative analysis to link the perspectives of strategy, marketing operations, organization and finance.
- Deal-making: although this is a crucial part of the process it is only one of the stages when things can go right or wrong. Also, during the deal-making process the strategic assumptions coming out of the first two stages will need extensive checking out.
- Integration (or post-acquisition management) and learning: during this phase any changes to management, operations and to strategy are implemented and there is further development via new opportunities or harvesting synergies.

Ten critical success factors for the acquisition process (which you should now match your current situation up with) are likely to be:

- You are very clear as a management team what your strategic goals are – and your own current strategic position.
- You are not doing it for the wrong reasons (for example, the pure pursuit of growth, sheer ambition, excitement, prestige, etc).
- The acquisition team project manager shows strong, clear leadership throughout the process.
- Other options are not closed down prematurely (for example, organic development, alliances, or other acquisitions).
- The team has a balanced mix of skills and can (as a whole) manage all the perspectives of strategic, financial, organizational, tax and legal
- The team is sufficiently experienced (in managing acquisitions and is not learning on-the-job).
- The team has enough spare time and capacity to devote to the process – without undermining their present jobs.
- The team does not succumb to the thrill or the pressure of the acquisition chase.
- Rivalry for the target (from other buyers) is not so high that 'V2' (the value generated, diluted or destroyed from the deal) becomes negative.
- In the urge to accomplish a deal you do not miss 'The One Big Thing' which is not so obvious, and which could materially hamper the success of the acquisition.

Acquisitions and shareholder value (4) – the acquisition strategy

Where acquisitions are concerned it is extremely dangerous to have an open, or 'emergent' strategy. In order to capture shareholder value from an acquisition it is imperative to have a strategy which is primarily 'deliberate'. A deliberate strategy is one where: 'There is a clear, deliberate and detailed plan of achieving our goals – and with competitive advantage'.

For acquisitions this involves having not only an idea of how your target will be developed in its external markets, but also internally: which embraces the integration strategy too.

The crucial additional ingredient here is the idea of competitive advantage, which means that an average plan does not really count as a strategy. What we really need is the cunning plan.

Many acquisitions do not succeed because they either have an average (and not a cunning plan), or perhaps a very incomplete plan for what happens next following the acquisition.

Things that might count as a 'cunning plan' might include:

- Doing management restructuring (as part of integration) at senior level to promote some thrusting, younger middle level managers and to incentivize them to achieve stretching, post-acquisition targets.
- Instead of moving in staff from the acquired company into our premises (and exacerbating cultural differences) to move all staff from both acquirer and target to a new, greenfield site.
- Prior to defining new business processes and structure (in detail), to benchmark world-class organizations to establish best practices which will be integrated with the best processes of both acquirer and acquired.

The final main ingredient in developing an acquisition strategy is to understand the target's market and competitive environment in more depth – especially short and medium term. Often within 12 to 24 months, sudden shifts in this environment can create new trading conditions – which will either help or hamper the delivery of assumed post-acquisition performance. Here environmental analysis does not have to be 'long-range' to highlight major threats or opportunities.

In the next sections we look at:

- understanding our goals and present position
- evaluating options
- determining criteria – the dos and don'ts
- detailed evaluation – external
- detailed evaluation – internal
- process considerations.

Understanding our goals and present position

Whilst many companies feel that that they know their own strategy and position quite well, this perception is often misplaced. Often this perception is based on some relatively basic strategy tools like SWOT analysis (strengths and weaknesses, opportunities and threats), and upon patchy data on the market and on competitors (which is mostly backward-looking, and subjective feelings and impressions about the business). It is not surprising that most strategies (and this is true right up to the very large company) are partially if not substantially 'emergent' (as defined by Mintzberg, 1994).

Where there are ingredients of a deliberate strategy, these are more commonly focused on goals – the 'why' of the strategy, and not so much as the 'what', the 'how' and the 'so-what?'.

Before acquisition options are explored, figure 10.3 now gives us a useful framework through which we can understand the overall strategy for acquisitions.

FIGURE 10.3: The acquisition strategy big picture

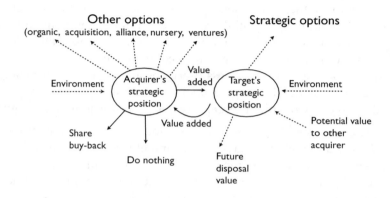

This highlights a number of critical things:

- First, you must be clear about how strong your own strategic position is prior to becoming committed to a specific acquisition, or to a strategy to acquire companies generally. This includes organic development, alliances, or setting up a special nursery unit for new ventures.
- Second, there may be a variety of other routes to corporate development other than to acquire a particular target.
- Third, do-nothing or simply to maintain your strategy is always an option.
- Fourth, a share buy-back may actually help you to utilize surplus capital without dissipating it on ventures which destroy shareholder value.
- Fifth, value should be added by yourselves to target (otherwise what value you bring to the party), and this value should be greater than that which other acquirer's would bring to this situation.
- Sixth, the target's own strategic options need to be understood fully.
- Seventh, environment changes in the external which might impact either yourself or your target need thinking through.
- Eighth, what disposal options are you likely to have should you have exhausted possibilities of adding value or be faced with better opportunities of adding value say in three year's time?

Evaluating options

To appraise acquisition options we again turn to the strategic option grid and the five key criteria of:

- strategic attractiveness
- financial attractiveness
- implementation difficulty
- uncertainty and risk
- stakeholder acceptability.

'Strategic attractiveness' can be defined according to a number of factors including:

- market growth (present)
- market volatility
- competitive intensity
- future market growth
- fit with own capability
- fit to our brand
- likely edge over competitors
- scale of opportunity
- focus or possible dilution of our strategy.

Financial attractiveness focuses on the key value and cost drivers which underpin a strategic option. Key criteria here could be:

- incremental sales volumes generated
- premium pricing achieved
- discounts avoided
- costs reduced
- costs avoided (for example one head office rather than two)
- strategy development is accelerated or retarded
- impact on share price.

Implementation difficulty needs to be anticipated over the total time of implementation, and not just during its early phase. Typical criteria (of difficulty) include:

- inherent complexity
- clarity of implementation strategy
- determination and commitment
- resistances
- availability of resources and skills.

Detailed factors for uncertainty and risk are diverse and specific to the context of a specific option. Some generic factors include:

- environmental uncertainty (will external conditions change?)
- management uncertainty (can we make it work?)
- cultural uncertainty (will people adapt?).

We can now take this to a more detailed level in the acquisitions criteria: the dos and don'ts.

Determining criteria – the dos and don'ts

When you have finally come up with a small list of candidates then is the time to apply your acquisition criteria to sort out which one may be worth approaching. These criteria are best expressed as acquisition dos and don'ts, rather than as bland criteria.

Among the criteria for an acquisition in the financial services industry, dos include:

- we must be able to negotiate a change of name (to the group)
- it must be of sufficient size (current profitability of over £5 million per annum) to be worth doing
- it must be a leader (as benchmarked by customers) in its particular niche
- we must be able to keep its strong management.

Don'ts include:

- it must not be dominated by a key individual
- the culture must not be rather different to our own
- we will not pay over £50 million for the acquisition.

These acquisition dos and don'ts takes some of the emotional heat and subjectivity out of acquisition evaluation, and help inject strategic thinking into it.

It is extremely helpful to do this from the point of view of dos and don'ts which should be spelt out prior to any acquisition appraisal.

Detailed evaluation – external

The detailed external analysis of a target focuses on understanding the inherent attractiveness of its markets – and of its competitive position. This can be achieved by using the GE (or General Electric) Grid.

Originally devised by General Electric, a highly successful conglomerate in the US, the GE grid answers the questions of 'which businesses are in the most inherently attractive markets?' and 'what businesses have the strongest competitive positions?'

Ideally, you would wish your business (existing and acquisitions) to be both inherently attractive markets and have very strong competitive positions.

The GE grid is used for a number of applications relevant to acquisitions:

- First, to get a better fix on your own strategic position first, as a prelude to looking at acquisitions and other options. This is split down by product/market segment.
- Second, to analyze and evaluate the strategic position of a target acquisition, and specially:
  - To compare and contrast it vis-à-vis your own strategic position. Is there overall consistency between both business portfolios?
  - To explore whether acquisition integration can materially re-position any of these businesses particularly in terms of relative competitive position.
  - To understand the basis of economic profit generation in the target's business, and to challenge whether this is likely to be sustainable.
  - To understand how much effort in integration and investment may be required to reposition the required business in order to improve its economic profit.

The GE grid is the best way of probing assumed 'strategic attractiveness' in the strategic option grid which we saw in the centre section on 'options'. Indeed, when we use the GE grid we may well need to go another level of analysis down – to set criteria for inherent market attractiveness and for 'competitive position'.

The significance of the positions on the GE grid means (in broad terms):

- northwest positions: a very major generator of economic profit
- southwest positions: a significant generator of economic growth – but with constant struggle
- northeast positions: a marginal generator of economic profit
- due south positions: a mixture between just break-way even in economic profit and some economic profit dilution
- southeast positions: significant if not major shareholder value distribution.

A step-by step guide worked example for the GE grid is now taken from the acquisition of Rover Group by BMW.

CASE STUDY: BMW'S STRATEGIC POSITION, 1994

BMW was a very successful company which has exploited important niches in the car market with a very strong, differentiation strategy. Originally renowned for its quality motorcycles post Second World War, it had diversified into small cars. Although once regarded as the poor relation to Mercedes, BMW had actually reached a position on a par with (and some could say ahead of) Mercedes. In late 1994 BMW has displaced Mercedes as the supplier of engines to the next generation of Rolls Royce cars.

BMW had built a very impressive brand by 1994. This was established by very clear market positioning, very high quality product, and service from its dealer network to match. The very success of BMW meant, however, that it had become a prime target for competitors to ambulate, possibly by moving into direct attack.

BMW's strategic position in 1994 was relatively strong, with its very strong marque, premium prices, dealer network and its relative quality levels.

But was BMW (as of the mid-1990's) capable of sustaining its competitive position against competitor attack from both Western and Far Eastern sources (such as from Toyota's Lexus marque)? There were some symptoms that led to a turning point reached in BMW's strategic health around the early 1990s.

First, BMW's reputation for quality had not been unblemished. Certain of the early 3 series models in the early 1990s had significant quality problems.

But besides the increasing threat of competition, BMW was moving in the direction of medium and smaller sizes. Although BMW sold a lot more 3 series than 5 series, and also a lot more 5 series than 7 series, it was actually the top of the range cars which are rated as outstanding by motor magazines. So was this a move to downsize a strategic temptation that would ultimately weaken BMW? Also, the competitive forces traditionally tended to be more acutely adverse when one considered the volume end of the car market.

But even before BMW had actively considered buying Rover it had decided to experiment with the smaller end of medium-sized cars with its BMW Compact, launched in 1994. So BMW did have organic options to its acquisitive strategy for Rover Group, at around 1994. Summarizing BMW's strategic position as at 1994, BMW:

- Had been (and still was) a very successful company which had achieved market leadership in executive, high performance cars in Europe.

- Had a worldwide reputation for quality which is now being imitated by a variety of players.
- Had a product line which was beginning to appear out of synchronism with the changing market environment, and which appeared somewhat limited and perhaps over focused.

But does this actually follow from our analysis? It is now worthwhile for you (the reader) to spend some time pondering what other options were available to BMW.

EXERCISE – BMW STRATEGIC OPTIONS

What options were available to BMW (as at 1994) (other than to acquire Rover as a central plank of its strategic development), and how attractive are these? You may wish to explore, for instance:

- Strategic alliances.
- Organic development (of new products) to broaden its range.
- Other acquisition options.
- Specific migrating its competitive strategy to have less emphasis (or even more emphasis) on differentiation.
- Maintaining and protecting its current niche position.
- Exploiting new technologies for engine and vehicle design.
- Specific options which you might have come up with are: acquire Porsche, Volvo, merge with VW Audi, a partnership with VW Audi, set up its own four-wheel-drive business, apply its engine technology into other markets (like boats, public transport).

Having analyzed BMW with considerable depth, we now turn to Rover Group.

CASE STUDY: ROVER'S STRATEGIC POSITION, 1994

Following a difficult history in public ownership, Mrs Thatcher's government sought to sell Rover Group off in the late 1980s.

The Conservative government clearly wanted to privatize Rover but for obvious political reasons did not want it to fail into foreign ownership (for example, of Japanese disposition). Then a deal crystallized with British Aerospace (BAe), which on purely financial grounds was rather favourable. BAe acquired Rover for around £150m in 1988.

Rover had sought to reposition itself during the period 1985 to 1993 and a big part of this success is attributable to the involvement of Honda which supplied Rover's key engines. Honda had taken a 20 per cent stake in Rover Group, and this strategic alliance appeared to be working very well. Honda began to see Rover as a central plank of its European strategy.

The Honda connection enabled Rover to tap into Honda's technology economies of scale. It was thus able to reach economic sustainability at a smaller size than it would have had to have been were Rover to be completely independent. The Honda link came at a price, however, as Honda's bargaining power enabled Honda to extract value out of the relationship through its technology licensing arrangement.

But the second and third major planks of Rover's attempted strategic turnaround were to reposition its product range to become much higher quality and also through productivity breakthrough.

In terms of products, Rover had previously had a product mishmash with large executive cars alongside the Maestro, Allegro, Metro and Mini. In the earlier 1980s Rover appeared to be trying to be a broad-based provider (with some niches) and simultaneously pursuing a differentiation and lower cost strategies. Rover (then BL) had made the mistake of being 'stuck in the middle' without a (then) clear competitive position.

But from the mid-1980s Rover sought to:

- move up-market
- have a much tighter focus on its car range.

The product range improvements made by Rover (prior to BMW's acquisition) included:

- The launch of the 200 and 400 series to gradually supplant and replace the Allegro and Maestro.
- The 600 series which was built on an identical platform to the Honda Accord, and commanded a price premium.
- The huge success of the Discovery range of four-wheel-drive.
- The re-badging of the Metro as the Rover 100 in late 1994, backed up with an advertising campaign attempt to give the car a feel of style (moving it from the 'grey market' – the over-50s – to the young market).
- A restored reputation for reliability.
- The partially restored marque of Rover.
- Its somewhat improved product range (in some areas).

But offsetting these relatively fragile sources of competitive advantage we can also identify:

- its relatively small size and dependence on Honda technology
- the need for investment on a scale which was difficult to finance through internal cash generation
- its high unit costs.

According to the *Sunday Times*, 6 February 1994, Rover also paid Honda substantial sums for the car floor plans and the engines for its larger models – plus a royalty for each jointly-developed car Rover sold. This agreement barred Rover from selling Honda-based models in markets Honda wanted for itself. So Rover was not allowed to sell the 600 in America.

The *Sunday Times* went on to say that Rover was caught in a Honda bear-hug: whilst Honda gave the British company protection, it prevented Rover's cars from breaking into real profit. The Rover–Honda strategic alliance underscores the risks which any medium or smaller-sized player exposes itself to when joining a strategic alliances with a larger and more powerful partner.

Rover's sales were still (in the 1990s) predominantly concentrated in the UK. Also, outside the UK its models have very low market share (even in continental Europe) and are sometimes not known at all.

So, overall, Rover had (as of 1994) a still fragile competitive position. Outside the UK its brand was weak, its market share was low and it lacked a strong distribution network. Its parent, BAe, was no longer fed by an entrepreneurial visionary, eager to develop an industrial conglomerate but by an ex-BTR, financially hard-nosed chartered accountant. With the government's five-year brakes on BAe's exit off (the terms of its agreement with BAe), the scene was set for the sale of Rover.

Given BAe's reluctance to continue as Rover's parent, Rover was left with a number of strategic options. Simpson (chairman of Rover) concluded that there were two options. These were:

- a full take-over by Honda
- a management buy-out.

Honda, at the time, seemed disinterested in Rover as a fully-owned subsidiary and a buy-out looked impossible to finance (as against Rover's thirst for capital – present and future – and its low rate of profit). This rate was woefully short of that required by venture capital.

Only Mercedes and BMW were likely candidates for the third option, as VW was still struggling to digest its late-1980s growth. So BAe turned to BMW for the strategic rescue of Rover Group.

But if one had been BMW, what sense would have been made out of acquiring Rover Group if one had applied the GE grid?

To get a better idea of Rover's strategic position, let us therefore look at the product/marketing positioning of the Group. To achieve this we will position Rover's products on the GE grid (which is invaluable for appraising acquisition targets). This maps product/markets in terms of their inherent attractiveness – which is a function of:

- vulnerability to PEST factors (or political, economic, social and technological factors)
- the rate of sustainable market growth
- Porter's five competitive forces (1980).

On the other horizontal we plot relative competitive position, factoring in here Rover's relative value-added (to customers) and Rover's unit costs relative to competitors.

Figure 10.4 now uses the GE grid (as of 1994) to analyze Rover's product/market niches. The 600 series are shown as being pushed to the right due to advancing competitive position. The 800 series is also weakly positioned.

FIGURE 10.4: GE grid: Rover at 1994

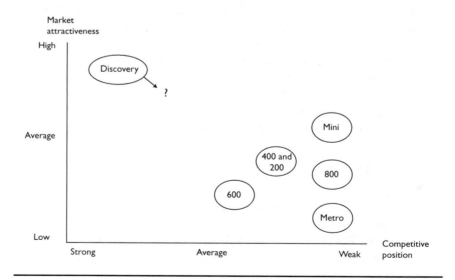

By contrast, the Rover 400 and 200 and Metro niches were in marginally more attractive markets (due to the assumed trend by customers to fewer smaller cars) although with weak competitive positions. The Metro and Mini are not seen as competitively strong and the Mini in particular is depicted (without new investment) as being dangerously close to the brink.

The overall profile (apart from the four-wheel-drive which is undisputedly in the northwest), is weak. Put simply, this analysis cried out for huge new investment. And this huge requirement was one of the big factors which blew BMW's integration plans off course. Even with the four-wheel-drive, competitive rivalry was increasing rapidly. If we add, on top of this, its vulnerability to fashion and the environmental factors (the Discovery is hardly a small car) it is perhaps less geologically friendly, longer term. We also detect further longer-term downsides (although these have yet to materialize by 2001).

A substantial part of Rover's current profits were reputed to be earned by the Discovery alone, so concerns on this score were important. Clearly BMW was banking on the growth drivers for four-wheel-drive winning out – as penetration of Europe is only 2.5 per cent (compared to 10 per cent in the US) there was still a belief that growth will win out.

Detailed evaluation – internal

The following key factors are important:

- What are the detailed competitive strengths of particular products or services?
- What are the strengths and weaknesses of underlying processes and systems?
- How are the key drivers of costs being managed?
- How flexible are organizational structures?
- What is the culture and mindset of the organization?
- What (if any) are its distinctive technologies as other scarce competences?
- Does the company have any other strategic assets which are hard for other companies to replicate or imitate?
- How dependent is the organization on particularly important or scarce skills (such as top management, IT, or other technology), or key account relationships?
- What are the strengths and weaknesses and vulnerabilities of the organization's supply base?

Developing an effective acquisitions strategy is an absolutely crucial part of the process.

Unless this is carried out effectively not only can you miss major downsides but you may end up enquiring the wrong acquisition target anyway.

Developing a successful and robust acquisition strategy needs to begin by defining our strategic position and plans for development (some of which may be acquisition, some may include acquisition, and some may not even involve acquisition). Using the strategic option grid one should be able to narrow down the focus of lines of enquiry.

Then by setting the acquisition dos and don'ts – the specific criteria for deciding whether an acquisition target is *prima facie* worthwhile investigating – one is perhaps somewhat less prone to getting carried away with the thrill of the chase, at least at this early stage.

Once one has narrowed down the options to one or more targets it is then appropriate to examine the target's strategic position. You should then use the acquisition dos and don'ts to help you perform a health-check to evaluate how the target will really fit into corporate goals and how it will enhance our own strategic position. At a more detailed level the GE grid then provides a more bottom-up view of its strategic attractiveness which you then proceed to check out in the next section in Evaluation – operations due diligence.

Mobilization is not only about becoming part of the team, however: it is about deploying sufficient time resource. Acquisitions are very time-consuming projects, and this can easily become a full-time job. It may well be essential to appoint a business unit manager as the full-time project manager – probably as a secondment.

Companies who fail to heed this advice frequently end up with either stressed-out senior managers, or a poorly-managed acquisition process, or both of these things. It is always worth reminding yourself that 'an acquisition is rarely a part-time job'.

Having covered mobilization let us now turn to the role of acquisition search. This takes us through:

- sources of target
- approaching the target.

Sources of target (1) – search

Before we go deeper into sources of target it is essential to say a few things about search.

The word 'search' could be taken to mean the process of exploring opportunities in both likely and less likely places in order to meet your objectives. This process of exploring opportunities can be structured or less-structured, it can be deliberate or accidental, ongoing or spasmodic.

We do know from more successful acquirers in the past (like Hanson plc) is that they do tend to be more structured (rather than less), more deliberate (rather than accidental) and more ongoing (rather than spasmodic) in their search.

The careful specification of acquisition criteria (which we discussed earlier) will help in providing more focus finding the optimal acquisition target. The development of an effective acquisition strategy generally will also weed out these areas of where not to look.

Indeed, the very notion of a less structured search in itself should give rise to concern. For it is hardly likely that one will come up with an acquisition which has a clear strategic logic that is not known to you already.

If you are going so far out of your product/market/core competence domain that you do not know your target at all (or even, relatively well) then this should ring major alarm bells. Equally, if you are to enter a new geographic region which you do not know very well, then this will clearly amplify risks.

Moving now onto sources of target, these might include two main types.

- market, competitive and competitor analysis
- financial brokers including merchant banks and accountants.

Sources of target (2) – market, competitive and competitor analysis
As we outlined in the earlier section on acquisition strategy, market and competitive analysis can help to tease out specific acquisition targets. For example, this can help you to identify:

- suppliers to acquire (through backward integration)
- distribution channels (or perhaps even customers) who might be advantageous to acquire
- acquisition targets in different geographic markets.

In addition, competitor analysis is often a source of specific acquisition targets. This source is often overlooked perhaps because companies often feel intimidated by strategic planning processes, often skipping over the amplifier analysis phase. This becomes a blind-spot.

Sources of target (3) – financial brokers
Financial brokers include merchant banks, accountants and other intermediates. These range from those who maintain an ongoing database of companies who might be available for sale to ones who just might happen to have knowledge of companies who are for sale. (Accountant-only firms tend to fall into the latter category.)

Merchant banks (and other brokers) may not always provide the trouble-free route to finding a suitable acquisition target which you are looking for. First, they will obviously have their database of companies who are potentially up for sale. These may or may not map onto your own acquisition strategy and criteria. More dangerously, where you lack a clear acquisition strategy and criteria, using this channel as the primary source of acquisition target could, potentially, be blinkered and dangerous.

Whilst they might also come up with suggestions for them to approach on a more proactive basis, this again will be dependent upon the quality and orientation of their contacts. Very quickly, this route can channel you in the direction of targets who may not fit your strategy and acquisition criteria particularly well.

Merchant banks and other acquisition brokers can be expensive in fee terms – which means that whilst hopefully you get excellent advice, you are adding to transaction costs. This inevitably dilutes and reduces the value which you can finally harvest from the acquisition.

In conclusion, there is probably no better substitute for yourselves being the prime driver of acquisition search, rather than relying upon third parties as the primary (or even secondary) route to find an acquisition candidate. This advice obviously needs to be put into the context of you having the necessary competence to screen acquisition candidates, and to make the initial approach, to which is now explored.

Linking strategy and valuation (1) – value segmentation

We have already seen one crude approach to understanding the value of an acquisition using the V1, V2, V3 typology, where:

- V1 is the value inherent in the business strategy itself
- V2 is the value added through the particular deal
- V3 is the value created or destroyed through post-acquisition management.

We have also seen how V1 can be understood more deeply through the GE grid, appropriately supported by the analysis from appendix I – operations due diligence. More specifically a number of techniques from that section help to provide better support for understanding current and future value generation, especially:

- The growth drivers – for understanding the sustainability of expansion in the market or in the companies turnover.
- The five competitive forces – this helps to understand the robustness of margins, and also to identify shifts in the industry structure, for example through new competitor's entering the market or through changes in distribution channel strategy.
- Target's competitive position: a weak position (like that of Rover in 1994) might entail considerable future investment.

But there are very many ways of understanding value which can be obtained by segmenting it in new ways. For example, consider the following segmentation of value into: future enhancing and protective value, future opportunity value, synergistic value and sweat value:

- Enhancing and protective value: the value which can be added either by strengthening the acquired business's current competitive position and scope; and the value to the acquirer of a defensive nature. For instance, in avoiding loss of economies of scale.
- Opportunity value: the value of the opportunity stream inherent in both the acquired company's markets and its existing platform. This value can come from possible new products, services, network channels or technologies, or simply through fast market growth generally.
- Synergistic value: the value of bringing together particular activities within the business value systems.
- Sweat value: the value released by pure reduction of costs or assets in the acquired company, or the potential disposal of whole businesses.

Here we draw up separate pictures for the major high-level value drivers and also the high-level cost drivers. Figures 10.5 and 10.6 show how this was used to understand BMW's acquisition of Rover more effectively.

FIGURE 10.5: Rover's value drivers

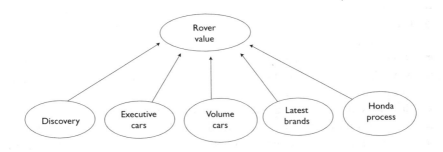

Notice on these figures the dependence of Rover Group on the value generation from the four-wheel-drive Discovery model. Also notice the number of major cost drivers reducing the value generation of Rover (figure 10.6).

FIGURE 10.6: Rover's cost drivers

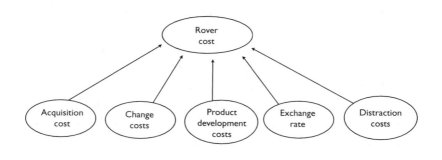

Linking strategy and valuation (2) – scenarios and risk

Risk analysis for acquisitions should be conducted not by standard, pre-set, sensitivity percentages, but by a deeper appreciation of the robustries of key variables – the value and cost drivers. To facilitate this is it useful to draw upon both scenario story-telling (about the future), using the uncertainty-importance grid – from chapter 2.

Figure 10.7 uses the methodology for BMW's acquisition of Rover Group. These show BMW's assumptions as follows:

- Rover's existing product range (volume cars) was reasonably strong
- the four-wheel-drive Discovery model would remain highly competitive
- Rover's unit costs were reasonably low
- Rover's depending on Honda could be removed without doubling or trebling existing investment levels
- Rover's existing management resources were 'strong'
- BMW would be able to get on well with Rover's management team
- the UK exchange rate would not strengthen them by over 20 per cent.

These became both more important and more uncertain, shifting both south and east.

FIGURE 10.7: Uncertainty-importance grid

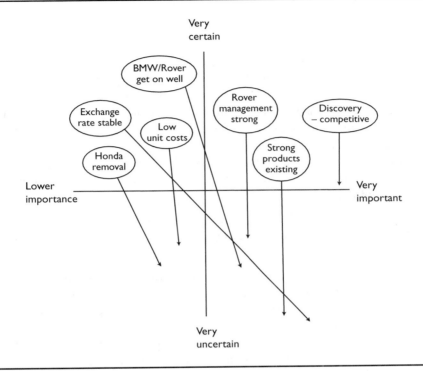

These shifts might have been anticipated before the event (see Grundy, 1995). The effect of these adverse shifts meant that BMW destroyed shareholder value (according to some sources – see for example, *The Independent*, 28 March 2001) of between £2.5 billion and £3.0 billion.

Yet at the time the acquisition of Rover (at around £800 million) was felt to be 'cheap'.

But with post-acquisition investment in Rover increasing from the £100 million to £150 million per annum level pre-acquisition to around £500 million this acquisition was anything but 'cheap'. In fact, this highlights another important issue – scoping the scale of the investment required post-acquisition to capture:

- 'protective' value
- 'enhancing' value
- 'opportunity' value.

This meant big increases in investment to protect the competitiveness of existing models, and to launch new models – notably the smaller, four-wheel-drive Freelander, the Rover 75, 45 and 25 – and a de luxe mini.

Linking strategy and value (3) – divestment

Divestment may be relevant from two perspectives:

- You may not necessarily wish to retain all the businesses' operations following an acquisition. For example, arguably, BMW should have divested of all or part of Rover's volume car business to concentrate on the four-wheel-drive business and niche cars like the MG. In that event, divestment valuation issues are of parallel interest to acquisition valuation.
- You will not always be the acquirer. Indeed, as we saw earlier it is usually the vendor who adds value during the acquisition process, and not the acquirer.

Even where a business area is profitable and has longer-term potential, four questions still need to be asked in the context of corporate development:

- How much shareholder value can be added by the group parent to this business unit in future?
- How does this compare with what other corporate parents could add to the business?
- Could we sell the business to another corporate group for more than what it is worth to us (based on real or perceived market value)?
- Could we generate incremental shareholder value by reinvesting the proceeds in more exciting opportunities ourselves? (And ones which we would unlikely to be able to fund otherwise.)

Sadly, there is still limited evidence that many managers take fundamental questions like this seriously – until they themselves are subject to a break-up bid.

Here are lessons for the divesting owners/management:

- What features of the market environment can you emphasize as being attractive (especially the growth drivers)? (V1)
- What past competitive strengths can you identify and extrapolate out into the future, emphasizing dominance or near dominance in key segments? (V1)
- What is your future opportunity stream and what would it be worth as an upside if you had more funds to invest (i.e. from the acquirer)? (V1)
- How can you create real or imagined rivalry for a deal and which new parent would it be worth most to? (V2)
- What is the lowest cost of capital which could be used to discount your cash flows (and how could you justify this)? (V2)

- What is the highest realistic terminal value at the end of the forecast time horizons, and how can we justify this? (V2)
- How can we best convey the impression that we are not in a hurry to do a deal – and we might not need to do one anyway? (V2)
- What are the particular agendas on the acquisition team's minds (especially personal and political), and how can we exploit 'loose bricks' in the acquisition team's bid strategy? (V2)
- What synergies with the acquirer's business value system (real or imagined) can you envisage and what 'best value' can be put on these? (V3)
- What is the best case for achieving sweat value for integration and how can this be built into our plans and forecasts – 'we will do it anyway'? (V3)

Managing the deal (1) – acquisition options and bargaining power

The deal-making process is a critical part of determining V2, which means the value added, diluted or destroyed during the negotiation. In this chapter the role of acquisition options and bargaining power are explored. This is then linked to the deal-making agendas which both parties to the acquisition may have. The role of scenario storytelling for the deal is then explored before a number of tips on deal-making dos and don'ts is elaborated. Finally we look at funding the acquisition and at the deal done by BMW in buying Rover.

Turning first to the role of acquisition options and bargaining power, just which factors will actually determine 'V2'? These can be distilled into five key influences.

- The strength of desire by the acquirer to buy.
- The strength of desire by the vendor to sell.
- The other options available to the acquirer – either through alternative acquisition, organic development or through alliance.
- The other options available to the vendor – either to dispose of the business to other parties, or to develop or turn the business around oneself.
- The relative time pressure to do a deal: is it more urgent to the buyer to do a deal, or is it more urgent to the vendor?

Figure 10.8 displays this as visually (along similar lines to Porter's Five Competitive Forces [Porter, 1980]).

FIGURE 10.8: Acquisitions: the five forces

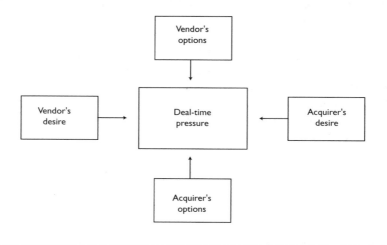

The acquirer's other options

- What options for organic development does the acquirer have?
- What alliance options does the acquirer have?
- What other acquisition options does the acquirer have?
- How attractive and flexible are these options?

The vendor's other options

- What options exist to develop and grow the business organically – without disposal?
- What other options – for example to sell to other parties – exist?
- What closure options exist for the vendor (in case of a forced sale)?
- How attractive are these alternative options?

The time-pressure to do a deal

- What specific timetables, deadlines or other corporate pressures are driving the acquirer to want a quick deal?
- What parallel time pressures does the vendor also face?
- Who is under most perceived time pressure – the vendor or the acquirer?

Following reflection on the bargaining power associated with the deal, the next stage is to examine the deal-making agendas of the various parties.

Managing the deal (2) – deal scenarios

The acquisition deal is a complex and sometimes unpredictable process whose course may not be easily forecast. Nevertheless it may be possible to anticipate some of its twists and turns by using scenario story-telling.

Scenario story-telling entails being able to imagine and anticipate the different moves which you and the vendor are likely to make during the deal. The professional advisers on both sides are also players in the drama. Just as any really good chess players focus around half of their attention on the intent of their competitors (rather than just on their strategy and moves), so in scenario story telling equal weighting is placed on the vendor's intent.

Using the 'out-of-body experience' and the deal-making agendas (see stakeholder analysis, chapter 5), now put yourself fully within the mindset, the feelings and the anxieties of the vendor. It may be helpful for one person in your team to actually role-play being the vendor.

Key phases of the deal which are fruitful to imagine and develop through interactive role play of the key players within the vendor's team include:

- The initial contact with the vendor (see also our earlier sub-section on 'Approaching the Target').
- The first full meeting with the vendor to explore a potential deal.
- The various stages of the due diligence process where you are likely to discover downsides and drawbacks and, especially to imagine the interactions which might occur as these downsides are discussed between yourselves and the vendor.
- Possible increases in the acquisition price – due to new, competing bidders for your target emerging.
- Possible reductions in the offer due either to unexpected due diligence issues emerging to, or due to deliberate tactics on your part to knock the vendor down in a 'forced sale' situation.
- Responses to 'deal stoppers' emerging at a very late stage in negotiations.
- Reactions of the vendor's top management and shareholders to discussions of 'who is going to be doing what' in the new company – especially where these are personally and politically sensitive (for example if the current chairman – currently a significant shareholder – might be asked either to step-down or to assume that role of non-executive director only, or as longer-term consultant to the company this might cause major difficulties).

Each of these situations is likely to be complex, uncertain, and yet decisive in the outcome of the deal process.

In order to perform scenario-story telling for the dynamics of the deal it is essential that you are able to be:

- Creative, in describing the future context of the story.
- Fluid, in linking one event with another (as a chain), and in thinking through the interactions between the various players, and their knock-on effects.
- Imaginative: in being able to develop a particular story-line right through to its results and implications.

CASE STUDY: BMW AND ROVER

The continuing case study of BMW's acquisition of Rover Group in 1994 now illustrates how the process can easily become subservient to the acquirer's drive to consummate the deal. Interestingly, Honda, Rover's (then) alliance partner did not seem prepared for BMW's 'surprise' bid, even though the five year period after being acquired in 1993. (The UK government, which had sold Rover to BAe, had stipulated that it could not be sold for at least five years.)

BAe had put itself in the position of having to sell Rover Group as a result of a weakening of both its civil aerospace markets (due to the ending of the Cold War). In addition, its new chief executive (who was previously finance director at BTR, the financially aggressive industrial conglomerate) took a highly commercial stance to BAe's future – its businesses needed to demonstrate their contribution to creating shareholder value. Finally, Rover Group needed considerable capital investment in its product development and production facilities, which BAe as a corporate parent was both unable and unwilling to provide. Whilst BMW had spotted this opportunity, it would appear that Honda had not. In that respect BMW had been good at monitoring the availability of acquisitions and had been skilful in pre-empting any bid by Honda.

This account is a summary of industry commentary at the time.

BMW offers Rover a new home

With £800m on the table from BMW, it took the BAe board less than five hours to decide that it would exit the car industry and put an end to its five-year relationship with Honda.

Mr George Simpson, Rover's chairman and the man who believed the relationship with Honda to be 'the natural path', was told by BAe to take the next flight to Tokyo to face a company which had thought its offer was a *fait accompli*. Six days earlier Honda had agreed to increase its stake from 20 to 47.5 per cent, pumping £165m into BAe and valuing Rover at £600m – 40 per cent less than the eventual winner.

Honda had started from a seemingly unassailable position, given its 20 per cent stake and its 14-year relationship with Rover. But ultimately, it was BAe's desire to find an exit from its five-year-old investment that proved the key.

BMW had done a thorough job in stalking Rover: BMW had identified Rover in September 1993 as a target that would extend its car range and achieve economies of scale in distribution, component sourcing and R&D.

Its initial offer to BAe was repulsed because of Rover's relationship with Honda. Dr Hagen Luderitz, director of corporate planning at BMW, said that BMW delivered a letter to Honda chief executive Mr Nobuhiko Kawamoto, stating its interest in Rover. Strangely, no response was received.

Mr Kiyoshi Ikemi, counsellor to Honda's president, denied any direct approach, claiming Honda received only indirect hints of BMW's intentions. 'We weren't informed properly until Friday last week', he protested.

By that time BMW had performed detailed operations due diligence on Rover: unperturbed by the original rebuff, BMW went ahead with its scrutiny of Rover. Mr Wolfgang Reitzle, BMW's research and development director, visited the UK plants and test drove the entire fleet. After two months, he decided that BMW had enough support to make a bid.

After BMW entered the competition, Honda responded rapidly. Having been informed of BMW's interest in Rover, Honda was under pressure. 'If we took a larger percentage, BAe said it would be a clear signal that the rest of the company was not for sale,' said Mr Ikemi.

On January 21, Honda agreed to increase its stake to 47.5 per cent. This offer was also before the BAe board on the Thursday morning.

But BMW increased its offer to what was felt would be a knock-out blow, but it was a fierce race to the finish. Mr Luderitz admitted that the speed of the deal limited BMW's ability to perform due diligence, although he was confident the synergies with BMW justified the £800m price tag – valuing Rover at £1 billion. He delivered the formal offer personally on January 26.

At 9.15 on the following morning, the BAe board of directors made their decision. Before them was the prospect of selling a business which was seen as non-core and required substantial capital injection. The BMW offer had a deadline of midnight the previous night. The BAe board decided it wanted out – and Mr Simpson travelled to Tokyo to see if Honda would make a better offer, thus playing off both potential acquirers against each other. Honda decided that it didn't want full control (at a price which beat the BMW offer).

According to commentary at the time, Honda's president Nobuhiko Kawamoto was visibly startled by BMW's revised bid. He protested, insisting that BAe had already agreed to sell Honda an additional 27.5 per cent stake in the Rover operating company, lifting its total to 47.5 per cent, and that they had a 'done deal'.

Simpson explained that he was sorry, but Western businesses had to deal with issues such as stakeholder value, and in that context it was extremely difficult to evaluate things like a 15-year partnership and moral commitments. When the sums were done the bird in the hand – the £800m – was worth much more than what Honda had offered.

Mr Kawamoto telephoned George Simpson at his hotel two hours later to say that there would be no deal on that basis.

When BMW originally began talks with Rover it offered around £550m (*Sunday Times*, 6 February 1994). But this figure was considerably less than Rover's book value of nearly £1.3 billion. Initially BMW made formal suggestions to Honda to co-operate in a Rover-BMW deal that would preserve the Honda-Rover link by direct association with BMW thus mixing a acquisition with a continued alliance. According to the *Sunday Times* (6 February 1994), Mr Kawamoto didn't reply to this proposal.

Honda's offer of £167m to move its stake from 20 per cent to 47.5 per cent valued Rover group at about £650m. This was beaten on two counts by a BMW offer in January 1994 of around £700m (for total control).

Then, on 16 January 1994, two Rover senior managers flew to Munich to meet BMW to enable BMW to make a full bid for the whole of Rover – for Rover's holding company (and not just the subsidiary, in which Honda had a 20 per cent stake). It was at this point that BMW went for the knock-out punch.

When the offer finally arrived at BAe's London office – at 5pm on Wednesday, 26 January – it had now been increased to £800m, but after 1 February the bid would be withdrawn.

The core bid value of £800m looked generous when stacked up against Rover's recent profits track record of pre-tax losses in 1991 and 1992 of around £50m, and a pre-tax profit of merely £50m in 1993. A price tag of £800m indicated that BMW saw considerable incremental strategic (and ultimately) financial benefits flowing through from Rover. These benefits can be seen (with hindsight) to have been elusive.

Even though BMW had out-manoeuvred Honda it still had another hurdle to jump. George Simpson and Bernt Pischetsrieder, BMW's chief executive, both saw Tim Sainsbury, the UK industry minister, to press their case. Tim Sainsbury was persuaded on the argument that Rover would be unattractive to private shareholders with the continuing involvement of a minority shareholder Honda, which had control of Rover's engine technology. (This is an interesting example of a strength in one argument being turned during the deal-making process into a weakness in another, to positive advantage.)

That BAe got a good price for Rover Group is undeniable. The *Sunday Times* (8 August 1993) foresaw (based on informed industry comment) that Rover would be sold for £400–500m plus debt, just over half the BMW price tag.

The case study on BMW's deal process in buying Rover highlights a number of key lessons:

■ The would-be acquirer needs to monitor potential acquisition targets continuously, not merely in terms of their performance and potential, but also in terms of the likely enthusiasm and pressure for sale. BMW achieved this very well, but Honda not so well.

■ There is an inevitable trade-off between the need to conduct thorough operational due diligence and the need to head off competing bids. Nevertheless, the rush to close the deal may not allow for sufficient reflection and dispassionate critique of the target so that an inappropriate deal is struck.

■ When there is competition in the frame, it is very easy to over-pay for the deal. Whilst a price tag of £800m on profits of £50m does not seem extravagant (in price–earnings ratio terms), if the deal were looked at in more prudent cash flow terms, the huge underlying investment need of

Rover would have made it very hard indeed to justify a positive NPV of this order.

■ Where competition exists it is essential to perform scenarios for the deal-making process of 'if we make move X, will they make a move Y, and do we then make move Z', and so on.

Post-acquisition integration – and learning

The integration process

The integration phase is one where value is often diluted or destroyed rather than created, and this requires further strategic thinking. This may be due to a variety of reasons, for instance:

■ Integration plans may be left to emerge and, if deliberate, are inadequately thought through to deal with obstacles to change.

■ There may be an abrupt change in management style, leading to lower morale and business performance rather than improved performance.

■ There may be no real change in the management when one is badly needed, leading to drift (as at Rover during 1995–1996).

■ The acquisition period itself is a distracting time for incumbent management. There may be a period of months or longer when new developments are deferred, costs are unwisely cut. During this period the normal attention to customer delivery may be lost.

■ New management might impose its own way of doing things and thus damage the acquisition's competitive strength. (At Rover Group BMW imposed its own notion of what 'Britishness' was about, mispositioning the brand.)

■ Key staff may leave, feeling (rightly or wrongly) that their career prospects are blunted.

The integration phase is important too as it is during this period when the acquirer has most opportunity to learn from the acquisition. This learning should obviously deal with the post-acquisition performance of the acquisition – financially and strategically. But it should also cover the acquisition process itself. A central question is how difficult and speedily did we integrate the acquisition relative to our expectations?

In this section the reasons why integration strategies may fail and succeed, are examined, along with the pros and cons of different acquisition integration styles. The need to maintain business continuity is then addressed. This leads on to the need to project-manage integration and the associated organizational issues. The need to monitor and learn from performance is then highlighted, and the links to post-acquisition learning and review.

Why they succeed or fail

Acquisition integration can fail for a large number of reasons. Figure 10.9 captures these reasons as a fishbone analysis. Using the fishbone, the key symptom of the problem is shown at the right hand side of the page – at the fish's head. The underlying root causes of the problem are depicted as the bones of the fishbone. (Note there is no special order to the fishbone analysis display.)

FIGURE 10.9: A fishbone analysis of failures in acquisition integration

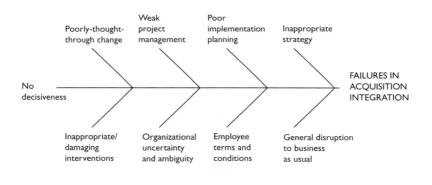

Figure 10.9 highlights some of the main reasons for failure. These range from there not being an effective and robust strategy in the very first place through to inadequate integration planning and project management and inappropriate organizational change. Typically, unsuccessful integration processes are characterized by a lack of decisiveness on the part of the acquiring management team or through inappropriate and damaging interventions.

After deciding 'who does what' in the new organization, the second most difficult stumbling block is likely to be around employee terms and conditions. Unilateral changes to salary structures and to benefits in kind just after the acquisition are likely to trigger significant disruption in the organizational process.

It is useful to examine (at a more positive level) what factors would need to line up to deliver a particularly effective implementation process. This is depicted in figure 10.10 (using wishbone analysis) Notice that while some of these alignment factors are reversals of the fishbone analysis, some of them are now, and all of them are not in any way average, but more superior or visionary.

FIGURE 10.10: A wishbone analysis of successes in acquisition integration

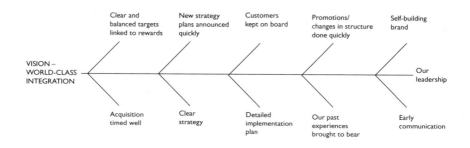

Figure 10.10 thus emphasizes the importance of having a best-in-class integrative process, with scenario story-telling, excellent integration project management, and a balanced set of performance measures.

Integration strategies – the pros and cons

Integration strategies can range along a continuum, from:

- leave alone
- to putting managers in to complement
- and to installing a new management team.

There are obviously choices too as to the speed of the intervention. Changes can be implemented immediately, or after a period of say six to nine months, or perhaps after around 18 months.

Whilst there can be no hard and fast rules of how to approach these changes the following recipes are well worth remembering:

- if you think you are going to need to make changes, do this as soon as possible – do not procrastinate
- the decision as to what extent you do need to make changes depend very much on:

- current management's strengths and weaknesses
- flexibility (or lack of it) of current management's mindset
- the requirements of the future business strategy and its associated competitive challenges
■ the value which you feel you can add to the acquisition, and your own team's existing competences
■ the amount of available management skills which you have, and the opportunity cost of deploying them on this particular acquisition.

The above points need some further expansion and qualification as follows. First, the most important consideration ought to be the current skills gaps of existing management and the future requirements. If these fall significantly short of needs it is not a good idea at all to action putting in additional management skills.

If you do not feel a need to inject fresh management skills at all this might raise a question over the acquisition logic anyway – if you are not going to make changes to develop the organization's capability, what value (V3) are you actually adding?

Often a leave alone or wait-and-see approach may lead to disappointing post-acquisition performance.

When you are going to make major changes another useful recipe is: 'Once you have made all of the changes which you propose to make, tell them you have finished'.

Unless you do this then organizational morale can easily go into a downward spiral. This can be represented in figure 10.11 where morale over time is plotted against organizational performance over time.

FIGURE 10.11: Integration dynamics

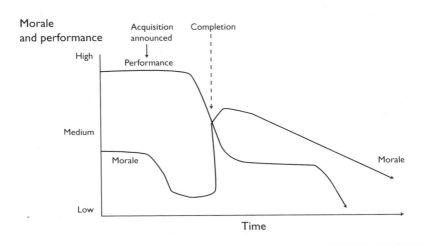

Ironically, whilst acquisitions are bought ostensibly in order to generate increased performance, in the short run this performance typically declines – due to organizational fear. Where an experienced acquirer is involved the opposite effect is frequently created: the integration situation gives management a new clarity and sense of challenge. The conglomerate Hanson plc's integration strategy was very much along these lines: here, newly promoted middle managers had a real appetite for delivery results, freed of the limiting mindset of previous senior managers.

Besides management changes (and associated structures) the second most important and difficult area to manage is the issue of routines, processes and procedures. For although there may seem less crucial they form an integral part of the culture of the organization. Even more changes to these can irritate and alienate current staff, especially if new processes are perceived to be inferior to the old.

A sensible idea is to define best practices for the new organization based on the best of the acquired business and the acquirer – and on best practices generally.

During the integration phase it is imperative to establish a detailed communication plan to deal with the expectations of key stakeholders.

Government and regulatory stakeholders can also be important as the following example at BMW/Rover highlights:

CASE STUDY: BMW SUFFERS AMNESIA – AND FORGETS THE BRITISH GOVERNMENT

In early 2000 BMW finally succumbed to the costs of post-acquisition losses at Rover Group. Approached by a venture capital firm Alchemy, BMW agreed a deal to dispose of Rover's loss making business – with major sweeteners as a pay-off. (The four-wheel-drive business was to be sold to Ford).

Whether by design or by accident BMW omitted to tell the British government of its plan. When the news was broken on television the Labour Government was absolutely livid that they had been kept in the dark over this deal. UK television was dominated by the news for 48 hours afterwards.

The UK Government had just cause to be angry as they had provided significant investment grants to BMW Rover to help fund new model launches.

The cost of the proposed deal with Alchemy was that BMW fell out of favour with the Government, sales of BMWs fell in the UK (BMW's number one export market) and BMW had to pay Alchemy compensation for switching the sale to rival bidders Phoenix.

To establish a full communication plan you will need to think through the following:

- customer communication, including:
  - telephone calls (preferably)
  - follow-up letters
  - selected meetings (very soon indeed after completion)
- supplier communication (as above)
- distributors (as above)
- management and staff:
  - letter (of the initial announcement)
  - meetings/presentations (in the first week post-completion)
  - individual interviews/meetings (within the first few weeks following completion)
- Government and regulating authorities:
  - selective communication, dependent upon potential impact.

You can see from the above that there is a great deal of work to do in the intermediate period following completion. This is likely to come very soon after the equally busy period of the negotiations. Management attention and effort can droop in the early post-acquisition phase and begin to destroy V3.

Post-acquisition learning and review

Most of the techniques for post-acquisition learning and review are now in place. One can now readily re-appraise the acquisition by examining a number of issues in the following exercise.

EXERCISE: ACQUISITION LEARNING CHECKLISTS

- The integration projects – were these as attractive and as easy as was assumed?
- Were interdependencies managed as well as they needed to be?
- Did new, external brakes on performance crystallize, and what was their impact?
- Were internal performance drivers managed as well as was hoped for, and did new internal brakes on performance materialize?
- Why did specific performance problems occur? (Fishbone analysis.)
- Were all the critical assumptions about the whole acquisition integration identified, and did we understand their importance/degree of uncertainty?
- What are customer or staff perceptions of the appropriateness of integration strategies or tactics and are these perceptions adverse or have deteriorated, and if so, why was this? (Fishbone analysis.)

EXERCISE: ACQUISITION LEARNING CHECKLISTS continued

More specifically (and based on lessons from acquisition lessons in from similar reviews of acquisition integration elsewhere), the following key questions can home in on some likely generic areas of difficulty or blockage:

- Was brand strategy (post integration) appropriate?
- Was the quality of target's management as good as what we thought?
- Did the changes to key individuals in the management team work and well, and if not, why not?
- Did we really understand pending competitive shifts in the environment?
- Were our assumptions about life-cycle effects impacting on the acquisition's product range valid – and also their competition strengths and weaknesses?
- Were assumed investment levels to deliver V3 adequate or not?
- Did we lose key personnel by mishandling the softer issues (for example, restructuring, management development, remuneration, perks, etc.)?
- Did we intervene inappropriately in operational practices – causing unnecessary disruption?
- Were we really clever in defining our integration strategy and integration projects or did these change considerably in scope and difficulty over the first 18 months?
- Did we devote enough time and attention to managing the acquisition integration?
- Finally, what lessons can we draw from this for integrating any future acquisitions?

The following checklists now take you through each of the key stages of acquisition:

Setting strategy and objectives

Many acquisitions lack a robust strategy. To avoid this please ask the following:

- What is our own strategic position (i.e. of the acquirer), and is it strong, average or weak?
- What strategic options (generally) for strategic development – alongside and including acquisition – do we have (including organic development, alliance, or buying-in the relevant skills directly)?
- Do we have the natural capabilities to screen and evaluate acquisitions (without getting carried away with the 'thrill of the chase') and also to negotiate a favourable deal and to integrate it effectively?
- Is this a good time for us to be thinking about acquisitions (for example in terms of the economic cycle, competitive conditions and those of financial markets generally)?
- More specifically, what are our most important objectives for an acquisition project, and are these good or bad?

    'Good reasons' for making an acquisition might include:

    - increasing our own shareholder value so we can add tangible value to the acquired business
    - to acquire scarce capabilities (for example management or technical skills) that we can apply elsewhere
    - to build our own competitive advantage.

EXERCISE: ACQUISITION LEARNING CHECKLISTS continued

'Bad reasons' for an acquisition project might include:

- to grow the business (as an end in itself)
- to enhance our own, personal careers
- because we feel threatened by increased competition
- because others are doing it, and we might get left behind.

■ How will this phase be project-managed?

Acquisition evaluation

Acquisition due diligence is often biased towards internal appraisal. To counter this please ask the following questions:

■ How inherently attractive are the markets which our target is on (consider its growth drivers and the level of competitive pressure)?

■ What is our target's underlying competitive position, and is it okay, average or weak?

■ What is the basis of its competitive advantage, and is this likely to be sustainable given anticipated market and competitive change?

■ How does it add distinctive value to its customers (if at all) and, if so, how does it capture this in the form of financial (and thus shareholder) value?

■ How competitive is its cost base (and as against existing players and new entrants and/or distribution channels)?

■ Are any of its products or markets moving into maturity or decline (life-cycle effects)?

■ What is the strength of its management?

■ How vulnerable is it likely to be to key staff leaving?

■ Given our integration plans, how difficult (and uncertain) is integration likely to be?

■ Where does the business currently make most/least money, and where does it destroy shareholder value (at the present time)?

■ Where is the business likely to make most/least money in the future?

■ What can we (genuinely) bring to the party in the way of value-added to the acquisition?

■ How will this phase be project-managed?

Negotiating the deal

The deal is the most important phase of the project – and one which may be poorly handled by the inexperience. Consider the following:

■ Do we have a strong and experienced acquisition team – especially in terms of due diligence skills and negotiation skills?

■ Will the team work well with each other – and avoid getting carried away with the 'thrill of the chase'?

■ What competition might exist for the deal, and is this likely to push up the price to a level at which we become indifferent as to whether to go ahead or not with the deal?

■ What is the relative balance in the bargaining power between buyer and seller – what is the relative pressure to buy or sell, and who has the most options?

■ How skilled is the vendor's team in negotiating – and where are their likely vulnerabilities and weaknesses?

EXERCISE: ACQUISITION LEARNING CHECKLISTS continued

- Are we absolutely clear as to what we are bringing to the party versus what value is already inherent in the acquisition (so we avoid, in effect, paying twice)?
- Are there in-built check-points within the deal-making process for whether we carry on or not?
- Who will have the ultimate say over what we are prepared to offer?

Integration

Integration is an activity where project management will pay off in a very big way. If it is not project-managed then acquisition value will almost invariably be destroyed. Please consider the following questions:

- What key synergies are anticipated to be harvested through the acquisition?
- What changes are required in order to achieve these synergies – to products, services, operations, systems and processes, structures and people?
- Who are the key people who are essential both to protect and develop the business?
- How can they be convinced that it is worth backing the organization follow-ing this period of pronounced uncertainty associated with the acquisition, for example through:
  - selling the benefits of the acquisition in terms of future opportunity for their own development and reward
  - providing them with a clear role in integration and further development;
  - spelling out openly the criteria for success and failure
  - protecting their self-respect through active incorporation of 'core best practices' into a new paradigm
  - having a clear and well communicated strategy for steering change?
- Is it planned to announce changes in leadership and structure quickly as opposed to playing a 'wait-and-see' game with the result of mounting uncertainty?
- Will changes in systems and control routines be handled with delicacy and sensitivity, and will sensible timescales be set to make changes? Where sys-tems and control changes are required from 'day one' are there arrangements to support this externally?
- How will the issue of any culture change be handled, especially where it is intended to integrate a large part of operations? Does this reflect any pre-acquisition diagnosis of the key differences in culture between both organizations?
- How will learning about the acquisition be secured in terms both of 'what we have got for our money' (both internal and eternal capability) and also on the effectiveness of integration process?
- How will the phase of integration be project-managed as a whole?

Conclusion

Acquisitions are frequently difficult, risky and political decisions which often go wrong because of an absence of, or because of inappropriate, strategic thinking. This chapter gives you an applied and tailored process for avoiding major strategic and financial catastrophes in managing acquisitions – from idea through to implementation.

Key points

The following are important key points from this chapter:

- acquisitions are a classic example of how managers can destroy value through not thinking strategically
- many of the techniques which we have seen elsewhere in the book (like the strategic option grid, the uncertainty grid, fishbone and wishbone analysis) are equally applicable
- strategic thinking helps the financial evaluation and the implementation process – and deal-making scenarios
- using an adapted form of Porter's five competitive forces helps understand any potential for over-payment
- the BMW and Rover case is a classic example of what can happen when strategic thinking is not applied rigorously – especially in destroying shareholder value.

References

Ansoff, H.I., *Corporate Strategy*, McGraw-Hill, New York, 1965.

Copeland, T., T. Koller, J. Murrin, *Valuation: Measuring and Managing the Value of Companies*, New York, J. Wiley, 1990.

Grundy, A.N., *Breakthrough Strategies for Growth*, Pitman Publishing, London, 1995.

— *Exploring Strategic Financial Management*, Prentice Hall, London, 1998.

Jemison, D.B. and S.B. Sitkin, 'Acquisitions: The Process Can Be A Problem', *Harvard Business Review*, March–April 1986, p.p. 107–16.

McTaggart, J.M., P.W. Kontes and M.C. Mankins, *The Value Imperative*, Free Press, Macmillan, New York, 1994.

Mintzberg, H., *The Rise and Fall of Strategic Planning*, London, Prentice Hall, 1994.

Ohmae, K., *The Mind of the Strategist*, McGraw-Hill, New York, 1982.

Porter, E.M., *Competitive Strategy*, Free Press, MacMillan, New York, 1980.

— 'From Competitive Advantage to Corporate Strategy', *Harvard Business Review*, May–June 1987, p.p.43–59.

Rappaport, A., *Creating Shareholder Value*, Free Press, MacMillan, New York, 1986.

Stewart, G.B., *The Quest for Value*, Harperbusiness, New York, 1991.

PART FOUR

Strategy in practice

CHAPTER ELEVEN

Strategic behaviour and the strategy process

Introduction

Name one company not facing considerably more external and internal change than it was 10 or 15 years ago. You will no doubt struggle to do this.

The brutal reality is that managers are facing increasing levels of change while also coping with increased complexity and, frequently, reduced levels of resources. Primarily tactical styles of managing are now outmoded and companies are awakening to the imperative to think – and act – strategically. Still, however, they find themselves held back by the quagmire of organizational politics.

Strategic management has become an expectation, not only on the part of the company but also the individual, who often feels as if they are clinging to a fragile and precarious management structure. At any moment, the fact that their own roles can disappear into an organizational black hole generates a good deal of defensive, political behaviour. This in turn drives out strategic thinking, as we saw in chapters 6 and 7 on The Value of Strategic Thinking.

That same behaviour also undermines the capacity of the organization to behave strategically. Thus, there is frequently a huge gap between the expectation that managers should manage strategically and the reality. Although managers know they are expected to act strategically, they frequently don't know what this entails – in short how to do it, and especially to behave strategically. This is not merely a case of lacking the necessary strategic thinking skills but is more fundamental as it requires ability to manage strategic behaviour and the wider strategic process.

To illustrate why we believe strategic management is much more than a matter of strategic thinking skills, consider an example from our own experience of a strategic thinking programme for a major technology group. This involved working with 40 senior managers to give them the necessary skills to put flesh on the strategy being developed at board level, and to prepare them for its implementation. After one of the workshops, one of the writers was given an off-the-record debrief by the human resources director about a particular senior director:

> You wouldn't believe it. After the programme, Sam (director of X Division), who was on the programme, came up to me and said, 'I want to do an MBA'. He was the last person in the company I thought would say that. He is just purely tactical.
>
> You know, there is more strategic thinking and behaviour in the average gerbil than he could ever have – with or without an MBA, but I'm sorry, that might be an insult to those furry creatures.

At the time one of the writers felt conflicting things about what was said:

- He felt sorry that a senior manager had shown enthusiasm for strategic thinking, but was regarded as inherently lacking competence in that area.
- He wondered whether or not the director was right – Sam was never going to be a brilliant strategic thinker, but this did not prevent him from achieving reasonable competence in that area; actually he was a bright manager.
- Maybe the biggest constraint Sam faced was the way in which his behaviour was constrained by that of the top team of which he was a member, and the behaviour of the wider organization, especially that which was political in nature.

So, if there was a strategic disability here, it was certainly not just down to Sam. This was not simply a case of a specific individual developing corporate strategic thinking in a relative vacuum. No, the main blockage appeared to be a behavioural one, and not just some impairment in individuals' management skills. In short, the problem was one of how the managers behaved strategically.

Sam is not an isolated case by any means. In fact, he is typical of many thousands of extremely well-paid, but occasionally very stretched, senior executives. Whenever we have worked in senior teams to facilitate strategic thinking, this impression is consistently reinforced: behavioural issues are both the most important and frequently the most difficult to overcome when trying to manage a team or an organization more strategically. Truly strategic behaviour seems to be an absolutely central part of the critical path in turning strategic thoughts into organizational reality.

Let us define 'strategic behaviour' as being the cognitive, emotional and territorial interplay of managers engaging in strategic thinking.

Mere 'behaviour' has been expanded here to encompass 'the cognitive, emotional and territorial interplay' of managers. This stresses that there are several factors at work here and that these are extremely closely interwoven. These interrelationships between cognition, feelings and territorial interplay are appropriately called 'the behavioural cocktail'.

So, if we now take it as read that strategic behaviour is the behavioural context for strategic thinking, why is it important?

Strategic behaviour is important in shaping strategic thinking and in turning it into a reality for the following ten key reasons:

- Informal decision-making. Too frequently, one (or more) manager is more vocal and dominant in a team than the others, resulting in the arguments and concerns of other members being marginalized or in them not even being expressed at all. This creates an unbalanced political climate within the team. Where strategic behaviour is managed well, then there should be a more favourable climate for well-focused strategic thinking which results in more informed and appropriate decision-making.

- Speed of decision-making. Relatively turbulent strategic behaviour is very likely to slow, or even halt, the progress of decision-making in a team. This produces a backlog of undigested strategic ideas. This also reduces the strategic responsiveness of the team, which has a knock-on negative effect on the responsiveness of the rest of the organization. It also gives an opportunity for the wrong kind of organizational politics to thrive.

- Decisions are actually made, not deferred. One of the biggest problems in senior management teams is that of actually coming to a decision, even once the strategic issues have been thoroughly explored. This was described graphically by the head of strategy of a well-known financial services group:

  When our management team gets together it is just like Heathrow. More and more aircraft [strategic issues] are coming in and the air traffic controllers seem to have given up. They just get stacked up and nothing ever seems to be landing.

- Creativity is encouraged. Where a team's strategic behaviour is more consciously orchestrated, there is perhaps a greater chance of its full creativity being harnessed. This applies both when a team is full of very creative individuals and when it is relatively deficient in that vital, creative spark. This helps avoid strategic thinking being purely analytical in style.

- Discussing the undiscussible. Many management teams find certain issues particularly difficult to deal with. These may be associated with strategic projects or programmes that are drifting or appear likely to fail. As soon as this occurs, the ripples of organizational politics begin to spread, building one on the other until they become waves. Where a team finds it hard to harness its strategic behaviour, these kinds of issues are likely to remain in the realm of the undiscussible. Unless this zone of debate is opened up strategic thinking will remain at best only partly effective. Thus strategic behaviour here influences the quality of strategic thinking.

- Mental maps are enriched. Managers in established teams sometimes tend to assume that everyone in the team sees the world in more or less the same way. The reality is, however, that, even in a mature team, they often do not. Managers may need to work hard in their interactive behaviour to explicitly share and compare their mental maps. Otherwise, they are likely to run into unduly (and often unnecessarily turbulent) strategic behaviour. Much of what we know as organizational politics is probably caused by mental maps being only partially exposed, thus generating either artificial or exaggerated areas of disagreement. Interestingly, more open strategic thinking thus leads to more harmonious strategic behaviour.

- Frustration is avoided and energy accumulated. In a management team facing many intractable strategic issues, and where team behaviour is not really under control, frustration can mount and mount. This frustration can be cognitive, emotional, political, and even personal. Energy then dissipates as problems are not solved, everything appears to take two or three times as long as it should and, very quickly, in these circumstances the team's behaviour becomes fractious. However, where the team can helicopter out of its behavioural difficulties, this can resolve the more business-related complexities and dilemmas. Where frustration builds unduly, top managers may be inclined (in their desperation) to 'drive through' strategies, which may short-circuit true strategic thinking. This sets up waves of (political) resistance, some of which could be avoided.

- Team commitment is increased. Even a relatively strong and open team may struggle when it has to deal with painful options, such as putting a major project on hold, refocusing activities or embarking on a significant downsizing. By being able to steer around the more awkward behavioural blockages, these decisions can be made not only with less difficulty but also with a better balance of evidence and judgement.

- Creating a platform for influencing. Many business teams find that they need to influence thinking and feeling about strategic issues elsewhere in the organization. Unless the team's own strategic behaviour is well-aligned internally, it may prove difficult for the team to exert its influence in the rest of the organization. In such instances, being able to harmonize its own internal strategic behaviour may reduce the political disadvantages of a department or business unit relative to its organizational peers.

- Internal politics are channelled more effectively. Although every team has to deal with its fair share of internal politics, if unchecked, political activity can debilitate it severely. As will be seen later in the book, many of the dysfunctional aspects of internal politics can be channelled into a more constructive debate.

EXERCISE: DIAGNOSING STRATEGIC BEHAVIOUR IN YOUR OWN ORGANIZATION

- To what extent is strategic behaviour not harmonious in your organization?
- Where this behaviour is not harmonious, why is this the case? (Please do a fishbone analysis.)
- What are the adverse consequences of this behaviour not being harmonious?
- What are the direct and indirect costs?

EXERCISE: REFLECTING ON STRATEGIC BEHAVIOUR IN YOUR OWN ORGANIZATION

To what extent are strategic decisions made in your organization:

- Primarily based on their inherent strategic logic, or the say-so of one or more dominant individuals?
- Made in such a way that it is clear when they were actually made (and by whom) rather than ambiguous?
- Made on a basis of an understanding of the existing situation rather than by creatively exploring the ideal situation?
- Communicated only in terms of the content of the decision as opposed to its rationale?

So, where does strategic behaviour fit into the strategy process? A particularly good way of picturing the strategic mountain is shown in figure 11.1 – the pyramid of strategic thinking. This shows the key pre-conditions of getting the value out of strategic thinking (like a kind of Egyptian wishbone analysis).

The base of the strategic thinking pyramid is made up of strategic analysis (including SWOT analysis, the five competitive forces and other techniques). Frequently managers and students of management alike (maybe 50 per cent) fail to ask themselves the 'so-what?' question, which is the next level of the pyramid.

FIGURE 11.1: The strategic thinking pyramid

Then, perhaps, another 50 per cent of the remainder fail to generate some truly radical and creative strategic options. As we have already seen (in chapter 4) these strategic options should include not only:

- the 'what' – strategic positioning externally
- but the 'how' – the implementation strategy.

The next level up from that of options is vision. Perhaps another 50 per cent of managers are too shy to really distil their strategies into a singular picture or message. Finally, perhaps another 50 per cent of those left still fail to translate this into clear action plans, and perhaps a 50 per cent of these fail to adopt strategic behaviour. So, in summary, our overall success rate could be:

Success rate = 50% (so-what) x 50% (options) x 50% (vision) x 50% (action plans) x 50% (behaviour) = 3.1%!

Arguably, the behavioural apex of the strategic pyramid is the zone which it is hardest to get right. This filter can finally kill off what remains of the value of strategic thinking delivered to that point. Let us look at this a little more closely with a very quick review of what has previously been said about the role of strategic behaviour in the strategic process generally.

EXERCISE: DIAGNOSING YOUR OWN STRATEGIC THINKING PYRAMID

Using the strategic thinking pyramid, what does this reveal about strengths and weaknesses and any major gaps in your strategic management process:

- Where are the biggest gaps?
- What is the 'so-what?' from this?

As we have seen, although much has been written about strategic decision-making, relatively little focuses on strategic behaviour specifically. For example, Johnson (1986, p59) says:

> It is perhaps surprising that…there are so few systematic studies of *the way in which the interaction of individuals* contributes to strategic decision-making. [Our italics]

Much of the previous thinking on how managers actually make strategic decisions is concerned with attacking rational and analytical models of strategy rather than actively creating new frameworks for understanding strategic behaviour. For instance, Mintzberg (1994) criticized the process of 'strategic planning' and the 'design school of strategic management' that promotes the development of strategy as an analytical process as simply not being what managers actually do. Strategic planning is also thought by some to be of very limited utility because of the sheer uncertainty generated by fluctuating economic and market demands, competitive activity and organizational change. This acute uncertainty crystallizes in chaos (Stacey, 1993). Most managers will recognize the havoc caused by uncertainty and chaos, but at the same time would clearly like to avoid seeing chaos as being inevitable.

Whilst accepting that Mintzberg has an obvious point, pushing it far is akin to criticizing the Drivers Highway Code for being unrealistic and unhelpful because most drivers break the speed limits, fail to signal properly on occasion, and frequently go through traffic lights on amber. What would it be like for a day if everyone actually behaved according to the Highway Code? Perhaps we would all get there quicker, safer and happier.

Other major strategic writers have experimented with the idea of strategic behaviour, but only in a relatively limited way. Ansoff (1987) describes how paradigms (how the organization unconsciously behaves and reacts to things) determine how organizations adapt to crisis in terms of their reactive behaviour. Sadly, however, at no point does Ansoff actually define strategic behaviour. Also, Dixit and Nalib's book (1991) asks in the opening chapter, 'What is strategic behaviour?' but then, unfortunately, does not actually define it. Strangely, managers themselves recognize it immediately. One wonders then, 'is strategic behaviour self-evident?' – certainly for us it warrants both definition and deeper understanding and how it drives strategic decision-making.

We have already defined it ourselves so we should now look at its impact on strategic decision-making.

In the following section we do take a little time reflecting on what has been said before by strategic management writers. Hopefully this will not be too onerous for management readers – we will touch lightly on their most important ideas.

Strategic decision-making

Many managers have a somewhat schizophrenic view of decision-making. On the one hand they see the ideal process in very rational terms – there needs to be a careful weighing up of alternatives prior to making a strategic choice, and then the whole must be dealt with rather than merely a part of the issues. However, actual experience is one of decisions made reactively in response to pressures and constraints. These pressures and constraints are frequently handled by compromise or by deciding to deal with only part of the issues or by simply delaying the decision.

So, there is a very great tension between the rational model of strategic decision-making and managers' everyday experiences. The rational model is a set piece approach to dealing with the fundamental messiness of strategic issues. However, before we throw it out as being unrealistic, let us first examine what it suggests, so that we can distil what is good about a rational perspective. Figure 11.2 explores how the key model assumes a deliberate and linear progression from thought to action, strategic decisions being the filter of strategic options and strategic resources being absorbed in the process.

FIGURE 11.2: Rational strategic thinking

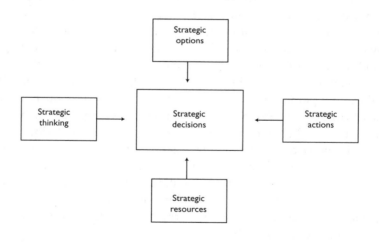

However, as earlier discussions have highlighted, strategic decision-making is, at best, a part rational, unpredictable, fluid and haphazard process. Some decades ago, Cyert and March (1963) called this 'satisificing'

behaviour (to draw attention to managers' tendencies to avoid the worst outcomes rather than seek the best outcomes). In everyday terms, we might call this avoiding cock-ups.

Cyert and March also suggested that management decision-making is effectively 'bounded rationality' – in bounded rationality some strategic issues were dealt with rationally while others not. Indeed, Cyert and March described the decision-making process more colourfully as 'the garbage can model' (Cohen, March and Olsen, 1972). Another writer, Brunsson (1982), went even further, suggesting that apparently 'irrational' decision-making procedures play a key role in shaping actual decisions. It would seem from this that the main influences on decision-making are non-rational (and may therefore be primarily rooted in the emotional and subjective) with an occasional glimmer of rationality creeping in. Many managers – and not necessarily pure cynics – might recognize that their own organizations are primarily governed by non-rationality and subject to only the occasional constraint of being rational.

Brunsson now helps us to understand the strategic decision-making process:

> Some actions are not preceded by weighing of (strategic) alternatives, evaluating alternatives or choosing.

Brunsson achieves a considerable understatement here. As management consultants we have often been asked to introduce the most basic of decision-making methods into senior teams (such as the AID grid – see chapter 5). Sometimes it is not at all easy even to define decisions as Mintzberg suggested because of the fluidity of the decision-making process. It may not even be fruitful to study 'decisions', as they are actually so hard to locate. As Mintzberg (1978) says:

> It occurred to us that we were in fact not studying streams of decisions at all, but actions, because those are the traces actually left behind at organizations.

This suggests once again the need, perhaps, to shift out concerns from strategic decision-making to understanding and managing strategic behaviour. However, if the situation managers face in strategic decision-making already seems hopeless, now let us throw in the additional problem of incrementalism (Braybrooke and Lindblom, 1963).

Incrementalism has been described as being 'the science of muddling through' or of dealing with one problem at a time, even though these problems are inextricably linked. Quinn (1980) highlighted how strategies tend to evolve in disordered steps that build on (and sometimes detract from) each other. These steps are frequently made without holistic pre-design. So, not only do we have partially formed, loosely defined and partly rational strategic decisions, they are also disjointed. They do not come together over a period of time to generate a coherent strategic vision, but represent many substrategies that are being pursued. Those substrategies are sometimes in conflict with each other, producing a state of 'stratophrenia' in managers (defined as being the confusion that occurs when two or more opposing strategies are pursued simultaneously).

Besides the problems of disjointedness in strategic decisions, we also have the final problem – that strategic decisions are often weakly implemented (which one could call the 'wimp' syndrome, standing for weak implementation). The problem of weak implementation is well documented. For example, Butler writes (in Hickson *et al*, 1986, p12):

> An interesting question is why some decisions achieve a greater degree of implementation than others... [perhaps] the original intention was only weakly implemented [or the gap] could arise when the implementation was of a completely different substance from the original intention.

In other words, implementation bears an almost accidental relationship to the original strategic decision (or, if a strategic decision is actually implemented, it might be because it is a fluke).

The strategic decision literature therefore suggests that it is the fluidity and disjointedness within the strategic decision-making process that makes it so hard to gain real clarity in strategic thinking and equally focused action. This underscores the need to explore how strategic behaviour can be harnessed more effectively to stabilize and direct the strategic decision-making process.

In summary, then, strategic decision-making:

- is at best, a partly rational process
- is frequently based on avoiding worst, rather than seeking best, outcomes
- entails carefully weighing decision alternatives in a systematic fashion only in exceptional cases
- often occurs as a continuous stream of discussion, without producing specific, tangible decisions
- generates strategy incrementally, rather than as an holistic pattern
- is frequently weakly implemented.

How does this stack up against the results of your second reader exercise in this chapter, which reflected on the style of strategic decision-making (and behaviour) in your organization?

Taking this further, figure 11.3 now shows a momentum-driven model of the linkages between strategy and action. It depicts external and internal events influencing strategic behaviour as a dynamic process. These events crystallize strategic action. Notice that also included is a zone of strategic inaction. Strategic inaction is not necessarily a weakness in the process – it allows management the space to do further strategic reflecting.

FIGURE 11.3: Momentum-led strategic thinking

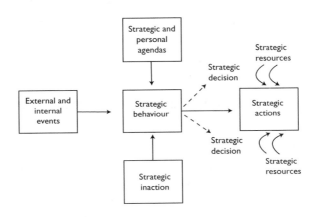

In figure 11.3 you will see a number of differences from figure 11.2, which was a more artificial, rational model. Figure 11.3 suggests that:

- Events themselves (rather than strategic thinking) are the prime drivers of strategic action.
- Agendas (personal and strategic) filter strategic decisions on a go/no-go basis, rather than a careful, rational weighing of strategic options – particularly their advantages and disadvantages – taking place.
- Strategic inaction plays an almost equally important role to that of strategic action (strategic inaction can be either intended or unintended – you can either decide not to do something deliberately or drift into it).
- Strategic resources are typically allocated primarily tactically rather than in a carefully programmed way.
- Strategic behaviour is highly influential in shaping the way in which strategic thinking crystallizes into action; it appears sometimes more crucial than the cognitive processes associated with making specific decisions, indeed under time and political pressure decisions themselves can become almost secondary, even a by-product of the mobilization process. This is likely to lead to inappropriate decision-making and/or implementation, weakening organizational performance.

At a helicopter level we are caught at this point between two apparent polarities:

a) between the need to spread more analytical and creative strategic thinking through the organization, and
b) the need to somehow harmonize its patterns of strategic behaviour.

Whilst b) clearly takes us into the behavioural and political domain, it is our contention that sorting out a) (strategic thinking) can actually help us to sort out b) (strategic behaviour). Also, by recognising and managing the behavioural aspects more effectively, we are also likely to get a better result in a) (strategic thinking).

Organizational learning and strategic change

Organizational learning and strategic change also offer us additional insights into strategic behaviour. Organizational learning received a resurgence of interest following Senge's work (1990), which looked at things from the perspective of systems theory. However, the main contributor to linking learning and strategic behaviour is Chris Argyris.

Argyris's theory (for instance, 1991) is fundamentally simple: managers protect themselves from error by means of a set of explanations (or 'espoused theories') of what they are doing and why. These espoused theories (their reasons for action) often differ dramatically from how they actually behave.

Argyris helps us to understand the role of errors in the strategic management process. Error-making is linked to organizational learning because managers are supposed to learn from their mistakes. However, Argyris again puts us right with his notion of 'self-sealing errors', which is another way of describing organizational cover-ups. Things that go wrong and which are then covered up might therefore be a key ingredient of strategic behaviour (see figure 11.4). Argyris sometimes calls this phenomenon the 'dead cat syndrome', likening it to finding a dead cat in your back yard. Instead of burying it and trying to find out why it died, you simply throw it into someone else's back yard. They discover the cat and repeat the process, throwing the cat into someone else's back yard. This results in a profound waste of energy.

When working with one services company as a consultant, one of the writers was drawn into saying:

Sometimes there are not just one or two individuals playing the game but whole teams. Thus they are in the organizational back yard with racquets, trying to get the dead cat back over someone else's wall – or effectively playing 'dead cat tennis'.

In the most extreme case, the 'dead cat' issue can become highly dangerous, characterized as being the 'nuclear dead cat' – one that is due to go off unless someone manages to defuse it.

Janis (1989) takes this theme further by focusing on errors that are especially damaging (the nuclear dead cat again). Janis lists a variety of sources of biases in judgement leading up to errors. For instance, he chronicles gross omissions in setting objectives or surveying alternatives, poor information, selective bias (misprocessing of information), failure to examine risks and, finally, failure to work out detailed implementation steps and devise contingency plans. When managers are under a lot of pressure their strategic behaviour defaults, according to Janis, to a 'wow grab it' mode – they jump at the first plausible solution (or alternatively, in the case of a dead cat, 'wow, get rid of it').

The role of strategic errors is shown in figure 11.4.

FIGURE 11.4: Strategic errors

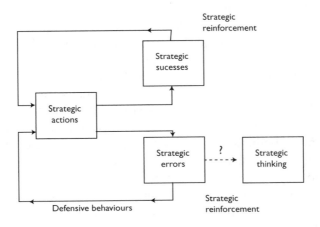

However, is Janis falling into the trap of adopting an (economic) rationalist perspective – depicting managers who exercise limited rationality as being 'foolish'? In reality, managers are buffeted by behaviours of others, their own feelings and perceptions that they have limited power and influence over events. Then, they might be acting quite 'rationally' – following the easiest (if 'erroneous') course of action.

Argyris describes many instances where espoused theory diverges from theory in use. For instance, during his study of the behaviour of strategy consultants (1986) he found that, on numerous occasions, they projected difficulties that they were having in interacting with their clients as 'client incompetence'. Argyris's point is that, far from being aloof from defensive routines, 'professional people' are actually more vulnerable to indulging in defensive routines (Argyris, 1991). (Perhaps this is yet another reason for 'being your own strategy consultant'.)

Turning next to organizational change, the idea of the paradigm is of interest. A 'paradigm' is defined as the deeper level of basic assumptions and beliefs that are shared by members of an organization, ones that operate unconsciously. These assumptions define, in a basic, taken-for-granted fashion, an organization's view of itself and its environment (Schein, 1986). The paradigm is also closely bound up with the management processes used to make things happen.

Much of the paradigm in practice works at an unconscious level in organizations. It forms a network or 'web' (Johnson) of taken-for-granted beliefs, assumptions and practices that shape both strategic decisions and implementation. Managers are unwittingly caught up in this hidden web that shapes and constrains their behaviour. In chapters 6 and 7 in 'The Value of Strategic Thinking' a lot of emphasis was placed on the problem of trying to generate fresh strategic thinking whilst the organization was trapped in an old and outdated paradigm.

Johnson (1992) distinguishes between a number of key ingredients within the paradigm. These include power, structure, controls, routines, rituals, myths and stories, thus ranging from relatively tangible to the intangible. Johnson also describes the importance of ceremonies in providing living form to the paradigm. (To some extent strategic thinking workshops have become new and fashionable ceremonies, with mixed benefit as once conducted they are often partly or completely forgotten.) Unless you consider these ingredients in formulating or implementing strategy, you will almost certainly fail.

Johnson also draws our attention to 'momentum building' (see also, Miller and Freisen, 1978) versus inertia-type behaviours. Clearly, creating and maintaining a momentum is a key part of the management of a senior team, and this momentum is threatened by apparently intractable strategic issues and dilemmas. Virtually every team has some concern with achieving progress (although one of the writers has been involved in some more intellectual teams where debate was an end in itself – thankfully, such teams are not overly common because of the pressures of the real business world). The idea of momentum building naturally leads us into the land of politics.

Politics and contention

Organizational politics is an inevitable ingredient of strategic behaviour. When individuals interact strategically, this is necessarily attended by extensive political influencing. We are inescapably drawn into analyzing and interpreting some of the key patterns of influencing behaviour that surround the strategy (Pettigrew, 1977). Strategy-making is an obviously highly political process (Johnson, 1980) and requires extensive negotiation between subgroups.

A helpful way of surfacing political influences (which we will explore in depth later) and agendas is the use of stakeholder analysis (Piercey, 1989) – see, again, chapter 5. Stakeholder analysis not only identifies the key stakeholders (on a particular strategic issue) and their likely position (in terms of both degree of influence and attitude), but may also help to surface agendas.

Stakeholders may also reposition themselves significantly in times of crisis, depending on their perceptions of the crisis, their ability to understand it and their capacity to respond to it in appropriate ways (Chilingerian, 1994).

Politics can also be a positive force in freeing up essential debate. For instance, both Kanter (1983) and Pascale (1990) emphasize the role of unleashing contention as a positive force in organizations. Unfortunately, these suggestions appear to be prescriptive rather than based on any well-grounded, empirical study. In the wrong hands, they can be an excuse for a specific individual in the team to be disruptive and destructive, with the intent of undermining the leader and becoming the centre of personal attention. However, if contention is suitably directed – and if managers can cope with the heat of challenge without going into Argyris's defensive routines – then there may be some real breakthroughs.

By using stakeholder analysis (see chapter 5) then perhaps organizations can withstand and channel a greater level of contention and challenge.

To summarize our review:

- In most organizations the strategic management process is disjointed, messy and produces very partial and fragmentary glimpses of the strategic road ahead.
- Behaviourally speaking, it is thus naturally a very difficult thing for strategic thinking to take root in the organization and its activities can become merely 'strategic ceremonies'.
- This difficulty is compounded by problems of actually turning strategic ideas into implementation and change, and in dealing with organizational politics.

So, having reached these perhaps unpalatable conclusions, where do we go from here? One approach would be to immediately throw in the towel and accept that strategy is at best highly emergent. But this would be to substantially abandon the value of deliberate strategies – and of the strategic thinking techniques outlined earlier in this book.

We do not believe ourselves that such a defeatist approach is either desirable or necessary. For there are, we believe, ways of coping with the distortions wreaked by strategic behaviour. But before we outline these, let us first examine the way in which strategic behaviour actually appears to operate. The frameworks which follow were derived from research into strategic behaviour in a top team at British Telecom (Grundy, 1997). This department was under severe pressure to produce strategic ideas and insights from a (then) highly ambiguous and somewhat political organizational position.

What forms does strategic behaviour take?

From our research, 'strategic behaviour' manifests itself in a variety of forms in practice (see figure 11.5) including:

- strategic tasks and problem analysis
- analytical and interpersonal processes
- team mix and individual characteristics
- team interaction and dynamic processes
- meta-behaviour
- organizational context
- outputs.

FIGURE 11.5: The system of strategic behaviour

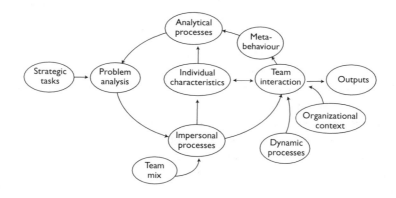

'Meta-behaviour' represents the higher order behaviours associated with strategic thinking, including summarizing, process management, reflection, etc.

These behavioural groupings are now analyzed with some helpful questions which will help you to diagnose strategic behaviour (and its influence) in your organization, as follows.

Strategic tasks and problem analysis

Strategic tasks are, essentially, the major strategic activities a team undertakes. These can include, for example:

- acquisitions
- business development programmes
- business performance reviews
- cost reviews
- divestment/rationalization decisions
- key management appointments
- reacting to external change
- resource allocation
- restructuring decisions.

During these activities, many problems can arise, including, for example, deciding whether to make a senior appointment internally or recruit externally, or, where there are many business development projects, determining which should be given priority.

EXERCISE

- What are the key strategy activities which your team faces over the next 6 to 12 months?
- Which of these activities are most crucial to the business in the:
  - medium term?
  - long term?
- How time-intensive are these activities likely to be, and how should they be programmed?
- What does the team need to do less of – or stop doing altogether – to devote sufficient time to its truly strategic activities?
- Which of these activities is liable to generate the most behavioural turbulence?
- What roles should key individuals within the team play (for a specific activity)?
- What specific problems and dilemmas are likely to come up, and how can these be addressed?
- What personal and strategic agendas (PASTA) factors are likely to come into play, and how should these be managed?

EXERCISE continued

- What major constraints are likely to be faced, and what options for getting around these are likely to exist?
- Where are these constraints likely to become virtually impossible to deal with, and how can these be headed off?

Analytical and interpersonal processes

To address these strategic tasks and problems requires both analytical and interpersonal processes.

EXERCISE

- How can problems and dilemmas be anticipated well in advance by the management team?
- How can your team ensure that it clarifies issues before debating situations, let alone creating options?
- How can your team avoid tunnel vision and achieve some genuine creative thinking when generating options?
- How will solutions be challenged and probed, without destructive picking apart?
- Who will summarize and synthesize a conclusion?
- How will your team ensure that where people do agree, they say that they agree?
- When members of the team disagree, will they be expected to also say, in the same breath, why they disagree?
- How will interruptions be managed so as not to disturb the flow of debate, yet still allow valuable, but lateral, thoughts to be heard?
- How will your key team members allow themselves to be influenced and won over (where appropriate), rather than taking up fixed positions?

Team mix and individual characteristics

Key questions

- Is your team mix genuinely in balance or is there a preponderance of one or two styles (for example, in Belbin terms, too many plants or chairmen; in Star Trek terms, too many Spocks or Klingons)?
- Is it worthwhile to get your team to check out its team styles (using some psychometrics)?
- Do individuals with pronounced team styles require one-to-one support (off-line, as it were) to adapt their behaviour or could they fruitfully simply try out another role?
- Where your team recruits someone new, what are their preferred team roles, and, assuming this replaces someone leaving the team, will this inadvertently unbalance the team mix?

EXERCISE continued

■ What other characteristics of particular individuals might distort the strategic behaviour of the team (for example, their idiosyncratic cognitive style or other personal traits)?

■ Does the professional background of your team members bias them towards certain types of behaviours (for example, towards picking apart)?

■ Are there particularly acute 'power contours' surrounding a particular individual (or individuals) and how can these be toned down (i.e. areas where an individual is particularly strong and also prepared to make a strong stance to the point of inhibiting or intimidating others from engaging in debate)?

■ What are the personal career ambitions of individuals within your team, and how might they influence or distort their behaviours?

■ Are there particular anxious, vulnerable or sensitive individuals, and how does this need to be managed?

■ Are your team members (either as a group or individually) just that little bit too serious, and is it necessary to oil the flow?

■ Who is likely to succumb to strategic frustration, and on which issues? How can this be headed off?

Team interaction and dynamic processes

Key questions

■ What is likely to generate a particularly high level of behavioural turbulence and how can these issues or interactions be navigated?

■ If there are specific threats of team breakdown, how can this be facilitated? (What could give rise to these breakdowns? Consider using fishbone analysis.)

■ Where known or likely areas of conflict or personality clash exist, how can these be averted or controlled? In which behavioural scenarios are these likely to arise?

■ How can levels of excitement be managed so that your team neither flags nor burns up too much energy? What is its 'energy over time' curve expected to look like?

■ Where there is real threat of one or more individuals dominating the conversation (and probably withdrawing), how can this be minimized?

■ Is there a tendency to dive into or rush the discussion of issues so that problem analysis is incomplete? If so, how can this be averted (for example, by more helicopter-like reflection)?

■ Can your team time be managed more effectively to avoid both slippage and allow sufficient time to debate the really big issues?

Meta-behaviour

Key questions

■ What facilitation is your team likely to need – when and how should this be provided?

EXERCISE continued

■ Would it be wise to ask your team (before discussing a particularly sensitive topic): what 'P' behaviours it wants to avoid (for example, being political, picky, pessimistic, and so on)?

■ Should your team use any strategic analysis tools or methodologies, and how can it learn to use these consistently? (For example, consider using fishbone analysis for any strategic problem.)

■ Could your team benefit by consciously trying to avoid 'rabbit hole management' and strive instead towards 'helicopter vision'?

■ Would stakeholder analysis or stakeholder agenda analysis be useful in surfacing agendas in your team?

■ How can your team target (in advance) the value of its outputs and monitor these subsequently (for example, by using the 'value-over-time' curve)?

■ How can your team take up the idea of value destruction and use this idea on an everyday basis to steer debate towards value added?

■ How should your team prioritize its decisions? (For example, by using AID analysis.)

■ How can your team build in time to reflect on the process (even if this is just five minutes at the end of a two-hour meeting)?

■ Can your team usefully introduce more humour to lighten its heavier strategic debates (without being frivolous)?

Organizational context

Key questions

■ Who are the key stakeholders (outside your team) with an influence on the team's strategic activities? What is on their agenda and how should these agendas be taken into account or proactively influenced?

■ How does the wider organizational and political structure influence what goes on in your team?

■ What factors outside your team are likely to result in inaction, inertia or distraction, and how can these be managed?

■ How does your team interact with strategic processes elsewhere in the organization, and how can these processes be managed more proactively?

OUTPUTS

Key questions

■ What specific outputs will be needed from key team meetings (for example, decisions to do things, new projects, decisions not to do things, and so on)?

■ How will these outputs be communicated to the rest of the organization?

■ How will the likely reaction of other stakeholders outside the organization be gauged? Will this cause your team to think through its positioning of those messages most carefully?

■ At the end of the day, what are those outputs worth – what value have they really added?

What are the key dimensions of strategic behaviour?

Figure 11.6 now explores some of the more important dimensions of strategic behaviour. Strategic behaviour is an amalgam of cognitive, affective and territorial elements, but, on top of these elements, behavioural momentum is a key variable of strategic behaviour.

FIGURE II.6: The momentum of strategic behaviour?

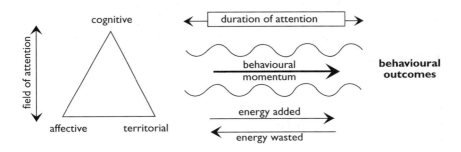

Factors that add energy include, for example, creative thinking, leadership or simply a sense of urgency. Factors that dissipate energy include having too little process in debate or interactions, generating considerable strategic frustration (for example, where the quality of listening is poor).

From figure 11.6 we can hypothesize that:

- With attention diffused under a wider range of issues, strategic thinking will be slow and ineffective.
- Where attention is narrow not only are thought-related outputs likely to be of higher quality but team behaviour will be higher, and energy preserved.
- Where territorial and emotional elements in agendas are dominant (either consciously or unconsciously), progress will be slower and energy wasted.
- Where mental maps (and priorities within them) within the team differ this will cause major frustration and a lack of progress.

- Where cognitive, territorial and emotional elements become interfused, it will become very difficult (if not impossible) to move forward.
- Cognitive confusion will tend to provoke emotional and territorial instability. Equally, emotional attachment and territorial ambiguity will aggravate cognitive confusion, resulting in a soup of strategic agendas.

Why and how is strategic behaviour important? – a summary

It is now possible to explore the more specific reasons for strategic behaviour's importance from managers' own perspectives – especially in terms of how it might add to or detract from value. These reasons include:

- the quality of strategic thinking
- sharing of mindsets
- creating an imperative to act
- possible change of territorial barriers
- building a platform for influencing
- time expended
- timeliness and utility of outcomes
- cognitive and emotional energy expended.

Where strategic behaviour is not particularly well-orchestrated, then management debate can, as a result, be too narrowly confined in scope, or too superficial (lacking depth) or fragmented (missing key interconnections). It might also fail to identify strategic blind-spots or it may identify them as vague, possible opportunities and threats, but not have diagnosed those sufficiently in order to add value.

Sharing mindsets

Linked to both 'quality of strategic thinking' and 'refocusing of attention', the commonality of mindsets also plays a major role in determining strategic outputs.

Strategic behaviour that is not underpinned by a continual sharing of mindsets may thus inhibit a healthy degree of challenge and testing during strategic debate. Poorly shared mindsets can lead to a hardening of personal strategic agendas, which can then frustrate decision-making action and change.

Mindsets are thus the frames of reference that provide a basis for creating shared strategic thinking.

Creating an imperative to act

Both managers and strategic management theorists alike are well aware of the frequent gaps that occur between strategic thinking and action, especially when dealing with apparently intractable problems. However, the consequence of this is that, unless the strategic behaviour within a team can create some need to act (even if this action is simply 'to investigate further'), implementation may well not be mobilized, even where it is an organizational imperative.

The feeling of there being a need to act is thus the precursor to action, as a tangible behavioural outcome.

Territorial barriers may be changed

An open and cohesive style of strategic behaviour may well be more conducive to reducing territorial barriers. Some of these barriers may be mainly organizational, and some may be mainly cognitive or even emotional, especially when issues exist that individuals have attachments to, given past experiences and investment of effort.

Building a platform for influencing

Once again, creating a platform for influencing is a precursor to achieving action.

Time expended

Time expended by teams generally will obviously govern:

- the number of issues the team cover
- the depth and thoroughness of their investigations
- how many issues exist where thinking is turned into action.

Timeliness and utility of outcomes

Where strategic behaviour becomes increasingly chaotic, this may obviously reduce the effectiveness of the strategy process, which might be frustrating from a team's own perspective. It may result in costly organizational delays as decisions are put off and opportunities slip. While a 'task-based' perspective is by no means the only one, nevertheless it still exists, and it should not be ignored simply because of the influence of other perspectives, such as the political.

The timeliness and utility of outcomes thus concerns the final outputs of strategic behaviour and how they are used by the rest of the organization.

Cognitive and emotional energy expended

Finally, a management team's mental and emotional resources may be depleted by the frustration of weak control over its strategic behaviour.

Potentially, unrelieved frustration levels in other teams might rise to the point at which there is an effective burn-out, especially when a particular issue becomes a 'strategic black hole'. This suggests that controlling strategic behaviour effectively requires 'energy management' activity. This concerns the less tangible and indirect effects of strategic behaviour rather than the more tangible outcomes.

In summary, strategic behaviour does appear to play a profoundly important and influential role in shaping strategic thinking. Not only does shaping strategic behaviour seem to yield potential benefits, but default behaviours do seem to have costs – for the organization, the team and also the individuals involved.

Conclusion

Strategic behaviour is another important dimension to strategic thinking. Many of the frustrations in getting the value out of strategic thinking are down to behavioural constraints.

In this chapter we were able to unravel many of the complex interactions and dynamics at work within strategic thinking.

In addition to this input, chapter 12 helps you at a practical level to gain more influence in this area.

Summary of key points

Key points from this chapter include:

- The strategic thinking pyramid is a useful diagnostic device to understand what needs to line up to get the value out of strategic thinking – and the role of behaviour.
- The strategic decision-making process is typically highly fluid and incremental – precisely because of the influences of strategic behaviour.
- This process can lead to errors, bias and to weak implementation.
- Strategic thinking requires an open approach to learning – which in turn requires more effective strategic behaviour.
- To manage strategic behaviour requires the management of power, for which stakeholder analysis is vital.
- 'Strategic behaviour' breaks down into a complex and interactive system, each part of which can be managed more effectively at a team level through the key question diagnostics.

■ Within the strategic thinking process it is crucial to focus the team's attention, to surface personal agendas, and share mental maps, and to monitor levels of energy and (potential) frustration – to avoid burn-out.

References

Argyris, C., 'Teaching Smart People How to Learn', *Harvard Business Review*, May–June 1991.

Braybrooke, D. and C.E. Lindblom, *A Strategy of Decision*, Free Press, Macmillan, New York, 1963.

Brunsson, N., 'The Irrationality of Action and Action Rationality: Decisions, Ideologies and Organizational Actions', *Journal of Management Studies*, 198 (1), p.p.29–44, 1982.

Chilingerian, J.A., 'Managing Strategic Issues and Stakeholders: How Modes of Executive Attention Enact Crisis Management' in H. Thomas, D.O. Neal and D. Hurst (eds), *Building the Strategically Responsive Organization*, p.p.190–213, John Wiley, Chichester, 1994.

Cohen, M.B., J.C. March, and J.P. Olsen, 'A Garbage Can Model of Organization Choice', *Administrative Science Quarterly*, 7, p.p.1–25, (1972).

Cyert, R.M., and J.G. March, *A Behaviour Theory of the Firm*, Prentice Hall, Englewood Cliffs, New Jersey, 1963.

Dixit, A.K. and B.J. Nalib, *Thinking Strategically*, Norton, New York, 1991.

Grundy, A.N., *Harnessing Strategic Behaviour – How Politics Drives Company Strategy*, Financial Times Publishing, London, 1998

Hickson, D.H., R.J. Butler *et al.*, *Top Decisions: Strategic Decision-making in Organizations*, Basil Blackwell, Oxford, 1986.

Janis, I.I., *Crucial Decisions*, Free Press, Macmillan, New York, 1989.

Johnson, G.J., *Strategic Change and the Management Process*, Basil Blackwell, Oxford, 1980.

— *The Challenge of Strategic Management*, Kogan Page, London, 1992.

Kanter, R.M., *The Change Masters*, Unwin, London, 1987.

Miller, P. and P. Freisen, 'Archetypes of Strategy Formulation', *Management Science*, 24, 1978, p.p.921–33.

Mintzberg, H., *The Rise and Fall of Strategic Planning*, Prentice Hall, London, 1994.

Pascale, R., *Managing on the Edge*, Penguin, London, 1990.

Pettigrew, A.M., 'Strategy Formulation as a Political Process', *International Studies of Management and Organization*, 7(2), 1977, p.p.78–87.

Piercey, N., 'Diagnosing and Solving Implementation Problems in Strategic Planning', *Journal of General Management*, vol. 15, no 1, (Autumn 1989), p.p.19–38.

Quinn, J.B., *Strategies for Change: Logical Incrementalism*, Richard D. Irwin, Illinois, 1980.

Schein, E.H., *Organizational Culture and Leadership*, p.6, Jossey-Bass, San Francisco, 1986.

Senge, P., *The Fifth Discipline: The Art and Practice of the Learning Organization*, Doubleday, New York, 1990.

CHAPTER TWELVE

Becoming your own strategy consultant

Introduction

Learning to think strategically for oneself is merely one of the qualifying steps to becoming your own strategy consultant in the round. In addition to being able to understand, to diagnose and to resolve key strategic issues effectively, you will also need to be able to accomplish the more difficult task of carrying others within the organization with that thinking.

Paradoxically, this can sometimes mean holding back from advancing your own strategic thinking too far – otherwise it may take too long for others to catch up. Also, there is a very real risk that you might close your mind off to other thoughts and perceptions which may come from others.

In addition, your mindset might be one of the Holy Grail strategy – that there is one single right and best strategy in any given business context. Usually there is more than one good strategy – and even where there is only one, there is invariably more than one way of implementing it.

In the final analysis, the process of strategy is more important than its actual content. If you are prepared to work hard to get the process right then the content (and in particular the outputs) of strategic thinking will largely look after itself.

In this chapter we look at how to plan, implement and review a process of strategic thinking within your own team or organization. This is set out as follows:

- the role of a strategy consultant
- designing a strategic thinking process
- cultural implications of strategic thinking
- the role of a strategic planning unit
- organizing for strategic thinking

- delivering value-driven output
- linking to implementation
- designing a strategic workshop
- conclusion.

The role of a strategy consultant

Whilst there has been much criticism of the role of strategy consultants in the past, nevertheless it is unlikely that they would exist if they did not have a function. There are many that are sceptical of their virtues, sometimes because of valuable scepticism and sometimes because of cynicism or envy. But just because they seem to have a current function, there is no reason why they have to be a permanent feature of management. Indeed, it is our contention that at least some of their expertise can (and perhaps should) be exercised by managers.

When one of our authors originally decided to write this book he was told by two eminent publishers that 'whilst the book is very attractive, we are not sure that it will not cause offence to strategy consultants'. (As it was not actually targeted at strategy consultants – one would not try to promote a book on 'The World Without Dodos' to the dodo – this might well be somewhat surprising.)

So, before we look at how the manager can be his own strategy consultant, let us look at how strategy consultants can add value generally.

The key ways in which an external strategy consultant can add value include the following thirteen activities:

- acting as an independent sounding board
- helping to set the strategic agenda
- asking the right questions – generally
- asking the questions that others dare not ask
- providing a process for thinking
- collating and interpreting data
- facilitating the thinking process
- generating or providing the teams with 'out-of-the-box ideas'
- acting as a catalyst for decision-making and for action
- constructively critiquing the output
- helping identify blind-spots
- providing energy and enthusiasm
- being a symbolic presence – to help people think and behave differently.

Some of the above activities may seem relatively self-evident – like 'providing a process for thinking' or 'collecting and interpreting data'. Others might be less obvious, such as the last two points of providing energy and enthusiasm and being a symbolic presence. Being a symbolic presence is an interesting activity – this involves value being added by simply being there. Minimalistically this presence sends signals that something different can happen and that it can happen in a different way from normal.

Also, note that some consultancies will focus on a relatively small number of the above activities – for example, on collecting and interpreting data. In our own case as consultants we would probably rarely be involved in collecting raw data ourselves – as we work principally as process consultants. This means that we primarily add value by facilitating the strategic thinking process. This is in contrast to the expert consultant – who is hired primarily because of his/her content expertise.

One area which we have not mentioned above – but which is one often commented on by sceptical managers – is:

- helping provide an official stamp on decisions effectively taken already by top management.

Whilst management is a political process and this is not something which consultants can escape, this does not mean that the consultant should be used in a covert, political role.

Turning back to the role of the internal strategy consultant, all of the thirteen roles can be exercised by an internal manager. The activities which might be harder to fulfil for an internal manager are:

- asking questions that others dare not ask
- constructively critiquing the output
- being a symbolic presence.

Whilst not impossible, the challenge is perhaps greater for the internal consultant. This challenge puts more stress on the internal consultant's self-confidence and indeed on his/her courage. Depending upon the situation this may mean that the internal strategy consultant may need to put the process first and thoughts about his/her longer-term career in the organization second. Paradoxically, success in this role is the ideal preparation for becoming a top manager. Alternatively, if a manager succeeds in this difficult role then there should be no shortage of job offers elsewhere!

Besides playing an official (internal) consulting role, every manager can also adopt this role by stealth or informally. Consultancy facilitation ought to be an integral part of a senior manager's skill-set.

To check out whether you have the natural capability to become an internal strategy consultant (whether formally or informally), now answer the following brief questionnaire in twelve questions:

	Very Strong 5	Strong 4	Average 3	Weak 2	Very Weak 1
What is my natural ability to see the very big picture?					
What is my ability to think outside the box?					
What is my ability in devising management processes?					
What is my level of political skills?					
What is my level of interpersonal skills – at senior levels?					
What is my ability at asking the right questions – and at the right time?					
What is my listening skills ability – and powers of observation?					
What is my ability to cope with the ambiguous and uncertain?					
What is my ability to handle personal stress under difficult challenge?					
What is the level of my all-round analytical ability?					
What is the level of my communication ability?					
What is the level of my own persistence and drive?	___	___	___	___	___
Total Score	___	___	___	___	___

Now calculate your overall score out of 120:

- Score 110–120: you might consider setting up your own consultancy (after some internal experience or with another firm).
- Score 90–110: this may be a full-time internal role for you.
- Score 70-90: you can add a lot of value through merely internal consulting by stealth.
- Score 50-70: don't give up! Work out a number of developmental activities to move this forward (especially pinpointing key projects or meetings as the vehicle for consultancy-by-stealth).

Designing a strategic thinking process

The key issues to consider here are:

- defining the key issues
- defining the outputs
- breaking down the process into stages.

The first step therefore is to define the key strategic issues. This can be done in a variety of ways. The classic starting point for defining the key issues is a SWOT analysis (see chapter 2).

As we have already seen, whilst SWOT analysis can be efficient in arriving at some key issues, it is frequently not particularly effective. SWOT analysis often merely highlights the more obvious opportunities and some of the more evident weaknesses. It does not necessarily surface all the key internal present weaknesses. It is even less likely to identify the emerging weaknesses – that is against the world of the future.

It is also normally introverted – seeing strategy from inside-out rather than from an outside-in perspective. Only by taking market, customer and competitor perspectives of the world can an effective SWOT be created.

Another helpful ancillary technique is to draw from a gap analysis (see chapter 2) some of the 'stretch' issues which will guide and target strategic thinking. Gap analysis can be deployed across a number of dimensions, especially:

- Scale: how big a business do you seek to achieve? Whilst sometimes being a misleading guide to the end-goal of the strategy, targeting future scale is one route to scoping strategic issues, especially in terms of: distribution channel requirements, determining the debate about acquisitions versus joint ventures versus organic growth, and also resources and skills requirements.
- Growth: the rate of anticipated growth gives another guide to which strategic issues might be most worthwhile focusing on. When, for example, you are seeking compound growth rates in excess of 30 per cent, then this inevitably raises issues such as future organizational structure, processes, skills, outcome and leadership styles. For corporations appear to meet transitions in their organic make-up when they reach certain growth and scale thresholds.
- Customer value: what is the gap between the average value-adding activities and in superior value creating activities? (This can be linked to customer benchmarking, i.e. asking them how well key motivator factors are delivered and hygiene factors are met.)

- Cost: unit cost levels can also be targeted. If cost reductions of over 5 per cent per annum (compound) are sought, then this is almost certainly a key strategic issue.
- Competitor positioning: using competitor profiling one can often generate a more incisive and important set of strategic issues than merely relying on a SWOT.
- Financial performance: profit before tax is often targeted in the gap analysis. Unfortunately this suffers from being focused on a short and medium measure – and one which may not correspond to economic value added.
- Value: economic value might provide a more workable and appropriate measure to target your gap analysis on. By focusing on value creation (essentially based on future cash flows) it is possible to avoid traps like:
  - Preferring acquisitions to organic development. (The former promotes speed and scale as goals, but these can be illusory as speed might be slower (especially due to integration constraints) and scale might just be associated merely with adding activities.
  - Going through the motions of strategic thinking and strategic planning without really giving due weight to medium- and longer-term share-holder value (especially value beyond a two-year time horizon).
- Capability: one of the most useful applications of gap analysis is to explore and scope the gap between present and future skills base.

The above techniques can be applied at a helicopter level before conducting them in greater detail, business area by business area.

Another important input is a quick look at some of the more pressing competitive and performance issues facing you. This may well invite a performance driven analysis along with a number of fishbone analyses to scope strategic problems and constraints. This adds a little more structure, scope and depth to what would otherwise be a strategic brain-dump.

Frequently issues may emerge during the strategic process – as follows.

CASE STUDY: COST AS AN EMERGENT STRATEGIC ISSUE

Just before the last recession a division of a major telecommunications company began to rethink its strategy. Issues such as inter-national development, the future of its local area network business, key account management and new technology development were all identified during the critical phase of issue analysis and gap analysis.

Six weeks into the review, three new issues emerged:

- Culture and mindset: was the company able to define its values and assumptions beyond a phase of thrusting, entrepreneurial development?
- Skills: how could the company retain and expand its innovative skills base?
- Costs: because the market was getting far more competitive and with increasing economies of scale, the old cost structures needed to be revisited, re-targeted and changed.

The first two of these strategic issues were then brought into the strategic process: culture and mindset cost base. Regrettably, the third issue – costs – was discounted.

Subsequently the issue of costs became pivotal in the thinking of top management in the division.

Some useful (generic) issues to contemplate are therefore:

- new markets
- new product development
- geographic market presence
- changes in distribution channels / impact of IT and e-commerce
- acquisitions
- alliances
- services strategy
- cost base
- restructuring
- scarce skill acquisition
- senior management capability
- competitor entry
- regulatory threat
- culture and style
- divestment and / or closure
- strategic controls and rewards
- the planning process itself
- the implementation process.

Having identified the key strategic issues we are now in better shape to design the process, which should be done by first defining the outputs. These might include:

- broader priorities of issues, specific areas for investment, performance improvement or turnaround
- specific projects or programmes which are then implemented in an ongoing way

- specific business areas where we are either going to exit, or just stop doing generally
- any fundamental restructuring plans
- an overview of likely sales, returns, and resources needed
- an analysis of key uncertainties and contingencies (including their impact and plans to avoid or minimize these)
- specific critical skills areas which, unless acquired in good time, could well delay the achievement of strategic development and change.

It is now possible to decide what mix of strategic thinking inputs is appropriate. Given the focus of the above outputs, consider the following example:

CASE STUDY: STRATEGIC THINKING – SHIFTING THE PROCESS

The managing director of a medium-sized services company began the review of his business area. This had both a challenging performance gap to fill and faced a particularly tough trading environment.

Initially, in his view, he sought to look at a number of key areas of input. These included:

- regulatory issue analysis
- innovative product design
- dealer network – relationship and management
- administrative cost base
- systems development
- competitor analysis
- customer need research.

He then delegated the task of collating inputs on each of the above issues to seven managers and, where appropriate, to sub-teams.

During discussions with his external strategy mentor it transpired that:

- The administrative cost base was not a key strategic issue – as it was actually not that large relative to bottom-line profit.
- The competitor analysis was unlikely to yield great insights. In this particular case it was not only well known how the competitors operated now (and were inclined to behave in the future) but they all had rather similar, less innovative ways of competing. So, despite some minimal embarrassment, the data collection in this area was stopped.

- On deeper reflection, much of the collection of detailed market research on current customer needs appeared to be either unnecessary or duplicated what was already well-known in the organization. Again, this was significantly curtailed.

To design an overall process now this is usually done by using a simple flow-chart – of the kind depicted in figure 12.1. This classic shows us starting with the issue/gap analysis, then collating market and competitor data alongside some scenario story telling of future competitive and technological patterns. By performing an outside-in examination of current capability this gives us a detailed overview of strategic positioning, business by business.

'Key options and decisions' then offers top management the opportunity to test out their breakthrough thoughts, both by further creative development and in terms of economic value and skills capability.

Finally, this output is reflected in strategic plans, budgets, in individual business cases, project plans, and recognition and reward targets.

FIGURE 12.1: A strategic planning process

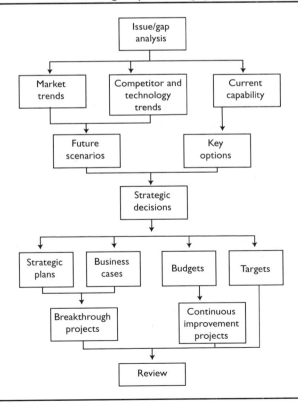

Whilst figure 12.1 is a useful framework for now breaking the process down into steps and sub-projects, it might imply an over-deterministic interpretation. For on some decisions it is inappropriate to begin with current issues/gap analysis. This may be either because you are starting from the wrong strategic space anyway or because you should work backwards from the future.

Alternatively, there may be times when the external environment and even the company's competitive and trading position is less crucial than its internal capability and resource constraints. Anticipating this fact is very, very important for the following reason: if one makes the (invalid) assumption that capability and resource constraints are likely to be a stopper vis-à-vis particular growth strategies, this realization might be repressed if there is already commitment to a major expansion. Once having spent a lot of time examining growth possibilities through external analysis it is then harder to pare down such plans – and to refocus the effort on internal development.

Cultural implications of strategic thinking

Strategic thinking therefore probably does not come naturally to most organizations. Most companies are caught up in tactical, everyday pressures and the attention therefore is on managing a kaleidoscope of horribly fragmented issues. This haphazard process is sometimes punctuated by attempts to take a quick look at the bigger picture, rapidly replaced by immersion in the detail once again.

The above situation is as if some air force trainees were let loose on flying a helicopter for the weekend, only they are told to save fuel (because of the petrol crisis which we began within chapter 1) and that this exercise can be accomplished by not taking off. So, instead of soaring rapidly to their destination they drive out of the airbase and onto the local motorway doing a steady forty miles per hour. When stuck in a traffic jam they take off temporarily but then land on the other side to resume their journey in the slow lane.

Whilst being overtly absurd, the helicopter-driving scenario is precisely what many attempts at strategic thinking amount to. Because it is not apparent what strategic thinking can achieve, first attempts at it are woefully under-resourced. Take the following case illustration as an example:

CASE STUDY: A MAJOR EUROPEAN INSTITUTION BEGINS TO 'THINK STRATEGICALLY'

One of the co-authors was recently asked to facilitate a strategic thinking workshop for a major European institution. The institution is very large and complex and the 'mission' is to run a strategic thinking workshop pilot within a specific business area.

The author (acting as consultant) first suggested that it would be immensely valuable if the workshop programme was tailored to the institution's context – and to focus on specific issues. A visit was proposed, but on budget grounds this did not happen.

Instead, the tailoring of design was done through a fifteen-minute telephone conversation, conducted partly by mobile telephone in a Cornish pub, and partly outside in the rain (as the signal was inadequate).

Notwithstanding this somewhat inadequate preparation (which also ruled out doing meaningful pre-work) the workshop ran exceptionally well. But although it ran well, a number of constraining forces impeded its effectiveness, as follows:

- The workshop was held in a very exclusive hotel but in a conference room, with no natural light (a 'strategic dungeon'). The consequence of this was that the participants rapidly lost energy and momentum in the afternoon (echoing our findings in chapter 6 on the importance of facilities for strategic thinking).
- The participants were served a three-course lunch with rich food and two or three glasses of wine. This took an hour and ten minutes, prohibiting any other form of exercise or fresh air (other than taken for smoking purposes).
- The purpose of the workshop was not positioned internally at the start, even though the business unit's general manager was present as a participant. Presumably his (laudable) intention was to be 'one of the team' but this meant that when difficult or sensitive issues came up the facilitator had to leave them substantially in suspense.
- At the end of the workshop the facilitator left it an open question as to what they might do next with the process, and once again there was no take-up on this theme. (This was notwithstanding the fact that the group had used the Champney's case – see chapter 8: 'Leadership and Strategic Change' as a prompt to their thinking that same day.)

The above case is by no means unrepresentative of most companies' first attempts at strategic thinking. Had this been our own direct client (as it was the work came through another channel), we would have insisted on more suitable preparation and follow-through.

The case also highlights the importance of getting some physical hygiene factors right (the room), and also the positioning of any strategic event. In the above case study it was as if the client had not even begun to realize that to introduce strategic thinking effectively in an organization requires a considerable culture shift. It cannot be achieved with a quickie, one-off strategic event (which inevitably becomes more a form of strategic entertainment rather than something which shifts the centre of gravity of thought in an organization).

To examine what we mean therefore by a strategic thinking culture, let us reflect on what it might look like, as follows.

Key characteristics of a strategic thinking culture might include:

- Key issues are not only clear on the top management's strategic agenda but are also openly discussed and reflected upon within the levels of the organization.
- All staff (at whatever level) are encouraged to practise strategic thinking at their own level – albeit within the bigger picture context.
- Strategic thinking genuinely is prized within the organization and is rewarded not merely through organizational progression but by individual recognition – both financially and non-financially.
- Strategic thinking is regarded as a critical management competence and is supported both through individual and group training.
- Key teams within the business take relatively regular days out to address emerging strategic issues and also to think strategically about implementation.
- There is a culture of asking the unconventional question about 'why are we doing things in this way?' – and a recognized process for dealing with new ideas once they come up.
- Key management processes are infused with strategic thinking rather than acting as brutal enemies. Particular processes which are aligned include: business planning and budgeting, management reporting, senior management meetings, organizational change and restructuring, cost management initiatives, performance reviews.

Is this a fabulous dream or a reality in your organization? One suspects it is probably the former. Certainly most companies seem to be a long way from this ideal at present. Despite the hype of the learning organization over the last decade or so, relatively little progress appears to have been made in terms of injecting strategic thinking into core management culture.

So where does a strategic thinking culture need to begin? Well, we will avoid the conventional prescription that: 'Strategic thinking must begin at the very top of the organization' if only because it may not take root initially at that strata. Sometimes it can blossom at the level just below board level, through ambitious thrusting managers seeking to initiate development or change. This – we have observed – is frequently supported by a sympathetic and eager human resources director, or other senior HR development staff.

Once some strategic thinking has been practised and has borne fruit, then this can spread naturally both horizontally (to other senior managers with similar agendas) or vertically and directly to the top team. In many instances in our experience the board has seen successful attempts at deliberate strategic thinking lower down the organization as a significant opportunity for themselves. For strategic thinking offers the top team a welcome escape for intractable dilemmas and overly microscopic thinking.

On occasion the CEO himself/herself is the catalyst for a strategic thinking culture. But when this is successful it is often accompanied in parallel by an infusion of strategic thinking across senior levels – as we have described above.

For strategic thinking to become truly embedded within the organizational culture it thus needs a number of things. Borrowing from the idea of the culture web/organizational paradigm (Johnson and Scholes, 1987), we see the following shifts as being necessary:

- Structure: strategic thinking is definitely not seen as only residing at the top of the organization.
- Power: all staff are given some power to think strategically – within their domain of responsibility.
- Controls: control systems based on financial and operational measures also reflect the strategic dimension.
- Routine: organizational routines (like meetings, reports, etc) reflect the imperatives of strategic thinking (like root cause and option analysis, prioritization, etc).
- Rituals: these are adapted to have a more strategic content – looking forward rather than backward (for example, company conferences).
- Symbols: managers are encouraged to use more strategic language – without this getting bogged down in artificial jargon.
- Stories: real strategic thinking successes are captured and circulated in the organization – in management presentations or by the Intranet.

Strategic thinking is not merely a set of analytical processes which can be grafted easily onto existing management activities. Rather, it demands a rather different style – one that is lighter, more imaginative and open to thoughts which transcend any particular ownership and power base. (We saw this underlined in chapters 6 and 7 on 'The Value of Strategic Thinking' where potential value was greatly inhibited without cultural alignment with its imperatives.)

This demands a number of important cultural shifts, which we see as follows in a from-to analysis (see chapter 5):

From	To
Thinking driven by what works in the past	Thinking driven by the possible and by the future
Top-down driven business planning	Thinking percolating freely through the organization
Really big issues not talked about (other than cynically)	Big issues, freely and constructively discussed
Plans as 'comfort blankets'	Plans drive actual action
Obsessive and narrow financial targeting	Measured, balanced sets or organizational goals
Lip-service is paid to 'empowerment'	Empowerment is genuine
A leadership environment, where 'what I say' is a strategy	Pluralistic ownership of the strategy

By any reckoning, introducing strategic thinking into all or part of an organization inevitably implies some culture change. Implementing those changes requires consistency. For instance, if one were merely to redesign the planning process and set a different agenda but without changing managers' expectations of what plans will be used for and who people will be judged against them, success will be fitful.

It is often helpful, in order to introduce a strategic thinking culture, to run a small number of strategic thinking workshops to equip staff with both the skills and the mindset. But it is important that initiatives like these are not just isolated but that they should be reinforced.

CASE STUDY: THE CASE OF THE FORGOTTEN STRATEGIC THINKING

A couple of years ago one major fast-moving-consumer-goods (FMCG) company, with highly innovative products, decided to develop its strategic thinking capability more. Staff from marketing and from one other support department attended two one-day strategic thinking workshops.

The key wins from this process were that:

- a number of new 'lines of enquiry' were identified and embryonic strategies to deal with these were worked out
- the two sub-teams picked up a number of techniques which they spasmodically used in the business.

The key losses from this process were, however, that:

- Some of the most senior managers involved moved to other roles, so they did not feel impelled to follow-up those strategic ideas.
- Several key areas – including product development and senior fulfilment – were not involved in the process. This failed to build a common language approach and philosophy across the company.
- The initiative was not followed through, indeed during the next training and development cycle this intervention was dropped from priorities.

The role of a strategic planning unit

In the past it became fashionable to set up a strategic planning unit as a kind of 'Think Tank' for helping top management to establish its future direction for the business. Unfortunately this rarely appeared to work because of a number of causes:

- The planning unit was often too remote from the business, especially if it was the corporate planning unit – at the corporate centre.
- Often it was given an unclear remit about what it was there for, and also what it was not there for.
- Once established, it began to grow its own routines and rituals – especially those personified in the annual strategic planning cycle (which was often a lot more 'planning' than 'strategic').
- Its activities were often resisted by powerful business heads, resenting the intrusion into their own domain.
- The planners often had ambiguous power and were therefore caught between acting as glorified administrators, being the 'corporate wise men' or as acting as genuine facilitators.
- The planners themselves often consisted of 'bright young things', perhaps those with newly minted MBAs or from consultancies. These staff had a different orientation (often being perhaps more academically

bright and more theoretical than their line management counterparts). This led to a chasm of misunderstanding between planners and line managers, the latter understandably either 'feeling thick' or alternatively regarding the planners as being 'wet behind the ears', or incapable of grasping everyday business realities.

The result of the above factors (along with periodic organizational culling) led to the demise of many planning units. In today's world, whilst some still exist, they are typically smaller and often just one- or two-person departments. Sometimes they are called 'business development' or just 'planning' – which may be better organizational titles as they are less prone to attack.

Ideally, the role of today's strategic planning unit is very simple. It ought to be to help to facilitate the strategic thinking process of the organization where this can add most value – and to develop this as a capability. Potentially, this can have immense value added as strategic thinking is not only a higher order skill but it is also inherently difficult to imitate. It can lead to a real competitive advantage through:

- speeding up the strategic responsiveness of the organization
- identifying more complete and coherent strategies for implementation
- creating 'unusual clarity of purpose' within the organization
- delivering the confidence to take the first steps into uncertain areas – where other competitors are frozen with fear
- avoiding huge corporate waste through investing resources in areas which have really not been fully thought through.

The third bullet point above is a particularly interesting one, as so few organizations have much clarity of purpose at all.

Diagnosing and meeting client needs

This short section just summarizes how the techniques found earlier in the book can assist in meeting the needs of either internal clients (if you are in a strategic planning role) or for external clients (where you are an external facilitator). We will focus on the ones which are most relevant. For diagnosing clients' needs the valuable tools are:

- fishbone analysis – for understanding the root causes behind a client's problem
- wishbone analysis – for helping clients to think through all the factors which need to line up to deliver the value of any actions which they now wish to take
- stakeholder agenda analysis and the 'out-of-body experience' – for understanding their deeper anxieties and drivers

- scenario development and the uncertainty-importance grid – for helping the client to see around corners and to anticipate alternative futures
- attractiveness-implementation difficulty (AID) analysis – helping to prioritize client options.

An interesting feature of assisting clients to develop and implement their strategies is the management of the emotional boundaries around these strategies. A facilitator may put a lot of energy into helping a client reach a point where not only a decision – but even action, too – is possible. The client may then falter from moving ahead because of a combination of strategic, organizational and personal uncertainty.

When the client does not follow through at this point it can be somewhat disappointing to the consultancy facilitator. The facilitator needs to manage his/her own emotional commitment at this point. After all, their role is simply to set the decision-maker up for the decision, and not to actively force the decision. This is akin to the role of the midfield player in football – if they put the ball sublimely at the striker's feet and the striker then proceeds to knock it over the bar, then at least the midfielder has done his job.

The consulting facilitator's primary role is therefore to stimulate and challenge the strategic thinking of his/her client – whether this is an internal or an external client. It is not primarily to come up with brilliant strategic ideas themselves.

This is an intensely political and also personally-sensitive process (as we saw in chapters 6 and 7 on the value of strategic thinking, and especially in chapter 11 on strategic behaviour) – and one that is extremely delicate to manage. As one's client – however tough on the outside – can internally be extremely sensitive, there are almost unlimited possibilities for the process going off-course. Besides the more analytical technical techniques in this book, there is never a substitute for the exercise of judgement, foresight and skilful persuasion.

Such a combination of skills is hard, if not impossible, to package – the more successful, larger consultancies manage still to exercise these skills as if the client is just dealing with one facilitation and not with a firm. Better still, the client makes very selective use of external facilitation, relying upon this on a just-in-time, rather than on a just-in-case basis. In its state of complete perfection, this is achieved within and by the client itself.

Organizing for strategic thinking

So, to summarize, in the past many organizations have actually made the planning process the responsibility of a strategic planning manager, creating some interesting sounding job titles (and associated scepticism and perhaps cynicism). However, to place the primary responsibility for planning in the hands of one specialist staff member may dilute ownership of any outputs. Indeed, it can potentially build up major resistances to what would --in another process/structure – have been seen as perfectly sound ideas.

Rather than to default to appointing a potentially full-time planning manager – with attendant bureaucracy – a perhaps more cunning plan is to project-manage it through the existing management team – and preferably with facilitator support.

A 'facilitator' would have a rather different role to a planner, as the following illustrates:

Planner	Facilitator
Issues the plans	Does not own or issue the content of plans
Focuses on planning process primarily	Focuses on thinking process primarily
Seeks a comprehensive picture and route to the future	Seeks to get the value out of a smaller number of lines of enquiry
Works through meetings and forms	Adds value through workshops
Is typically part of the management team	Is certainly not a member of the management team
Will be internal	Could either be internal or external, dependent upon need
Is invariably full-time	Works on assignment or is part-time
Analytically skilled	Behaviourally skilled

The above table contrasts quite markedly the role definition, skills set and fit of planner versus facilitator. Here the facilitator focuses mainly on orchestrating the process of strategic discovery, rather than with the heavier task of planning administrator.

Sadly, it is hard to find the ideal blend of someone with analytical and creative techniques, and also the behavioural and political skills. Whilst it may be possible to find many of these skills through external consultants and have the advantage of them not being 'native' to the organization, this may well run into the problem of looking like a 'nice to do' initiative.

Ideally this requires training up someone to do the internal facilitation itself. Here it is actually more important that they have process and behavioural skills rather than either in-depth operational knowledge or MBA-level skills. Equally important is their inner political confidence – which could be non-existent if there were any possibilities of future job security being threatened by how a facilitation process was handled.

In order to define your role as facilitator it is necessary to select from a number of styles. A useful way of understanding these styles is to reflect on figure 12.2, which displays two axes:

- expert versus process facilitator
- analytical versus behavioural.

The 'expert' role can stem from your knowledge of the business, or of specific technical issues, or it can be an expertise purely in strategic thinking and analysis.

The 'facilitator' role is concerned with management of the process, including time management, achievement of targeted output, managing the behaviour of the team, and controlling key stakeholders. There are also some practical aspects, such as chairing feedback sessions, setting the agenda for group work, and acting as scribe.

FIGURE 12.2: The strategic adviser: different styles

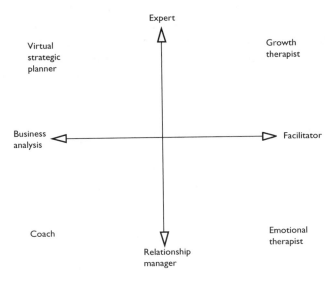

Figure 12.2 thus suggests four styles of facilitator:

- expert/analytical
- expert/behavioural
- behavioural/process facilitator
- analytical/process facilitator.

The expert/analytical role is a very common role, and one which an internal planner or an external consultant/adviser is inclined to play as a default style. The expert/behavioural role is often that taken by a human resource development person, where they are likely to make interventions which draw people in who are quiet, or to harmonize team behaviour. Such a facilitator is likely to play either in this role or in that of behavioural/process facilitator. The analytical/process facilitator could be a former accountant or market analyst or an external or internal management consultant.

Even when showed these different role styles and asked to reflect upon them, advisers/facilitators still tend to stick with their default styles – the ones which they are most used to. Unfortunately the style adopted may not marry well with the specific situation at hand.

For example, taking a workshop focusing on a restructuring, this is likely to require a very heavy bias towards behavioural/process facilitation, due to the obvious sensitivities. Where the facilitator opts for an expert/analytical style this may be inappropriate and counterproductive.

Also, where a workshop focuses on acquisitions, the main need might be for an expert/analytical style. Here an HR development person might not be able to deal with the variety of issues that may arise.

In order to identify your default facilitator style, let us first analyze some of the key capabilities which go along with each of the styles: Expert/analytical:

- knowledge of the business
- knowledge of possible technical solutions
- problem-solving ability
- analytical knowledge of strategic thinking
- integrative skills – seeing the bigger picture.

Expert/behavioural:

- knowledge of the people involved – informal
- knowledge of the people (psychometric)
- knowledge of team processes.

Behavioural/process facilitator:

- listening skills
- intervention skills
- influencing skills
- providing energy to the group.

Expert/process facilitator:

- expertise in the strategic thinking process
- creative thinking
- questioning skills
- summarizing skills
- providing inspiration to the group.

EXERCISE: YOUR DEFAULT FACILITATION STYLE

For the key facilitation styles now covered, how would you rate:

a) which role you like playing:

- expert/analytical
- expert/behavioural
- behavioural/process facilitator
- expert/process facilitator.

b) which role others would see you as good at:

- expert/analytical
- expert/behavioural
- behavioural/process facilitator
- expert/process facilitator.

FIGURE 12.3: The advisory circle: the client

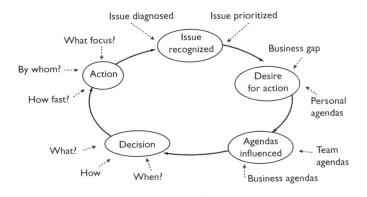

Another important area for the budding facilitator to be aware of is that of the issue recognition cycle. Figure 12.3 shows how this operates.

During any workshop new issues may well surface. A strong facilitator will be able to sense the potential of this issue (either as a problem or opportunity) and of its implication on other issues or aspects of the business. Such a facilitator will also be able to think through (a) how long it might take to explore that issue; (b) what techniques might help to analyze and discuss it; (c) how bumpy the process and associated behaviour might be en route, and (d) who might cause problems or be of help. This demands very quick thinking and a well-honed intuitive sense of the workshop dynamics.

In getting up to speed with this level of facilitation there is no substitute for getting lots of facilitation experience. Facilitation is never a boring task as both authors will testify. On one particular occasion a team of eleven managers insisted on working together (without splitting into groups) for two whole days and an evening. They refused to go along with the facilitator's advice, making little progress and wearing themselves out. In the 16 years of that author's experience as a facilitator, this was a first.

On another occasion the top manager in one organization told one of the authors that 'this will be the most difficult project you have ever undertaken'. Unfortunately he neglected to say that it was he who was going to make it so difficult. A very strong, forceful manager by nature, two hours into the strategic workshop when we were just finishing off checking out the current strategic position, he exploded volcano-style:

> Tony, when is the helicopter thinking going to start, if we don't get airborne soon I will bloody-well take off in my helicopter for Japan and the Far East, where the real growth is!

Author's historical note: this workshop was in the mid-1990s whilst Japanese and Far East markets were in boom and just before this boom turned to bust.

Coming back to figure 12.3, unless the facilitator recognizes that even where an issue has been discussed in detail, there is no guarantee that any action will ensue unless all the preconditions for actually doing something are met.

A second area for thought is the simple logistics of running strategic thinking events effectively. Often the arrangements for such a process are determined by the managing director's PA's decision on hotel accommodation. It is not unusual for facilitators to be told that a workshop is to be run for two days in an hotel room without external light, hardly encouraging visionary thought.

Or a 'workshop' might be planned for the top 30 managers of a specialist department, without thinking about (a) whether this is actually viable or not (physically and intellectually), or (b) whether it is significant that all the middle managers have been left out.

Alternatively, where workshops are held on site there are often inadequate catering arrangements (signalling that this workshop is not really that important). Or, managers drift back to not only the mobile telephones but even to their e-mails between sessions, causing major distraction.

Before an event is held its purpose and intended outputs (and next steps) need to be tightly defined in advance. When a facilitator is to be used, then they need to be appropriately positioned. This also means that they should not be over-positioned. (One of the authors was once rather flatteringly described as being 'A leading European thinker', setting unrealistic and inappropriate expectations in the management team – they expected a cross between Superman and Einstein.)

It is also important to pre-define who will collate the outputs from a workshop. Unless these are typed up quickly not only is the sense lost but also the immediacy. Ideally the output should be available within three working days of the workshop.

In an effective, well-facilitated workshop there can be quite a volume of output. Whilst the more critical decisions and analyses are probably contained in a dozen or so flipcharts (over a two-day period), there may be another two dozen or so sheets of ancillary thinking, which provides helpful context.

One of the central roles of the facilitator is to capture that thinking with a flipchart pen (or on acetate) so that the rest of the management team can have both their hands, and their minds, free. This part can be harder for an internal facilitator, who might make value-laden interpretations (either intentionally or unintentionally) of what is said.

Delivering value-driven outputs

Conventionally, many managers are happy to just see some strategic outputs rather than necessarily ones of the highest quality and value. As we argued in chapters 6 and 7, on the value of strategic thinking, there should be economic value of strategic thoughts – at each and every stage.

It is a helpful learning discipline therefore to set aside five to ten minutes at the end of a strategic thinking session simply to put a value on some of the outputs. Whilst this value may be highly approximate and broad-brush, it is healthy to review whether real value has begun to come out yet or not.

This routine also helps to underline the need to actually implement the strategic plan, rather than to just have a number of temporarily exciting strategic thoughts.

Just to recap, the major categories of the value of strategic thoughts from chapters 6 and 7 were:

- the meaning (of strategic thinking)
- business value
- context
- thought value
- prioritization
- core process
- process drivers
- supporting structure and skills
- supporting processes
- soft value.

Linking to implementation

Having established at last some clarity of decisions and of key priorities, it is necessary to actually implement strategic actions. Many managers bemoan the lack of guidelines – either from business school thinkers or from management consultants in how to approach this crucial phase of strategic thinking.

There are a number of important recipes to achieve successful links to implementation, as follows:

- to focus on a number of key strategic breakthroughs which are tangible and actionable (and not just broad-brush ideas)
- to set some clear parameters on the outputs of the strategic break-through, for example in terms of:
  - scale
  - competitive benefits
  - profitability and/or economic value
  - shifts in capability
- to use the key implementation techniques of:
  - fishbone analysis (for problem diagnosis)
  - from-to (or FT analysis) (for exploring the scope of implementation)
  - wishbone analysis – to examine what needs to line up to deliver effective implementation
  - forcefield analysis (for exposing the scale of implementation difficulty), possibly with the value-over-time curve

- stakeholder analysis (and agenda analysis) – for understanding who you need to communicate with, who to involve, who to influence, and how to influence them
- urgency-importance analysis and / or attractiveness–implementation difficulty (AID analysis)
- the importance / uncertainty grid (for exposing key implementation vulnerabilities – and addressing these proactively
- the project management techniques coming in chapter 13
- scenario story telling, especially for how future implementation might go well versus not so well. Also using this to work backwards from future implementation success

■ devising a set of key questions to work through.

Taking a closer look at the final point above, a typical list of questions to work through is found in the following exercise:

EXERCISE: IMPLEMENTING A STRATEGIC BREAKTHROUGH

For one area of implementing your strategy, either at the corporate, business, departmental, project, team or individual levels:

■ Where this is a problem, what are its root causes (fishbone)?
■ Where this is an opportunity, what is its vision and what factors (both within and outside your control or influence) would need to line up to deliver this vision?
■ For this breakthrough, what is its targeted, economic value? (Think about its likely net costs into the future)
■ Where the breakthrough comprises a number of discretionary actions or activities, where are these positioned on the attractiveness-implementation difficulty (AID) grid?
■ What is your cunning plan now for implementing it?
■ How difficult will it be to implement (forcefield analysis)?
■ Who are the key stakeholders involved during the lifetime of this breakthrough?
■ Where are these stakeholders likely to be positioned, given your cunning plan, in terms of (a) attitude (for, neutral or against) and influence (high, medium or low)?
■ How do these patterns of attitude and influence shift for different areas of implementation? (Here you might need to do separate stakeholder agenda analyses for each action or sub-project.)
■ Given the agendas of key stakeholders (use stakeholder agenda analysis), how might you influence them either to (a) be more favourable, or (b) to reduce the influence of those who are against?
■ Given all of this thinking, what scenario stories can you tell about:
  - the implementation going very smoothly
  - the implementation being somewhat turbulent
  - the implementation going completely wrong.

Designing a strategic workshop

Strategic workshops can be used for a variety of strategic issues, including:

■ acquisitions
■ alliances
■ new organic business development
■ restructuring
■ cost management
■ organizational design (and futures)
■ organization and people strategy
■ scenarios (generally)
■ specific strategic projects
■ shareholder value management
■ strategic thinking awareness
■ competitor intelligence
■ financial strategies, e.g. marketing, logistics, IT, finance.

EXERCISE: TARGETING STRATEGIC WORKSHOPS

Based on the possible areas of workshops described in this book:

■ Do you presently run workshops in this area?
■ Should you run workshops in this area?
■ If you did, what would their targeted value be?

We now give you some very practical advice on design, running and getting maximum value out of strategic development workshops.

Although workshops can generate disproportionate value (and vision), this can be diluted considerably where:

■ there is inadequate pre-planning (of issues, process and outputs)
■ there is no facilitation or where it is ineffective
■ there are no plans in place to deal with the output and to move it on into the next phase
■ there are no tools to help managers make progress (use the tools and checklists contained in this book).

Twelve key questions on 'how to run a workshop' are as follows:

■ What is the objective of the workshop?
■ How does it relate to other initiatives?

- What are seen as the key outputs (learning, problem definition, action plans, behavioural shift, etc), and how will these be documented and communicated, and to whom?
- Who needs to be involved?
- How will it be positioned in the organization and by whom?
- Who will facilitate, and are they seen as competent and impartial?
- Where should it be held and what facilities are required?
- What are the next steps following the workshop likely to be?
- What key barriers and blockages may arise, and how will these be dealt with, and by whom?
- What specific activities will be undertaken and what will this input require?
- How will these be broken down into discussion groups and who will be in each one?
- How long is required to make substantial progress on each issue and what happens if tasks are incomplete?

Experience shows that it is essential to consider all these questions at length, rather than rushing into a workshop on a particular issue with merely a broad agenda. The questions emphasize both content and process, and involve thinking through how these interrelate. They also involve analyzing both current and future context – this provides high quality feed-in of data, and also helps to think through feedback into the management process in detail and in advance.

It is vital to structure the content of each workshop to contain key questions. An example of this for a bank is as follows:

Morning:

- What is our current position in derivatives trading?
- What options exist for us to develop new products for new or existing markets?
- What competitive advantage would we be able to achieve and sustain, and how?

Afternoon:

- What would the implementation implications be, and what would the direct and indirect costs be?
- Broadly speaking, what are the likely financial implications (and risks) of any new developments?
- What are our next steps?

Conclusion

A key lesson from this chapter is that you do not have to be a full-time consultant (either externally or internally) to be your own strategy consultant. Being your own strategy consultant requires merely a willingness to step outside the pure content of strategic issues and to then design, plan, target, resource and perhaps facilitate a strategic thinking process.

This requires some familiarity with a few strategic thinking techniques, sensitivity to organizational politics and agendas, and a structural process – and one which includes at least some workshop elements. It does not require being Superman or Supergirl.

Summary of key points

- The process of strategy is often more important to focus on than its content.
- A strategy consultant can add value in a diversity of ways: from being a sounding board to providing out-of-the-box ideas and from being a symbolic presence and energizer to being a facilitator.
- Asking the right questions and even unthinkable questions is a key role – and one which it is hard for an internal manager to fulfil operating within a conventional mindset.
- You will also need a variety of stretching competencies to fulfil this role – requiring training, development and, potentially, mentoring.
- Establishing a process requires being able to identify strategic issues, to target the outputs, and to select the necessary techniques.
- Data analysis needs to be focused on the situation and on the particular outputs sought, rather than spread thinly.
- The strategic thinking process needs to be project-managed.
- Strategic thinking requires cultural alignment with greater empowerment.
- Planning units can find it very difficult to act as effective facilitators when asked to operate in a conventional operational environment where there is no real strategic culture.
- Their effectiveness can be materially enhanced if they develop their facilitation skills and roles. Ultimately it is line management's primary role to have, and then to own, the key strategic thoughts.
- Even a facilitator's role is complex, requiring a number of different high-order skills.

- Every facilitator must be aware of the process of strategic issue recognition, and how to maintain the focus on a small number of issues.
- A continual focus on 'what value is coming out' of strategic thinking is essential.
- Very clear links to implementation are always required.
- Strategic workshops can be applied to a diversity of strategic issues – from acquisitions to business development and to organizational strategy.
- Each workshop needs careful planning, structuring, key questions, targeted output, positioning and project-managing.

Reference

Johnson, G. and K. Scholes, *Exploring Corporate Strategy*, Prentice Hall, 1987.

CHAPTER THIRTEEN

Managing a strategic project

Introduction

Most managers have not integrated project management with their everyday management activities. Despite increasing demands on them due to performance challenges and business change, project management is now an essential skill for today's senior manager.

Project management techniques can be applied at the level of the business strategy itself, or to operational change programmes, or to even more tactical programmes aimed at improving short-term business performance.

Strategic projects themselves necessitate a new analytical tool set relative to those found in traditional project management disciplines. This chapter gives a comprehensive account of those processes. This enables managers the ability to deal with:

- cross-functional projects
- projects within a particular function
- specific issues faced within their own role over the next 12–18 months.

Indeed, in many companies the role of co-ordinating strategic projects is very much located within a specialist function – in operations or finance. This chapter helps all managers – of whatever discipline – to manage business projects more effectively through strategic thinking.

Here we take you through:

- the strategic project management process
- managing strategies as projects
- project objectives and milestones
- managing strategic projects – checklists.

The final checklists are particularly relevant for doing any MBA project.

The strategic project management process

Strategic project management (or SPM) is defined as:

> The process of managing complex projects by combining strategic thinking, business analysis and project management techniques in order to implement the business strategy and to deliver organizational breakthroughs.

These business analysis techniques include strategic, operational, organizational and financial analysis.

Conventional project management is very much the offspring of Taylorian scientific management. Although the idea that management is a science and should be managed as such is no longer much in vogue, the rationalist assumptions embedded in project management carry on.

Outside the land of major construction projects the real issue is far less the management of interlocking detail. Instead it is about making sure that managers do not lose sight of the really big picture, for which strategic thinking is an imperative. 'Why are managers even doing this project and not another one?' is a very real question often to ask. Where projects are riddled with uncertainty the relatively precise definition of activity durations becomes first an academic irrelevancy. Worse, as business projects are particularly vulnerable to knock-on effects, the most important critical success factor seems to be to identify how projects can be made more resilient generally rather than worrying about whether a particular activity might over-run by 10 per cent or so.

Let us now begin to draw the contrast between conventional and strategic project management.

	Conventional Project Management	**Strategic Project Management**
Links with business strategy	Vague and distant	Direct and explicit
Project definition	Usually portrayed as a 'given'	Highly flexible, creative, depending on options
Project planning	Follows on directly from project definition	Only done once a project strategy is set
Attitude to detail	Absolutely central – it is all about control	Important but only in context – try always to see the big (helicopter) picture
The importance of stakeholders	Emphasis on formal structures – project manager, team sponsor	Far-reaching stakeholder analysis; requires continual scanning
The importance of uncertainty	Coped with through critical path analysis (after activity planning)	Do uncertainty analysis first, then plan activities

In addition to the more traditional aspects of project management, equally important in managing strategic projects are:

- problem diagnosis
- looking at options – not only for which projects to do but how to do them (especially acquisitions)
- managing stakeholders – those individuals with an interest in the project
- dealing with uncertainty
- trading-off not merely tangible but also less tangible value
- creating a strategic vision for the project
- identifying key implementation difficulties.

The above areas reach beyond the domain of traditional project management, carrying us explicitly into the land of strategy, finance and organizational analysis, and into strategic project management.

The following checklists now help you to manage projects using strategic thinking.

Managing projects and strategic thinking

- Why is the project actually needed and what are you looking to get out of it, what are the overall deliverables?
- What options are available to create these deliverables?
- What further projects (or mini-projects) will also be required to reach these deliverables?
- What key taken-for-granted assumptions have you made, and what could go wrong, when and how, if these are not fulfilled?
- Should you be prepared to say 'No' to the project (or to sub-projects) as it is maybe either not fundamentally attractive or are too difficult – given your resources or other reasons, or both?
- Have you identified all of the mini-projects (such as improving team morale) that are on the 'soft' critical path?
- Have all the complex activities been identified as actually complex enough to warrant thinking about as a sub-project?
- For each key activity, what is the likely value that this particular activity will create?
- How should you best position each part of the project effectively within the organization so that it gets the attention it deserves?
- What personal agendas of both yourself and of others exist which are associated with the project, and how should these be managed?

The strategic project management process contains five key stages (see figure 13.1). These stages include:

- defining the project
- creating the project strategy
- detailed project planning
- implementation and control
- review and learning.

FIGURE 13.1: Strategic project management: the process

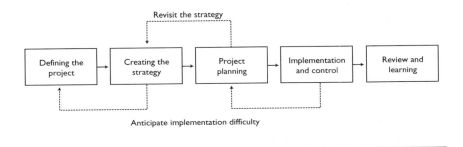

Figure 13.1 emphasizes that project management may require the project to be redefined or the project strategy to be revisited. It also highlights the need to anticipate the project's implementation difficulty – at the planning stage and even earlier.

Defining the project involves:

- diagnosing any key problems which gave rise to the project in the first place
- defining the project's scope and main focus
- clarifying any key interdependencies
- creating an overall (at a very high level) vision for the project, and its key objectives
- thinking through, at least initially, who the stakeholders might be.

Key strategic tools which we would use include:

- fishbone analysis
- wishbone analysis
- stakeholder analysis.

The above reveals that defining the project is not something which is done in five minutes – and is self-evident. Project definition involves a good deal of reflection about the purpose and context of the projects.

Creating the project strategy entails:

- Exploring the external and internal environment for the project at greater length.
- Defining more specifically the key strategic goals of the project.
- Examining strategic options for a) what to do, and b) how to do it, including 'push' versus 'pull' strategies (a 'push' strategy is one where little discretion is allowed to those stakeholders impacted on by the project. A 'pull' strategy is one where the degree of discretion is higher, either over the project's goals or the project's process, or both) .
- A preliminary appraisal of the project's overall attractiveness and implementation difficulty.
- Further thinking about the positioning of key stakeholders, and how these might be influenced.

Project strategy demands even more thought than project definition – as there may be many ways of implementing the project. Key strategic tools to be used here include:

- the strategic option grid (see chapter 4)
- wishbone analysis (see chapter 3)
- stakeholder analysis (see chapter 5).

Detailed project planning requires:

- A detailed analysis of the key activities and / or sub-projects which the overall project strategy requires.
- An analysis of how these activities are networked in a sequence, given their interdependencies and also an analysis of their critical paths.
- An appraisal of key uncertainties along with contingency plans and impact analysis.
- A financial appraisal of the project's value and cost drivers, along with an overview of the financials.

Key strategic tools thus needed here include:

- how-how analysis (see chapter 5)
- interdependency analysis
- attractiveness-implementation difficulty (AID) analysis (see chapter 5)
- the uncertainty grid (see chapter 2)
- value and cost drivers (see chapter 5).

Other useful tools include forcefield analysis and stakeholder analysis (chapter 5).

Whilst this is the core of traditional project management, project plans will only ever be as good as the project strategies they are based upon.

Implementation and control necessitates:

- definition of project milestones and responsibilities
- key implementation difficulties highlighted and counter-measures built in to resource action plans
- some preview of likely project dynamics.

Implementation and control requires continual checking back to the project's strategy and vision to ensure that apparent delivery of milestones is actually fulfilling the original purpose of the project. Particularly useful techniques here include forcefield analysis, stakeholder analysis and the uncertainty grid.

Review and learning involves:

- Revisiting the project to assess whether the targeted deliverables were achieved, whether the implementation process went smoothly or not, how effectively the project was positioned politically, and other behavioural lessons.
- And, also, how could the strategic project management process itself be improved?

Relevant tools at this stage include fishbone analysis (for problem analysis – chapter 5), wishbone analysis and the uncertainty grid (for key project vulnerabilities), value and cost drivers (for attractiveness) and forcefield/stakeholder analysis (for implementation difficulty and support).

Review and learning is thus not merely a peripheral part of the process, but is the driver of continuous improvement in the project process. Generally speaking, review and learning is frequently the weakest link in the strategic project management chain.

Managing strategies as projects

Business strategy can be looked at more dynamically as a stream of projects. Whilst strategy is – in practice – often made incrementally, rather than seeing this a threat to strategic planning (as does Mintzberg, 1994), we can now see the project as being an important unit of strategic analysis. Strategic project management thus becomes a way of emergent strategy becoming deliberate. Henry Mintzberg has criticized conventional strategy theory, which is based on the notion that strategy is deliberate. He has suggested that most of the manifestations of strategy are very much implicit, fragmented and fluid. Mintzberg's definition of strategy is therefore one of 'a pattern in a stream of decisions or actions'.

Whilst many 'decisions' or 'actions' may not be identified as projects, certainly if they are truly 'strategic' then they ought to be projects, whether this is made explicit or implicit. For if we go back to the classic definition of a 'project', which is:

> A project is a complex set of activities with a predefined result which is targeted over a particular time and to a specific cost.

then strategic decisions (or actions) are necessarily projects.

'Business strategy' is thus effectively a collection of mutually aligned projects designed to create a specific competitive positioning. In effect, this recognizes that most strategic thinking should be done at a smaller scale level than is typically appreciated. We call this level that of the 'Mini Strategy'. This approach is helpful because it enables management (at all levels) to get a better grip on business strategy, especially so that they actually get on and implement it.

Whilst Mintzberg's extension of the types of strategy from one to two (deliberate and now emergent) is laudable, these two forms simply do not go far enough. We have therefore added three additional forms: the submergent, the 'emergency' and the 'detergent'), giving:

- deliberate
- emergent
- submergent
- emergency
- detergent.

FIGURE 13.2: The strategy cycle and the strategy mix

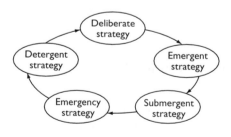

These forms of strategy are depicted in figure 13.2 which shows a deliberate strategy at the start, often moving into an emergent phase. Unless its duration and implementation is steered, it may drift into submergent or 'emergency' phases, or even 'detergent' (where it is tidied up). A 'submergent' strategy is a deliberate or an emergent strategy which has ceased to work. In this phase managers often re-double their efforts, putting in more time and resource without questioning the original scope of the project, and the basis of the project strategy.

An 'emergency' strategy is one where there is so little coherence to action that there is no real sense of direction at all.

Finally, a 'detergent' strategy is one where a strategy which has not worked in the past is now being re-thought, and its various parts which did not work in the past are being discarded, or changed (Grundy, 1994).

Any strategy can be analyzed to discern which stage of its evolution it is presently at. A strategy which is in two or more of the above phases simultaneously is said to have a 'strategy mix'.

Besides asking oneself where the business strategy and the project strategy is, vis-à-vis the strategy mix, it is also imperative to examine the strategy mix as it changes over time. Taking a typical project, initially there may be an intensive phase of deliberate strategy but quite quickly this opens out into a number of emergent strategies. Some of these strategies fan out, losing their sense of direction and thus becoming submergent or even emergency strategies.

The strategy mix can be used for diagnosis at a number of levels, for example for projects at a:

- corporate strategy level
- business strategy level
- the breakthrough programme level (i.e. involving a number of inter-dependent projects which will combine to support the business strategy)
- at the project level itself, which is what we concentrate on here.

Due to the importance of the various forms of strategy, it is worthwhile defining each strategy type out further, as follows.

Deliberate strategy

A deliberate strategy is one which has a very clearly formulated idea of how to get from A to B. Deliberate strategies, if innovative and skilfully crafted, can offer a more direct route to your strategic objective for growth. The proviso here is that any deliberate strategy needs to anticipate both pending external change and complexities of implementation.

Emergent strategy

An emergent strategy (as we have already mentioned) is one which is hard to detect as an explicit strategy at the time. Emergent strategies are more commonly ones whose pattern can only be detected virtually after the event, once the pattern has been knitted together. Emergent strategies vary in terms of (1) how coherent this pattern is after the event, (2) whether they exploit opportunities in different strategic directions thus, in effect, partly cancelling each other out. In the former case emergent strategies are helpful, whilst in the latter case they are positively unhelpful.

Submergent strategy

A submergent strategy is one which was either originally a deliberate strategy which has gone wrong or an emergent strategy which has got itself into real trouble. The submergent strategy is an unrealized strategy which has led to damaging results.

Emergency strategy

'Emergency' strategies are characterized by very little longer-term pattern in strategies with these being mainly reactions to short-term pressures or temptations. Emergency strategies are 'off the highway' of achieving longer-term strategic direction. An emergency strategy would hardly count as a strategy at all unless it was so prevalent as it is in everyday reality.

Detergent strategy

A detergent strategy is often called 'refocusing' strategy. The idea of detergent strategy is perhaps more powerful as it links directly to cleaning up a mess left after an emergent, submergent or emergency strategy. A detergent strategy can be found either as part of a major and dramatic turnaround, or as a more localized attempt to prepare a more solid basis for new deliberate strategies.

A key conclusion from the notion of the strategy mix that no single form of strategy is therefore appropriate to managing strategies in different contexts. Deliberate, emergent (and even detergent) strategies need to be managed together in a deliberate juggling act.

The above forms of strategy are all extremely important to business projects as a) the strategy mix may be predominately of an emergent, submergent or emergency nature, meaning that it is very difficult, if not impossible, to make linkages between the project and its higher level business strategy, and b) the project itself may be in a more emergent, submergent or 'emergency' state. Although this is clearly undesirable, it is by no means an inconceivable state. Many projects lack sufficient clarity of purpose and inherent advantage to actually succeed.

Where the business strategy is very fluid it is then that much harder to engender a logic and clarity at the project level. Equally, where key business projects have the habit of not being terribly well thought through, then there is perhaps an even greater tendency for the business strategy to become fuzzy and ill-thought through.

Business projects are often seen by managers as relatively separate activities, unlinked to one another, but in reality many business projects form part of bigger programmes which in turn form a central part of the business strategy. These linkages between projects will be much stronger where there is a relatively clear and primarily 'deliberate' business strategy. Very substantial and important projects (or clusters of projects) can thus aptly be called 'strategic breakthrough projects'. A strategic breakthrough project is defined as:

> A strategic project which will have a material impact on either the business's external competitive edge, its internal capabilities or its financial performance – or all three.

As we saw earlier, there should only be a relatively small number of strategic breakthroughs. By restricting the number of 'breakthrough' projects to a minimum, the following advantages are likely to accrue:

- critical mass of resources is more likely to be achieved;
- marginal projects will not be undertaken;
- organizational attention and communication will be focused on a much smaller number of things at any one time;
- the organization is less likely to wear itself out on many very difficult projects.

FIGURE 13.3: Business strategy as a stream of projects

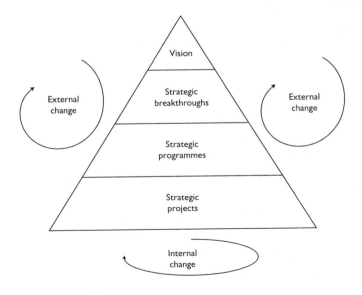

Figure 13.3 now illustrates how a business strategy can be seen as a stream of projects. This 'stream' of projects is not static but represents rather a flow of projects over time – which collectively shifts or transforms the business. An important insight here is that strategic thinking is often best focused on the level of a strategic project, rather than on developing comprehensive, catch-all business strategies top-down. Each individual project is then linked with the overall strategic vision of the business.

Project objectives and milestones

Now we have thoroughly diagnosed the context for the project using a selection of project diagnosis tools, we can now define the project's key objectives with greater clarity. Whilst this may seem to be an obvious and self-evident part of the process, it is often not. There may be several dimensions of the project's objectives, including:

- strategic objectives
- operational objectives
- organizational objectives
- financial objectives.

For instance, strategic objectives might include:

- penetrating a market to gain a certain percentage of market share
- gaining a particular competitive position
- creating new opportunities for strategy development
- generating tangible synergies or spin-offs in other areas of the business.

Operational objectives – for their part – might include:

- improving efficiency levels
- resolving performance difficulties or bottlenecks
- simplifying operational processes
- achieving world-class operational standards
- achieving very high customer service standards, or zero defects
- developing new processes.

Organizational objectives might include:

- building existing competencies
- creating entirely new competencies
- improved team-working
- increasing organizational responsiveness and flexibility
- simplifying the organization

- creating specific behaviours – for example, leadership, creativity, strategic thinking
- shifting the organizational mindset
- making it a genuinely international organization.

Financial objectives might include:

- improved rate of return on assets
- improved return on sales or margins
- reduced costs
- payback over a particular period (for an investment)
- net present value (the economic value of the future volume of net cash flows less investment).

Whilst every project will have its core objectives (which will almost certainly be multiple), there will almost certainly be some secondary objectives. Although a sub-set of these objectives may be reasonably self-evident, there will be some ambiguity about what the strategic project is actually about. It is therefore imperative to define the primary and secondary objectives explicitly rather than leave them to the risks of miscommunication and misunderstanding throughout the organization.

It is invariably useful to tease out the full range of objectives of a project – both financial and non-financial.

Having established greater clarity on project objectives it is then worthwhile to go back to our earlier diagnosis, whether this was achieved using fishbone, wishbone or performance driver analysis. At this earlier stage the probable scope of the strategic project should have begun to emerge, potentially in the shape of an embryonic strategy. This scope can then be tested against the project's objectives, for example to address these questions:

- Will achievement of the objectives deal fully or only partly with the problems or potential opportunity unearthed in the diagnosis phase?
- Are the objectives sufficiently complete to achieve this?
- Are the objectives becoming so complex that we may well need to think of splitting the project into separate projects, or at least into sub-projects?

The clearer the project's objectives are then the easier it is to interrelate the project to other projects, and also to begin to compile a business case for the project. It also becomes easier to decide on the most appropriate project management skills that will be required. Also, control measures can be more readily derived. Finally, it becomes much easier to communicate the project and to position it with key stakeholders.

Milestones form the key methodology for project control. A project milestone can be defined as the time by which some specific project deliverable has been achieved.

When planning a project one normally works backwards from the milestones to the present, rather than vice versa. This means that one is less inclined to indulge in spurious or dilutive activity. Specialist functional managers, being disciplined by training and (usually) by nature, are well-placed to ask for milestones across not just activities normally regarded as projects, but also for other activities too.

Sadly, many managers become overly preoccupied by project milestones and neglect the 'how' of the project – its project strategy and plan. These are crucial and to some extent are more important than the project milestones themselves. Remember that the whole point of a project is to achieve the result in least time and cost.

Where a project fails to achieve its designated milestone, then the next step is, unsurprisingly, to do a fishbone analysis of the root cause of its failure.

Besides specific project milestones for certain projects (like change management) where it is harder to define more specific milestones, it is as well to also specify some key indicators. Key indicators are some of the softer and more qualitative deliverables of the project. So, for example, with a culture change project we would need to examine each of the key shifts which were the goal of the project and then ask the question what are the key indicators for this shift to have actually occurred?

A guiding principle overall is to ensure that project milestones and indicators do not become a bureaucracy. Their whole purpose is to energize, mobilize and focus, not to become ends in themselves.

Managing strategic projects: checklists

In this final section we will give you some detailed checklists for managing strategic projects:

- organic business development projects
- projects involving strategic and financial planning
- restructuring projects
- information systems projects
- management buy-out projects
- alliance and joint venture projects
- operational projects.

These checklists are useful for live business projects and also for MBA coursework and MBA projects and dissertations.

Organic business development projects

These checklists will help to flesh out some of the richer content issues which you may well come up against in evaluating projects. Whilst managers may feel they are well-versed in these organic development projects, they may well look too myopically at the more obvious areas of inquiry.

Organic business development projects can be aimed at a number of areas including:

- new products
- new markets – by sector or by geography
- selling more to existing customers
- new value-creating activities
- new distribution channels
- new technologies.

Turning now to some core checklists for each of the areas outlined above:

New product projects

It is often said that nine out of ten new product ideas fail either because they are not thought through sufficiently in themselves or (and more commonly) the product concept does not quite match market need. These checklists (coupled with wishbone analysis) should help you get a better steer. Our questions now are:

- How fast is the market for this type of product growing?
- How much competitive pressure exists in its market?
- How well does the product meet its target customer needs; what are the turn-ons and turn-offs from a customer point of view?
- Which other products is it competing with and what are the relative advantages/disadvantages between each?
- How (if at all) does the product need servicing, and what are the relative competitive advantages here?
- How complex is the product, and will this level of complexity mean it is a) harder to launch, b) less flexible to change subsequently?
- Are there any wonderfully innovative features (which add real value) of the product?
- If these exist, how easily can these be imitated?

- How consistent is the organization's capability and mindset with this product, and what implementation issues might this raise?
- What skills training is required to support this product effectively?
- Are the product's long-run unit costs likely to be sustainable longer term?
- What other changes in the organization (for example to key business processes or to organizational structure) are needed?
- Will the sales force and distribution channels accommodate the new product effectively – without destruction, disruption, a dilution of sales of other products?
- To what extent might the product cannibalize on other existing products?
- To what extent will the product's innovation be project-managed well?
- How can its introduction be positioned and accelerated in the organization?

New market projects

New market development projects may overlap to some extent with new products. Nevertheless, we include some new questions to supplement those on new products:

- Have you systematically prioritized which (of potential new markets) it would be most attractive to address (for example, using the AID analysis, or the strategic option grid)?
- How inherently attractive is this market (consider its growth drivers and the level of competitive pressure in it)?
- How difficult is it to operate within that market (generally)?
- Do we have the natural competencies to do well in that market?
- Is this market culturally vastly different to our current core markets?
- Is this a market especially prone to discounting, high costs of satisfying customers or distribution channels, or low margins generally?
- Have we got a genuinely 'cunning' entry strategy (or just an average one)?
- What channel strategy options exist and which of these is a) most attractive inherently (in terms of its use and value-added generally), b) one where we have greatest competitive advantage?
- What are the most critical uncertainties about that market and how can we minimize our exposure to these?
- Will entering this particular market foreclose options to enter other markets?
- To what extent will market conditions vary internationally, and which of these markets should we really give highest priority?

Selling more to existing customers

Selling more to our existing customers may well be a neglected strategy but, nevertheless, one which might be both highly attractive and relatively easy:

- Which of our existing customer base could we potentially sell more to?
- What could we sell them, why and how?
- What things have prevented us from selling as much as our true potential to existing customers – in the past?
- What latent, existing needs could we satisfy – and which we are not currently satisfying?
- What latent, future needs could we satisfy – and how?
- How might selling more to our existing customers strengthen our relationship with them and gain lock-in?
- Are there other buyers within the customer's organization which we can sell to (e.g. another management function, another division, etc)?
- What specific sales or other incentives would encourage greater penetration of our existing customer base?
- Which of our key competitors is currently active within these customers and how can we erode their share?
- How can we make it unbelievably easy to buy from us (and to buy more from us)?
- How can these improvements be project-managed?

New value-creating activity projects

Adding value in new ways may offer exciting project opportunities but ones which managers may find it difficult to think through:

- Are there new ways in which we can add value to the customer (value-creating activities)?
- How much additional value is likely to be created for them – from their perspective?
- How will we be able to capture or share this value creation given our relative bargaining power and our longer-term strategy?
- To what extent should new value-creating activities be in- or out-sourced, and why?
- How readily might new ways of adding value be imitated by competitors?
- To what extent will customers seek to do these value-creating activities themselves (assuming they are worth having)?
- What is our natural level of competence for adding value in these new ways?

- Can we easily pilot these new value-creating opportunities?
- How will we project-manage developing these new value-creating activities?

New distribution channel projects

Opening up new distribution channels avoids the difficulties of new product and/or market innovation – and may well be cheap. But in order to avoid diluting our strategy and shareholder value, we will need to be relatively selective:

- How much margin are we likely to obtain from a new distribution channel?
- How difficult is it likely to be to deal with?
- What are the key alternatives to dealing with this particular channel (for example by the Internet, sales force, an alliance, etc)?
- Will this particular channel lead to conflict with any other distribution channels and, if so, how will we manage it?
- Are we likely to get a high level of returns or other quality problems through this channel?
- Will the channel actually understand our product sufficiently well?
- How much support will this channel put behind our product – relative to that of other products?
- Does this distribution channel have something that fits our natural competencies and our culture?
- How competitive is this particular channel relative to other pathways to market?
- If we do not use this channel, what (if anything) is the biggest downside?
- How would we project-manage new entry to that channel?

New technologies

New technologies may be a turn-on to middle managers but a turn-off to top managers (whose main focus is to extract short and medium-term values out of the business). We may therefore need some testing questions in order to screen innovative technology projects:

- Does the technology actually fit with our present or emerging definition of 'what business(es) we are in'?
- Do we really understand the technology?
- What other things (other than technology) all have to line up to deliver real value? (Use a wishbone analysis)

- Are we doing the project mainly because of its sheer technological edge, and because it is inherently exciting – or because it will generate real value, and value that we can actually harvest?
- What key value and cost drivers are impacted on by the new technology?
- What new skills do we need to fully exploit any new technology?
- To what extent do we have to change our mindset in order to get the very best out of the new technology?
- Where the technology relies heavily on the Internet, how easy is our business model copied or imitated?
- How quickly will the new technology spread and where there are customer turn-offs in its use, how can these be mitigated or removed?
- How rapidly might the technology be superceded by further technologies and how vulnerable does this therefore make our strategy?
- What substitute technologies are available which are in many respects better right now?
- How should we project-manage the introduction of the new technology?

Projects involving strategic and financial planning

A strategic (and financial) plan is a complex activity which involves a number of outputs and a variety of stakeholders – with different involvement. This is an area for project management par excellence – and yet one which is only peripherally touched on by most strategy text books. It is also an area frequently managed poorly within organizations generally.

- Does the 'strategic' plan genuinely take into account the impact of external change?
- Does it involve the specific measurement of competitive advantage or disadvantage in terms of value added (and at what cost) to target customers vis-à-vis key competitors?
- Is it consistent with 'mission' and is this 'mission' credible given the risk and uncertainties in achieving strategic goals?
- Is financial appraisal used to evaluate the economic value of business strategies (i.e. in cash flow terms – and not just 'reported' earnings projections) or are these strategies left untested in terms of shareholder value?
- Is the strategy feasible given current financial constraints, and do these 'constraints' need testing themselves?
- Does the strategic plan reflect the organizational and operational capability (strengths and weaknesses) of the business – can we excel in what we propose?

- Are there clear strategic and financial milestones for success which link to quarterly or bi-annual business performance assessment?
- Is the 'strategic plan' communicated in appropriate detail to sufficient relevant levels of management and staff responsible for implementation?
- Is there adequate scope for 'emergent strategies' to develop within the overall strategic and financial framework – i.e. in-built provision for innovation and exploitation of hard-to-foresee opportunity?
- Are adequate change project mechanisms set in place to implement the strategy (for example, change project teams, off-site review workshops, rewards for actions to implement change, etc.)?

Restructuring projects

Restructuring projects are now undertaken on an almost routine basis by most larger organizations. Restructuring is often managed in relative isolation from other projects and is also positioned as geared towards delivering more shorter-term benefits. Restructuring – if managed as a strategic project – can be handled much more effectively than this, especially if the following questions are addressed:

- Is the rationale for the restructuring fully thought through and does this reflect not merely current needs but anticipate pending changes in the business?
- Is there a history of frequent re-structuring which has resulted in a permanent (and unnecessary) state of instability in the organization? (If so, how can this be managed more strategically in the future?)
- Has the restructuring put managers into 'artificial' positions without genuine business benefits which are patently transparent and which will aggravate organizational ambiguity?
- Are new appointees genuinely capable of being effective in their roles given their skills, their style, and also the degree of team-working within the organization?
- Has the restructuring been communicated in such a way to lay bare the business-led reasons for the restructuring?
- What is the timing of announcement of restructuring – has it been deliberately timed so as to prevent reflection and debate and could thereby result in simmering resentment?
- How does the restructuring complement other projects or initiatives in the business and how should it be managed alongside these?

Information systems projects

Life in today's organizations is almost unrecognizable with the expansion of office technology and communications. Information systems projects are demanding at a business, technical, cultural, and especially political level. Therefore consider the following:

- Are all projects aimed at changing information systems part of an overall information strategy which is, in turn, linked to both business strategy and intended organizational change?
- How have the cost/benefits of any change project been evaluated in terms of both internal and external benefits and costs, including:
  - customer value
  - access to markets
  - customer 'lock-in'
  - improving responsiveness
  - operational efficiency and capacity?
- Are changes in information systems seen as a) primarily of a technical issue, versus b) as also generating important and more difficult people-related and political issues? In the latter case, does the organization have the necessary tools (like stakeholder analysis) and processes to gain maximum ownership for change?
- Who are the key stakeholders: a) of the end outputs of information systems, and b) as agents within the change process itself?
- Is there a risk of over-run against required timescales which might result in an expensive and disruptive 'crash programme' or a dilution of project benefits?

Management buy-out projects

Management buy-outs may rank as one of the most difficult projects which you may ever choose to contemplate undertaking. To help avoid this becoming mission impossible, consider the following:

- What are the main objectives of the buy-out project and to what extent are these shared by key management stakeholders, for instance:
  - freedom from head office *diktat*
  - the possibility of making a significant capital gain
  - protection of job security
  - challenge of developing the business into new areas
  - opportunity to renew the management team?
- Has the proposed management team the ability and balance to produce a quantum improvement in business performance or does it smack of 'more of the same'?

- What tangible changes will be made to support the symbolic event of the buy-out – for example, changing the company name, relocating premises, throwing out all the old stationery, reorganizing managers' old office layout, removing unnecessary status symbols, and how will these be project-managed?
- Is there a robust strategy for improving the competitive position of the business or are the buy-out plans mainly aimed at producing 'the right set of numbers' to please venture capitalists? How will this strategy be project-managed?
- Has the buy-out team got clear milestones for progress which are achievable but stretching?
- How will the issue of an 'exit route' to sell the business on (where this is applicable) be managed by the management team throughout the lifetime of the buy-out. (Are we managing the buy-out 'result' effectively?)

Alliance and joint venture projects

We will give you checklists on acquisitions in chapter 10.

Whilst acquisitions (chapter 10) capture the headlines in the financial press, many organizations move their corporate strategy forward in a slightly more stealthy fashion through alliances (otherwise known as 'joint ventures'). A 'strategic alliance' can now be defined as:

'A longer-term strategic partnership between two or more organizations where there is investment in the venture by all of those partners, sharing both reward and risk.'

Alliances may be thought of as being less risky than acquisitions. It is true that often the exposure of an alliance partner may be less (due to sharing of risk and the fact that the commitment, although longer-term, is usually not quite so permanent). However, the riskiness of an alliance (sometimes known as a 'joint venture') can be higher due to:

- the very looseness of the arrangements
- the need for a good deal of co-operation and openness
- the fact that alliance partners may often have different aspirations (and possibly ones in tension or conflict), or different levels of bargaining power
- the possibility that the strategies of partners may change over time (and alongside that the personal agendas of key players in top management)
- the liklihood that the alliance itself will evolve and change as will its competitive environment.

Having said all this, alliances can be extremely profitable, for example witness Securicor's alliance with British Telecom to form the mobile telecommunications company Cellnet. Cellnet became so successful that Securicor's total shareholder value (as a group) was substantially increased, independently of performance in Securicor's traditional businesses.

Some key questions to reflect upon for any alliance (split up into the phases of formation and development) are as follows:

Formation

- What is the fundamental purpose of the alliance – what distinctive value does it add?
- Why is it likely to be better than other possible alliances?
- What are the different options for structuring and resourcing the alliance?
- To what extent is the alliance well-timed?
- How are the various needs and competencies of the alliance partners genuinely complementary?
- To what extent are these needs and competencies in tension or in potential conflict?
- To what extent is the alliance genuinely therefore a 'positive-sum game' (or an arrangement where all parties are significantly better off through participating in the alliance)?
- What is the potential for the alliance leading on into a full acquisition, longer term?
- Culturally, are the alliance partners likely to get on with each other: well, satisfactorily or, perhaps, badly?
- Have all partners got sufficient interest and commitment in the alliance to make it genuinely effective?
- Will our entering into an alliance with another partner(s) only give us a temporary advantage – as it is likely to trigger other alliances in the industry?
- What are the potential risks and downsides to sustaining our core competencies by depending upon the alliance?
- Can we learn about how our partners do things really well and apply them elsewhere in our business without our partners becoming antagonistic?
- How long – realistically – do we think the alliance is likely to last?
- Who – if anyone – is likely to become the more dominant partner in the alliance, and if this is not likely to be us, what is the potential value of us being in the alliance?

- Do any arrangements for potential divorce adequately safeguard our interests?
- How will the formation of the alliance be project-managed?

Development

- What investment is the alliance likely to require over time, and are alliance partners both able and willing to commit this when the time arrives?
- What senior management (and other scarce skills) is the alliance likely to need, and who will support this requirement?
- How will alliance partners conduct any reviews of performance and steer the strategy forward?
- In the event that the alliance takes off even more successfully than anticipated, how will it cope with this, particularly with regard to:
  - people
  - structures
  - financial resources.
- What processes for change of partners (including new ones coming in, old ones leaving or changes in partner stakes) be managed?
- How will alliance development be project-managed (for example, what will its key milestones be)?

Operational projects

Besides the more purely 'strategic' projects including organic development, acquisitions and alliances, there may also be some major operational projects. These can be grouped (for convenience) under the two main headings of:

- operations expansion
- cost management and efficiency.

Operations expansion

- Based on the checklists dealing with selling more to existing customers/selling to new customers, etc (from 'Organic Development'), what is the potential for relatively easy-to-do expansion?
- To what extent can capacity be increased:
  - by physical expansion?
  - without physical expansion (and by the 'cunning plan')?
  - by appropriate outsourcing?

- What productivity targets (by each and every incremental resource) need to be established?
- How will expansion be project-managed?

Cost management and efficiency

- How cost-competitive are we against our existing competitors (now)?
- How cost-competitive are we against any new entrants (now)?
- How cost competitive are we likely to be (on current plans) vis-à-vis existing competitors and potential entrants?
- What are the key cost drivers within our current operational set-up and how can these be a) incrementally improved, b) radically challenged (for example with zero-based approaches, i.e. working up from a situation of nil resources)?
- What are the key value drivers of the business and how can incremental value be added – and harvested – from a lower, or equivalent, or (preferably) a changed cost base?
- How can key business processes be re-engineered and simplified to make operations more efficient?
- Which other companies should we benchmark and learn from – either from inside or outside the industry – to become more efficient?
- By customer benchmarking are there areas of activity that add little real customer value that we can reduce?
- How might cost management and efficiency initiatives be project-managed?

Conclusion

Business projects are one of the main opportunities for practising strategic thinking. Whether these projects are very large and complex or actually more of a micro-level, it really does not matter.

Whilst you may well be involved in the strategic planning cycle (probably once a year), strategic projects are likely to come up at a rate of potentially more than one per quarter.

Finally, now that you have digested this chapter, please go back to the checklists for your very next strategic business project and spend 20 minutes or so thinking through the issues.

Summary of key points

- Project management is an essential medium through which strategic thinking can create action and real results in the management process.
- Strategies can be fruitfully understood – and managed – as a stream of projects.
- Each project may have a diversity of objectives – it is crucial to define and elaborate these at length, and to communicate them.
- Each area of a strategic project demands its own special recipes – for this see the extensive checklists – which work just as well for 'live' strategic projects as they do for MBA projects.

References

Grundy, A.N., *Breakthrough Strategies for Growth*, Pitman Publishing, London, 1995.

Mintzberg, H., *The Rise and Fall of Strategic Planning*, Prentice Hall, London, 1994.

CHAPTER FOURTEEN

Conclusion: everyday strategic planning (or ESP)

Introduction – applying strategic thinking every day

The central theme of this book has been that strategic thinking is not something which one does intermittently, and especially only in off-site, set-piece events. It is an ongoing activity of continual reflection, which one does on a day-to-day basis.

Strategic thinking can be applied to a number of levels – corporation, business, departmental, the project, and the individual, and to a huge diversity of issues. It should not be confined merely to strategy formulation but also to its implementation. Indeed, in many ways it is during implementation that it can often add most value – as every strategic project faces change and uncertainty during strategic action.

It is not only relevant to your life and your job but also to your social and personal life generally. In fact, practising it in your personal life can help you develop this capability through:

■ demonstrating its personal value, in a variety of ways
■ reinforcing the patterns of thinking which underpin it.

Particular areas of application where we have found strategic thinking has been invaluable at a personal level include:

■ 'Relationship demergers' (or, more crudely, a divorce, where one of the authors used strategic thinking to create a workable marital settlement which was fair strategically and financially to both sides – and within four weeks).
■ Relationship acquisition (where strategic thinking helped to create criteria for seeking and choosing a new partner).

- Relationship migration (one of the authors used the strategic option grid to evaluate whether, having found a new partner, to marry now, delay getting married, stay single, etc).
- Family issues (for deciding whether to fund – privately – a replacement kneecap for an elderly relative or to wait for the NHS to come up with the goods – which would possibly have been too late anyway).
- Leisure issues (for deciding which gym we should use following a house move).

Expanding upon just one of these illustrations – the last one – let us examine how strategic thinking proved helpful for one of us, having found a new partner.

CASE STUDY: STRATEGIC THINKING – THE NEW GYM

In 2000, after having lived together for two years, we decided to consolidate our two, separate four-bedroom houses situated 78 miles from each other, into one home. This entailed selling one, buying a larger one, and then selling off the second one – over a nine-month period.

One of our major life interests was going to the gym. Indeed, one of the authors could admit to being 'addicted' to the gym.

We had previously lived in Buckinghamshire, near to an excellent gym, accessed by a four-mile, ten-minute drive along wooded lanes. The gym had a huge pool, plenty of modern equipment, a steam room and excellent yoga classes. This gym had been acquired by a larger company and service standards were now slipping significantly. In particular, it had some rather special pieces of equipment, called cross-trainers. These enabled one to do a full upper and lower body work-out simultaneously, and in around 20 minutes.

We found our new house in Goffs Oak, Hertfordshire (famed only because of frequent visits by Posh Spice, Victoria Beckham – whose mother lives approximately 245 yards from our front door, sadly just beyond David Beckham's passing range). This obscure place is not too far from anywhere, but not near either. This presented problems when choosing a new gym. Indeed, one of the authors actually identified this as a stopper to the move process – as without a gym that was at least as good as the one which we had left, then there would have been major dissatisfaction with the move.

So, we set out to search for the ideal gym, in Spice Girls' strategic terminology, 'what do we really, really want?' Using the strategic options grid as a starting point we defined our key criteria, which ran as follows:

- quality of gym facilities generally
- cross-trainer
- distance
- time and quality of journey
- late evening opening
- general ambience
- parking
- TV facilities in gym
- pool
- sauna/steam room
- friendly service
- value for money
- flexibility of membership
- yoga (see later for unexpected events).

We had double the number of criteria here relative to a generic strategic option grid, highlighting how complex the decision was likely to be.

Initially, two options sprung to mind: a new gym in Potters Bar and an older gym in North Enfield. Both had similar journey times and the more modern one at Potters Bar would have been a certain choice had it not been for having no cross-trainer.

At the time of moving house we were led to believe that a new gym was opening up just off the M25, where the Tesco Country Club was formerly. This was to have modern equipment which would fit our core criteria for strategic choice. Unfortunately, and just after we had begun to move in, one of us telephoned them only to find that not only had the project not been completed but it had not even been started! This meant that the core option which we had banked on was now lost.

Our new next-door neighbours suggested another country club, further out of London. Whilst having a palatial swimming pool and golf course (the latter being of not interest to us), its facilities were scant.

Realising that our core two options (see now table 14.1) were not really up to scratch, we decided to widen the search. Surprisingly there were no suitable gyms within easy reach at the edges of North London nor due north of us. However, there was a sister gym to our old one just at the edge of St Albans.

TABLE 14.1: A tactical strategic option grid

	Former Gym –	Potters Bar	North Enfield	Country Club	St Albans 'Kanuns'	Grundy Park	Esporta
Quality of general facilities	✓✓✓	✓✓✓	✓✓	✓	✓✓	✓	✓✓✓
Cross-trainer	✓✓	–	✓✓	✓	✓✓	✓✓	✓✓✓
Distance	✓✓✓	✓✓	✓✓	✓✓	✓	✓✓✓	✓✓
Time and quality of journey	✓✓✓	✓✓	✓✓	✓	✓	✓✓	✓✓
Late evening opening	✓✓	✓	✓✓	✓	✓✓	✓	✓✓✓
General ambience	✓✓✓	✓✓✓	✓	✓✓	✓✓✓	✓	✓✓✓
Parking	✓✓✓	✓	✓✓	✓✓	✓✓✓	✓	✓✓
TV facilities in gym	✓✓	✓✓✓	✓	✓	✓✓	✓✓	✓✓✓
Pool	✓✓✓	✓	✓	✓✓✓	✓✓	✓	✓✓
Sauna/ steam room	✓✓	✓✓	✓	✓✓	✓✓	✓	✓✓✓
Friendly service	–	✓	✓✓	✓✓	✓✓✓	✓✓	✓✓✓
Value for money	✓✓	✓✓	✓	✓✓	✓✓	✓✓✓	✓✓
Flexibility of membership	✓✓	✓✓	✓✓	✓✓	✓✓	–	✓✓
Yoga	✓✓✓	✓	✓	✓	✓✓	✓	✓✓✓
	33	24	22	23	29	21	37

✓✓✓   Very good
✓✓   Average
✓   Poor

Whilst being far from ideal journey-wise (15 miles away and 25 minutes drive) we felt we could use the St Albans 'Kanuns' gym as a 'holding option'. By reducing our visits from six times a week to, say, four, and staying longer, we could substantially get our intended strategy through different implementation options.

But this was still far from ideal. Using scenario story-telling we imagined making that journey on cold, dark, frosty evenings – the picture was not a particularly appealing one. At this point we introduced another option: only two miles away was a public gym which did have cross-trainers, had been modernized some-what and was very good value for money. (This gym was called – ironically – 'Grundy Park' – an unusual name and identical to that of one of the authors.) We were just about to sign up with the gym and then suddenly it emerged that they required signing up for twelve months. This would have locked us into a facility which did not quite have the ambience of a private gym. So we did not go ahead, and decided to think a bit harder about our options.

So whilst one of the authors was walking through London's West End he began the following line of though enquiry:

'What do we really, really want from this? Well, my partner really, really wants a cross-trainer. Why don't we just go out and buy one – our new house could accommodate one. We could still belong to the St Albans gym, perhaps going twice a week – and my partner can still get her daily dose of exercise at home. Or, we could create our own gym and just use that. In five years we would have spent £5500 on gym fees and possibly another £2500 in mileage costs – what can you get for £8000? Probably a lot.'

Investigations revealed that to purchase the kind of machine we had used in the gym would cost a mere £4000 plus. Still, that would be much less than moving house again and paying stamp duty to the UK Government, which would be a considerable multiple of £4000.

But were there any sub-options for acquiring a cross-trainer? We discovered that whilst £4000 would buy you a cross-trainer guaranteed to run ten hours a day for five years (approximately 18,000 hours), even my partner's usage would be a minute fraction of this. There was a model with similar performance (but of slightly less durability) for around £2000. We could even get an ex-display model for £1500 (or approximately 14 months of gym fees). This now began to look like a rather promising solution. My partner was looking more relaxed about this by the minute.

It still seemed odd, however, that there was no really suitable gym within a five to ten mile drive. The final breakthrough came when one of us was running a strategy programme at Cranfield in the evening. The client director who was there at the meal lived about seven miles away from us in Enfield. One of the authors – in a moment of reflection – asked the client director:

'I just remembered, you live in Enfield. Do you know of any really good gyms which might have opened recently?'

She turned to me and said:

'Yes, there is perhaps one, called Esporta. I have not been there myself but I believe it is very nice, although quite expensive.'

At nine o'clock the next day I called Esporta and (almost disbelieving) was told, 'Yes, we have cross-trainers – lots of them –

and a swimming pool, sauna and steam room. We just opened two months ago. Actually if you are able to join this weekend there is a special deal to avoid membership fees.'

So, Esporta came to our salvation. The gym has been truly a Pareto-style improvement (Pareto improvement is one where you make a number of improvements but the main thing is that in no critical respect are you made worse off through the change.) The only adverse feature of Esporta turned out to be minor parking charges before 6.30pm – hardly a strategy stopper.

Figure 14.1 (which is a version of our handwritten option grid of that time) highlights how complex strategic choice can be for everyday projects and decisions. Also, one frequently has to spend quite a bit of time to define and refine the strategic criteria which apply to a particular decision and its context.

Notice, too, how sensitive the decision-making process was to specific criteria. St Albans was undesirable because of the considerable journey (but was otherwise okay). 'Grundy Park' would have been fine, with better ambience. Potters Bar would have fitted almost perfectly if we had managed to persuade them to buy some cross-trainers.

Also, observe how the grid helps to widen the search for further options rather than being satisfied, say, with just two.

Even by implementing options in a different way (for example by going to St Albans five times a week and by buying our own cross-trainer, or doing the same with Potters Bar, we did arrive at satisfactory solutions).,

Also, by displaying this as an option grid it was easier to view this more dispassionately. Never once did we have an argument over this issue. Asked afterwards what might have happened had we just gone to one of the other gyms, like North Enfield or Potters Bar, Laura reflected:

'Oh, I don't think I would have been really happy there at all. Yes, it probably would have made me think of not moving in fully, and maybe of going back to my old place.'

The case therefore rests here – there certainly is value to be had from strategic thinking.

Postscript – what is the one 'big thing that you forgot?'

In June 2001 one of us was late to a yoga class and decided (with encouragement from Esporta staff) to go into the class 25 minutes after it had actually started. This generated some complaint, escalating into what is now known at Esporta, Enfield, as

'Yoga Wars', a battle between ourselves and Esporta's 'Yoga Police'. The moral: to paraphrase Monty Python's 'The Spanish Inquisitor's Sketch' in strategic thinking: 'always expect the unexpected' – or analytically, do not go without your 'uncertainty grid'.

Using strategic thinking every day – its scope and applications

Besides the big (and potentially scary) issues which we mentioned in the Introduction, there are a large number of other areas in everyday life where it can be equally fruitful. Areas of past use include:

- choice of holidays
- choosing whether to do an MBA or not
- repairing and upgrading a patio
- applying for a job/career change.

Let us take a look at each in turn.

Choice of holidays

A holiday is a complex set of activities which are set in a future and often uncertain environment – and with many interdependencies. It is prima facie in desperate need of a strategy. Yet it would appear that few holidays are subjected to the process of strategic thinking, as we can see from a story by one of the authors.

CASE STUDY: THE NORWEGIAN HALF-TERM BREAK

When my son James was eight, my wife (now my ex-wife) told me of her plans to go to Norway for a week during half-term. She has seen an interesting advert in the Cambridge Evening Post of a cruise/coach tour.

I asked her (strategically):

'Ann, what are you looking to get out of the holiday?' to which she replied:

'It would be nice to be with just James for a week – I believe Norway is quite beautiful. Also, we can see the wildlife which James is interested in.'

This particular holiday happened to entail:

- two days on a ferry
- much of the time spent on a coach

And of course this was February.

> Embedded in the holiday strategy were a number of key assumptions which I was prompted to think about, using the uncertainty-importance grid.
>
> I teased out these assumptions, as follows: 'Ann, it seems an attractive idea, but there might be a few drawbacks. For instance, how much daylight is there in Norway in mid-February?'
>
> 'I don't know – I guess not much' she replied.
>
> 'And are most of the animals likely to be still hibernating at that time of year?'
>
> 'Probably, yes.'
>
> 'I wonder too whether James would get bored on such a long journey – and I can't quite see how he will play football in the snow.' I continued.
>
> 'Actually, I am beginning to go off the idea,' Ann murmured.
>
> Having been on a number of 'holidays from hell' with my family I was concerned to spare my wife the agony of living through a frozen week in the northern wastes.

Whilst some readers may be much more organized with their holiday than the above case, how many of us have not thought through, when contemplating a holiday strategy:

- Why we want to go on it?
- What value (specifically) is it likely to add to us?
- What value might it certainly dilute or destroy?
- What needs to line up to deliver 'what we really, really want' out of it (the wishbone strategy)?
- What is the 'cunning plan' of getting the most out of it?
- What are the key assumptions which underpin its success, and how certain/uncertain and high/low importance do these have?

EXERCISE: EVALUATING YOUR HOLIDAY OPTIONS USING THE STRATEGIC OPTIONS GRID

For one or more holiday options, which you might be currently contemplating, what do the above key questions highlight about their relative attractiveness?

Now let us now turn to whether to do an MBA or not.

Choosing whether to do an MBA or not

An increasing proportion of aspiring managers now think, at some stage in their careers, about doing an MBA. Once again, as we found with holidays, the amount of thinking that people do about why they want to undertake such a project (MBA could be described as a 'Mega Big Activity') is typically very limited. In truth, many MBA students are driven by the idea of having those luscious letters after their name. Whilst greater salary is often somewhere on their shopping list, 'how much' extra salary they aspire to is often left vague, and little time is spent in researching what pay rises newly-qualified MBAs actually get.

If ever there was a case for doing a wishbone analysis for the MBA project, then this is it.

Both authors have gone through this experience, so let us examine ourselves under our own microscope.

Often one gets hooked onto such a project in a 'defining moment' – which may not have been subsequently subject to the rigours of strategic thinking.

Laura's MBA

I was travelling on a mission to deliver some European training. I can't even remember the airport I was at, but certainly my plane was delayed. I picked up a magazine and it had an article on MBAs which did, I confess, make an impression on me.

Previously I had worked for many years in the pharmaceuticals industry in a relatively technical role. I had partially broken out of that into a training role, which I had enjoyed but was beginning to get restless. I also wanted to take on more responsibility in the organization. My boss was reasonably astute financially, whilst I had limited experience in that area so I felt that an MBA would help me catch up and become both more competent and confident in a senior role.

Here, Laura's immediate strategy could have been accomplished by a series of short courses and self-study. But, on top of these issues, there were latent goals like:

- adding to her qualifications
- preparing for a possible move into consultancy
- becoming more strategic
- becoming less dependent upon the industry and her company and, possibly, in leaving both

- adding to longer-term job security and flexibility (in the pharmaceuticals industry it has become really difficult to keep up to date).

Now, turning to our other author.

Tony's MBA

The first time I really appreciated the significance of an MBA was as long ago as 1972. I was being interviewed to train as an accountant with Arthur Young (now Ernst and Young). The newly-qualified accountant I talked to (one of the Cadbury family) said that 'even more impressive than being a chartered accountant is to have an MBA as well'.

Sadly, in some ways, I took the chartered accountancy route, which was hard to escape from, and in those days, frankly, was slightly tedious. At my first line job in BP I was still very much trapped in the financial function. Then, when I joined a French retailer, Charles Jourdan, operations managers seemed hell-bent on keeping me in the accounts department and out of the commercial domain. Sometimes it is said that 'the accountant's role is to count the dead after the battle' – which I believe is a totally inappropriate mindset. Even within KPMG's consultancy (which I remember fondly as 'Keeping Partners' Money Growing') we were still (in those days) very much accountants playing at being real consultants – our reports were heavily numbers-orientated and lacking in vision (in the 1980s).

In 1981 I decided I really wanted to do an MBA. I would have given my back teeth to do the full-time MBA at Cranfield (where I later got a PhD and now teach) but finances (and an emergent family strategy) precluded this. I therefore waited until 1985, when I could get some funding from KPMG, and did a part-time 'evening' MBA at City University, which has since, sadly, substantially burnt down. My main goal was to broaden my career options and, in particular, to become a strategy consultant.

Looking back there is no way that I would have had the confidence to have done many strategy consulting projects without the 'MBA', which I think (perhaps erroneously) means: 'Must Be Assertive'.

Reflecting on the above cases we were struck by the fact that whilst our goals were reasonably clear at the time, their degree of clarity was probably not sufficient to justify the investment of over one thousand hours of our time each and, at today's prices, an investment of £12,000 each. Also, our search for different options was somewhat limited (although in 1985 this was partly a function of the limited level of sophistication of the MBA market at that time).

For in doing an MBA there are a whole variety of options (which you can evaluate using the strategic options grid). These include:

- Going to a major, prestigious school or one that is in the next two divisions.
- A UK, European (non-UK school), or one in the USA.
- Full-time, part-time, evenings, distance learning options.
- Instead of doing an MBA, to unbundle the learning process by doing a number of short courses, phased over a three- to five-year period (we sometimes call this the MBA 'By-Pass' market).

EXERCISE – FOR THOSE CONTEMPLATING DOING AN MBA

Using the strategic options grid, how do the various options for doing an MBA (or by-passing one) score?

How do these scores look if tested bottom-up, for example using value and cost drivers, forcefield analysis, the uncertainty grid, and stakeholder analysis?

NB: You need to factor in the economic value/opportunity cost of the time you might need to spend on the MBA.

Turning next to a more mundane example, let us look at the strategic issue of the patio.

Repairing and upgrading a patio

It may seem a simple task to deal with a patio but this one was of such a scale as to easily warrant the term 'strategic'.

THE CREEPING PATIO PROJECT

When we moved to our new house we discovered a most unusual configuration. Our front garden was immaculate, with a centre-piece of a large pond with goldfish. To the side of the house was an area of astro-turf: laid out as a mini football pitch.

The previous owners had a special interest in football, having a most well-known name – being relatives of one of England's most famous players ever – now continuing his career on TV. Because of the success of the former owner's business (which was a series of leisure outlets with a football theme) they had time on their hands.

So, our back garden was an area of lawn which had been used as a miniature golf course (the owner's previous all-consuming hobby) and a delightful Wendy House which displayed a number of holes, larger in size than golf balls. The garden was otherwise an empty space of green and (presumably to reduce mowing) was bounded by a massive patio area, sufficient to host a team of football players and their wives.

Rather naively, we had not even noticed that something was seriously up with the patio area – both before and after we moved in – and even during the landscape gardener's visit.

Our first visitors rapidly zeroed in on the patio problem:

> Oh look, this patio is sinking and the cobbles are coming up. And your brickwork is wet here, and here. The patio is obviously not level so the water is running towards, and not away from, your house.
>
> And it looks like this bit was re-laid and in such a way that the water cannot run through the blocks, so it is being directed into your brickwork. Also, right around the back of your house the patio has been laid just above, rather than just below, the damp course, which is an additional concern.
>
> It would be a really big and expensive job to re-lay the patio again – even with the existing tiles. Have you ever thought about 'decking' – using a wooden surface? That would be much cheaper.

So, we asked the landscape gardener to quote for the work. True to form, the quote was a day late. The quote to our amazement and shock was … £5500!! (and three weeks work).

In a state of such shock the natural human reaction was to take it on the chin and think of how we could fund it. After a couple of hours the shock had worn off and – quite independently – both of us had begun to think about the other options.

'We should certainly get some more quotes,' said Laura.

'I agree, and one thing that concerns me was that they did not seem terribly relaxed, either when I met them or when they left. And that joke about the granny who went for a cheaper quote and the cheaper contractor who ran off with her money…' said Tony.

So, we commissioned three quotes, and here they are:

Option 2   Quote 2:
To re-lay all of the tiles across the whole patio and to reduce the level so that the damp-proofing would be above the patio level; to knock a small wall down.

COST: £3700 (two weeks work – one person)

Option 3   Quote 3:
To re-lay all of the tiles across the whole patio, but to put in a drain at the edge of the house so that the water could run away – making it possible

to have the patio at the current level; to remove the former owner's massive dog kennel – free.

COST: £1800 (three days work – with a team)

Option 4   Quote 4

To do the same as Option 3, except only to re-lay the blocks partially. (This would have worked temporarily but we would have been left with an area with no needs growing between the cracks and another area with loads of weeds.)

COST: £1850 (three days work – with a team)

(And to move the dog kennel: two rounds of drinks for the lads.)

To do the whole patio under Quote 4 would have cost an additional £1000.

So, effectively, this quote was £2850.

The result: we went with the cheapest and the most innovative quote.

Besides the obvious variation in costs (of 300 per cent), the interesting thing is that allegedly experienced contractors seemed unable to think strategically about the problem. Only the innovative contractor (who had perhaps the least polished sales pitch) was able to resolve the problem at least with regard to cost. A cynic might say that the other contractors were not trying to do this. But they did know that they were in a competitive bid situation and that their edge in providing the optimal solution was clearly going to be one of the most important criteria in choosing who would do it.

Strategic thinking helped us to be less emotionally tied up with this issue, and the result was not only a saving of up to £3700 but also a more durable solution. (The wooden decking would have probably looked old and slimy after, say, ten or more years.)

But what was the 'one big thing we had forgotten'? Our contractor was not particularly trustworthy. We paid him £1700 when it was almost finished and he got so drunk that he never returned. This underlines the need to police your assumptions (per the uncertainty grid) constantly – in fact it is a very good idea to imagine that (during implementation) you are the 'Strategy Police'.

Applying for a job/career change

The strategic options grid is a useful way of evaluating both new job opportunities and career changes. This can be achieved by examining a number of possible future career routes against the criteria of:

- strategic attractiveness
- financial attractiveness
- implementation difficulty
- uncertainty and risk
- stakeholder acceptability.

For example, if we take the case of a young chartered accountant (aged 28) contemplating different career options, these might include:

- financial controller/financial director of a strategic business unit
- corporate treasury
- acquisitions and mergers specialist (merchant banking)
- management consultancy.

Figure 14.1 now appraises these options. Whilst financial controller/financial director scores 'medium' on strategic (or longer-term) attractiveness, and on implementation difficulty, and 'low' on uncertainty and risk, for this particular person it is low on acceptability. This is because the thought of a more traditional, mainly reporting role is less of a turn-on. (Score of 9 overall)

FIGURE 14.1: Strategic option grid: for career strategies

	Financial controller/FD 1	Corporate treasury 2	Acquisitions and mergers 3	Management consultancy 4
Strategic attractions	√√	√	√√√	√√√
Financial attractions	√	√√√	√√√	√√
Implementation difficulty	√√	√	√√	√√
Uncertainty and risk	√√√	√√√	√	√
Stakeholder acceptability	√	√√√	√√√	√√√
Total scores	9	11	12	11

On the other hand, a career in corporate treasury is very attractive financially, but very difficult – counterbalanced by being low uncertainty and highly acceptable. (Score of 11 overall.)

A career as an acquisitions and mergers specialist scores very high on strategic and on financial attractiveness, and on acceptability to this stakeholder, but highly uncertain and of medium difficulty. (Score of 12 overall.)

Finally, a management consultancy career is highly attractive strategically and highly acceptable, but of medium financial attractiveness, medium difficulty and high risk. (Score of 11 overall.)

So, by a narrow margin, acquisitions and mergers specialist comes out the best. But hold on a minute. If this person was relatively risk averse, subjectively this career might lag the corporate training and management consultancy options. Also, if we learn that this accountant is especially keen on a sixth option, 'career flexibility', then the options might score on this new criterion as follows:

Financial controller/financial director:	High (3)
Corporate treasurer:	Low (1)
Acquisitions and mergers specialist:	Low (1)
Management consultancy:	High (3)

Then we get the following scores (summing up all six criteria):

Financial controller/financial director:	12
Corporate treasurer:	13
Acquisitions and mergers specialist:	13
Management consultancy:	14

Now we have management consultancy coming out highest, followed by corporate treasurer and acquisitions & mergers specialist (in joint second place). Financial controller/financial director has caught up considerably.

The closeness of these scores is a reflection on the subtlety of human decision-taking, and not a weakness of the technique.

Because of the emotional sensitivity of difficult career choices, it is imperative to use some form of quasi-objective technique like the strategic options grid to discriminate between options. The technique allows some of the trade-offs to be examined, and will help to test out underlying assumptions and values.

EXERCISE: WORKING ON YOUR OWN CAREER STRATEGY

For a number of career options (or, more specifically, job roles) which you have in mind:

- Do these rate on the strategic options grid?
- Given the relative weight which you place on these different options, how does this affect your overall view of the relative attractiveness of these options?

Other strategic issues, which you might well encounter in everyday life, include:

- options for a wedding
- which university your children might go to
- buying a holiday home
- downsizing your home
- moving area
- turning around a relationship
- setting up your own business
- which hobbies to keep – or drop – as your family expands, etc.

EXERCISE: EVALUATING STRATEGIC OPTIONS IN EVERYDAY LIFE

For one of the options covered above:

- What does the strategic options grid tell you about its relative attractiveness?
- How can you make specific options more attractive with 'the cunning plan'?
- How sensitive are particular options to key assumptions about the future?

Having now covered everyday opportunities for strategic thinking thoroughly, in the remainder of this chapter we consider:

- scenario, behaviour and stakeholder analysis
- managing personal strategic thinking
- 'helicopter' programmes for one-to-one personal strategic thinking.

Scenario, behaviour and stakeholder analysis

One of the most fascinating areas in strategic thinking is that of story-telling the future behaviour around a strategic issue and also the associated stakeholder analysis.

Whilst we have already covered stakeholder analysis, stakeholder prioritization analysis, the out-of-body experience, and importance and influence analysis in chapter 5, there are further areas to explore.

Scenario story-telling puts a dynamic into the analysis, which begins with the out-of-body experience.

Remember that the out-of-body experience involves seeing the world through the eyes, thoughts and feelings of:

- all key stakeholders attending the event
- individual stakeholders.

This gives managers a first cut of stakeholder positions. Where a number of issues are likely to be discussed, then this analysis can be done quite distinctively for each issue. Obviously this opens up quite a considerable area for potential thinking. Here is it appropriate to identify those issues that are likely to be particularly sensitive – the 'hot' issues.

Further, it may be useful to look at how individuals may interact (given their agendas) on a specific issue. This can be used to draw out behavioural scenarios of how the debate will actually run. Here it may be fruitful to do some 'story telling'. For example:

> On the diversification issue, Peter will begin by highlighting concerns about the proposition 'If we don't do it, we will be vulnerable to reduced turnover in our car business', while Sandra will express her fears about whether or not we have the competences to diversify effectively, particularly as in her last role this kind of strategy was attempted but proved to be a disaster.

To construct a behavioural scenario, first identify what is likely to be on the agendas of each and every stakeholder. Then imagine how the issues will come up in the workshop or meeting and tell yourself stories about how the key players will interact, with what outcomes. For example, imagine you are about to facilitate a strategy workshop with the top team of a major communications business. The team has a new chief executive (who, although promoted internally, is anxious to make a real impact in moving the business forward over the next few years). His predecessor moved on to become group chief executive and is a hard act to follow.

The team falls into two main camps. There is a new finance director and a new technology director (both appointed from outside) and a newly promoted commercial director (Europe). The administration director, services director and commercial director (Far East) were on the old team, and are long-standing appointments.

Two of the long-standing appointments are still sceptical of the value of having a strategic plan anyway, feeling it will become bureaucratic and unwieldy. The new appointees (right) wanted to preserve those things that had made the core business so successful in the past. However, these differences in views could be more apparent than real.

In my behavioural scenario 1 – 'muddling through' – the more sceptical directors feel threatened by the sense of challenge to what has worked in the past and begin to pick away at attempts to generate some genuinely new strategic thinking and breakthroughs.

In this scenario, frustration mounts as the team is unable to progress through the agenda. The chief executive tries to intervene to state that he really does believe the discussions have merit. The facilitator ends up having to go for a much more modest outcome: resolution of three major strategic dilemmas and action planning for how another four areas will be dealt with subsequently. However, we fall short of a strategic plan framework and the workshop is rated as 'overall, good – better than past meetings'.

In scenario 2 – 'Golden breakthrough' – the pre-interviews that the facilitator conducted paid off. There is, quite surprisingly, uniformly high buy-in to the process. Some discussions have to be tightly facilitated (as all members of the team are particularly bright, articulate and want to have their full say), but we do cover 80 per cent of the key issues and dilemmas.

In this scenario, during the two-day workshop, a couple of key challenges dawn on the team. Not only do they believe it was fruitful, but, even before the workshop closes, they have ordered a second one to deal with implementation analysis.

Having done this (high-level) behavioural scenario analysis, the facilitator would then begin to think about how he/she could leverage scenario 2 into scenario 1. The facilitator would also go through each one of the key strategic questions, imagining just how much thinking is required to design (and run) a strategic workshop in a particularly challenging situation.

Value and 'difficulty over time' curves

It is also wise to anticipate the likely value that will be added over time during the strategic event. This might be added principally during the 'analysis' part of the workshop or the generating new 'options' phase or in making strategic choices or in discussing the implementation issues (and plans).

Equally, at what point in the day will the greatest difficulties be encountered? How does this relate to the running order of the issues, the stakeholder positions and agendas, and the behavioural scenarios imagined in the previous section? In the earlier illustration of the com-munications business, the facilitator imagined that the greatest difficulty would occur when debating where future resources should be prioritized both in external development (late in day 1) and in developing internal capability (early in day 2).

Managing personal strategic thinking

Personal strategic thinking is a habit that should be continually cultivated. When managers come on the three-day 'Breakthrough Strategic Thinking' course at Cranfield (phased over two workshops, three months apart), we send them away with some very important suggestions on strategic thinking.

Strategic thinking: some suggestions

Dos	Don'ts
Spend time regularly to devote to a specific strategic issue	See strategic thinking as a 'once a year, or infrequent activity
Focus on just *one* issue at a time	Worry about the value of what will come out
Use odd moments – e.g. in traffic, hotels, before meetings – to work on a specific issue	Allocate *too short* a period of time to move the issue forward
Collect small and rich amounts of data (from customers, competitors, etc.)	Struggle with difficulty without asking 'why is this issue so difficult?'
See yourself as a confident, strategic thinker	Have the mindset 'I am not good at this'

The above guidelines help to translate the key imperatives of strategic thinking into practice. The specific point about collecting small and rich amounts of data is that to get the required insights you often do not have to collect vast amounts of data. But most of these points concern the way in which mental attention is focused on strategic thinking, rather than on its mechanics.

There is also a need to orchestrate a number of inputs in the quest for strategic thinking. These include:

■ Helicopter thinking: this is about taking the bigger picture, rather than getting lost down rabbit-hole details (see, again, chapter 1).
■ Strategic process: this concerns the management of behavioural interaction, facilitation, the actual location and facilities, who will be there, their expectations, etc. The 'p's refers specifically to the kind of 'p' behaviours (e.g. political, personal) that we don't want to have (see chapter 11).

Key questions and steps

It is imperative to pre-plan the key questions you will need to cover (to focus discussion and thinking). These will map out the steps in the thinking.

Tools and techniques: whilst the tools and techniques of chapters 2, 3 and 5 play a very big role these do not (of themselves) create both the necessary and sufficient conditions for generating strategic thinking.

Questioning and creative thinking: in many ways it is just as important to ask the right questions (during interaction) rather than to say 'I think...' or 'It is...'. This should be very much the role of a facilitator but not confined to him/her. This creative thinking angle is equally important to analysis and questioning (see chapter 4).

Energy and time: enough time should be set aside for the session and managers have to bring sufficient energy to be truly engaged. (Starting a workshop at 7pm in the evening after a long meeting on tactical issues is not such a good idea.)

Turning to the kind of question structure which is useful, the following gives a good illustration of the kind of sequence of questions which it is helpful to work through during the implementation phase of the strategy. These questions can be used for an individual (40 minutes) or for a pair of managers working in parallel on two separate issues (60 minutes), or a single team on a single issue (90 minutes).

Implementation analysis: key questions

- For one area of breakthrough within your own business:
    - do a root cause (fishbone analysis)
    - what options are available to address this area (radical, creative thinking)?
    - how attractive/difficult to implement are these options likely to be (AID analysis)?
- For the same breakthrough (and for one option only):
    - what is the underlying implementation difficulty (forcefield analysis)?
    - who are the key stakeholders? What is on their agenda, and how are they positioned on the attitude/influence grid?
    - given this, how could you make the breakthrough easier to implement?

Finally, as a generic process for managing mini-strategies, we also import a process used on the Cranfield programme (see figure 14.2). This takes you through a number of steps beginning with problem definition to developing the objective and then the strategy. AID analysis then helps with detailed evaluation and prioritization followed by forcefield and stakeholder analysis.

FIGURE 14.2: A process for managing mini-strategies

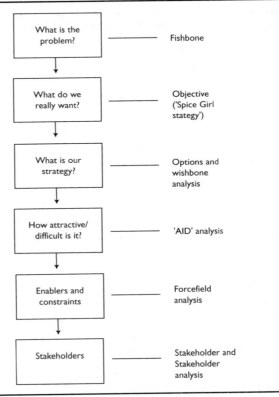

The strategic options grid can be used instead of, or alongside, the wishbone and AID analysis, where there are a variety of complex options. (This is done by doing the strategic options grid first, then the wishbone for one or more strategic options separately, and then the AID analysis to prioritize ingredients of each wishbone.)

This process is not mechanistic; there may be times, for example, when you either do not need to do a fishbone analysis (as there is more of an opportunity rather than a problem). Also, stakeholder analysis is sometimes useful to do early on and up-front.

Helicopter programmes for personal strategic thinking

'Helicopter programmes' is an idea which came out of some strategic thinking. Six years ago, one of the authors was on holiday at Centreparcs in the UK (an environmentally friendly home where you can swim in hot pools in the depths of a delightfully odd and damp British winter).

CENTREPARCS GIVES BIRTH TO 'HELICOPTER PROGRAMMES'

For once, my two children were not threatening to drown themselves in the tidal wave which comes every half hour. I had a twenty-minute run at strategic thinking.

Since leaving KPMG and PA Strategy Consultants I had worked on some very interesting strategy facilitation assignments with some major companies. But I found that the work came to me when it wanted me, rather than being something which one could easily and proactively encourage.

My diagnosis (fishbone analysis) of the root causes of this revealed that:

- Fundamental strategy reviews were not something practicable, and were often a case of sorting out a strategy which had gone wrong, or gone into drift rather than were forward-thinking.
- Managers did not (then) perceive the need for a strategic thinking process (it was rather like trying to sell someone a car, when no-one has ever seen what one looks like and ridden in one).
- Whilst there was (then) occasional demand for strategy facilitation, this was often seen as a nice-to-have, last minute thing. By the time a client contacted me the diary was often busy with other things – especially management development programmes.
- Clients loved to 'think about doing real strategic thinking' (as was often the case on courses) but seemed less inclined to actually do it for real. I suspected that some of this was down to potential embarrassment that they had not done it properly before – and they therefore preferred to attend learning/feel-good events. This was rather like continually going to confession to feel better rather than actually going about the world and doing some good.
- The early 1990s recessionary climate had cast a shadow (still) over managers' thinking imaginatively about the future.

- Where there was a need, clients had to scurry around to find a budget to fund a proper strategic thinking event and purpose.

Whilst this was a pretty good fishbone, I still felt I had not got down to the bottom of things. So, whilst the waters of the Centreparcs lagoon lapped at my ankles, I then had the out-of-body experience of 'what it is like to be a client, buying in a process and facilitation of their strategic thinking'.

The thoughts which I had (in my client mindset) ran as follows:

I haven't done this before – will facilitation actually work?

I am letting go control to someone from outside the organization – this makes me feel anxious, especially if it wobbles or falls over and I have hired him/her.

It is embarrassing having someone in because it feels like an admission that we can't do this very important thing very well – 'strategic thinking'.

So, instead of actually finding a suitable facilitator, managers flock to business schools.

So, realising that there is a very substantial latent need for strategic thinking and bearing in mind the state of organizational readiness to take on board strategic thinking, I hit on a way of reducing the psychological barriers to engaging in the strategic thinking process.

This is called 'helicopter programmes' to:

- symbolize that this is about helicopter thinking and about stepping back from the day-to-day
- make strategic thinking less frightening, also to sound less difficult and make it more user-friendly
- help incorporate inputs from other spheres of analysis – such as organizational diagnosis and personal strategic management, and not just big-picture strategic thinking.

The concept of helicopter programmes is one of a number of half-day, one-to-one sessions, either held on- or off-site to help a senior manager to work through a number of strategic issues. This occurs in a 100 per cent, politically safe environment. It is also zero-embarrassing, as no-one else in the organization needs to know that the individual is having assistance. Also, as they can be seen to be performing better than previously, they then get to take all the credit themselves rather than share the glory with the facilitator.

Since then a considerable number of senior managers and directors have benefited from the helicopter programmes, either as stand-alone assistance or as a means of easing into the strategy process with their team, either with or without a facilitator.

In terms of our earlier chapters 6 and 7 on the 'Value of Strategic Thinking', value comes in several areas, particularly from:

- creating thought space
- providing a thinking framework
- business value – improved decision-making
- prioritization
- personal value, especially in terms of confidence, clarity, reduced anxiety, and greater preparedness to act.

But whether or not you ever wish to seek help of this kind, it is essential that you recognize that this is a need of most senior managers and directors. Without setting aside enough personal strategic time to think about your issues – and with sufficient support processes (perhaps including a helicopter programme or equivalent support at least once in your career), you may be destined to be swept along by the torrent of management activity.

AN EXAMPLE OF A HELICOPTER PROGRAMME

A few years ago a very senior Tesco manager was looking for a strategy and marketing programme at a major business school. Unfortunately the only programmes available which met his requirements were of one to two weeks duration and involved travel outside the UK. The total cost (including travel) was in the region of £3500 to £6500.

The manager could not really afford the time out of his stretching job, which he was new to.

Instead of attending a long programme of this nature he took the opportunity of a helicopter programme. This enabled him to work on:

- scoping and prioritizing his own role
- making any necessary adjustments to his personal style
- learning how to use 'helicopter' (or strategic) thinking
- developing a key, innovative strategy for Tesco
- defining the role (and value added) of his department
- scoping and beginning to implement a restructuring, and developing his change management capability.

So before we finally conclude, it may be time for you to spend a few minutes thinking about how you can now develop your own personal strategic thinking capability. Try this next exercise, which simulates aspects of the helicopter programme.

EXERCISE: PERSONAL STRATEGIC THINKING

- What business am I in – in my role?
- What value do I add, and what are my key value-creating activities?
- What are the key strategic issues I currently face in my role?
- What key strategic issues am I about to face over the next six to eighteen months?
- What are my options in dealing with these issues?
- What lines of enquiry might I go down in order to resolve these issues?
- Who I can bounce my ideas off or seek facilitation from, in order to develop strategic thoughts on these issues?
- If I was to have a 'personal strategic plan', what would be in it?
- How can I set aside more dedicated time for personal strategic thinking, and how can I create the discipline and process to develop my own personal helicopter programme?

Reference

Grundy, A.N. and L. Brown, *Strategic Project Management*, Thomson Learning, London, 2001.

Acquisitions evaluation:
operations due diligence

'Due diligence' can be defined as :

> The process of detailed evaluation of an acquisition to ensure that you are getting what you think you are getting and that there are no hidden and unexpected downsides.

The process of due diligence is very much like that of doing a survey on a house before you agree to buy it. Having established that a property fits your strategic needs and appears to be the most appropriate option you now wish to ensure that it is both structurally intact and that you are not going face far more work than you thought to integrate it. Also, as with a house purchase it is a method of checking out that the valuation is both realistic and reasonable.

If you find that what you are trying to buy is not quite what you thought it was, then you may decide either not to go ahead, or that you have good grounds to re-negotiate the price. And as with a house move, you need to make sure that you do not get so psychologically committed that you are therefore unable to back off and re-negotiate.

Our next step is to look at each perspective individually. This entails a combination of analysis tools and of also asking some key diagnostic questions.

Markets and marketing

To understand our acquisition target's markets we need to understand its relative competitive strength across the range of its product/markets segments (see figure A.1). This can be conveniently evaluated by using a scoring technique as follows:

- three ticks = very strong
- two ticks = average strength
- one tick = weak
- no ticks = no presence (in that product market).

FIGURE A.1: Acquisition target's positioning

Products \ Markets	1	2	3	4
1				
2				
3				
4				

Further analysis can be performed by looking at the relative attractiveness of the various product/market segments. This is based on the following major criteria:

- environmental volatility
- future growth rate (or 'growth drivers')
- relative competitive pressure.

Again we would have for market attractive:

- three ticks = very attractive
- two ticks = moderately attractive
- one tick = low attractiveness.

A third piece of analysis can be performed (where sufficient data is available for business and financial performance). Again we would score:

- three ticks = strong performance
- two ticks = average performance
- one tick = weak performance.

Note: there is usually a strong correlation between product/market segments which are both highly attractive where there is a strong competitive position – and with strong business and financial performance. Likewise there is a strong correlation between product/market segments which are less attractive and with a weak competitive position and weak business and financial performance.

To illustrate this, look at an overlay of these grids for Rover Group at 1994 (see figure A.2). (Here, business and financial performance has been inferred.) This highlights not only the considerable spread of Rover's product/market portfolio but also its depending upon the Discovery four-wheel-drive model. This also helps to highlight complementary and fit with the product/market segments of the acquirer.

FIGURE A.2: Rover group: positioning as at 1994

Markets Products	Small– niche	Volume– small/medium	Volume– larger	Niche– larger	Sports	Four wheel drive	Criteria
Metro		√ √ √					Attractiveness Strength Performance
Mini	√ √ √ √ √ √						Attractiveness Strength Performance
200 and 400		√ √ √					Attractiveness Strength Performance
600 and 800							Attractiveness Strength Performance
MGF		√ √ √			√ √ √ √ √ √ √		Attractiveness Strength Performance
Discovery						√ √ √ √ √ √ √ √ √	Attractiveness Strength Performance

Products and services

The detailed appraisal of target's products and services entails some competitive benchmarking of its strengths and weaknesses.
To understand customer value we need to explore:

- What gets the customer locked in (the 'motivator' or distinctive turn-ons), and the 'hygiene' factors (this is value which is assumed will be added to the customer – but which if not delivered can result in the customer switching to an alternative supplier).
- How relatively important are these factors?
- How well does the company actually deliver these?

This comparison may need to be performed separately for different product/market segments, but especially for the 20 per cent of those segments which add 80 per cent of value.

The comparison of relative costs is more difficult because internal data may be harder to come by, especially without unethical espionage. However, where there are good proxies for understanding cost drivers, a reasonable estimate of relative cost is usually feasible. Useful proxies include:

- salary and wage rates relative to industry norms
- likely labour productivity, given the quality of the labour force and manufacturing and other processes
- relative economies of scale (especially for manufacturing and materials costs)
- head office and site location (is this de luxe or modest?)
- corporate mindset (is this relaxed or stringent on costs)
- attitudes to financial control and to commercial management generally.

To bring together this analysis, the competitive profiling technique, what we say in chapter 3, is a helpful way of displaying competitor positioning.

Had Rover been positioned on the grid as at 1994 it would have emerged as being strategically weak and highly vulnerable – the four-wheel-drive division excluded.

Technology

Technology capability is another critical area of operations due diligence. Technology may underpin the targets competitive advantage in a number of ways:

- Customer lock-in: IT systems which make it ultra convenient and cheap for the customer to deal with the company rather than others.
- Product superiority: hard-to-imitate advantages inherent in the product (whether patented or not).
- Brand advantage: what is its contribution to a 'high-tech' image, like at Dyson Appliances? These advantages can still be beneficial long after any advantages from being the first to do something new have expired (for example with the Sony Walkman).
- Service delivery: using technology to minimize customer's life-cycle of costs.
- Transaction processing: highly cost effective use of IT.
- Customer intelligence/marketing: clever customer databases which can secure additional sales.

A company's technology is embedded in its physical products, in its processes and in manifest too in the thoughts and the behaviours of its staff. Technology due diligence thus requires an appraisal of all these manifestations – to identify not just 'what our target has got?' in the way of technological edge but also 'how effectively is it using it?'.

This approach is a somewhat different concept from conventional technology due diligence. The latter is inclined to focus on the tangible, and is particular with checking out 'will this existing technology work in the future?' Obviously, identifying key areas of existing technology gap is important, but not having a major current gap should merely qualify the target for potential acquisition.

Operations and people

The due diligence of organization and people is one of the most important areas for scrutiny. Whilst we have already touched on some of the skills areas – and organizational mindset – in earlier questions there are a number of more detailed areas to probe.

But before moving into the detailed considerations which an acquirer will need to make an organization and people, let us go back to the case of BMW and Rover Group.

Organization and people – at BMW and Rover Group

BMW expected to find a relatively strong management team in place at Rover Group. This led them to believe that a more hands-off integration strategy vis-à-vis organization and people change was appropriate. Unfortunately these assumptions turned out to be misplaced.

This had a number of significant impacts:

- First, BMW had to replace a number of Rover's top management team. This was implemented after delay – only beyond 18 months following the acquisition – which lost BMW a good deal of time.
- Second, BMW managers had to spend considerable amounts of time to help develop Rover Group's brand strategy. Arguably, Rover's skills in this area were not up to the task ahead.
- Third, both the loss of technology input from Honda and the need to fundamentally revise Rover's product strategy meant that BMW had to support Rover's redesign effort to an unexpected degree. This entailed a considerable number of BMW's R&D staff being seconded to the UK. This was said to have kept the airlines very busy and the Holiday Inn, Coventry's occupancy very healthy for a long period.

These gaps were not only expensive to address but also carried with them a significant opportunity cost. How many new BMW models could have been designed using this scarce resource and investment – over the period 1995–1999, had BMW not acquired Rover?

Misalignment of organization and people with that of the acquired company (especially during the integration phase) is one of the main reasons why acquisitions fail - and especially for destroying 'V3', the value added during integration.

It is therefore imperative that this aspect of due diligence is handled with care, with rigour, and yet with sensitivity. The following case study highlights the costs of not managing this stage – and from it evolving an effective implementation strategy, well.

In addition to the core areas of operations due diligence (access all companies) there are also more specific data requirements for manufacturing operations. These invite the following questions:

Manufacturing facilities

- What are the principal items of machinery and equipment?
- How up-to-date are these?
- How do these compare against competitor's facilities, both in the UK and elsewhere?
- What condition are these in?
- What degree of utilization do these have?
- What is their replacement cost, and net book value, and their depreciation rates?
- In the future, do these give a basis for competitive advantage?

Manufacturing processes

- What are the key manufacturing processes and how advanced are these technologically?
- Do these rely on 'just-in-time' production?
- Are there methods of ensuring zero defect?
- How standardized are procedures?
- Are cycle times competitive?
- How reliable are sub-contractors?

Purchasing

- To what extent is the company prone to industry shortages?
- How competitively are supplies being sourced?
- How does the company monitor and control the quality of purchases?
- Are purchasing procedures robust enough in terms of internal control?

Managing the acquisition deal

Deal-making dos

A fruitful way of helping manage the negotiation process more effectively is to ponder the following deal-making dos and don'ts: these dos and don'ts have been compiled with the help of the distilled experiences of over 150 managers with acquisition exposure in acquisition seminars throughout Europe. Additional explanatory comments are shown underneath each section in italics.

Clarify the deal rationale – dos

- understand the reason for and underlying pressure driving the vendor
- be clear what it is that you are getting
- the 'walk-away-from' price must allow a good margin of worth to you of the deal.

Although these are three simple points, they should be branded on the foreheads of the acquisition team.

Track the deal fundamentals – dos

- know your 'tradables' in advance of the negotiation
- get early agreement on the essentials
- keep ongoing track of the benefits (value) of the deal and total costs of the deal as any changes occur.

These three points need continual work and a great deal of stamina. In particular, you cannot assume that the accountant on the team can necessarily capture all the implications of fast-moving negotiations in real time.

Managing the deal process – dos

- Hold a pre-negotiation meeting(s) before deal-making with your advisers.
- Remember that the deal is a learning process: you may learn things which cast new light on (a) attractiveness of the target, (b) attractiveness of the deal and (c) potential post-acquisition management difficulties.
- Establish a series of check points at key stages to stand back and take an objective look at the proposition.
- Take time out from negotiations if a log-jam exists and go back to essentials/tradables.

Because of the momentum which the deal process acquires, you need to invest considerable effort to manage the process in a calm, structured way.

Managing the communication process – dos

- work hard at communication – within 'the team' and with the vendor
- focus all information through one key point
- be absolutely clear on who has the final say.

These points are again easier said than done. Acquisition negotiations can become extremely complex and the opportunities for miscommunication abound. These opportunities are multiplied further with cross-border decisions where at least one side works in a second language.

Managing the relationships with the vendor – dos

- Keep on thinking 'I am not here to make friends'.
- Have a 'negotiation game plan' in place in advance – especially to give advantage over an unsophisticated/inexperienced vendor.
- Exploit disagreement or fragmentation of views in the opposition.
- Where an unsophisticated vendor is involved, be prepared to provide support:
  - to talk them through the key stages in advance
  - when it all begins to seem 'too much' at later stages
- Avoid alienating key managers you wish to retain.
- Make provision for continuity of employment, systems etc., where you are buying part, not all, of a business.

It is not possible to offer rigid prescriptions in the area of managing relationships – essentially these should be managed on a situation-by-situation basis. However, the above six points flag up some important pointers.

Achieving tactical advantage – dos

- look for skeletons (by continual probing)
- be prepared to 'go for the extra' at the last stage of negotiations (the vendor's emotions take over here)
- reflect on your negotiating skills and style, and its strengths and weaknesses before finalizing the team
- encourage candour from managers of target
- keep out of any areas clouded by lots of subjectivity on the part of vendors
- be aware of who thinks they are driving the deal but without necessarily letting them influence the out-turn of negotiations (you can still be proactive!)
- be prepared to use financial tools as both valuation tools and as negotiating weapons.

Obviously point 2 needs to be weighed against the situation – late, deal-wrecking tactics are not being advocated here. Point 5 stresses the need to avoid getting into debates which involve lots of feeling about what the business might be worth – always go back to the strategic, financial and other facts.

Managing the acquisition team – dos

- appoint an 'acquisition project leader' (and, if necessary, a manager – to co-ordinate detailed information flows)
- involve 'the integrator' at key stages – indeed, consider making the integrator the project leader
- ensure that the maximum experience of acquisitions is within the team, e.g. where the leader lacks 'experience' this needs to be counterbalanced
- adjust your normal duties – it is not a part-time job
- control the players in the team and the commitment 'up to the top'.

The organizational issues surrounding acquisition teams cause endless debate, often of a heated variety. It is imperative that roles and responsibilities are very well-defined, otherwise there is a very real threat of going down the slippery slope into political in-fighting (points 1, 2 and 5). Also, point 4 actually means what it says – you can't lead a complex acquisition effectively at the peaks of activity alongside a heavy operational role – something has to give.

Deal-making don'ts

Managing the deal process – don'ts

- assume that your professional advisers individually know 'the whole picture'
- allow ambiguity to persist in key areas, particularly in leaving it until too late to raise key legal, tax, pension or related issues
- see the deal in any sense as 'final and agreed' until formal closure.

The final point is critical – as soon as you think you have 'won' you may well have lost – in value terms.

Managing relationships with the vendor – don'ts

- get involved socially with vendor and representatives without a clear strategy (particularly for the inexperienced)
- give vague assurances of continuity of employment which you may not wish to be held to.

These speak for themselves. Sometimes experienced acquirers greet point 1 with incredulity. But it does happen. Situations have occurred where an acquisition manager and the vendor's representative even swapped stories about their mistresses – maybe this was harmless intimacy, or maybe it was not.

Achieving tactical advantage – don'ts

- put all of your cards 'up front' on the table (be prepared to ask them what they are looking for – depending on the context)
- be stampeded by artificial deadlines
- become impatient with apparent haggling over minutiae – this can be very important and have a big impact on value
- give in to the temptation of 'giving in to' perfectly sound arguments without a fight
- conceal skeletons where it will be evident you have been obviously manipulative as the concealment will be transparent.

Points 1–5 above again appear self-evident, but remember acquisitions can become very much an emotional experience where reason gets left behind unintentionally.

Managing the acquisition team – don'ts

■ let any of your team display excessive enthusiasm
■ air your team disagreements in front of the opposition.

These issues are picked up very quickly by an experienced opposition, especially through unconscious, non-verbal behaviour.

General references

Ansoff, H.I., *Corporate Strategy*, McGraw-Hill, New York, 1965.
— 'Managing Strategic Surprise by Response to Weak Signals', *Californian Management Review* XVIII (Winter 1975), p.p.21–23.

Argyris, C., 'Teaching Smart People How to Learn', *Harvard Business Review*, May–June 1991.

Braybrooke, D. and C.E. Lindblom, *A Strategy of Decision*, Free Press, Macmillan, New York, 1963.

Brunsson, N., 'The Irrationality of Action and Action Rationality: Decisions, Ideologies and Organizational Actions', *Journal of Management Studies* 198 (1), p.p.29–44, 1982.

Chilingerian, J.A., 'Managing Strategic Issues and Stakeholders: How Modes of Executive Attention Enact Crisis Management' in H. Thomas, D.O. Neal and D. Hurst (eds), *Building the Strategically Responsive Organization*, p.p.190–213, John Wiley, Chichester, 1994.

Cohen, M.B., J.C. March and J.P. Olsen, 'A Garbage Can Model of Organization Choice', *Administrative Science Quarterly* 7 (1972), p.p.1–25.

Copeland, T., T. Koller and J. Murrin, *Valuation: Measuring and Managing the Value of Companies*, John Wiley, New York, 1990.

Cyert, R.M., and J.G. March, *A Behaviour Theory of the Firm*, Prentice Hall, Englewood Cliffs, NJ, 1963.

Dixit, A.K. and B.J. Nalib, *Thinking Strategically*, Norton, New York, 1991.

Dyson, J., *Against the Odds*, Orion Business, London, 1997.

Goldratt, E.M., *Theory of Constraints*, North River Press, Great Barrington, Massachusetts, 1990.

Grundy, A.N., *Corporate Strategy and Financial Decisions*, Kogan Page, London, 1992.
— *Implementing Strategic Change*, Kogan Page, London, 1993.
— *Breakthrough Strategies for Growth*, Pitman Publishing, London, 1995.

— *Exploring Strategic Financial Management*, Prentice Hall, London, 1998.

— *Harnessing Strategic Behaviour – How Politics Drives Company Strategy*, Financial Times Publishing, London, 1998.

Grundy, A.N. and L. Brown, *Strategic Project Management*, Thomson Learning, London, 2001.

Hickson, D.H., R.J. Butler *et al.*, *Top Decisions: Strategic Decision-making in Organizations*, Basil Blackwell, Oxford, 1986.

Janis, I.I., *Crucial Decisions*, Free Press, Macmillan, New York, 1989.

Jemison, D.B. and S.B. Sitkin, 'Acquisitions: The Process Can Be a Problem', *Harvard Business Review*, March–April 1986, p.p.107–16.

Johnson, G.J., *Strategic Change and the Management Process*, Basil Blackwell, Oxford, 1986.

Johnson, G. and K. Scholes, *Exploring Corporate Strategy*, Prentice Hall, 1987.

— *The Challenge of Strategic Management*, Kogan Page, London, 1992.

Kanter, R.M., *The Change Masters*, Unwin, London, 1987.

Lewin, K., *A Dynamic Theory of Personality*, McGraw Book Company, New York, 1935.

McTaggart, J.M., P.W. Kontes and M.C. Mankins, *The Value Imperative*, Free Press, Macmillan, New York, 1994.

Miller, P. and P. Freisen, 'Archetypes of Strategy Formulation', *Management Science* 24 (1978), p.p.921–33.

Mintzberg, H., *The Rise and Fall of Strategic Planning*, Prentice Hall, London, 1994.

Mitroff, I.I. and H.A. Linstone, *The Unbounded Mind*, Oxford University Press, Oxford, 1993.

Ohmae, K., *The Mind of the Strategist*, McGraw-Hill, New York, 1982.

Pascale, R., *Managing on the Edge*, Penguin, London, 1990.

Peters, T. and R.H. Waterman, *In Search of Excellence*, Harper and Row, New York, 1980.

Pettigrew, A.M., 'Strategy Formulation as a Political Process', *International Studies of Management and Organization*, 7 (2), 1977, p.p.78–87.

Piercey, N., 'Diagnosing and Solving Implementation Problems in Strategic Planning', *Journal of General Management* 15 (1) (Autumn 1989), p.p.19–38.

Porter, E.M., *Competitive Strategy*, Free Press, Macmillan, New York, 1980.

— 'From Competitive Advantage to Corporate Strategy', *Harvard Business Review*, May–June 1987, p.p.43–59.

Quinn, J.B., *Strategies for Change: Logical Incrementalism*, Richard D. Irwin, Illinois, 1980.

Rappaport, A., *Creating Shareholder Value*, Free Press, Macmillan, New York, 1986.

Schein, E.H., *Organizational Culture and Leadership*, Jossey-Bass, San Francisco, CA, 1986.

Senge, P., *The Fifth Discipline: The Art and Practice of the Learning Organization*, Doubleday, New York, 1990.

Stewart, G.B., *The Quest for Value*, Harperbusiness, New York, 1991.

Stalk, E., *Competing Against Time*, Free Press, Macmillan, 1990.

Index